The Australian Women's Weekly

COMPLETE BOOK OF

HOME
HINTS

The Australian Women's Weekly

COMPLETE BOOK OF
HOME
HINTS

VIKING

Viking
Penguin Books Australia Ltd
487 Maroondah Highway, PO Box 257
Ringwood, Victoria 3134, Australia
Penguin Books Ltd
Harmondsworth, Middlesex, England
Viking Penguin, A Division of Penguin Books USA Inc.
375 Hudson Street, New York, New York 10014, USA
Penguin Books Canada Limited
10 Alcorn Avenue, Toronto, Ontario, Canada M4V 3B2
Penguin Books (N.Z.) Ltd
182–190 Wairau Road, Auckland 10, New Zealand

First published by Currey O'Neil Ross Pty Ltd 1984
This paperback edition published by Penguin Books Australia Ltd 1987

10

Typeset by ProComp Productions Pty Ltd, Adelaide
Printed by Australian Print Group, Maryborough, Vic.

National Library of Australia
Cataloguing-in-Publication data

The Australian Women's Weekly complete book of home hints

   Includes index.
   ISBN 0 670 90036 2.

   1. Home economics. I. Rolfe, Patricia. II. Australian women's weekly.
640

CONTENTS

THE WEEKLY AND THE HOME

ROYAL WEDDINGS and royal babies come and go, beautiful film stars have their brief season. The backbone of most women's magazines is not the entertaining news stories or the lavish colour pictures but the service departments. Cooking, home decorating, sewing and knitting, caring for family, pets and plants, these are the reasons why copies of the *Australian Women's Weekly* are carefully filed away for future reference, mailed to other countries, or passed from hand to hand, even at times, from generation to generation.

The *Australian Women's Weekly* for many years after it began in 1933 was more or less a self-contained world. As season followed season, year followed year, the magazine's service departments catered to imaginative cooks with warming food for winter and with summer delights, to keen knitters and sewers with new styles, and it kept readers up to date with changing ideas in decorating. However, it left no more permanent record of itself.

In the past decade the magazine has begun to assemble some of this valuable material in book form. First, there were booklets within the magazine. Then the first soft-cover books were published. These have been an outstanding Australian publishing success with sales of individual books well over one million copies.

The time had come to put basic information about homemaking into one volume. Similar books on the market are of foreign origin and are not suited to Australian conditions or climate or to the Australian way of doing things. The *Australian Women's Weekly*, with Currey O'Neil Ross, is in a unique position to cater to the needs of Australian homemakers.

This book is not, however, simply a reprinting of material from the *Weekly*. The aim was to cover as wide a range of needed subjects as was possible in one volume. Such sections as the law and consumer affairs, budgeting and finance, natural disasters, emergencies and first aid were compiled specially for this book.

The *Complete Book of Home Hints* is directed at a wide range of homemakers, both women and men. It tries at all times to be practical and specific, but to avoid suggesting that there is one 'correct' way of doing things.

When it comes to cleaning and other routine chores, some people like to be equipped with a battery of aerosol cans and electrical appliances and to proceed in what they believe is a scientific and efficient way. Others feel that they can get the same effect more cheaply, and perhaps just as easily, with nothing more than a bottle of methylated spirits and some clean rags. These are matters of personal preference. If a certain method works for you and suits your temperament and ideas, that is the correct way for you. Homemaking is a very individual thing.

The chapter on etiquette makes allowance for different ideas. What may seem old fashioned to some people, others will regard as the only way to do things. There are also considerable differences in behaviour between people of different racial origin.

Nonetheless, there are many areas in this book where the *Australian Women's Weekly* might claim that if you follow its advice you can hardly go wrong. Allan Seale's advice on indoor plants draws on his vast experience and knowledge over many years. The decorating chapters are based on material from the *Weekly*'s homemaking department. Much of the chapter on food relied on material from the *Weekly*'s Test Kitchen, pre-eminent in its field. Sandra Symons, who compiled the chapter on fitness and diet, drew on years of experience in writing on this subject.

1
THE KITCHEN

WHETHER you prefer a kitchen with austere laminated surfaces or with natural textures such as pine and quarry tiles is largely a matter of taste. But whatever style is right for you, efficiency of design will be one of the main considerations in planning a kitchen.

Today there is such a wealth of kitchen appliances, utensils and tableware on the market that it's hard to know what to buy. This section will help you to decide which of these are best for you, and how to look after them.

PLANNING YOUR KITCHEN

A kitchen which really suits the family's needs can save considerable time and make life easier and more enjoyable. The layout of your kitchen should be designed to give you the most efficient working space possible within the limitations of the room.

No matter how large or small the kitchen, the first point to bear in mind is the work triangle: the path you tread between sink, stove and refrigerator. Try to keep these three items within a couple of steps of one another. Relegate even one of the three to a corner and you will clock up unnecessary kilometres. Another point to bear in mind is through-traffic. Try to plan a kitchen in which people going from the interior of the house to the outside are not continually distracting anyone working in the kitchen.

BASIC LAYOUTS

There are some basic layouts for kitchens but these do not suit every situation. In old houses and small flats many variations are necessary.

L-shape This is a convenient layout for a shared kitchen-dining area, or a very small kitchen. The sink and stove should be positioned in the centre of each length of bench with the refrigerator at one end.

U-shape This layout gives an unobstructed work triangle. To avoid wasting corner cupboard space choose double-hinged cupboard doors for maximum access to a swinging shelf system.

Galley kitchen Ideal for narrow rooms with

9

U-shape

L-shape

Single-line

Island

Galley

doorways at either end, the galley kitchen has parallel work benches with a passageway in between. One of the benches may be designed to become a breakfast bar if the kitchen opens on to a dining or family-room. The stove and sink should be kept on the same side, to avoid crossing the traffic path.

Single-line kitchen Because all work areas are arranged in a straight line this kitchen works best in small apartments. Place free-standing range and refrigerator at either end to avoid the work space.

Island kitchen If your kitchen is large and fits into none of the previous categories an island bench could be the solution. A central bench is used to create a useful work triangle and save unnecessary walking.

RENOVATE OR REMODEL?

Everyone who watches television has a clear idea of what to do with an old kitchen: you simply get in one of those companies which advertise so freely, ask them to wave their wand, and the whole area is transformed.

REMODELLING

Even if that is what you can afford there are a few cautions. Do not put yourself in anyone's

hands completely. Have a very clear idea first of the sort of kitchen you want and where you want everything to go. Do not, above all, be talked into something more elaborate and expensive than you can afford.

Plumbing, door openings and windows will probably dictate where sink, stove and refrigerator will have to remain. You might think of enlarging windows to brighten a gloomy room or rehanging doors so that they open away from the kitchen and give you more space. It may be possible to remove part of a wall to connect the kitchen with a dining or family-room by making a breakfast bar or servery.

Draw up your own plan using graph paper. Experiment with layout of work benches and cupboards. It is almost impossible to have too much bench or storage space. If your existing kitchen is a disaster, work out what is wrong and try to avoid the same mistakes.

Companies selling custom-designed kitchens have showrooms so you can see before you buy. However, shop around before you choose. Inspect finishes and detailing carefully and get several precise quotes, with no hidden extras. Sometimes you will find that a local carpenter can do the job as well, if not better. Some companies give you the option of installing the cupboards yourself. This can save money if you are a competent handyman.

RENOVATING

If you cannot afford a complete remodel, you can still do a very respectable job on an old kitchen with renovation. Again, draw up a plan on graph paper to see what may be possible, at a price. Unless you decide to replace your sink with something more modern and efficient you may be able to do most of the renovating yourself.

A handyman can fit cupboard units or can line and face existing cupboards, if necessary. Extra storage space may be all that is needed to make the kitchen work efficiently.

After that you can do wonders with paint. If the walls are old and pocked, be wary of high gloss paints. They will show up any marks. To enlarge a small kitchen, paint walls and ceilings in white or cream and use colour on cupboards and shelves. Very high ceilings can be scaled down by marking a line around the walls to a height of 2½ metres and painting the ceiling and above the line in a darker colour.

Wallpaper can camouflage old walls efficiently. The vinyl-coated papers are washable. You might even give an old refrigerator a new look by painting it with several coats of glossy paint.

Self-adhesive tiles are a relatively cheap and easy way to change the flooring. They are available in many colours and patterns including simulated cork and slate. If the old flooring is resilient and in reasonable condition you may be able to stick the tiles onto this. Otherwise use an underlay. Cushioned vinyl and cork tiles are more expensive but need little care.

Small touches, such as replacing old cupboard door handles, can make quite a difference, Pleasing touches, such as a herb or two in a pot, temporarily brought indoors, or baskets of fruit and vegetables, make a kitchen much nicer to visit and work in.

LIGHTING AND POWER POINTS

Check on the exact positions of benches and cupboards before installing new wiring. You may find you lose a power point in a storage cupboard or behind a wall oven.

The amount of light necessary will be determined by the distance between light sources and the amount of reflection from bench surfaces. Fluorescent tubes attached to the undersides of overhead cupboards will illuminate work areas well. A pelmet will screen tubes. Spotlights on a track can be angled to specific areas. It is also a good plan to have a light above hotplates if there is no range hood with accompanying light.

You should have enough power points for electrical appliances, both for convenience and for safety's sake.

STORAGE

Careful planning is needed to make the most of your kitchen space. Most frequently used items should be placed within easy reach.

Heavy appliances should be kept as close as possible to where they will be used to avoid too much lifting. An appliance work centre at bench level complete with power points and doors which close around it saves a lot of effort.

Small items should be kept on narrow shelves for easy location. Large deep drawers are useful for storing bulky utensils such as saucepans and casseroles.

Cupboards should be planned for easy access. Cupboards above bench level should be no deeper than 300mm and should be set around 400mm above the work surface for head room.

Storage is not just confined behind cupboard doors. Today open shelves, butcher's hooks hanging from a rack or beam, cup hooks and racks offer decorative opportunities. It is useful to remember, however, that if you have hardworking utensils they will rarely look as decorative as they do in photographs in glossy homemaking magazines.

Bi-fold doors and swinging shelves make it easy to reach everything. Shelves within cupboards should not be too deep to allow easy access to the back.

If you have space, when planning remember that the most carefully contrived cupboard and bench space cannot beat the pleasure and convenience of a walk-in pantry.

BENCHES

Height The Australian standard for bench-top height is 900mm but you may want to adjust this to suit your height. A guideline for comfortable height of work benches is 150mm below your bent elbow when you are standing.
Work surface If you do not want to worry about putting a hot pan from the stove onto the work surface you will have to have stainless steel or ceramic tiles. These are expensive. Care is needed with the grouting between tiles so that water does not seep through and cause the particle board below to swell and the tiles to crack.

Timber bench tops are attractive but should be well sealed.

Plastic laminates are very popular and hardwearing bench-top surfaces. A velvet-finish plastic laminate surface doesn't show scratches and marks as readily as a shiny surface.

Plastic laminate work benches need only an occasional wipe with a damp cloth. Any stains can be removed with household detergent or liquid household cleanser.

THE SINK

Stainless steel has long been accepted as the most sensible and hard-wearing material for a kitchen sink. There are now, however, attractively coloured sinks in bright or muted shades of vitreous enamel, which is chip resistant; and in copper.

The size of the family and the size of the work top will determine whether you choose a double bowl or the space-saving one-and-a-half size, whether you have draining space on both sides or on one side only. Modern sinks have their own accessories, including chopping boards, drainers and baskets.

Taps should be efficient and designed so as not to collect deposits of grime. A high, curved spout will make it easy to fill a bucket or large utensil.

Clean stainless steel sink surrounds with a cloth moistened with vinegar. Do not leave on too long. Rinse, dry.

Stainless steel sinks will shine if rubbed very hard with wads of crumpled up newspaper.

Kitchen sinks are more likely to stay unclogged if drains are cleaned regularly. Dissolve 3 tablespoons of washing soda in boiling water and pour the solution into the drain.

Don't pour coffee and tea grounds into the sink, as kitchen waste will eventually accumulate and clog it.

WASHING UP

Washing up is easier if dishes are scraped and rinsed after use and stacked according to size. Remove left-overs from pots and pans as soon as food is dished up and soak utensils.

It is practical to begin with the least dirty and most fragile items when washing up: glasses, glass dishes, cutlery, non-greasy plates and dishes, greasy plates and dishes, and cooking pots and pans last.

Use large plastic ice-cream containers filled with hot water when you have only a small number of utensils to wash. It saves water.

Buy liquid cleaners in the most economical size (not always the largest) and decant into old squeeze-top or spray-top plastic bottles. Use a squirt instead of pouring out a large amount.

GARBAGE

Check your garbage for bottles, aerosol cans and batteries before putting it in the incinerator. They can explode or give off toxic fumes.

A waste disposal unit will help eliminate wet garbage from your kitchen.

If possible, do not keep a dustbin near the kitchen door. It will attract flies, ants and cockroaches.

A few mothballs in the garbage tin will help ward off dogs and insects. Ammonia also keeps the garbage tin odour-free and keeps away pests.

Pierce a hole in the lids of plastic garbage bins and tie them to the handle to stop them from blowing away, or being crushed.

THE WELL-STOCKED KITCHEN CUPBOARD

Perhaps this looks a bit lavish for the average family, but it is a useful checklist.

Herbs, spices and savoury seasonings
Bay leaves, chives
Black olives, bottled (if opened and not all used, tip off any liquid and cover with salad oil: they will keep for 3–4 weeks)
Bouillon cubes, chicken and beef
Breadcrumbs
Chutney and pickles
Herbs and spices, choice of: basil, marjoram, sage, thyme, rosemary, mixed herbs, black and white pepper, cayenne pepper, cinnamon, cloves, curry powder, ginger, paprika, mixed spice
Peppercorns: black and white
Mustard: English and French
Parmesan cheese, grated
Salt: cooking and table, sea salt
Pickled onions
Tomato purée and paste
Cake ingredients, dried foods, sugar and sweet flavourings
Almonds, whole (unblanched)
Candied peel

Glacé cherries, vanilla pods
Almond and vanilla essence
Arrowroot, cornflour, rice flour, gelatine
Baking powder, bicarbonate of soda, cream of tartar
Dried fruits: apricots, prunes, currants, raisins, sultanas
Coconut
Dried milk, evaporated milk
Flour: plain, self-raising and wholemeal
Pasta
Rice
Sugar: castor, granulated, loaf, soft brown
Oatmeal, cereal

Vegetables
Haricot beans, lentils, instant mashed potato, dehydrated peas

Canned soup, fish, meat, vegetables and fruit
Soup: consommé, tomato, asparagus, oyster, pea
Fish: anchovies, crab, salmon, prawns, sardines, tuna, smoked oysters, kippers, pilchards
Meat: ham, corned beef, pâté de foie, steak and kidney pie, ox tongue, lamb tongues
Vegetables: artichoke hearts, carrots, celery, mushrooms, new potatoes, pimento, spinach purée or leaf, sweetcorn, tomatoes
Fruit: morello cherries, apricots, pears, peaches, prunes, raspberries

Biscuits, fruit juice, coffee, tea, preserves etc
Biscuits: plain for cheese; sweet (your own choice)
Coffee (vacuum-packed and instant), tea, chocolate, cocoa, Milo, Horlicks or Ovaltine
Fruit juices: grapefruit, lemon, orange, pineapple, black currant, lime
Tomato juice
Jams, preserves: golden syrup, honey, marmalade, jams of your choice
Vinegar: malt, red and white wine, cider
Wine: red and dry white for cooking. Buy half bottles unless keeping cask wine.

KITCHEN APPLIANCES

The range of kitchen equipment is so extensive and handsome these days that it often seems almost indecent to ask if it will do the jobs it was designed for properly.

Taste and pocket have a good deal to do with what you want in your kitchen but there are some practical points.

REFRIGERATOR

A refrigerator is a major household expenditure, so the type purchased should suit the way the family lives. If the household consists of a working couple, freezer space, or a separate freezer to cut down on shopping time, becomes more important. Consider carefully the size of refrigerator you need. A too-large refrigerator wastes power and a too-small one wastes food. A practical point is to determine whether you need a door opening to the left or right. The two-door refrigerator, with freezer above, below or beside the refrigerator, is the popular choice in Australian homes.

The small bar refrigerator is a useful adjunct. If you spend a good deal of time around your pool or in a family-room, or if you have a teenager or elderly person living somewhat of a separate life in the household, it can be more sensible and economical to cut down on the size of the kitchen refrigerator and install a bar refrigerator where it will get plenty of use.

REFRIGERATOR MAINTENANCE
The fridge is so much taken for granted in Australian households that people expect it to go on working efficiently with almost no care or attention. In many cases it does. Today's refrigerator is as close to care-free as any appliance can be. You would only have to talk to someone who remembers the old ice-chest to appreciate this.

Some maintenance is essential, both to save energy costs and to get the best use of your refrigerator. Wash and dry inside and outside often. Switch off and remove food racks and vegetable crispers. Sponge walls with warm water and a very little detergent, rinse thoroughly and wipe dry. Wash trays and racks in soapy water, rinse and dry.

Wiping out the interior with a cloth dipped in vinegar will prevent mildew.

A quarter of a cup of ammonia mixed with cold water in a spray bottle is a good cleaner for the refrigerator exterior. Waxing will prevent soiling.

The coils (usually located at the back of the refrigerator) should be vacuumed regularly. Keep dirt from collecting under your refrigerator. A square cut of lino to fit underneath can easily be slipped out and washed.

Leave an open box of bicarbonate of soda in the refrigerator. It will banish food smells for about six weeks. Vanilla poured on a small wad of cotton wool is also effective for removing musty food smells. Wipe it on interior walls. Do not use disinfectant as it will taint food.

Your manufacturer's booklet will tell you how to defrost your refrigerator, if it needs manual defrosting. When defrosting the refrigerator cover the lowest shelf with foil turned up round the edges. Make a small hole in the centre of the foil and place a bowl underneath to catch all drips. To defrost a refrigerator quickly, use a small hair drier.

FOOD STORAGE

Food to be stored in the refrigerator should be tightly wrapped to prevent odours of one food drifting across to another and to prevent food from drying out.

Refrigerated food should be placed so cold air can circulate around it. Containers with lids prevent food and liquids drying out. In frost-free models particularly, moisture is drawn from uncovered liquids, causing the unit to work harder.

FREEZER

If you want to store quantities of food for long periods, a freezer can save you money. Also, by preparing large quantities of food ahead you can reduce preparation time for meals. A freezer, however, will work more efficiently if it is kept filled. It is not something you can use effectively from time to time.

The most convenient spot is not always the best one for a freezer. If the only place available in the kitchen is next to the stove, the freezer may have to be banished to another, cooler place in the house.

A chest freezer is usually cheaper to run than an upright model. Cold air does not escape as quickly when the door is opened. Chest freezers do, however, take up more floor space. Upright freezers are much easier to organise although sometimes they will not take bulky items as easily as a chest freezer.

SOME HELPFUL HINTS

Most foods, fresh or cooked, can be preserved by freezing. Read the manufacturer's instruction manual carefully and follow it.

Freeze only fresh food of top quality.

Cooked food should be freshly prepared and allowed to cool before freezing.

In general, pack foods in quantities for one meal.

Interleave chops, steaks or fish fillets with foil or freezer paper to make them easy to separate.

Don't put fresh food in contact with frozen foods.

Foods for freezing must be packed in containers or bags or wrapped in foil to exclude all air. This avoids freezer burn, loss of colour or flavour and allows you to keep aroma of one food away from others.

Tape over the switch of the freezer's power point to prevent anyone 'borrowing' the point and turning off the freezer.

Tidy storage is easier if certain areas of the freezer are set aside for particular foods. In a chest freezer different coloured plastic string bags can be used to store different items.

If the freezer is without power for some time but the food is not completely thawed, it can be refrozen but will not have the same storage life. Use it as quickly as possible. Many items can be salvaged by cooking them, cooling, then refreezing.

BUYING FROZEN FOODS

Shop last for frozen food and get it home quickly. In hot weather, carry an insulated cooler in the car for more protection.

Go to a supermarket with a brisk turnover to ensure stock is fresh.

Do not buy packages with ice or frost on them.

Vegetables, except spinach and broccoli, should be free flowing in the bag. If they are frozen solid, they have been thawed and refrozen.

Choose opaque in preference to transparent packaging. Fluorescent lights can cause colour changes in frozen food.

FREEZER MAINTENANCE

A fully loaded freezer represents a large investment so it is important to know how to keep your freezer working efficiently.

If you want to monitor your freezer you may consider having an alarm system fitted to warn the household of a rise in temperature in the freezer. These alarms work by battery so that if power is cut off the alarm will still work. Even without power, food in a fully loaded freezer will stay frozen for up to 48 hours if the lid or door is closed. If you expect an interruption to power of some duration, pack dry ice around the food or seek emergency freezer space.

If you are moving house, let the removalists know in advance that they will be taking a freezer. It is better to keep the freezer full. The removalists should then put it into the van last, cover it with insulating material, and unload it first at the other end. It can then be plugged in at once.

If you are going away for a short holiday you may think it worth while to ask a neighbour to check your freezer from time to time. If you will be away for some months, then the freezer should be emptied, food disposed of, the cabinet cleaned and dried and left with the door or lid open to prevent stale odours developing.

As with the refrigerator, an open package of bicarbonate of soda left in the freezer will help remove odours. Replace every two months.

If the freezer is without power for some time and the food inside begins to decompose, the smells will be dreadful. Everything must be removed and the cabinet washed with two tablespoons of bicarbonate of soda dissolved in one litre of water, making sure that shelves and the door gasket are wiped clean. Then you should obtain a disinfecting product from the freezer supplier and repeat the washing process.

Defrosting the freezer

A freezer should be defrosted about twice a year, or when the ice is about 1cm thick. Ice is an insulator and a freezer cannot keep low temperatures if too much ice has accumulated on its walls or shelves. The freezer section of a cyclic defrost refrigerator should be defrosted four or five times a year.

Most of the frost can be removed with a plastic scraper so that it is not necessary to empty the compartment of food. If the ice is so hard that is it impossible to remove it with a scraper, it is necessary to switch off the freezer and remove the food. Cover the frozen food with several thicknesses of newspaper while defrosting is taking place.

A thick stack of newspapers should be placed on the floor of the freezer and a bowl of very hot water put on the newspapers. Close the door or lid of the freezer and let the steam rise and soften the ice. Change the hot water as it cools. It could take 30 minutes for the ice to begin melting.

When all the ice and water have been removed, wash the freezer with two tablespoons of bicarbonate of soda in two litres of warm water. Dry with a soft cloth, switch on again and after 10 minutes reload the frozen food, making sure that items which have been stored longest are nearest the door or lid.

FREEZING AIDS

Correct wrapping is important. There are two groups of wraps.

Group 1: high density polythene bags (crisp feel, opaque appearance); low density bags of heavy gauge plastic (flexible and clear); heavy gauge plastic film with clinging properties made expressly for freezer use; and good quality aluminium foil.

Group 2: high density plastic film or wrap; butcher's slap wrap; light gauge plastic bags; and clinging type plastic wrap.

Group 2 wraps are used for interleaving of wrapped portions. These should be used only in conjunction with group 1.

You will also need a vacuum freezer pump for extracting air from packets, freezer tape, a felt-nibbed pen containing waterproof ink or a wax crayon. A clipping device with aluminium clips for airtight seals on plastic bags is useful.

When you are short of freezer containers, put a freezer bag inside a container, then fill the bag with stewed fruit, soups or stews. Seal and freeze. When frozen, lift out the bag, and use the container again.

Freeze soup, stock or other liquid in clean milk cartons. These are easy to stack in the freezer and the carton can be peeled off.

LOADING YOUR FREEZER

If the unit has a fast freeze setting use this; if not set the controls on the lowest temperature setting. Place packages on cold surfaces (base, sides, refrigerated shelves, etc.) as much as possible. Ensure that you leave adequate air space (10–15mm) between packages.

Until recently it had been recommended that no more than 10 per cent of the freezer's capacity be loaded with fresh food each 24 hours. The meat industry claims that tests have shown that as far as meat is concerned it is acceptable, safe and certainly more convenient to load fresh, chilled meat to 60 per cent of the capacity of the unit at one time. This does not necessarily apply to other foods. Plan each bulk meat purchase to be up to 60 per cent of your freezer.

Plan to restock your freezer when it is almost empty. The temperature of frozen food rises temporarily with the addition of the fresh meat. Big temperature rises in frozen foods cause loss of quality and shorten storage life. With the freezer almost empty it is no problem to defrost, if necessary, before reloading.

Keep frozen food well separated from food which is being frozen. Before loading fresh meat, place all frozen foods on the top shelf of an upright freezer or in the top basket of a chest freezer.

After you have packed the freezer open it as little as possible over the next 48 hours.

STOVE

The choice is between gas and electric. It is up to you whether you make that choice on the basis of economy or in the belief that one fuel gives a better cooking result.

Separate hotplates and wall ovens look attractive but an upright stove takes up less space. Whichever you choose, try to have work bench space on both sides. The console model with grill and hotplates on one side next to the oven enables you to cook without backache when baking and roasting. It is a compromise between the conventional upright stove and hotplates and wall oven.

These days, decisions about your stove are more complex. If you are planning a new kitchen or renovating, you will have to make decisions about whether a microwave oven will enable you to cut down on the size and capacity of your stove. You should also investigate ovens with interior fans which, makers claim, enable you to cook faster, more evenly and cheaply.

When using the oven, open the door as rarely as possible. This lets heat escape and wastes energy.

To save fuel when using your stove, match the size of pots and pans to the size of surface units.

Flat-bottomed pots and pans produce good results on an electric stove because they make complete contact with heating elements. This is not so important with gas.

STOVE MAINTENANCE
If the oven is not too dirty or scorched with food, ammonia is effective in cleaning. Warm oven for 20 minutes then switch off. Put a saucer of full-strength ammonia on the top shelf and a large pan of boiling water on the bottom shelf. Close the door and leave overnight. Open the door for half an hour in the morning then wash off softened grease with hot water and detergent.

For big clean-ups, commercial cleaners

which are sprayed or brushed on the oven are best. Wear rubber gloves to protect hands from caustic burns and cover floor near oven with newspaper—drips may mark surfaces. Do not get caustic spray on surrounding paintwork.

Wipe oven surfaces, rinsing cloth often in hot soapy water, in this order: top, back, sides, bottom, door.

Clean stainless steel oven-shelves by dissolving ½ cup of laundry detergent in a laundry tub of hot water. Leave the shelves to soak a few hours or overnight.

To restore transparency to glass door of oven, wring out a cloth in warm water, dip in bicarbonate of soda and wipe over glass. Allow to dry and buff off with a soft dry cloth. When you have cleaned the oven and there is still an odour, heat some orange peels inside.

After cleaning tiles behind the stove, apply furniture polish and buff to a shine. Grease will then wipe off easily with a paper towel.

The back of a stove near a wall provides a retreat for cockroaches, mice and other pests. Householders handling their own pest control should spray in this area.

microwave oven can and most of the things a conventional oven can, such as browning, crisping and baking.

MICROWAVE OVEN MAINTENANCE
Read instruction book carefully.

Make sure power is off and the stove cool before you begin to clean any part of your microwave oven. Splashes inside the oven can be wiped off with a paper towel or damp cloth. Remove grease with a cloth dipped in soapsuds. Rinse and dry.

Never use a commercial oven cleaner in a microwave oven.

Never remove the cover over the stirrer fan of a microwave oven for cleaning.

To ensure a tight seal around the door, all metal and plastic parts must be wiped often with a damp cloth. A build-up of soil could cause a leakage of microwave energy from the oven. Do not use abrasive cleaners. Rinse and wipe off any cleaning materials thoroughly.

If you drop your microwave oven, or it does not seem to be working properly, get in touch with the manufacturer.

MICROWAVE OVEN

Microwave ovens are popular and the trade believes that they will not be just a fad but a permanent feature of most kitchens.

Microwave energy is a type of high-frequency radio energy. It enters at the top or side of the oven and is distributed throughout the oven. Microwave energy is reflected away from metals, goes through glass, ceramics and paper and is absorbed by food.

The most important part of your microwave oven is the magnetron tube. This converts electrical energy to microwave energy. The waveguide is a metal tube which directs the microwave energy from the magnetron tube into the oven cavity. Many microwave ovens have a stirrer fan beneath the plastic or glass cover at the top of the oven. The stirrer fan distributes the microwave throughout the oven cavity, but there are other systems of doing this. When the oven door is opened all microwave activity stops.

Microwave technology is constantly changing. Most microwave ovens sold now have a rotating turntable for more even cooking. The newest segment of the market is the convection microwave which can do everything a

SMALL APPLIANCES

There are more than two hundred small appliances on the market in Australia, catering for every purpose and whim in kitchen and household.

They are an important segment of the consumer durables market. It is true, however, that many are given as gifts, for Christmas or Mother's Day, and because the recipient may not be too enthusiastic about the gift, nobody in the household may ever take the trouble to find out exactly what the appliance can do and how it works most efficiently.

Beater-mixer Use just one beater in a hand-held mixer when beating small quantities so the mixture is easier to get at.

Blender To clean a blender, fill about a third full with hot water and add a drop of detergent. Cover and turn on for a few seconds. Rinse and drain dry.

Can opener Read instruction book carefully. Turn power off before wiping and cleaning. Wipe with a damp cloth after each use. Remove the cutter assembly, following directions, to clean. Wash can opener with a soapy small brush, rinse and dry.

Coffee pot Clean a coffee pot thoroughly every time you use it to remove oil traces that make coffee bitter. Fill the pot with water to about 3cm from the top, cover and bring to a boil. Add detergent, stand for at least 15 minutes. Scrub with a brush and rinse well. Clean the percolating tube and spout with a narrow brush. Do not immerse the heating section of an electric percolater in water.

Food processor Read instruction book carefully. After unplugging the food processor, wipe the motor base with a clean, damp cloth after use. Never immerse the base in water or other liquid. Wash other attachments in hot sudsy water.

If custards and gravies are lumpy, cool slightly and, using the chopping blade, process until smooth.

A food processor is suitable for preparing pet food. Left-overs can be added to cheaper cuts of meat and minced in a few seconds.

When partially freezing steak for slicing in a food processor, mould or cut it into a shape that will fit into the feed tube before freezing.

Jugs and kettles Do not put more water in the kettle than you need, but be careful to cover the element of electric jugs.

Put an enamel dish under an electric jug so water does not leak onto bench tops when it boils.

Empty a kettle after use to prevent the inside furring up.

Bring equal parts of vinegar and water to the boil in a kettle stained with lime deposits. Stand overnight.

Toaster Read instruction book carefully. Turn off after using. Wipe with a soft damp cloth and dry. Do not use abrasive cleaners.

Remove loose raisins or nuts from bread before toasting.

Do not use a fork or sharp instrument to dislodge a stuck slice of bread. Disconnect toaster. Press knob down to lower the bread lifter. Turn toaster upside down and gently shake to remove crumbs.

Clean crumb tray regularly, following instructions.

To reheat cold toast, just put it back in the toaster. It will quickly pop up again hot with little colour change.

SMALL APPLIANCE SAFETY
Some rules of safety and sense are common to most electrical appliances:

Keep instruction booklets, guarantees and manufacturers' service information provided with appliances together in a file.

Always turn power off at the outlet before removing plug. Remove by grasping the plug. Do not yank the power cord.

Never immerse any electrical appliance in water.

Do not operate any appliance with a damaged power cord or after the appliance has been dropped or damaged.

Do not use appliances near flammable material, such as curtains or quantities of paper.

Do not use accessories which are not designed specifically for the appliance.

Do not use outdoors or in damp areas unless the appliance is specifically designed for these purposes.

Do not place on or near a hot gas or electric burner, or touching a hot oven.

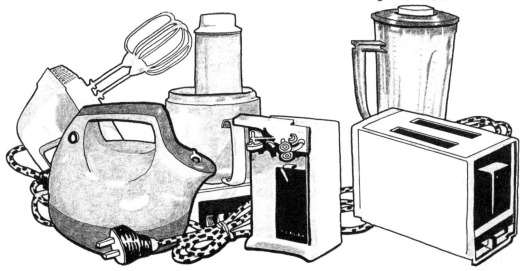

Do not touch hot surfaces of appliance.

Supervise children using or near appliances.

If you store several appliance cords together in a drawer, write the name of the appliance to which each belongs in felt pen on a snap-on tag from a bread pack and attach.

DISHWASHER

Given their function, it is surprising that dishwashers are not in more Australian households. The problem is often the cost of installation. If your kitchen is awkward, it may cost almost as much to install a dishwasher as it does to buy it. No wonder people are deterred.

It is much easier if you are planning a new kitchen and can incorporate the dishwasher in the design.

A dishwasher may be built into the cupboard area, it may be free-standing or, when space does not allow operation of a permanent fixture, some come with a mobile kit as an optional extra. The machine can be rolled forward and when you have finished it is rolled back.

The dishwasher must be the easiest appliance in the kitchen to clean. Most models do most of the work themselves. They have filters which remove food particles from the water as the machine operates. These have to be removed and cleaned.

TROUBLE WITH THE DISHWASHER?

Too much foam in the wash Increase detergent dosage. Use suitable detergent which will stop protein-based foods foaming.

White spots, streaks, film Check on amount of detergent used.

Tarnishing of silver Avoid contact with dry powder.

Tarnishing of aluminium Remove before final rinse. Heat affects the colour of aluminium.

Poor results generally Check filters, spray arms, powder dosage and water temperature.

Poor drying Check rinse aid dispenser. See that air vent in machine is free and water is fully drained. Check stacking of dishes. Never put crystal glass, antique china, glazed decorations, glued-on handles, bone, wood and some plastics or coloured aluminium in your dishwasher.

UTENSILS AND TABLEWARE

This list is simply for guidance for the new homemaker. Some people like nothing more than browsing through kitchenware shops, buying as other people might buy books. For the average person, however, it is unwise to buy anything for the kitchen until you are sure you are going to use it regularly. Many items, such as casseroles and cake-making equipment, are bulky and take up a lot of space.

ESSENTIALS

3 saucepans of graduating size
1 frying pan with lid
1 can opener
1 bottle opener with corkscrew
1 rotary beater
1 set of wooden spoons
1 set of mixing bowls
1 wooden chopping board
1 grater
1 rolling pin
1 set of metric measuring cups

1 set of metric measuring spoons
1 set small steel skewers
metal and plastic spatulas
1 flour sifter
1 strainer
1 vegetable peeler
1 egg slice
1 potato masher
1 baking dish
1 colander
1 kitchen fork

1 pair kitchen scissors
1 lemon squeezer
1 pair tongs
kitchen knives (bread knife, chopping knife, vegetable knife, carving knife and fork)
1 ladle

OTHER USEFUL UTENSILS

pie plates, 20cm and 23cm
pastry brush
draining spoon
meat mallet
omelette pan
double saucepan
wok
vegetable steamer
casserole dish
1 or 2 cake coolers
1 or 2 scone slides
lamington tin, 28 x 18cm
loaf tins, 20 x 10cm and 23 x 12cm for cakes and meat loaves
springform pan, 20cm
1 set patty tins (for cakes and tartlets)
set of scone cutters
1 nylon piping bag, with plain and star nozzles
1 garlic crusher
weighing scales
quiche tin/flan ring
2 sandwich tins, 20cm
soufflé dish

POTS AND PANS

There is some intolerance about saucepans. Some people swear by one material to the exclusion of all others. The right saucepan is the right saucepan for the job. If you do not do a great deal of slow, winter cooking, there is not much purpose in investing in expensive heavy saucepans. Read carefully any label or booklet which comes with new saucepans and follow the maker's instructions.

Some pans will stand up to dishwasher treatment, but pans with wooden or plastic handles should not go in the machine unless the manufacturer says so.

If food has burnt on the inside surface of a pan, it is better to try to soak it off with a bicarbonate of soda paste or an enzyme washing powder, than risk damage by harsh abrasives.

Wipe excess grease from a pan with a wad of kitchen paper or newspaper before cleaning.

Omelette pan Do not wash an omelette pan. Wipe round it with kitchen paper after use.
Electric pan Fat and salts left in an electric pan will discolour it. Clean after each use with hot soapy water.
Wok Smear your wok lightly with cooking oil when not in use. This will prevent rust.
Crock pot To clean a crock pot, unplug cord from outlet, wipe base. Do not immerse base in water. Clean porcelain inside and out with hot soapy water and sponge. Do not use steel wool or abrasives.
Pressure cooker To wash a pressure cooker, remove pressure control weight from cover and immerse cooker in hot soapy water. Scrub inside with steel wool and soap. Never immerse electric heat control on cookers. Check steam vent in cover to make sure it is not clogged. A pipe cleaner will clear it.
Casseroles Generally casseroles made from oven glass, ceramic glass, pottery, stoneware, earthenware and porcelain can be washed in hot water and washing-up liquid. Soak before washing to loosen food morsels. Use a nylon brush to free any stuck-on bits.

Check when you buy whether a casserole is dishwasher proof. Read any labels and leaflets which come with the ware. For casseroles made of materials for which details are given below, follow those instructions.

ALUMINIUM

Do not leave food or water in an aluminium pan for longer than the cooking period. It can cause the surface to pit. Wash up in hot water and washing-up liquid as soon as possible, rinse and dry.

Use a nylon brush to loosen food which has stuck and a soap-impregnated steel wool pad to burnish the surface from time to time. Do not use a steel wool pad on non-stick or mirror finishes.

When washing aluminium pans in a dishwasher make sure they are placed so that the water can reach all the surfaces of the pans to rinse off detergent completely.

Discolouration of aluminium pans may be due to mineral salts in the tap water. This can be removed by boiling up half a lemon or some apple peelings in the pan. Do not use bleach.

Fill an aluminium pan from the cold water tap, letting the tap run for a few seconds first, if the piping is copper. Traces of copper salts in contact with aluminium can pit the surface. Use a wooden spoon. Metal spoons cause scratches and may cause pitting.

Do not put an empty aluminium pan on a hotplate or gas burner. It will overheat quickly. And do not put a hot aluminium pan into cold water or hold it under a cold tap. It may buckle.

Rub aluminium pans with crumpled foil to restore shine.

STAINLESS STEEL

Clean stainless steel pans with hot water and washing-up liquid, using a nylon brush to remove food. A stainless steel cleaner will remove any stains. Do not use bleach.

Stainless steel does not conduct heat evenly so pans usually have a base of another metal. Clean an aluminium base as for aluminium, and a copper one as for copper.

If washing stainless steel in a dishwasher make sure it does not come in contact with powder detergent. Make sure there is room enough between pieces for them to be washed and rinsed properly.

VITREOUS ENAMEL

Wash enamel pans with hot water and washing-up liquid. If the inside becomes stained, fill it with water and add a teaspoon of bleach. Leave for a few hours then wash in the usual way.

If an enamel pan has a non-stick surface, treat as for non-stick ware.

COPPER, LINED

Wash inside of pan with hot water and washing-up liquid. Clean outside with a copper cleaner or apply a paste of vinegar, salt and flour. Wash off. It is important to have pans re-lined as soon as the copper begins to show through.

NON-STICK WARE

Keep and follow labels or leaflets which come with non-stick pans. Some non-stick pans can be washed in hot water and washing-up liquid but others can be washed in hot water only. Do not use abrasives, steel wool or scourers on non-stick ware. From time to time rub over with a nylon or plastic pad to remove any grease clinging to the surface.

To remove stubborn stains boil two tablespoons of bicarbonate of soda with half a cup of vinegar and a cup of water for 10 minutes. Rinse.

CROCKERY

Fine bone china is best washed by hand in a weak solution of washing-up liquid and warm water. Do not use bleach, abrasives or soda. It is easy to damage the surface and dull the pattern, particularly gold decoration. Line the sink with a towel to lessen the risk of chipping or breaking, or use a plastic bowl for washing-up. Rinse in fresh water, drain, dry and polish with a clean, soft teatowel.

Scratching can result from stacking wet pieces of china one on top of the other. Use a plastic-covered rack and make sure each piece is supported separately.

Check that your better quality china is dishwasher proof. Old and hand-painted china should always be washed by hand. If you are using the dishwasher, do not overload and make sure the washing powder is suitable.

After washing, store your delicate china carefully, if possible with cups not touching and adequate room between all pieces, and perhaps tissue or paper towels between plates and saucers. An old glove thumb over the spout will stop your best teapot being chipped.

Acids, such as vinegar and fruit juice, in contact with some decorated china may cause damage to some colours. If possible, wash up, or at least rinse, as soon as possible after using.

Sticky marks on glass and china from labels will come off if rubbed with a little methylated spirits, cooking oil or pre-wash stain removal spray.

A dampened brush dipped in cooking salt will remove tea and coffee stains from cups. Stains in cracked china can sometimes be removed with a cotton bud dipped in peroxide. Rinse well.

Marks on china from it coming in contact with metal objects, such as cutlery, can usually be removed by rubbing with a damp cloth dipped in borax.

MENDING CROCKERY

Broken china can be mended at home. Do not try to mend valuable antique pieces yourself. Take them to an expert. Do not subject mended china to hard wear.

Fresh fractures, involving no splintering or crumbling away, are the easiest to mend and the most likely to result in near-invisible repairs.
Adhesives Many adhesives are suitable for mending china. Most are the epoxy adhesive type, and many are quick setting. Adhesives

for china and pottery are generally colourless when dry. Anything that shows up on a mended article as a dark line is dirt, not glue.

Cleaning Dark lines occur when a piece has been broken and left for a period before being repaired. It is important to mend the article as soon as possible.

Dirty edges will also occur if a piece breaks along a previously mended join, and this may be a little more difficult to clean. Try immersing the item in near-boiling water—do not simmer — or in acetone or methylated spirits. If it proves immune to each in turn, stop trying to clean it. The piece has been glued with an old-type shellac glue.

Once you have removed the old glue (it must be removed), use a strong solution of household detergent in hot water, with a small amount of bleach dissolved (about 1 tablespoon to 4 litres) to clean edges. Leave stubborn items submerged for days or even weeks, but do not increase the strength of the solution.

Gluing and clamping Apply adhesive sparingly—too much will tend to keep the edges apart. You will need to clamp the edges; hand pressure alone is not enough and is hard to keep up for more than a few minutes. Clear cellulose tape will work for short periods, but a brown-paper tape will shrink as it dries. This is a good thing for the break, as long as it is taped evenly on both sides.

Broken handles on cups and mugs are a frequent problem. To support a simple break while the adhesive sets, use tape. Fix it crosswise and lengthwise around the handle.

PLASTICS

Plastic cups, saucers and plates should be washed as soon as possible after use. Some foods and drinks, particularly tea and coffee, will stain.

Do not use serrated knife blades on plastic plates. These can mark and dull the surface.

Some rigid plastics can be washed in a dishwasher but most flexible plastics, such as those used for food storage, must be washed by hand. The high temperatures of water in a dishwasher will affect them.

GLASSWARE

Antique or fine glassware can be kept looking its best with regular cleaning and maintenance.

To unstick a glass stopper in a decanter, apply a drop or two of cooking oil round the edge and stand in a warm place. Tap the stopper gently on both sides with a wooden spoon handle. The stopper should come out easily.

To unstick a glass from the inside of another, fill the top one with cold water and sit the lower one in hot water. The top one will twist out without shattering.

Put a towel in the bottom of the sink when washing fine glass and precious ornaments.

Slip delicate glasses into hot water sideways, not vertically, to prevent cracking from sudden expansion.

Fill dirty decanters with a solution of laundry stain removal powder and water and leave for several hours. Rinse well with warm water and dry upside-down in a wide-necked jug. Or, fill decanter with water and crushed eggshell and leave overnight. Shake vigorously, empty and rinse in warm water. Other remedies are to shake with a mixture of half warm water, half vinegar and half a cup of sand, or lead bird shot and water.

Washing beer glasses in detergent or soap makes the beer flat. Just rinse and drain

glasses—don't use teatowels to dry them.

Crystal will gleam if it is washed in one part vinegar to three parts water.

Or, add a few drops of lemon juice to water when washing glasses.

Put a silver spoon in a glass when pouring in very hot liquids to prevent the glass cracking.

MENDING GLASSWARE

Glass can be repaired the same way as china, but as glass is smoother than china the edges of the broken pieces need to be roughened a little to provide a better 'key' for the adhesive. Use a diamond scratch to do this.

Important Do not repair glass containers that could be used for food or drink. Tiny splinters can break away from the join with use. This is very dangerous.

Very fine sandpaper or an emery board will smooth out a tiny nick in the rim of a glass.

A little toothpaste on a soft cloth will remove scratches from glass.

Picking up the pieces Use a wad of wet cotton wool to pick up splinters of broken glass. Enclose in a strong plastic bag. A cut off piece of soap is also good for picking up fragments of glass. Discard.

materials. Wash these by hand and keep the handles as dry as possible. Hold the handles in your hand while you are washing these. Rub your silver and silver plate with a soft cloth after washing.

There are various dips and polishes on the market for cleaning silver. These are better than old-fashioned methods.

You can make rags for polishing silver and plate by boiling 60g ammonia powder in two cups of water. Soak small squares of damask in the liquid, and dry.

Remove discolouration from teaspoons used for boiled eggs by rubbing with a little salt or ammonia.

To clean wax drips from silver candlesticks, put them in the freezer. Wax will peel off when it freezes.

Polish silver frequently if you live by the sea. Sulphur compounds in the air cause silver to tarnish.

To remove stains from inside silver teapots, put a teaspoon of borax into the teapot, add 2½ cups of hot water and leave for about two hours. Pour liquid from pot, wipe clean, then wash in warm, sudsy water and rinse.

Silver to be put away for a time should be wrapped in the special acid-free tissue paper or tarnish-proof bags which you can buy from jewellers. Then store the wrapped silver in a dry place, in an airtight box if possible.

CUTLERY

SILVER

Silver cutlery should be washed as soon as possible after use, dried immediately and polished with a soft teatowel. Tarnishing and discolouration result from contact with salt, egg, vinegar and other acid foods.

Silver is a comparatively soft metal. Harsh abrasives will scratch silver. Use a liquid or paste specially made for silver cleaning. Clean fine old ladles and spoons slowly and carefully, taking care not to bend handles. A silversmith can repair some pits in antique pieces. However, collectors of antique silver often believe that it is one piece of silver constantly touching another which results in their valued pieces gaining a subtle and beautiful patina. So use your silver daily.

Washing-up liquids and dishwasher detergents are all harmless to silver provided they have been dissolved completely, and almost all sterling and silver plate can be washed in a dishwasher. An exception is cutlery with hollow handles or handles made from wood, horn, ivory, mother-of-pearl and some other natural

STAINLESS STEEL

When silver or stainless steel is put into a dishwasher with worn silver plate or copper, the colour from the exposed metal base of the plated pieces or of the copper can transfer to the silver or stainless steel. It is better to wash them separately. If the colour does transfer, use a silver polish or stainless steel cleaner to remove.

Stainless steel cutlery should stay bright without special care provided it is washed up after use. Prolonged contact with salt and acids can cause discolouration and may cause pitting. Knives should not be left in water. Some slight corrosion or water-spotting may occur.

KNIVES

Fine quality kitchen knives are a great investment. Protect them.

Make sure no one touches your special-purpose knives for odd jobs around the house.

Have drawers slotted so knives are separ-

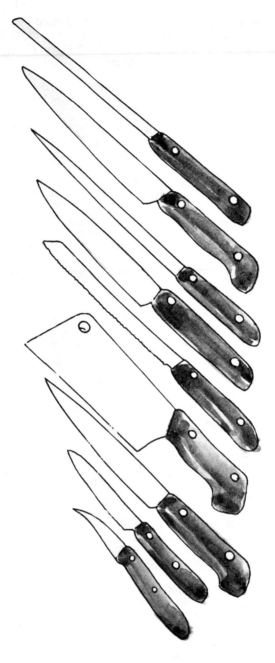

ated from each other. The best thing is a magnetic rack, or a wooden slotted one, standing, or hanging on the wall. Knives flung anyhow in a drawer can be damaged, and can be dangerous.

Do not put knives in the sink. Hot water can weaken the bond between the blade and handle.

An occasional professional sharpening is worthwhile.

Dry knives immediately after washing to retain brightness.

A piece of wet cork dipped in scouring powder will clean stained or rusty carbon steel knife blades. Once used, however, their shine will never be as bright as when new.

White bone knife handle Bleach lemon juice or salt on a damp cloth will remove some stains from white bone knife handles, but often is not successful when knives are old. If handles are yellowed with age, the yellowing will apear as a thin skin. Remove by rubbing with toothpaste on a soft cloth or use the finest grade sandpaper. Wipe handles and buff with silicone cream.

WOOD

Salad bowls Do not immerse a wooden salad bowl in water. This can make the wood dry out, warp or crack. Wipe the bowl round with a paper towel or a cloth wrung out in warm water and let it dry naturally.

Wipe over the surface of a new salad bowl with a cloth moistened with salad oil. Corn oil is good because it never goes rancid. The oil seals the wood and may help prevent the penetration of staining juices.

Rub stains with a nylon scourer dipped in water. Bad stains may need to be rubbed with sandpaper.

A thick paste of instant coffee and cold water rubbed into wooden bowls and platters will help remove scratches. The wood will glow.

Cheese boards Wipe cheese board with a cloth wrung out in warm water and leave it to dry in an airy place, propped up so air can circulate around it.

2
MARKET TO TABLE

THE MAGNIFICENT array of food now available in our markets and shops is one of the many bonuses of Australia's post-war immigration policy. When confronted with dozens of enticing cheeses, unfamiliar cuts of meat and exotic-looking vegetables it's not always easy to know what to buy.

This guide to buying, storing, freezing and cooking or serving food has been divided into major groups: meat; poultry and eggs; seafood; fruit and vegetables; herbs and spices; dairy foods; pasta and rice; and bread, cake and pastry.

MEAT

Today, most people are aware of the need for a varied diet, and that meat is not a necessary part of every meal. However, meat still plays an important part in the diet of the average Australian household.

Low or modified fat diets do not necessarily mean that meat must be rejected. The protein in meat is a valuable energy source when fats and carbohydrates are reduced. The right meat cuts—that is, those with little fat within the muscle and easily trimmed selvedge fat—can be incorporated in a low fat or reduced kilojoule diet.

The cuts of meat given in this section are mostly what the average Australian butcher does. Many of these are standard descriptions, following an industry code of practice for the display and advertising of meat. It is to ensure that the customer gets what he or she asks for. These days, however, many butchers cut carcasses in an entirely different fashion. Some cater to Italian or Greek or other European markets, some supply Chinese and other Asian people.

FREEZING MEAT

BULK BUYING

Consider what your family likes and eats before ordering bulk meat. When you take delivery of bulk meat, pack as much as possible into the refrigerator, leaving it in its original wrapping. Meat should not be left at room temperature. It quickly absorbs heat. If it won't all fit into the refrigerator use a portable insulated cooler.

The ideal way to buy bulk supplies is ordered to your requirements, prepared, packed, labelled and frozen by your supplier. You can, however, save money by buying specials already prepared. These have to be repacked in smaller or meal-sized portions before freezing.

WRAPPING MEAT FOR THE FREEZER

Each package should carry a label showing the name of the cut, weight or amount and date of packing. Air should be expelled either by pressing it out as you wrap or with the aid of a pump. Twist and seal bags with a strip of masking tape.

Expelling air is most important, particularly if the meat is cured, for example, corned beef. Oxygen left in the package accelerates oxidisation of fat, giving the meat an 'off' flavour after prolonged storage.

Over-wrap meat from supermarket meat cabinets if necessary.

Trim fat from meat to a maximum 5mm selvedge if possible. This may not be possible or desirable with pork or cured meats, but storage times given for these meats allow for this.

If meat has been pre-packed for freezing pack into the freezer all at once. When packaging meat yourself, handle each primal cut (rump, loin, etc.) separately. Batches of packaged cuts should be prepared before opening the freezer to pack them inside. This avoids excessive opening of the freezer during loading.

STORAGE

Sliced bacon, ham and smallgoods not recommended.

COOKING MEAT FROM THE FREEZER

Steaks and chops (grilling) Cook from frozen state. Brush with oil or butter, grill under high heat for 3–5 minutes each side to seal, reduce heat to medium or lower grill tray and continue cooking until done to taste. A vertical grill may be used if the meat is flat enough to fit into its basket.

Roasts Large joints should be defrosted slowly. Loosen wrap at base, place joint on a rack set in a dish and put into the warmest section of the refrigerator. Allow 10 hours per 500g. If defrosted at room temperature there is more drip loss and greater risk of microbial growth. If cooking from the frozen state, use a

Meat	Storage at −15°C or below
Rolled beef roasts	6 months
Solid beef joints	6 months
Steaks and cubed beef	6 months
Beef mince, lean	3 months
Beef mince, fat	1 month
Beef and pork sausages	1 month
Lamb and mutton joints	6 months
Lamb and mutton chops	6 months
Pork joints	3 months
Pork chops	3 months
Veal joints	6 months
Veal chops and steaks	4 months
Corned beef, lamb, mutton, tongue (raw)	6–8 weeks
Corned beef, lamb, mutton, tongue (cooked)	8–10 weeks
Offal	1 month
Bacon, unsliced, in medium to large pieces	2 months
Ham in pieces commercially vacuum packed	3 months
Smallgoods	1 month
Stock	6 months

meat thermometer. Any roast from the freezer, whether defrosted or frozen at time of cooking, should be cooked to a minimum internal temperature of 70°C.

With beef joints in particular, roasting from the frozen state causes excessive juices to seep out of the meat. These coagulate around the base of the meat and will not dissolve in the finished gravy—strain gravy before serving.

Corned meats Result is more satisfactory if defrosted before cooking. If cooking from the frozen state, add one tablespoon salt to the cooking liquid.

Stewing and braising meats It is generally preferable to defrost these meats for easy preparation. Follow instructions given for roasts.

Sausages Defrost in refrigerator as for roasts, or unwrap and place in cold tap water, providing sausages have been left in links.

Pork Remove pork from freezer to refrigerator and let it thaw evenly overnight before cooking. Cooking pork while frozen tends to loosen the juices which will coagulate with an unattractive appearance although the pork itself is quite edible.

COOKING MEAT

When using one of the dry heat cooking methods (roasting, grilling, frying or barbecuing), do not salt meat. Add pepper or other flavourings, cook and salt afterwards. In roasting, salt may be rubbed on the fat surface so that the pan juices are flavoured; even if you put salt on the meat, it would not penetrate.

ROASTING

Wipe meat with damp cloth or paper towels. Season with salt and pepper on fat surface, pepper only on meat surfaces. Place joint fat side up on a rack in roasting dish. This ensures heat circulation during cooking. If rib bones are present in a joint, these form a natural rack. Lean joints may need fat spread on top surface and frequent basting during cooking.

Roast at moderate heat only: 160–180°C. Smaller cuts such as rib eye and fillet may be cooked at a higher temperature. Roughly calculate cooking time at 50 minutes per kg. At end of this time, remove roast to bench, insert a meat thermometer with tip in the centre of the thickest part of the meat. Wait until the indicator stops. If insufficiently cooked, remove

thermometer and return roast to oven for further 30 minutes for each 5°C under the desired internal temperature.

When roast is cooked, rest meat in a warm place for at least 15 minutes before carving. Make the gravy and complete the cooking of vegetables during this time.

French roasting A variation of dry roasting for special flavour. Proceed as for roasting, without a rack. Roast for 30 minutes in a moderate oven. Pour special stock and/or wine over joint and continue to cook, basting joint often with liquid. Skim fat from juices in dish, strain and serve in a sauce boat. Roast should be rested before carving.

Traditional trimmings Beef: Yorkshire pudding. Veal: forcemeat. Mutton: red-currant jelly. Lamb: mint sauce. Pork: apple sauce, baked or fried apples, cranberry sauce. Poultry: bread sauce (chicken or turkey); apple sauce (duck or goose); cranberry sauce (turkey or goose); orange sauce (duck).

GRILLING

When grilling or barbecuing meat, always turn with tongs. A fork pierces the sealed surface of the meat and lets the juices out. Dry meat is tough.

Preheat griller, place meat on grill rack and season with pepper, and perhaps herbs or garlic, but no salt. Brush meat surfaces lightly with oil or melted butter. Grill under high heat until top changes colour (2 minutes), turn with tongs and grill for further 2 minutes. Reduce grill heat or lower grill tray and continue to cook until done to taste, turning meat occasionally. Season with salt and serve immediately. Grilled meat should not be kept hot for long periods or reheated.

Grilled to suit your taste Here are the accepted degrees of cooking of grills:

• Very rare (*bleu*): the meat is cooked enough to sear all the surfaces and offers no resistance when touched. Used for steak and some game.

• Rare (*saignant*): turn the meat when the blood has come to the surface and brown the other side. The meat offers little resistance when touched and feels spongy. When cut, it is deep pink inside. For steak, lamb, game and kidneys.

• Medium (*à point*): before the meat is turned, drops of juice are visible on the surface, showing that the meat is warmed through. When pressed with a finger, the meat resists because it is cooked enough to have contracted. When

cut, it is rose pink inside. For steak, lamb, kidneys, liver, veal and duck.
• Well done (*bien cuit*): the meat is very firm to the touch because heat has reached the centre. When cut, there is no trace of pink inside. For pork, chicken, fish and shellfish.

PAN-GRILLING

For meats with a fat selvedge e.g. T-bone steaks, lamb chops.

Heat frying pan or griddle over medium heat. Utensil should have a thick base for even heat distribution. Lightly grease pan or griddle with fat, butter or oil.

Season meat with pepper if desired, place in pan, cook on medium heat, turning occasionally with tongs. Adjust heat if necessary so that meat cooks without boiling in its juices. Drain off fat as it accumulates, and continue cooking until meat is done to taste. Season with salt and serve immediately.

PAN-FRYING

For lean steaks and crumbed meats.

Heat pan over moderately high heat, add enough butter or oil to just cover base of pan. Add meat and fry until meat juices begin to appear on top surface, turn with tongs and fry until cooked to taste. Remove meat from pan and season with salt. Juices in pan may be used as a basis for a quick sauce.

Note: For rare beef, fry on high heat for 2–3 minutes each side only, time depending on thickness of steak.

Frying in oil and butter A combination of oil and butter gives the best of both frying worlds: the flavour of butter is imparted to the food, and the addition of oil means that the food can be cooked at a higher temperature than if it were cooked in all butter, so eliminating the possibility of greasy food. The oil helps prevent the butter from burning when the temperature is increased.

The proportions vary depending on individual requirements of recipes, but generally about double the amount of oil to butter will give a good result; for example 60g butter to ½ cup oil.

Frying crumbed meat The pan should be heated, then the oil (or oil and butter), added and heated, then crumbed pieces of meat added one at a time, allowing the oil to regain some of its heat before adding the next piece. Any food which has been egg-and-breadcrumbed will cook much better if refrigerated

30 minutes before it is cooked. This encourages the egg mixture to absorb and hold the crumbs firmly on the food.

BRAISING

Cut meat if necessary into serving portions. Coat with seasoned flour if desired. Brown in a small amount of hot fat or oil. Do a single layer of meat at a time and remove to a plate as it browns. Add flavouring vegetables if used and sauté gently for 10 minutes.

Return meat to pan, add salt and pepper to taste and other flavourings such as herbs, spices or sauces. Add a small quantity of stock, water, wine or other liquid specified in recipe. Meat juices will increase liquid content. Cover firmly with lid and simmer gently on low heat, or cook in a slow oven, 160°C. Add other vegetables if required during the cooking period.

When meat is tender, thicken if necessary with a flour or cornflour and water paste. If a generous amount of chopped vegetables has been used, thickening will not be necessary.

SIMMERING

Wash meat under cold, running water. Corned meats do not require soaking as butchers today do not use strong brine solutions.

Place in a large pot and cover meat with warm water. Add whole peppercorns, a blade of mace, bay leaf and flavouring vegetables such as onion, carrot, celery etc. Bring to simmering point—i.e. when an occasional bubble rises to the surface. Skim at this point if necessary. Cover pan and simmer gently until meat is tender.

Large pieces of vegetables may be added during cooking time. Add cabbage 20 minutes before end of cooking time.

Remove meat and vegetable accompaniment to a warm platter. Carve sufficient meat for the meal, returning remainder to pan to cool in the liquid. When cool, drain meat and place in a container. Seal and store in refrigerator.

STEWING

Cut meat into cubes unless chops are being used. Coat with seasoned flour if desired. Brown meat in a little hot fat or oil, placing a single layer of meat in pan at a time. Remove to a plate when browned. Add onion and other flavouring vegetables to pan and sauté gently for 10 minutes.

Return meat to pan. Season with salt and pepper and add herbs, spices or sauces specified in recipe. Add liquid: stock, water, wine, tomato purée, or a mixture of some of these. Do not add too much liquid: 1 cup to 1 kg meat is sufficient as meat juices will add to liquid content. Cover tightly and simmer on low heat until meat is tender. Other vegetables may be added during cooking. Thicken if necessary with a flour or cornflour and water paste. Adjust seasoning and serve.

Casseroles Same procedure as for stewing, only meat is placed in a casserole dish after initial browning. Cover and cook in a moderately slow oven, 160°C until meat is tender.

For quick-to-prepare casseroles, coat meat with seasoned flour, layer meat in casserole dish with flavouring vegetables and add liquid such as red wine, stock, tomato purée. Cook for 30 minutes, then check liquid level and add more if necessary. Continue to cook until meat is tender.

POT ROASTS

Coat meat with seasoned flour if desired. Heat a little fat or oil in a heavy pan or Dutch oven, add meat and brown quickly on all sides. Remove to a plate. Reduce heat and add onion and other flavouring vegetables. Sauté gently for 10 minutes.

Return meat to pan and add a small quantity of liquid: stock, wine, water, tomato purée. Meat juices will increase liquid content. Add seasoning, herbs, spices or other flavourings. Cover pan tightly and simmer gently on low heat until meat is tender. Turn meat over during cooking.

Larger pieces of vegetables may be added during cooking period.

Remove pot roast and larger vegetables to a warm platter and keep hot. Skim fat from liquid in pan and reduce if necessary over high heat. Thicken with a flour or cornflour and water paste or pass through a fine sieve, pressing flavouring vegetables through into the sauce to make it thicken. Carve pot roast, spoon some sauce over meat and serve remainder in a sauce boat.

CARVING

Carving is largely a matter of practice and common sense, but it helps to have a plan in mind as well as a very sharp knife.

BEEF

Sirloin of beef To serve, place the thickest end on the left of the carver with the undercut underneath. Lift the joint and turn, bringing undercut to front. Cut undercut downward toward bone on a slight angle in fairly thick slices. Carve the upper part parallel with the ribs in long slices. Detach slices by inserting knife between bone and meat. A round of beef should be cut in thin slices.

LAMB AND PORK

Leg of lamb or pork The small end of the leg should be on the carver's left, with the thick part to the far side of the dish. Insert the fork in the thickest part and lift the joint slightly toward you. Start at the thickest part and cut medium slices down toward the bone. Detach slices from bone with knife, working from the thickest end toward the bone. Serve a small amount of fat or crackling with each portion. In the case of a leg of pork, the crackling is generally removed before carving.

Saddle of lamb Use a long-bladed knife and make long cuts on each side of the chine. Run the knife down between the meat and the bones, lift onto carving board and cut in thick slices. Turn saddle over and remove the fillet on the underside. If saddle includes the chump, carve this first, then remove the loin meat.

Loin of lamb or pork Start to carve with the thick part away from you. Cut through meat between bones to separate cutlets. If kidneys are still attached to loin, serve a small piece with each portion.

Shoulder of lamb Place on dish with skin side up. Insert fork in fleshy part and lift joint slightly. Cut slightly curved slices from outside to centre, down toward bone. Cut in a straight line from centre to right edge toward bone. Turn joint over and carve underside.

Ham Begin as for leg of lamb. Using a thin sharp knife, cut through thickest part from back edge toward bone. Cut thin slices toward both ends of the bone. Ham can also be cut in thin slices from the knuckle toward the thicker end.

CHICKEN

Remove all trussing equipment, such as skewers or thread, from the bird. Place the chicken breast-up on a carving board large enough to allow for easy handling. Have a plate close at hand to hold pieces as you remove them.

Pierce the chicken firmly with the carving

fork. With a sharp knife, cut the skin between leg and breast. Ease the knife into the leg joint at the back and cut through the thigh joint to remove whole leg from body. Cut through the joint to separate the drumstick and thigh. Place fork into the breast near the breastbone and cut off the wing close to the body. Begin slicing the whole meat from the top of the breastbone and cut down toward wing joint.

TURKEY

Remove the drumstick and thigh by cutting between the bones at the joint. Place the leg flat on carving board and cut it in half at the joint. Holding the end of the drumstick, carve the meat down into slices. Cut the other piece (the thigh) into slices.

Cut across the top of the wing into the carcass but do not remove wing. Carve the breast in thin slices down to the cut made at the top of the wing; this makes it easy to remove slices. Start each slice a little higher up on the breast. As you carve you will come against the bone of the carcass; cut small slices from near the breastbone. Toward the end you will be able to cut through the stuffing so it is incorporated into each slice. You can serve the remaining stuffing separately.

To remove wing, make a cut beneath it and cut between bones. Wing may be carved as the drumstick.

LAMB

Perhaps because Australia produces so many sheep, Australians have always eaten a good deal of lamb and mutton. It was relatively cheap and plentiful. If these days you eat in a restaurant which specialises in *cuisine nouvelle* and your lamb is perhaps half a dozen paper-thin slices of pink meat it will seem very different from the traditional Sunday roast leg or shoulder.

While lamb carcasses are required by law to be marked, these markings are not always visible once the lamb is broken down into the various cuts. In order to recognise the various sheep meats, look for the following characteristics.

Lamb 3–12 months old. Fat: firm and pinkish white. Flesh: fine grain and velvety in texture. Pinkish-red colour. Bones: red colour showing in certain bones such as ribs.

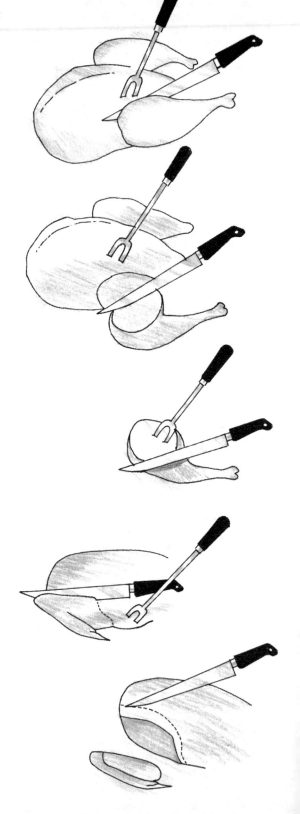

Hogget 1–2 years old. Fat: firm and white. Flesh: fine to medium grain and texture. Light red colour. Bones: slight red colour in bones.

Mutton 2 years and over. Fat: very firm and white. Flesh: medium grain and texture, red colour. Bones: no red visible in bones.

Hogget and mutton are not widely available these days. Country people who raise sheep often prefer mature meat themselves for a more substantial meal and a slightly stronger taste. Hogget and mutton should be aged for four or five days before using.

If for any reason you are cutting down on fats, choose lamb cuts which can be easily trimmed of fat. Leg of lamb is by far the most useful cut for low-fat cooking.

LAMB CUTS AND COOKING USES

Leg Whole, including short leg, fillet and long leg (i.e. leg with chump on): roast, simmer. Whole, corned, or corned and smoked: simmer. Whole, tunnel-boned: tie and roast with or without a stuffing; pot roast. Whole, boned and opened out (butterflied): roast, barbecue.

Chops and steak: grill, pan-grill, pan-fry, barbecue. Cubed: cooked on skewers (kebabs, etc.); braise, stew, casserole.

Chump Whole: roast.

Chops: grill, pan-grill, pan-fry, barbecue, braise, stew, casserole.

Mid loin Whole, bone in or boned: roll up and tie with or without a stuffing and roast. Fine skin covering fat should be removed; if bone in, chine (backbone) should be sawn at intervals.

Chops: grill, pan-grill, barbecue.

Rib loin Whole, untrimmed: roast (remove fine skin on fat). Whole, rib bones Frenched (trimmed), known as racks: roast, barbecue; if cut in 2-rib portions (double cutlets), can also be grilled or pan-grilled with medium heat. (Remove fine skin on fat.)

Cutlets: grill, pan-grill; pan-fry or oven-bake with crumb coating.

Forequarter Whole: roast. Must be oven-prepared by butcher, i.e. with rib section on underside sawn into chops. Whole, boned out: roll and tie with or without a stuffing and roast or pot roast. Cube for kebabs, stews, casseroles.

Chops: grill, pan-grill, barbecue, braise, stew, casserole.

Shoulder Whole: roast. Whole, boned out: roll and tie with or without stuffing and roast or pot roast. Cube for kebabs, stews, casseroles.

Chops: grill, pan-fry, barbecue, braise, stew, casserole.

Best neck Chops: braise, stew, casserole.

Cutlets: pan-fry with or without crumb coating; braise, stew, casserole.

Neck Chops (halved neck) or rosettes (whole neck): braise, stew, casserole, soup.

Breast Whole, boned: roast, rolled with sausage or other stuffing.

Whole, bone in or cut in strips: braise, soup, barbecue (after braising in own juices to tenderise meat).

Shank Whole, bone cracked if desired: braise, stew, casserole, soup, barbecue (marinate first).

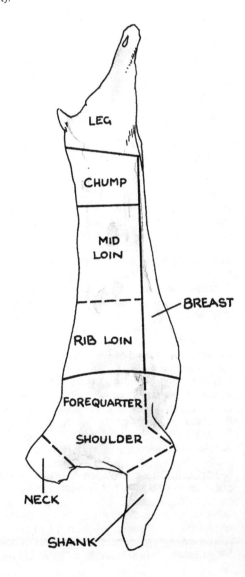

SPECIAL LAMB CUTS

Saddle of lamb This must be ordered ahead, before the butcher splits the lamb carcass. Saddle is descriptive of the cut and is the full back of the lamb, appropriately trimmed. It can extend from the chump to the neck end of the rib loins (small lamb); include the mid and rib loins or mid loins only (larger lamb). The breast is removed and the fine skin covering the fat pulled off.

Boned saddle of lamb for stuffing should come from a large lamb, and can be mid loin only or mid and rib loin. Pull off fine skin from fat, then cut the meat away from the bones, freezing the fillet first, then the loin meat from the rib and chine. Take care when freeing the chine from the fat along the centre of the saddle, as it is the thinnest part of the fat. Fill with stuffing, roll, tie and roast.

Noisettes These are formed from boned mid or rib loin. Pull off fine skin from fat. Roll up firmly beginning from the thicker side of the loin. Skewer in place then tie with white string at 3cm intervals with end ties 1.5cm from each. Cut between the ties. If desired 2 halved and cored lamb kidneys may be placed along the centre of the loin before rolling. Grill or pan-grill.

Racks These are the rib loins, 'Frenched', that is with the rib bones trimmed of fatty flap. Butchers prepare these *en masse* for cutting into cutlets, and in so doing usually cut off the blade bone at one end, leaving this end without a covering of fat. If you want 8-rib racks, then order ahead and ask the butcher to remove the blade bone without spoiling the fat cover.

Guard-of-honour This is made with two racks, each of 6–8 ribs, positioned with rib bones interlacing, fat-side out. Tie in place and fill tunnel thus formed with stuffing if required, then roast.

Crown roast Again this is 2 racks, usually of 8 ribs each. The butcher makes these on request, so order ahead. Ask him to remove some of the fat covering before forming the crown roast. As the fat ends up in the centre of the roast, it does not brown during cooking. Place a jar or bowl in the centre so that shape is retained during cooking, otherwise fill with stuffing and roast.

Medallions These are lean nuggets of meat cut from the rib loin, but should come from a large carcass, about 22kg at least. If from a small lamb, medallions are too small. Remove meat from rib bones then trim off all fat. You will be left with a roundish, long strip of meat. Slice meat and quickly sauté, or tie whole piece

at intervals, brown in butter then finish for 10 minutes in a very hot oven. Slice to serve.

BEEF

Beef appears on the Australian menu more often than any other meat. Although one aspect of the industry's promotion is aimed at increasing consumption, another and important promotion is educating people to combine beef with vegetables, dairy products, rice, pasta and other accompaniments to get a varied and satisfying diet.

BEEF CUTS AND COOKING USES

Knowing which cuts to use for a particular cooking purpose is essential so that you can make the most of your beef purchase. A beef carcass has the fewest tender cuts of any domestic animal carcass so these prime cuts are higher in price. Their advantage is that they suit the convenient dry heat cooking methods such as roasting and grilling.

However, there are other beef cuts which are also suitable for such cooking methods, less expensive and just as satisfying. Steak recognition and its ideal cooking use (and alternative cooking use) are where confusion exists.

Beef roasting cuts From hindquarter: wing rib, sirloin, fillet, rump, corner-cut topside and .fresh silverside roasts.

From forequarter: standing rib roast, rolled rib roast, rolled roast, rib eye and bolar blade roasts.

Beef grilling (and frying) cuts From hindquarter: sirloin, T-bone, rump, fillet steaks; the first 4 slices of round steak and the first 2 slices of topside steak are less expensive grilling cuts. If the beef is yearling, all the round steak is suitable for grilling, and though topside is also suitable, it can be drier because of the nature of the muscle.

From forequarter: rib steak on the bone, rib eye, bolar blade, cross-cut or blade steak on the bone, oyster blade steak.

Beef braising cuts From hindquarter: round, topside, fresh silverside and thick skirt steak.

From forequarter: bolar blade and blade steak, beef spareribs.

Beef stewing and casserole cuts From hindquarter: round, topside, fresh silverside, thick skirt steaks, shin or gravy beef.

From forequarter, bolar blade, blade, chuck and thin skirt steaks, beef spareribs, shin or gravy beef, fresh brisket (boned, fat removed and cubed).

Beef pot roasts From hindquarter: round, topside, fresh silverside pot roasts.

From forequarter: bolar blade, rolled chuck and rolled fresh brisket pot roasts.

Beef cuts for simmering From hindquarter: corned silverside.

From forequarter: corned brisket, usually boned and rolled, sometimes left on the bone in a piece.

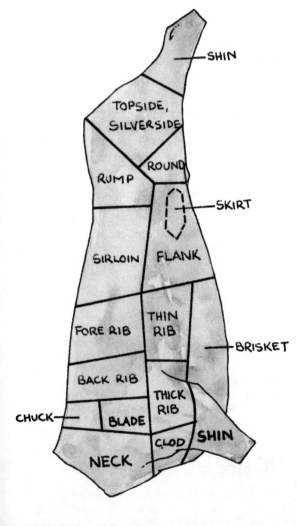

VEAL

The production and consumption of veal in this country tell a good deal of what has happened to Australia's population in the past generation or two. Veal consumption has gone up greatly and people are now familiar with European-style veal as well as the traditional Australian veal.

Veal comes from young beef carcasses. It is generally a by-product of the dairy industry. Cows must give birth in order to keep up milk production. Bull calves and heifers not needed in the herd are milk-fed until they are ready for the meat industry. This is light veal, pale in colour with very little or no fat. Medium and heavy veal generally comes from the beef industry when young calves need to be sold. Veal production units are increasing in number. These usually buy very young calves from dairy herds and raise them to produce the 'white' veal which is the European taste and tradition.

VEAL CUTS AND COOKING USES

Rump From light veal, the rump is usually part of a leg roast. Rump steak from larger veal can be grilled, fried or sautéed. If the whole leg is cut into steaks, the rump is included in these when the veal is seamed (see Schnitzel).

Loin The whole loin may be roasted, but a neater roast is obtained if the loin (or part of it) is boned out and rolled with or without a stuffing. The rib end of the loin can be prepared as a rack for roasting. A very tender veal cut.

Loin chops and cutlets are tender and almost half the price of leg steak. Grill, fry or use in braises, stews and casseroles.

Leg Leg roasts, with the bone in, are generally from light veal and often cut in half for smaller roasts. From medium and heavy veal, the primal cuts of round, topside and silverside can also be roasted.

Steak slices can be taken from any part of the leg excluding the knuckle. With light veal, the topside and silverside are usually taken off together for steaks of reasonable size. As steaks are usually prepared beforehand by the butcher, it is advisable to order ahead if thicker steaks are required. All veal steaks may be grilled, fried or sautéed. See Schnitzel for further details.

Shoulder, forequarter Bone in, or boned and rolled with or without a stuffing, the shoulder from light veal is an economical and tender roast. From medium or heavy veal, the whole shoulder is much too large for a meal-sized roast, and may be available in pieces, much like rolled beef roast. Rolled shoulder can be used for pot roasting and simmered veal dishes and as an economical substitute for nut of veal.

Depending on the size, the shoulder can be cut into chops on the bone, or boned out and cut into steaks suitable for grilling and frying. The steak cuts from medium and heavy veal are similar to beef cuts, e.g., blade steaks (bone in or boneless), but smaller and more tender than their beef counterparts.

Other chops can be cut from under the shoulder; these are best neck chops and are best suited to cooking with moist heat — stews, braises and casseroles.

Neck From light veal, the neck can be boned out and netted for a lean cut suitable for pot roast or cooking in an oven bag. However, it is frequently cubed, as is the neck from larger veal.

Knuckle The hind and fore shanks are usually sawn in thick pieces on the bone for stews and casseroles. The butcher often sells these as osso buco and, indeed, the knuckle is the only cut suitable for such a dish as it contains the marrow bone. It contains a lot of gristle (collagen) so the cut requires long, slow cooking to soften this into gelatine.

Breast From light veal, the breast is quite thin and, though lean, it contains a lot of connective tissue and bone. When boned out, it can be filled with a stuffing and rolled to make a roast. From medium veal, it is better to cook it by moist heat (pot roast or in oven bag). Generally the breast is trimmed and cubed for stews and casseroles.

Cubed veal The neck, best neck and breast are usually trimmed and cubed, and sold as stew and casserole meat.

Minced veal Trimmings from the carcass are minced, though frequently these are mixed with pork trimmings for veal and pork mince. If pure veal mince is required, use shoulder or cubed veal and either have the butcher mince it, or do this at home.

SPECIAL VEAL CUTS

Nut of veal Recipes often call for this cut. It is usually the whole round from the leg, carefully trimmed, though it can be the topside. Size varies according to size of carcass. Used for roasts and special dishes. It may be necessary to order ahead.

Schnitzel Thin slices taken from the leg, and the most popular veal cut by far. Schnitzel is preferred with as little connective tissue as possible separating the muscles.

Butchers break up the legs of light veal by following the seams, rather than according to primal cuts. These pieces are then sliced and flattened. Some slices have the grain running lengthwise, but this is unavoidable. The alternative is to slice in the traditional way, although slices may then break up in cooking. As the veal is so tender, a lengthwise grain does not affect quality.

Often butchers buy legs from medium and heavy veal for schnitzel, and these are cut thinly in the traditional manner. The colour is usually a deeper pink to light red, but, once cooked, the veal colour and flavour are evident.

Escalopes Small pieces of thinly sliced veal about 8–10cm square. Cut leg steaks into pieces. Use for sautés.

Medallions Round or oval-shaped slices of veal from the loin or fillet. As the fillet from light veal is very small, and there is very little in a carcass anyway, the loin offers the only alternative.

Ask for a whole loin, or half a loin if only a small amount is required, and have it boned out. Remove the 'tail' and outer skin or fat selvedge leaving the eye of the loin and a separate small fillet. (Use the 'tails' for stewing.) Slice loin meat about 1.5cm thick and fillet on the bias. Use for sautés.

The eye of the loin may also be left in the one piece, or cut in half if too long, then browned in butter, flambéed and finished in a hot oven for 10 minutes, or until cooked through. Use the pan juices for a sauce, deglazing with Madeira and veal stock.

Smoked veal Topside or silverside from medium or heavy veal is cured, smoked and cooked. A lean meat with a delicate smoky flavour, it is an excellent substitute for ham. A relative newcomer on the smallgoods market, it is available from large delicatessens.

PORK

The pig was introduced to Australia in the very early days of white settlement. In recent years the pig industry's association with dairying has all but vanished. Today nearly all pigs are produced in grain growing areas and grains are the principal ingredient in pig food.

A pig carcass should be hung in a cool room for at least 24 hours to allow the meat to firm before being cut. If pig meat is cut and sold too fresh, the flesh is rather floppy and wet. It is quite safe to cook and eat but its appearance is less attractive.

The colour of fresh pork varies depending on the size of the animal and the part of the pig it comes from. The ideal weight for good colour is about 65kg, but all cuts of pork can come from a smaller pig.

What is known as New-Fashioned pork was developed to offer the consumer a wider choice of cuts of pork.

PORK CUTS AND COOKING USES

Cooking methods suited to each type of pork cut are quite flexible, more so than for animals which graze, such as beef, lamb and veal. Because they do not graze, pigs do not develop tough muscles. They are fed with formula feeds which ensure a more even quality and texture of meat fibre. While all cuts of pork can either be grilled, barbecued or casseroled successfully it is more cost efficient to use the cheaper cuts for long, slow, moist methods of cooking.

Leg Leg roast (boneless silverside): roast, pot roast. Diced pork: grill, stir-fry, casserole, braise.

Rump Steaks: grill, barbecue, pan-fry. Schnitzel steaks: pan-fry, shallow fry, stir-fry, barbecue.

Loin Loin pork piece (boneless): bake, roast. Fillet pork: grill, pan-fry, bake, roast. Rack of pork (cutlets): bake, roast. Spareribs: grill, barbecue, bake, stir-fry. Butterfly steaks and medallion steaks: grill, barbecue, pan-fry, bake.

Shoulder Roast (boneless forequarter or Scotch boneless neck): roast, pot roast. Diced or minced: pan-fry, stir-fry, casserole, bake, barbecue. Steaks and chops (foreloin): barbecue, pan-fry, braise, casserole.

STORING PORK

Fresh pork Freshly cut from your butcher: can be stored covered in the coldest part of your refrigerator (without actually freezing) for three days.

Pre-packaged from your supermarket: store in refrigerator for two days,

Cooked pork Should be covered or wrapped and kept in coolest part of refrigerator about one hour after cooking and will keep perfectly for several days in an efficient refrigerator. Or can be suitably covered and frozen quickly at −17°C up to one month.

Smoked pork Store in original wrapper or can in coldest section of refrigerator until ready to serve unless otherwise stated on product packaging. If necessary, smoked cuts of pork can be frozen for short period in freezer at −17°C if wrapped in foil. However, pre-packed smoked convenience products should not require freezing e.g. luncheon sliced pork meats.

Pickled pork Pickled pork or fresh pork in brine can be stored in coldest section of refrigerator for three days. Soak in clean water a few hours prior to cooking.

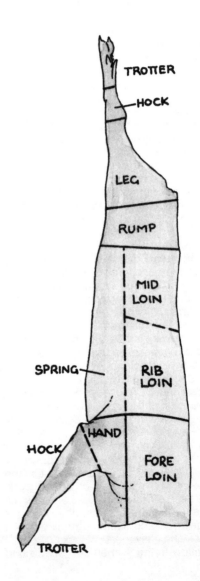

COOKING PORK

Roasting For gas and electric ovens, allow approximately 1 hour per kilo of boneless pork, slightly longer for pork with a bone, cooked in a moderate oven. We recommend that the internal temperature of the pork is checked and this should read 76°C.

The rindless pork roast should be seasoned, placed on a rack over a pan of water and baked in a moderate oven until the correct internal temperature is reached. This reduces shrinkage and fat intake, and the pork carves easily. Oven bags for rindless pork roasts will shorten the cooking time and give a moist result with less shrinkage. Allow roast to stand 10 minutes before carving, otherwise juices will escape and pork will be tougher.

For best results in cooking the crackling, it is suggested that the rind is removed from the roast (your butcher can do this for you), scored and then rubbed with oil and salt. Roast separately in a hot oven to puff and crispen. Serve broken pieces as a garnish.

Grilling It is impossible to cook pork with the rind still on and achieve tender, juicy meat. We would suggest that the rind is removed and cooked separately under a hot griller. When cooking the meat, always pre-heat the griller with a medium heat with the grill or rack in position according to the thickness of the pork. Grill the pork approximately 5 minutes each side according to thickness, but do not overcook it. Brush over a marinade or juices during the cooking.

Barbecues Pork should be handled similarly to chicken and lamb with regards to temperature and this should be a medium heat. Ensure that any excess fat or rind is trimmed off, as this creates flames and heavy smoke, particularly over open fires. It is necessary to cook over glowing embers or hot coals with even, gentle heat. Take care not to cook pork too quickly; basting and turning often will keep the meat moist and flavoursome.

Pan-frying Choose a heavy based, lightly greased frying pan to brown meat both sides over a medium to high heat, then lower the heat and partially cover the pan if desired to completely cook the pork. Turn often to prevent juices seeping out. Allow approximately 7 minutes each side according to thickness.

Stir-fry Pre-marinated or spiced pork which has been cut into thin slices or strips will stir-fry in approximately 5 minutes. Add prepared vegetables and sauce ingredients to make a quick and easy meal.

Shallow-frying A medium, deep-sided frying pan with about 3cm of hot oil or lard is ideal for cooking breaded pork schnitzels, battered, diced pork, pork mince patties or rissoles. Turn the items often to cook through evenly with a good golden colour. Drain well before serving.

Deep frying Use a suitable deep frying saucepan which will enable the use of a frying basket containing about 10cm clean hot oil. Ideal to quickly cook small savoury dim sims, spring rolls, light tempura battered pork, or pork mince combinations wrapped in pastry.

Casseroles and stews Best results achieved if the pork is sautéed or first browned and cooked with highly seasoned sauces, herbs and vegetables to create a complete meal.

MINCE

The cooking of many countries makes use of minced meat. Any cuts of meat, from fillet steak down, can be minced. Most butcheries carry three or four varieties of mince. Quality varies with price.

Beef mince Pure beef mince with beef fat included is often sold in at least three grades: a finely minced low-fat content product, a finely minced higher fat content product and a coarse mince with variable fat content. Fine mince is best for meatballs, meat loaves and hamburgers. Coarse mince serves for stews, pies and meat sauces. Fat in mince is necessary for flavour and improves the texture of meat loaves, meatballs and similar dishes. Coarse mince can be browned and drained of excess fat before making up.

Hamburger mince This is usually a combination of finely minced beef, lamb, pork and veal. You can use this in recipes calling for finely minced beef, if you wish.

Lamb mince This is not widely sold but most butchers will prepare it on request.

Veal and pork mince This is a fine mince containing veal, pork and a small quantity of pork fat for flavour.

Sausage mince This is usually beef and lamb off-cuts with cereal and seasonings. Proportions of fat and cereal content are controlled by State laws.

MINCE IT AT HOME

Almost any meat can be minced. Chuck steak has an ideal flavour and fat content for mince. And it is inexpensive. Round and blade steak mince well. You can remove the fat if you are on a low-fat diet. Gravy beef can be minced but needs a long cooking time.

Fat-free If you are using an animal fat-free mince, add 1 to 2 tablespoons of cooking oil to the mince when making meatballs and meat loaves.

OFFAL

Fancy meats, variety meats as they are known in America, or offal as they are generally referred to in Australia, are not everyone's idea of a taste sensation. Those who do enjoy a dish of brains, liver, kidneys and so on in restaurants, however, often are deterred from serving fancy meats at home because they are unsure of their preparation.

Offal is highly perishable and must be bought and used while it is as fresh as possible. For this reason, many butchers sell it frozen. Fresh offal will keep 24 hours if it is lightly covered to allow some air circulation and refrigerated immediately after purchase. Frozen, it will keep safely for one month.

Do not freeze offal if you suspect it already has been frozen and thawed for sale. To thaw, place wrapped on a plate on the bottom shelf of the refrigerator for 24 hours. To speed up the process, place in cold water and change the water occasionally. Do not thaw oxtail or liver quickly or they will lose too much juice.

BRAINS

Lamb brains are the most common. Place in lightly salted water for 30 minutes then carefully pull away membrane covering brain. Do not remove membrane if brains have been frozen or they will disintegrate: cut away on underside so blood can escape. Change water after first soaking and leave for an hour. To cook, poach (do not boil) and serve with sauce or vinaigrette, or crumb cold poached brains and sauté in butter or oil. Cold poached brains may also be grilled or braised. Watch carefully if grilling to prevent overcooking and keep well basted with butter or oil.

HEART

Order in advance to ensure quality and freshness, as hearts are popular for pet food. Hearts are strong flavoured and their muscle structure makes them dense in texture. If heart has not been cleaned, split open and remove lobes, flaps and membrane between cavities. Wash away any blood clots. Soak heart in cold water with a dash of vinegar for half an hour. Rinse and dry.

Overcooking will toughen heart. Slice and grill gently, basting well with butter or oil. To roast, stuff whole heart with bread or forcemeat stuffing and sew up. Cover with strips of fat or bacon to prevent heart from drying out.

Lamb hearts take about 45 minutes in a moderate oven, veal an hour and ox 1¼ hours. Baste frequently. Hearts may also be braised.

LIVER

Calf liver has the sweetest flavour and is also tender. Lamb's liver, or fry, is tender but has more of the characteristic bitter liver taste. Ox liver is both coarser and stronger in flavour. Liver is best bought in the piece and sliced when you are ready to use it.

Rinse briefly under cold tap. If in one piece, pull away membrane carefully, holding flesh so that it does not tear. Soak in cold water if membrane does not easily come loose. Pat dry, slice and cut out any large tubes. A one hour soak in milk will take away some of the strong taste from ox liver.

Grill, brushing well with butter or oil, or flour and sauté gently in butter and/or oil. Overcooking toughens liver. Chopped onion and crushed garlic sautéed in the pan before the liver is added will greatly improve its flavour.

KIDNEY

Look for rounded, well-formed kidneys. Colour can vary from light brown-red to dark, according to the age of the animal. Cut membrane, if still attached, and pull towards fatty core. Cut kidney in half and remove fatty core. Rinse well in cold water or soak in water with lemon juice for half an hour if you do not like a strong kidney flavour.

Grill halves, brushing well with butter or oil, or slice or cube and sauté gently and serve with sauce. Onions and mushrooms enhance the flavour of kidneys. Two wooden skewers inserted through kidney halves about 3cm apart will prevent curling when grilling. As with heart, kidneys will toughen if overcooked. They should be just pink inside.

OXTAIL

One of the tastier, more accepted forms of

offal. Its rich, sweet flavour makes it ideal for casseroles, stews, braises and soups. If the oxtail is not jointed when you buy it, cut through the natural indentations between vertebrae.

Cook oxtail for at least 3 hours. It has a high fat content, so dishes will need to be skimmed before serving, or left to become cold so that fat can be removed in the piece.

SWEETBREADS

The thymus glands of calves and lambs, consisting of a centre lobe (the heartbread) and two side lobes (the throatbreads). Soak for two or three hours in salted water with a dash of lemon juice to remove blood. Poach as for brains, then plunge into a bowl of cold water and remove membrane and tubes. Then cook as for brains.

TONGUE

Another more popular form of offal, tongue represents excellent value for money because so little is wasted or discarded after cooking. Fresh or corned lamb, calf and ox tongues are available, also smoked ox tongue.

Soak fresh tongues for 1 hour in lightly salted water with a dash of vinegar to remove extra blood. Corned tongue needs only a thorough wash under cold water; some people recommend soaking smoked tongue for 5 hours or so to soften it before cooking. Wash after soaking.

To cook, cover tongue (fresh, corned or smoked) with cold water in a good-sized pan with the seasonings of your choice: a quartered large onion, black peppercorns, a few cloves, chopped parsley and salt if using a fresh tongue. Do not salt corned or smoked tongue. Bring slowly to the boil and immediately reduce to a simmer. Cook covered. Cooking times vary: as a rough guide allow 2 hours for lamb tongues, 3 for calf and 4 or more for a big ox tongue.

Meat will offer no resistance when pierced with a skewer or fork when it is done. Remove cooked tongue to a platter to cool a little, then peel off thick outer skin while still warm. Remove bone and gristle from root end. Reheat in cooking liquid if necessary.

Serve sliced when hot, or cool and use as cold meat. Tongue may also be set in aspic incorporating some of the strained cooking liquid or it may be pressed.

TRIPE

Honeycomb is the most common variety of tripe (the stomach lining of cattle) available in Australia. It may be white or deep cream, but colour bears no relation to quality.

Blanching will improve tripe before you cook it, although it is ready to use when you buy it. Cover with cold water and bring to the boil. Drain and repeat. Tripe is often cut into small squares before cooking. Boiled tripe is simmered, after blanching, with milk, water, onion, vegetables and seasoning until tender (about 1½ hours) and the cooking liquid thickened before serving. It may also be incorporated with a sauce after simmering until tender in milk, water or stock.

Tripe breaks up if it is overcooked. Plain cooked tripe can be drained, cooled, and dipped in flour, egg and breadcrumbs then deep fried.

POULTRY AND EGGS

Chicken and turkey are no longer the occasional treat. Figures released by the Australian Bureau of Statistics for the year 1979–80 show that, on a per capita basis, Australians ate 20.3 kilograms of poultry. They also ate 220 eggs per head. Poultry has the virtues of being cheaper than red meats, low in fat and extremely versatile. Eggs are a high-protein alternative to meat.

POULTRY

BUYING POULTRY

It does not matter whether you buy fresh or frozen poultry. Fresh chicken is better for sautéed and fried dishes as chicken which has been defrosted tends to spit and the flesh may stick to the pan. A fresh chicken or turkey should be used within two to three days. Don't buy a fresh chicken or turkey for freezing. Mass frozen poultry is safer and better.

How much to buy   The first decision is whether it will be more economical to buy pieces. This depends on the dish you are planning: for roasting or frying allow about 375g per person; for grilling or barbecuing half a small chicken is best; for casseroles and other made-up dishes allow about 250g to 500g per person, depending on what else goes into the dish.

For salads allow 1 cup of cut-up cooked chicken per person. You should get a cupful from each 500g of uncooked meat.

Chicken sizes   A size No. 15 chicken is 1.50kg, a size No. 9 is 900g and so on. Sizes 12–21 are best for roasting and pot roasting; sizes 10–12 are best for frying and sauté dishes; sizes 5–9 are best for grilling and barbecuing. These smaller chickens are also better if you intend to give each person half a roast chicken.

Chicken pieces   Breasts and half-breasts are the most expensive. They can be bought boned. They are used for Chinese cookery and for dishes with sauces. If you are serving chicken for a special dinner party it must be breast for a first-clas result. Drumsticks can be barbecued or fried and are popular for parties. Marylands: this is a thigh with drumstick attached and is good for barbecuing and crumbed dishes. Thighs are ideal for curries and casseroles. Wings are used for barbecues and grills. Chicken livers are excellent for paté and other first courses.

FREEZING POULTRY

Put frozen poultry in your freezer as soon as possible. If it has begun to thaw, cook it as soon as it is thawed and then freeze it.

Do not buy fresh poultry and freeze. There is a possibility that what seems to you a fresh chicken has already been frozen and thawed. Uncooked food should never be frozen twice.

EGGS

BUYING EGGS

Eggs are graded and sold according to their

Poultry	Store at −15°C or below
Chicken—whole	6 months
Turkey, duck, goose	4 months
Giblets	4 months
Chicken pieces	4 months
Chicken pieces crumbed	4 months
Cooked pieces	2 months
Cooked casseroles, pies and made-up dishes	3 months
Chicken stock	6 months

minimum weight. This means that in a carton of 55g eggs, the minimum weight of any egg is 55g and in fact the average weight is 56–58g. The standard grades are as follows: 45g, 50g (small); 55g (medium); 60g, 65g (large).

All *Australian Women's Weekly* recipes use 60g (large) eggs.

Buy the freshest eggs possible.

Test for freshness Place the egg in sufficient cold water to cover it. Fresh eggs will lie flat in water. Slightly stale eggs will tilt a little; they can be used for frying or scrambling without ill effect. Stale eggs will sit upright in water; discard these.

STORING EGGS

Whole eggs Eggs should be stored in refrigerator or cool cupboard, with pointed ends down; when the yolk rises, the air space in the rounded end protects it from touching the shell. If storing in cupboard, ensure there is good circulation of air. Eggshells are porous and should not be washed before storing, because this removes the fine covering film. They tend to absorb strong odours, and should not be stored near strong-smelling foods.

Left-over eggs Store yolks in refrigerator, covered with cold water. Store whites or whole eggs out of shell in covered container in refrigerator.

Freezing eggs If stored at −15°C or below whites will last 9 months, yolks 6 months, and whole eggs 6 months.

COOKING WITH EGGS

There are five basic ways of cooking eggs: boiling, poaching, steaming, baking, frying. Eggs are coagulated by heat, and are best cooked slowly at low temperature. High cooking temperatures toughen the protein contained in eggs, and overcooking results in a tough, dry dish or, if any liquid has been added, curdling.

Before adding eggs to other ingredients, check that they are fresh by breaking them into a cup.

To separate egg whites from yolks Use a small funnel. Open the egg over the funnel. The white will run through and the yolk remain. Or, break the egg into a saucer, upturn a small glass over the yolk and pour off the white.

Beating eggs Eggs beat up fluffier when not too cold. They should be at room temperature for best results.

Before beating egg yolks, rinse the bowl in cold water. Beaten yolks will slide out easily.

Beaten egg whites will be more stable if you add one teaspoon cream of tartar to a cup of whites.

A small pinch of salt helps strengthen the albumen when whisking egg whites. Too much will make the whites watery.

Heat the beater before use and egg whites will beat up faster.

Egg whites will not whisk with the slightest trace of grease in the bowl or on the beater.

Rub a cut lemon around the inside of the bowl before whisking egg whites to get more volume.

SEAFOOD

Australians are blessed with a great variety of seafood and freshwater fish. There are more than 2000 species of fish in Australian waters. Of these, only about 10 per cent are commercially acceptable, but that still leaves about 200 species sold in our fish shops and markets.

BUYING SEAFOOD

Buying a whole fish is more economical than buying fillets. The trimmings and head can be used to make soup or sauces.

A rough guide is: whole fish, 450–500g (for 1 serving); gutted—had, fins, tail, removed,

450–500g (for 2 servings); steaks or cutlets, 500g (for 2–3 servings); skinned fillets, 500g (for 2–3 servings).

There are several points to look for when buying seafood.

Whole fish Flesh should be firm and spring back when touched, eyes bright not sunken, skin bright and lustrous, gills bright red.

Fillets and cutlets Flesh should be shiny and firm, not dull and soft; flesh should not be water-logged, no discolouration.

Shellfish Lobsters, crabs, Balmain bugs should have no discolouration of joints; prawns should have no discolouration along the edges of segments or legs; shells of molluscs, such as scallops and mussels, should be tightly closed.

STORING SEAFOOD

If seafood is stored correctly, it will keep perfectly. It is advisable not to use plastic wrap as this causes the fish to sweat.

Whole fish Scale, remove gills and gut. Wash in cold water and dry well. Wrap in foil or place in covered container. Store in refrigerator and use within 2 or 3 days.

Fillets and cutlets Wash in cold water and dry well. Wrap in foil or place in covered container. Store in refrigerator and use within 2 to 3 days. To keep fresh fish overnight in the refrigerator, sprinkle lightly with salt and wrap in foil. Put in the coldest part of the regrigerator, away from butter, cream or any food which absorbs odours.

Smoked fish Wrap in foil or place in covered container. Store in refrigerator and use within 7 to 10 days.

Shellfish Wrap in foil or place in covered container and keep in refrigerator; use within 3 days. Live mussels, oysters, pipis and cockles will die in the refrigerator. It is best to keep these in a damp hessian bag in a cool dark place. During cool weather they will stay alive for about 4 days. Discard any that open before cooking.

FREEZING SEAFOOD

Seafood should be absolutely fresh when purchased for the home freezer.

Fish Freeze whole fish only if you want to serve it whole, as filleting a frozen or thawed out fish does not produce satisfactory fillets. Gut and gill whole fish before placing in freezer. Wrap each fish, fillet or cutlet individually in plastic wrap; this enables you to thaw out exactly what you require. As soon as the fish is frozen, remove and dip in cold water (this forms an ice glaze) then return to freezer. This helps protect the frozen food from drying out and developing 'off' flavours.

Freezer life for fish is up to 6 months with the exception of mullet (3 months due to fat content). All frozen packages must be labelled and dated.

Shellfish Clean and remove inedible portions. Wash and wrap large portions. Wash and wrap large specimens such as lobsters or crabs separately. With small species such as prawns, it is best to freeze in block form. Place prawns in freezable container, cover with cold water and freeze.

Label and date. Freezer life for shellfish is up to 3 months; do not use after 3 months, as shellfish tends to deteriorate.

COOKING SEAFOOD

Fish can be cooked in a wide variety of ways. While there are no set rules about which method to use for a particular type of fish, certain textures and flavours are more suited to one or two methods of cooking.

For example a soft-fleshed fish is better baked than poached or steamed, as its flesh can fall apart very easily. Oily fish are more suited to grilling or oven baking. If a dry fish is

Seafood	Storage at −15°C or below
Lean fish and oily fish treated with ascorbic acid solution	3–4 months
Shellfish	3 months
Oily fish (untreated)	2 months
Cooked fish (patties, croquettes, etc.)	2 months

being grilled, it should be basted regularly so the flesh will stay moist. Fish with a delicate flavour are better simply grilled or pan-fried with a little butter, whereas a very coarse-fleshed fish is ideal in soups, stews and casseroles.

The most common methods of cooking fish are baking, grilling, steaming, poaching, pan frying, deep frying and barbecuing.

Do not overcook fish. It has very little fat content and is penetrated very quickly by heat. Over-cooking dries the flesh out and destroys the flavour. Fish is cooked when the flesh flakes easily when separated with a knife, which should go right through the flesh to the other side. Also, the translucent quality of raw fish should change to an opaque white when cooked. Once cooked, serve fish immediately.

Cooking fish seems very easy when you see vast quantities being plunged into boiling oil at the local fish and chip shop. Handling small quantities at home is not quite as easy. However, there are ways of simplifying and improving the cooking process.

Plunge fish into a bowl of boiling water for a minute or two to make scaling easier. Or rub with vinegar before scaling.

Thawing frozen fish in a bowl covered with milk helps give it a freshly-caught flavour.

To coat fish or meat with flour, place ingredients in a plastic bag and shake gently.

Add a dessertspoon of cooking oil to beaten egg before dipping fish: the breadcrumbs will stay on.

When crumbing fish, add lemon juice instead of water to the beaten egg. It improves the flavour and eliminates the fishy smell.

For best results with crumbed fish, refrigerate fish for 30 minutes before cooking.

Add a dessertspoon of vinegar to the oil or fat when it begins to bubble. This stops the fat being absorbed into the fish.

When frying fish, use a heavy-based pan as fish has a tendency to stick to pans because of its high water content. Always heat the empty pan first; this dries out the film of moisture from the air which has settled on the pan's surface. Now add the oil, and heat again, to the point where the oil looks perfectly still. Add the fish one piece at a time, allowing the heat of the oil to rise again before adding the next piece of fish. Another way to stop fish sticking to the pan is to heat two teaspoons of salt in the pan and then wipe away before frying fish Or, sprinkle fish with salt and leave for a few hours.

When grilling kippers, put a tablespoon or

two of water under them to keep them moist.

Reduce the saltiness of anchovies by soaking them in milk for an hour.

Shellfish will open easily if washed with cold water, then put in a plastic bag in the freezer for an hour.

Wash hands in warm tea to get rid of seafood odours.

Prawns Drop green (uncooked) prawns into boiling salted water; they will turn pink and float to the surface when cooked. If freshly caught drop them into fresh water first for 15 minutes so that all sand in the prawns is disgorged. Green prawns can also be sautéed, braised, fried, grilled and used in many international recipes.

Green prawns should be used where specified in recipes; cooked prawns will toughen if heated again.

Fresh lobster To drown lobster, place it in a bucket of tepid fresh water for 30 minutes. Bring a large saucepan of salted water or sea water to the boil, drop lobster in, reduce heat, simmer until cooked (about 20 minutes, depending on size).

Then drop lobster into cold water immediately to cool quickly and remove any scum on shell.

Scallops These must never be overcooked. If sautéing or frying, dry scallops thoroughly first; then cook for 3–5 minutes. Never boil scallops; poach them gently in well-flavoured stock for 4 minutes, then use as recipe requires.

Mussels Discard any with shells open. Scrape shells clean with a knife, then place on griller rack in pan and cook under a pre-heated griller. Remove mussels from heat as soon as they open.

Only mussels found at the bottom of the sea are edible; it is not advisable to eat any found on wharves or rocks.

Abalone Removed from its shell, abalone resembles a large oyster, and is tough and rubbery. First pound it well with rolling pin around the tough outer edge. Then cut into slices, cook in hot butter with a squeeze of lemon juice, about 3 minutes each side.

FILLETING A FISH

With a sharp boning knife remove head and pectoral fin. Cut off tip of tail. Slit the skin at the beginning of the tail section and cut around fin edges so skin can be removed more easily.

With tip of knife separate skin from flesh. Grasp skin firmly and pull it back toward head of fish. Pull and ease until skin is free as far as head section.

Working from head to tail, run knife down centre of fish against backbone. Hold knife flat against the bone and separate the fillet from bone gently. Repeat with other fillet. Then turn fish over, skin the underside and repeat filleting process.

Note: When skinning fish, dip your fingers in water then salt to grip the skin.

VARIETIES

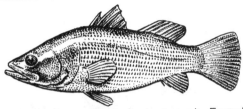

Barramundi Also called: giant perch. Found: N.T. (all year), Qld, W.A.

Regarded as one of Australia's top fish for eating, barramundi's moist, white flesh and excellent flavour suits almost any cooking method. Due to high demand, it is often misrepresented by lesser-known species.

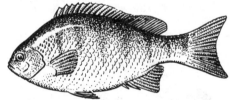

Blackfish Also called: luderick, sweep (Tas. and S.A.), black or rock prch (Vic.), black bream (Tas. and Qld). Found: all States.

A good inexpensive table fish if properly prepared, blackfish can develop a strong 'weedy' flavour if not skinned and filleted. Grilling and frying are both good methods of cooking.

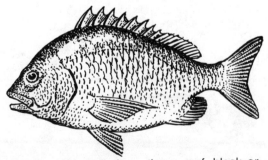

Bream Also called: southern, surf, black or blue-nose bream. Found: Qld, N.S.W., Vic., W.A. Silver or greyfin bream. Found: N.S.W.

There are six species of bream in Australia. Black (or southern) bream is generally considered the best eating fish, although in N.S.W. silver bream is more popular. A versatile and readily available fish, it has excellent keeping qualities.

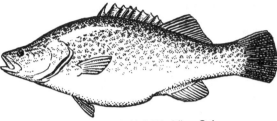

Cod, Murray Found: N.S.W., Vic., S.A.

The most prized of Australia's inland freshwater fish. Murray cod has a delicate, slightly oily flesh, which keeps well and can be cooked many ways; baking, grilling and poaching are popular methods.

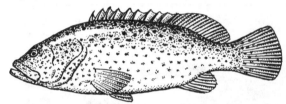

Coral cod Also called: coral trout, leopard fish. Found: Qld (March–July).

The coral trout and coral cod are often confused with each other. Both are beautifully coloured reef fish from Queensland and are sought after for their delicious flavours and firm, moist flesh.

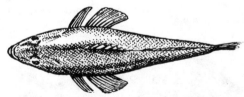

Flathead River flathead. Found: Qld, N.S.W., Vic., W.A. Sand flathead. Found: Qld, N.S.W., Vic., S.A. Tiger flathead. Found: N.S.W., Vic., Tas.

All three species of flathead have a good flavour. Both the tiger and sand flatheads have tender, white flesh. The river flathead is a little dry but has firm, flavoursome flesh and ranks high as a food fish.

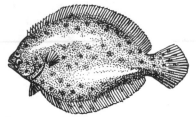

Flounder, greenback Also called: southern, Melbourne or New Zealand flounder; sometimes sold as sole, tongue sole or Qld halibut. Found: N.S.W., Vic., S.A., W.A.

Flounder is an excellent table fish with succulent, fine-textured flesh. These qualities deteriorate quickly, so it should be eaten fresh. It is ideal for cooking whole.

Garfish Sea garfish. Found: all States except N.T. River (splinter) garfish, snubnosed (snub) garfish. Found: N.S.W., Qld.

A sweet-tasting, small, bony fish, highly prized for its firm, delicately flavoured flesh, garfish—sea, river and snubnosed—tends to come on the market in gluts and is an excellent buy. It is best cooked whole, grilled or fried.

Gemfish Also called: hake, king barracouta, Tasmanian kingfish, barraconda. Found: N.S.W., Vic.

An increasingly popular species, gemfish has firm, chunky flesh and a distinctive flavour. Between June and September great quantities are caught and can be bought very cheaply. Usually sold in fillets, it is also available smoked. It keeps well in refrigeration but does not freeze well.

Gurnard, red and latchet Found: all States.

Closely related fish species with a rather dry flesh, both red and latchet gurnard are cheap, meaty and good in stews and soups. Skinned and filleted, they are sometimes marketed as flathead. Latchet has a coarse, tough skin.

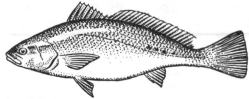

Jewfish (mulloway) Not to be confused with Westralian jewfish. Also called: butterfish, kingfish, silver jew, dewfish, river kingfish. Found: N.T., Qld, N.S.W., S.A., W.A.

Excellent table fish if chosen and prepared correctly. Mulloway can grow to more than 50kg. Between 1 and 3kg, their flesh is firm-textured and delicious. Smaller fish tend to be soft-fleshed and larger fish can lose flavour and be coarse and flaky. Dry cooking such as baking or barbecuing is ideal.

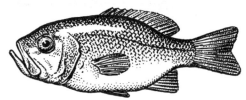

Jewfish Westralian Also called: dhu. Found: W.A. only.

A reef fish which is actually related to the pearl perch, Westralian jewfish's white flesh has a superb, delicate flavour, a very fine texture and excellent edible quality. Bake or lightly pan-fry.

John dory Found: N.S.W., Tas., Vic., S.A., W.A.

Extremely popular for its delicious, succulent flesh, the name John dory is applied to several species of Australian fish such as Queensland butterfish, but true John dory is caught mainly around N.S.W., with limited quantities available in some States. Available filleted or whole, but remember the head weighs almost as much as the body.

Kingfish, yellowtail Also called: Tasmanian

yellowtail, kingfish, yellowtail. Found: Qld, N.S.W., Vic., S.A., Tas.

Found in large schools off the east and south coasts of Australia, yellowtail kingfish can grow to 2.5 metres and is regarded as excellent sporting fish. However, the flesh becomes coarse as fish grows larger, although when smaller it has a delightful flavour and is ideal eating. Usually bought in steaks.

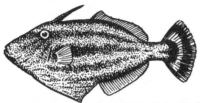

Leatherjacket Found: N.S.W., S.A., W.A.

A very easy fish to catch, the leatherjacket is considered a pest by most fishermen. It is pleasant enough to eat, with a firm, chunky flesh and a mild, almost bland flavour. It needs to be skinned before eating.

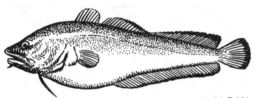

Ling Also called: rock ling. Found: N.S.W., Vic., Tas., S.A.

A member of the cod family, ling's moist white flesh is similar in texture and appearance to that of barramundi and has been sometimes sold as such. However, ling is milder in flavour and is, in its own right, a versatile and usually inexpensive table fish.

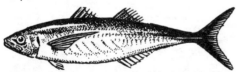

Mackerel, jack Also called: horse mackerel, cowanyoung, scad. Found: N.S.W., Vic., Tas., S.A., W.A.

A rather oily, dark-fleshed fish with a strong, distinctive flavour, jack mackerel is ideally suited to smoking, pickling and canning. Younger fish are sold as yellowtail or scad and can be delicious fried in batter.

Mackerel, Spanish Also called: kingfish. Found: N.T., Qld, N.S.W., W.A.

Common in Queensland waters, Spanish mackerel, a slightly dry, firm-textured and well-flavoured fish, is usually bought in cutlet form and is ideal for baking, barbecuing and marinating.

Mirror dory Also called: silver dory. Found: N.S.W., Vic., Tas., S.A.

A cousin of the John dory, mirror dory is similar enough in taste and appearance to be used as an alternative. Abundant in winter months and an excellent budget buy, it grills, fries or bakes whole.

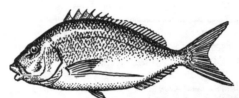

Morwong Also called: sea bream, jackass fish, teraki, queenfish, queen snapper, black or silver perch (Tas.), magpie morwong, sweetlips, rubberlips. Found: N.S.W., Vic., Tas., W.A.

Several species exist, but the jackass morwong is most popular for its firm, delicately flavoured flesh. A good eating fish similar to bream, although a little stronger in flavour, red morwong is much oilier than the jackass species, but both are suited to a variety of cooking methods.

Mullet Flat-tail mullet. Also called: tiger, jumping or brown-back mullet, wankari. Found: Qld, N.S.W., Vic., S.A., W.A. Sand mullet. Also called: lano, Wide Bay mullet. Found: all States. Sea mullet. Also called: hardgut, river, grey or sand mullet, poddy. Found: N.S.W., Vic., Tas., S.A., W.A. Yellow-eye. Also called: Coorong or freshwater mullet, pilchard, sea mullet (Tas.). Found: N.S.W., Vic., S.A., W.A., Tas.

There are many species of mullet in Australia but these are the common commercial species. They are an oily fish with a rich flavour and tender, well-textured flesh. The sand and yellow-eye mullets are the most popular.

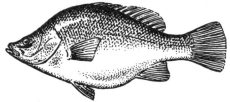

Perch Golden perch. Also called: yellowbelly, callop, tarki, freshwater bream (Vic.), Murray perch. Found: Qld, N.S.W. Pearl perch. Found: Qld. Silver perch (grunter). Qld, N.S.W.

Perch is a common name for a variety of freshwater and marine fishes. Among these, the golden, pearl and giant perch (barramundi) are very popular for their excellent edible qualities. Golden perch, while officially named 'golden', is more widely known as yellowbelly or Murray perch. It has a firm, sweet, rich flesh and is regarded as one of Australia's tastiest freshwater fish. Similarly the pearl perch, which is directly related to the popular Westralian jewfish, is highly prized for its fine-textured flesh and delicate flavour. It is a marine fish caught off the east coast of Australia. On the other hand, silver perch can be quite a contrast to the moist, rich flesh of the golden and pearl perch. It is a rather dry fish, although still good eating.

Red emperor Found: Qld, W.A.
Found only on the Great Barrier Reef and off the coast of Western Australia, red emperor is acclaimed as one of Australia's best eating fish. It is strikingly coloured and has a firm texture and fine flavour.

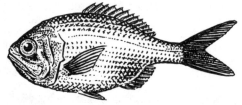

Redfish Also called nannagai, nannygai.

Found: N.S.W., Vic., W.A., Tas.
Marketed mainly as redfish fillets, the tender, white flesh of the redfish is often confused with that of small snapper, although its flavour is not as fine and its texture coarser. It is a cheap and popular table fish with a mild flavour.

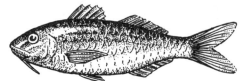

Red mullet Also called: goatfish. Found: all States.
No relation to the mullet family, the red mullet is in fact a member of the perch, bream and bass group of fish. It is known throughout the world as a choice eating fish with a delightful distinctive flavour. Its liver is also regarded as a delicacy. The fish is best grilled, baked or lightly fried.

Salmon, Australian Also called: bay trout. Found: N.S.W., Vic., S.A., W.A., Tas.
Australian salmon should not be confused with the highly-regarded freshwater species of salmon. Although it is known as bay trout, it is actually a type of sea perch. It can be eaten fresh-baked, poached or grilled but the flesh tends to be dark and a bit coarse. Most of the catch is canned.

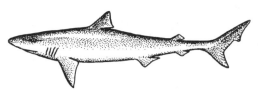

Shark Gummy shark. Also called: flake, sweet William. School shark. Also called: flake, peg-tooth (Tas.), snapper shark. Both found all States.
Although several species of shark are marketed commercially (generally as flake or 'fish fillets') the gummy and school sharks are regarded as the best for eating. The flesh is firm, white and boneless with a good meaty texture. It can be cooked almost any way but is particularly good battered and deep fried. It has excellent keeping qualities and if bought

very fresh may have a faint ammonia smell when cooked—so should be stored in the refrigerator for a day or two.

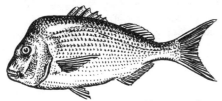

Snapper Names change with age, size and locality and include cockneys, pinkies, red bream, squires. Found: Qld, N.S.W., Vic, S.A., W.A.

A classic table fish with firm, tasty white flesh, larger snapper (more than about 4kg) tend to have coarser flesh and taste rather dry. If bought whole, the head and bones make an excellent fish stock.

Snook (barracouta) Also called: snoek, sea pike, short-finned pike, dingo fish. Found: N.S.W., Vic., Tas.

Of the barracouta species, it is the short-finned snook (found in southern waters) which makes the best eating fish. It has soft, white, fine-textured flesh which can be cooked in many ways. However, care should be taken not to overcook, as it can become rather dry. Normally the flesh is quite oily.

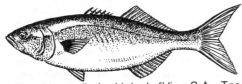

Tailor Also called: skipjack (Vic., S.A., Tas.), pombah (Qld). Found: Qld, N.S.W., Vic., S.A., W.A.

A popular, versatile fish with a slightly oily, dark-coloured flesh, tailor is excellent smoked and is readily available in this form. It keeps very well and is best grilled or barbecued, served with a piquant sauce.

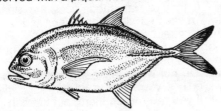

Trevally Also called: skipjack (W.A. only), silver bream (Vic.), silver fish (Tas.), silver or white trevally (N.S.W.). Found: all States.

An inexpensive fish with a firm, dry flesh, few bones and a subtle, sweet flavour, trevally does not keep well and should be eaten fresh and cleaned as soon as possible. It is excellent smoked.

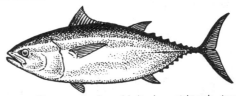

Tuna Also called: skipjack, striped tuna. Southern blue fin tuna. Also called: bonito, Spanish mackerel (W.A. only). Found: all States except N.T.

Most of the tuna in Australian fish shops is of the skipjack variety, the southern blue fin being mainly canned. It comes on the market sporadically but is bought quickly. Larger tuna are cut into steaks, but in both cases the skin, which has a strong taste, should be removed. Tuna must be very fresh, otherwise it loses its flavour and becomes pulpy.

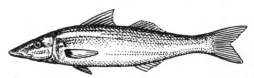

Whiting King George. Also called: spotted or S.A. whiting. Found: N.S.W., Vic., Tas., S.A., W.A. Sand (or silver) whiting. Found: Qld, N.S.W., Vic, Tas., W.A. School (red-spot or trawl) whiting. Found: all States except N.T.

Sometimes the term Australian whiting is used for this well-regarded species of native fish. They are related to the perch, bream and bass and bear no similarity to European whiting. King George or spotted whiting is most popular. It has fine-textured white flesh with a slightly sweet, delicate flavour. Sand and school are also good eating.

OTHER POPULAR SEAFOOD

Anchovies, whitebait Most abundant season: winter-spring. Optimum cooking methods: fry, bake. Description: tiny fish about 3cm long, slightly oily.

Balmain bugs Most abundant season: all year. Optimum cooking methods: boil. Description: similar in taste to lobster, a little richer, medium texture, white meat.

Cuttlefish Most abundant season: all year. Optimum cooking methods: bake, fry. Description: similar to calamari in taste, a little tougher (marinate in lemon juice for a few hours to tenderise).

Lobster Most abundant season: all year. Optimum cooking methods: boil, barbecue. Description: segmented, white flesh, local variety preferred.

Octopus Most abundant season: all year.

Optimum cooking methods: poach, fry. Description: good sea flavour.

Prawns Most abundant season: summer. Optimum cooking methods: grill, fry, barbecue. Description: delicious sea taste.

Sardines Most abundant season: winter. Optimum cooking methods: grill, fry, bake, barbecue. Description: oily dark flesh, good distinct flavour.

FRUIT AND VEGETABLES

Fruit and vegetables can give you all the nutriment, vitamins and basic minerals needed. As well, they can add great variety in flavour and colour to every meal. It is often a matter of custom and choice whether a particular variety is botanically or gastronomically regarded as fruit or vegetable. A good cook uses the best combinations for the dish.

In recent years, many people have gained new ideas on how to prepare and cook fruit and vegetables so that their maximum vitamin content—and flavour—are retained. Some of these methods clash with traditional methods in Australia but it is worth noting that many of these 'new' ways have been used for centuries in countries such as China and Japan.

Choose fruit and vegetables which are crisp, look fresh and which retain good colour.

FRUIT

Most fruits, so long as they have reached some weight and size and have some colour, will ripen after picking. You may have trouble with early-picked berries and stone fruits.

To ripen green fruit, such as bananas, tomatoes, pears, Kiwi fruit and so on, lightly wrap in a plastic bag together with a couple of apples. The apples give off ethylene gas which helps other fruits ripen.

STORING AND USING FRUIT

Apples Stored apples stay fresh longer if they do not touch one another.

When stewing apples, first boil peelings and cores, strain and pour over sliced apples and stew in usual way. This conserves vitamins and produces more jelly substance. Another method is to add two tablespoons of red jelly crystals instead of sugar. This turns the apples pink and gives a rich syrup.

A few slits in apples before baking stops the skin from wrinkling.

About 450g of cooking apples will produce

300mL of apple purée.

Use a potato masher to crush stewed apples for apple sauce in the pan rather than a blender.

Peeled apples will not turn brown if you put them immediately into some water with salt or a little lemon juice added for five or ten minutes.

Avocados Store cut avocados with the stone inside. Brush with lemon juice to stop fruit going brown and cover tightly with plastic wrap. Put the stone back in an avocado mixture, too, to stop it discolouring. Cover with plastic wrap. Remove the stone before serving.

Avocados will ripen more quickly if you put them in a brown paper bag and place them in a warm position.

Bananas Freeze bananas that are on the verge of going bad. They make delicious ice blocks. If they've darkened, peel and beat slightly. Freeze in a plastic container and use in banana cakes.

Green bananas ripen more quickly if put with overripe ones.

Berries Do not wash raspberries and strawberries unless you have to. It can spoil the flavour. If you must wash them, put them in a

colander under the cold tap.

Wash strawberries before hulling or water will make the berries mushy and less flavour-some.

To enhance the taste of strawberries, put them in a dish with the juice of an orange and leave for a while before serving.

Melons Refrigerate melon only long enough to chill it or the flavour will be lost.

Oranges and lemons Add grated lemon or orange rind to a jar of castor sugar and use to flavour cakes and puddings.

Lemons smeared with candle grease will keep indefinitely. Melt candle and rub wax over peel. When ready to use, crack the wax off.

Lemons in a plastic bag will keep for one week at room temperature, or for six weeks in the refrigerator.

Store lemons in a tightly sealed jar of water in the refrigerator. Change the water every few days. They will yield more juice this way. If you soak a lemon in hot water for 15 minutes or warm it in the oven for a few minutes, you'll get more juice from it too.

When you need only a small amount of lemon juice, make a hole in a lemon with a skewer or cocktail stick, squeeze out the quantity you need. Then either leave the skewer there until you want to use the lemon again, or wrap the lemon in kitchen foil and put in the refrigerator.

A juicy orange gives approximately 60mL (4 tbspn) juice and a juicy lemon about 45mL (3 tbspn) juice.

To remove pith from oranges put them in hot water for about five minutes. The pith comes away quite easily with the skin.

If you do not own a zester, remove rind from oranges and lemons with a potato peeler.

Grate or pare the skins of oranges and lemons before using the fruit. Store the skins in a carton in the freezer for future use.

Dried grapefruit, orange and lemon rinds added to a pot of tea, hot chocolate, or a pot of soup give a piquant, refreshing flavour.

Lemon juice is easily applied to fruit slices if you put it in a spray bottle.

Squeeze lemon juice into the cooking water of apples, cauliflower and Jerusalem arti-chokes to prevent discolouration of the vegetables.

Do not store oranges and lemons together or both will become mouldy.

Peaches To skin a peach put it in a pan of boiling water and count to 15 before removing and peeling it.

Pineapple Core fresh pineapple slices by pressing a small round pastry cutter firmly over the core of each slice.

Rhubarb Reduce the acidity of rhubarb by cooking it in cold tea.

FREEZING FRUIT

Use perfectly clean, just-ripe fruits and freeze them as soon as possible. Refrigerate for no more than 24 hours.

Fruits that discolour readily, such as peaches, nectarines, apples and apricots, can be treated with an anti-oxidant such as ascorbic acid or lemon juice before freezing if you wish to preserve the colour. Blanched fruits or those which are cooked before freezing will not discolour.

A satisfactory formula to stop fruits dis-colouring is either 1000mg ascorbic acid tablets, crushed and dissolved, or juice of two lemons in 1 litre of water.

All fruit must be cold before being put in the freezer.

Leave head-space of about 1cm for 500g fruit when packing in plastic containers with lids.

If artificial sweeteners are used, add them after the fruit has thawed.

There are several methods of preparation.

Syrup pack Make a light syrup by boiling together 1 part sugar to 4 parts water. Prepare the fruit, place in containers, then pour over syrup, leaving head-space.

Sugar pack Suitable for berry fruits. Sprinkle with castor sugar in the ratio of 125g per 500g fruit.

Blanching Wash and halve or quarter the fruit and remove stones and seeds. Drop pieces into boiling water and leave for two minutes for large, 1 minute for small. Transfer to iced water for same length of time. Open freeze until hard then transfer to plastic bags or containers.

Fruit	Preparation and packaging	Storage
Apples	Peel, core and slice. Pack in plastic bag with 125g castor sugar per 500g fruit	6 months
	Or, prepare and stew lightly. Pack in plastic container	6 months
	Or, prepare and blanch. Pack in plastic container	6 months
Apricots	Wash, halve and pit. Stew lightly. Pack in plastic containers	6 months
	Or, prepare fruit and blanch. Pack in plastic containers	6 months
	Or, prepare fruit and cover with light syrup. Pack in plastic containers	6 months
Avocados	Remove flesh, mash with juice of two lemons per 500g pulp. Pack back in shells, wrap in plastic, then pack in plastic bags	1 month
Bananas	Peel and mash with ½ cup lemon juice to each 1kg fruit. Pack in plastic containers	6 months
	Or, cut fruit into large pieces and roll in lemon juice. Pack in plastic bags	2 months
	Or, peel and wrap ripe bananas in plastic cling wrap. Serve to children as ice blocks.	2–3 days
Cherries	Stew with or without sugar. Pack in plastic containers	6 months
	Or, pit and sprinkle with sugar. Pack in plastic containers	6 months
	Or, pit and cover with light syrup. Pack in plastic containers	6 months
Citrus peel	Grate or dice. Pack in plastic bags	6 months
Dried fruit	In humid weather freezing will prevent mould developing on dried fruits. Freezing will also protect from weevil. Pack in plastic bags	12 months
Figs	Wash and remove stems. Cover with a light syrup. Pack in plastic containers	6 months
	Or, prepare and stew with or without sugar. Pack in plastic containers	6 months
Gooseberries	Top and tail, dry and freeze. Pack in plastic bags	6 months
Grapefruit	Peel. Remove pith. Separate into segments. Sprinkle with sugar. Pack in plastic bags or containers	6 months
Grapes	Freeze only seedless grapes. Split into small bunches. Pack in plastic bags	6 months
	Or, cover with light syrup. Pack in plastic containers	6 months
Kiwi fruit	Peel and slice. Sprinkle with sugar. Pack in plastic containers	6 months
	Or, prepare fruit. Cover with light syrup. Pack in plastic containers	6 months
	Or, slice thinly. Freeze on a tray. Transfer to plastic bags. Use for drinks	6 months

Fruit	Preparation and packaging	Storage
Lemons	Best frozen as juice Pour juice into ice cube trays. When frozen, remove to plastic bags	6 months
Mandarins	Peel, remove pith. Separate into segments. Cover with a light syrup	6 months
Mangoes	Peel, slice and sprinkle with castor sugar. Pack in plastic containers	6 months
	Or, prepare fruit and cover with light syrup. Pack in plastic containers	6 months
Melons	Peel and remove seeds. Shape into balls. Cover with light syrup. Pack in plastic containers	6 months
Nectarines	Peel and slice. Cover with light syrup. Pack in plastic containers	6 months
	Or, peel and slice. Sprinkle with castor sugar. Pack in plastic containers or bags	6 months
	Or, stew or blanch. Pack in plastic containers	6 months
Oranges	Early Valencias are best Freeze the juice. Pour into ice cube trays. When frozen, transfer to plastic bags.	6 months
	Or, freeze whole or in quarters. Pack in plastic bags and serve to children as ice blocks	2 months
Passionfruit	Remove flesh and freeze in ice cube trays. When frozen transfer to plastic bags.	6 months
Pawpaw	Peel and remove seeds. Slice. Cover with light syrup. Pack into plastic containers	6 months
	Or, prepare fruit. Sprinkle with sugar. Pack into plastic containers	6 months
Peaches	As for nectarines	
Pears	Do not freeze well	
Pineapple	Peel, core and slice. Cover with light syrup. Pack in plastic containers	6 months
	Or, prepare fruit. Sprinkle with castor sugar	6 months
Plums and prunes	Pit. Stew with or without sugar. Pack in plastic containers	6 months
	Or, prepare fruit. Cover with light syrup. Pack in plastic containers	6 months
Purées	Very ripe or blemished fruit can be puréed and frozen Pack in plastic containers	6 months
Rhubarb	Wash and trim. Cut into convenient pieces. Spread on try to freeze. When frozen pack in plastic bags	6 months
Strawberries	Wash, hull and freeze whole. Pack in plastic containers or bags. Use for jam	2 months
	Or, wash, hull and drain. Cover with light syrup. Pack in plastic containers	6 months
	Or, prepare fruit and sprinkle with castor sugar. Pack in plastic containers or plastic bags	6 months
	Or, prepare fruit and purée. Pack into plastic containers	6 months

VEGETABLES

Vegetables may be roughly grouped as follows. When planning meals it is preferable to combine vegetables from as many groups as possible in each meal.

Greens Leafy vegetables or leaves of root vegetables. These are rich in vitamin C.

Roots Edible tuberous roots, including potatoes, carrots, turnips, parsnips.

Onions Vegetables made up of concentric layers of skin. They include leeks and garlic.

Pulses Peas, beans and other seeds from pods. They are high in protein and vitamin B.

Fungi Best known are mushrooms but there are many varieties.

COOKING VEGETABLES

There are many possible ways but here are a few basic rules.

Cook vegetables quickly to keep them crisp.

Use the smallest quantity of water possible so that vitamins do not leach out. For preference, cook in a little butter or oil.

Store juices remaining after vegetables are cooked in jars in refrigerator for use in soups, stews etc.

Steaming Wash vegetables and shake dry, then place in saucepan with a knob of butter. Cover saucepan tightly. Vegetables can be cooked quickly but pan must be shaken to prevent vegetables sticking. Some green vegetables, such as cabbage, should be blanched first. Place them in a colander and pour over boiling water.

Stir frying Use enough oil to cover the bottom of a frying pan. Vegetables, cut in small pieces, are placed in the hot oil and stirred and turned constantly. Fry only small batches at a time and give them only 1 minute. Some vegetables need to be parboiled first. Drop them into boiling salted water for a few minutes.

Deep frying Vegetables may be blanched or parboiled first then drained and dried. They are then deep fried in hot fat until light brown.

Marinating Vegetables may first be marinated in wine to which has been added chopped onion, salt and spices. Drain, roll in flour then in beaten egg. Then place in a pan with a little stock and wine and allow them to braise for about 5 minutes. The vegetables are then removed, the liquid is thickened with a little flour and served as a sauce over them.

STORING AND USING VEGETABLES

Do not peel root vegetables (e.g. potatoes, carrots, pumpkin). Vitamin content is usually close to the surface and should not be lost. Wash under a cold tap to remove surface dirt, if necessary scrubbing lightly to remove soil in cracks. Peel after cooking.

You can revive green vegetables by soaking in iced water for half an hour or so. First remove outer leaves. A tablespoon of vinegar in the water will help, and will also remove insects lurking in the recesses of the vegetables.

Artichokes To prevent artichokes turning pots grey, soak them in water with a tablespoon of vinegar before you cook them.

Asparagus To cook asparagus, tie in bundles and cover the tips with kitchen foil. Wedge the bundles upright in a tall pan containing enough boiling water to come three-quarters of the way up the stalks so that the stalks are poached and the tips steamed.

Beans If beans are a little wilted, refresh them by chilling in a plastic bag in the refrigerator.

Brussels sprouts Brussels sprouts have a finer flavour when cooked in chicken stock.

Cabbage Add about a tablespoon of sugar or a slice of lemon to the water when cooking cabbage, cauliflower or sprouts to kill the smell.

For cabbage with a more delicate flavour and texture, poach in milk instead of boiling in water. Sprinkle with nutmeg or cinnamon.

Capsicums To skin capsicums, turn constantly under a hot grill until the skin blackens and blisters. Plunge them straight into cold water, then rub off the charred skins.

Cauliflower A cup of milk added to the water when cooking cauliflower improves the flavour and helps keep it white. A strip of lemon peel will have the same effect.

Celery Freshen celery by standing upright in a jug of cold water.

Remove the string from celery with a potato peeler. Simply run it up and down the sides.

To make the celery curl, cut stalks into 5cm lengths, then make vertical cuts at narrow intervals almost to the base. Leave to curl in cold water.

Corn To remove the silk from sweet corn, dampen a paper towel and brush downwards on the cob.

Add a teaspoon of lemon juice to the cooking water of sweet corn a minute before taking from the stove and it will stay yellow.

Do not salt the cooking water when cooking corn; it will toughen it.

Eggplant Remove the bitterness from eggplant by sprinkling the slices with salt.

Garlic Crush garlic with the salt you will use in the recipe. It softens the bulb and makes juicing easier.

Pound garlic cloves with the side of a heavy knife or meat pounder. Skins will come away easily.

Leeks If a sauce contains leeks, first simmer the leeks in milk or a mixture of milk and stock. Drain and use the liquid for the sauce.

It is sometimes difficult to clean leeks. Cut off the green part just above the fork and remove the outer leaf if it is tough. Make a slit down one side and, pulling apart the leaves at the slit, wash under the cold tap.

Lettuce Lettuce and celery should be stored in paper rather than plastic bags. Do not remove outer leaves of lettuce until ready to use. Store a lettuce whole in the refrigerator. The stem ends will go brown if it is broken up.

Lettuce and celery will crisp up in a pan of cold water with a few raw sliced potatoes or a slice of lemon. Put in the refrigerator.

Mushrooms Never salt mushrooms until they are cooked as this draws out the juice.

Wipe mushrooms with a damp cloth. Soaking in water impairs the flavour.

Purée left-over mushrooms in the blender with a little water. Freeze in ice cube trays and use for stews, soups and casseroles.

Onions After peeling onions get rid of the smell on hands by rubbing with salt. Or, try peeling under cold running water, freezing or refrigerating the onions first, or pouring boiling water over them. Onions for a salad will be tender and almost odourless if you pour boiling water over them.

Onions brown faster if you add a little sugar to the frying pan.

Part-cook onions before adding them to stuffing, or they will not reach a high enough temperature to cook thoroughly.

. Cover chopped onions with water and add butter to the pan for a quick fry. Boil until the water evaporates. Reduce heat and cook until golden.

Peas Peas and beans will not boil over if you rub around the inside top of the pot with butter.

Potatoes Keep potatoes fresh longer by scraping off sprouts as they appear.

New potatoes don't store well. Never buy more than three days' supply.

To store potatoes, remove from plastic bags, put into a strong brown paper bag, box or tray in a dark place to prevent greening.

If you have too many peeled potatoes cover them with cold water to which a few drops of vinegar have been added. Refrigerated they will last for 3 or 4 days.

Put peeled potatoes in cold salted water and they will not discolour while waiting to be cooked.

Mix skim or whole powdered milk with some of the potato water for mashed potatoes.

Cut potatoes for chips and stand an hour in cold water. Dry thoroughly to prevent splattering by fat. Fry for a few minutes and drain, then fry until golden.

Pumpkin Cook pumpkin with its skin on; then skin is easier to cut off.

Pumpkin will keep fresh if you remove the seeds and sprinkle pepper over it.

Salad Place an inverted saucer on the bottom of the salad bowl. This stops the dressing forming a pool and making the salad soggy. Dress the salad just before serving. Don't use too much dressing.

Oil and water do not mix so salad greens must be dried before they are dressed. Wash lettuce leaves—do not soak them—and dry

53

loosely in a tea towel or on paper towelling.

Rub the inside of the bowl with a cut clove of garlic to give salads a subtle garlic flavour.

Tomatoes Ripen green tomatoes in a warm dark place with a ripe tomato in among them. Putting them in the light will make them soft, not ripe.

If you slice tomatoes down and not across they will stay firm and not make sandwiches soggy.

To peel tomatoes, place them in a pan of boiling water for 1 minute, then remove to a bowl of very cold water for several minutes.

If tomatoes are a little soft and overripe, soak in salted iced water for about half an hour.

FREEZING VEGETABLES

Steam blanching Use a steamer or metal colander over a saucepan of water. When the water is boiling rapidly, put up to 500g of prepared vegetables over the steam, cover and leave for the recommended time. Blanching times in the chart below are for water blanching. For steam, add one minute.

Have ready a bowl of water with ice cubes in it. Tip the blanched vegetables into a colander and stand in the iced water for the same length of time as they were blanched, stirring from time to time. Drain, then place in the freezer in a single layer for about 30 minutes. Pack in plastic bags.

Water blanching In a large saucepan bring enough water to the boil to cover 500g vegetables. Add vegetables in a blanching basket, or a mesh salad basket. Blanching time is from the moment the vegetables are added, not when the water boils again. As soon as blanching is complete, follow the same ice-water procedure as for steam blanching.

Vegetable	Preparation	Blanching	Storage	To cook
Asparagus	Trim, cut into 5cm–15cm lengths	3 minutes	6 months	Cook directly from freezer in boiling water
Beans, green	Trim, break into 2–3cm pieces	3 minutes	6 months	Cook directly from freezer in boiling water
Broccoli	Divide head into small sprigs	3 minutes	6 months	Cook directly from freezer in boiling water
Brussels sprouts	Trim and cut a cross in stem end	3 minutes	6 months	Cook directly from freezer in boiling water
Cabbage	Trim and shred	2 minutes	6 months	Put frozen cabbage in pan over low heat
Capsicum	Remove seeds. Leave whole or cut in rings	Unnecessary	6 months	Stuff when frozen. Can be used for salads
Carrots	Scrape and cut in pieces	3 minutes	6 months	Cook directly from freezer in boiling water
Cauliflower	Separate into sprigs	3 minutes	6 months	Cook directly from freezer in boiling water
Celery	Wash and trim. Cut into 2cm pieces	2 minutes	6 months	Add directly from freezer to soups etc.
Corn on the cob	Remove husk and silk	5–7 minutes	6 months	Thaw, then cook in boiling water
Corn, whole kernel	Remove husk and silk, blanch then cool and cut off kernels	5–7 minutes	6 months	Cook directly from freezer in boiling water

Vegetable	Preparation	Blanching	Storage	To cook
Eggplant (aubergine)	Cut into slices, salt and let stand 20 minutes, fry, let cool		6 months	Reheat directly from freezer in frypan with little butter
Mushrooms	Freeze cultivated mushrooms without preparation. Field mushrooms should be wiped and trimmed		6 months	Cook in butter or add to prepared dishes
Onions	Peel and chop or freeze in their skins	Unnecessary	3 months	If chopped, cook directly from freezer in fat or oil. If whole, hold under cold water to loosen skin, peel, chop
Parsnips	Peel and cut into large pieces	3 minutes	6 months	Cook directly from freezer in boiling water
Peas	Pod	1 minute	6 months	Cook directly from freezer in boiling water
Potatoes, chipped	Prepare and deep fry until just cooked but not brown. Drain thoroughly		3 months	Spread on tray and place in moderate oven
Potatoes, new	Scrub and cook until nearly tender		1 month	Reheat in a small quantity of melted butter
Pumpkin	Peel and cook until tender. Mash		3 months	Put in moderate oven to thaw, finish cooking
Spinach and silver beet	Wash and trim	1 minute	6 months	Reheat gently in small quantity of water
Tomatoes	Wash, cut in portions or dip in boiling water to remove skins		6 months	Use to add to cooked dishes
	Cook until soft, sieve, cook until reduced		6 months	Use as flavour
Zucchini	Wash, but do not peel. Slice, sauté in butter		3 months	Return to pan and cook in a little butter
Herbs	Pick sprigs or leaves, wash and shake dry		6 months	While still in plastic bag rub between the hands
	Or chop and pack in ice cube trays. Cover with cold water			Add to cooked dishes
Garlic	Separate cloves from bulb		3 months	Peel and use as usual

HERBS AND SPICES

A wide range of herbs and spices is now commonplace in the Australian kitchen. In spite of their culinary value, herbs and spices should be used only sparingly. A little goes a long way. Also, the traditional combinations of certain herbs and spices with certain foods generally turn out to be the most effective.

MAIN FAMILIES

Culinary herbs in general belong to two families. The Labiatae have leaves impregnated with volatile oil. The oil is also present, but to a lesser extent, in the flowers. This class includes balm, basil, lavender, marjoram, mint, rosemary and sage. They produce a fragrance when leaves are crushed.

The Umbelliferae have oil present mainly in the seeds. These include anise, caraway, coriander, cumin and dill. Exceptions in this family are parsley, fennel, chervil and lovage where leaves are more fragrant. Tarragon belongs to the Compositae, borage to the Boraginaceae.

In hot climates where they originated, spices not only provided flavour, but were used as preservatives or to disguise food which had been ineffectively preserved. They also stimulate the appetite and activate the sweat glands in hot climates.

Herbs by numbers The basic three are: parsley, mint and bay leaf. Add the following two for the 'best-known five': thyme and sage. Add the following five for the 'best-known ten': dill, basil, savory, marjoram and tarragon.

The 'garden ten' are: borage, chervil, chives, lemon balm, lemon thyme, lemon verbena, lovage, marigold, nasturtium and spearmint.

The 'gourmet's two' are: rosemary and saffron.

STORING, FREEZING AND USING HERBS AND SPICES

Keep spices and herbs in the refrigerator if possible.

Light and heat affect the flavour, colour and freshness of herbs and spices. Do not sprinkle them over a steaming saucepan. Sprinkle into the hand, then into the pot and screw on lids tightly after use. Store dried herbs in dark jars.

A jar of seasoned flour is useful for coating liver, chicken pieces or fish fillets. Add dry mustard, paprika, dried herbs and salt.

If making herb butter with dried herbs, first put the herbs in a muslin bag and steep in boiling water for a minute. This improves the flavour.

Freeze any garden or market garden glut of leafy herbs (parsley, mint, dill, chives, etc.). Select young sprays and wash quickly. Blanch in boiling water 10 seconds only; chill in ice water 1 minute; pat dry quickly between towels. Freeze in single use quantities in small plastic bags. Use as fresh herbs in cooking, but not for salads and garnishes, as they look limp when thawed.

Parsley Freeze parsley sprigs in a bundle. Crumble off the amount required when still frozen, and return the bundle to the freezer.

Parsley can be preserved in salt and stored in the refrigerator. Pack the dry stalks between layers of salt in a plastic container with a well-fitting lid.

Parsley can also be chopped and frozen in cubes of ice, which are quickly thawed.

Crush parsley stalks for maximum flavour and add to soups, marinades and casseroles.

Left-over parsley stalks and celery leaves add flavour to stock.

BOUQUET GARNI

Make up several bouquet garni at once. They are a good small gift. And make up several combinations, labelling each.

For soup: ½ teaspoon each savory, marjoram, basil and ¼ teaspoon crumbled bay leaves.

For chicken and cheese dishes: ½ teaspoon each thyme, sage, marjoram and rosemary.

For creole dishes, chilli con carne and curries: ½ teaspoon each cloves, rosemary, thyme and 2 hot small dried chillies, chopped.

Don't be afraid to experiment with your own combinations.

Put the herbs into muslin bags, tie with a long piece of cotton, leaving the end out of the pan for easy removal.

VARIETIES

Allspice Seeds of West Indian pepper-myrtle or pimento plant. It is said to combine flavours of cinnamon, cloves and nutmeg. Used in game and pultry stuffing and in pickles, marinades, stews and chutneys.

Angelica Crystallised stalks of plant, used to decorate cakes and puddings.

Anise Mediterranean origin. Seeds are used to make aniseed. Used in cakes and custards and in Asian dishes.

Balm Perennial with lemon-scented leaves. Used in poultry stuffings. May be used to make tea or infusion.

Basil

Basil An Italian favourite, perfect with tomatoes and tomato sauces. An annual plant originally from India.

Bay leaf Leaves of bay tree, often used dried. Added to milk puddings and custards and used when cooking meats.

Capsicum Fruit of an annual plant, originally from Central America. Paprika is made from the red ones.

Cardamom Small black seeds of several tropical plants belonging to the ginger family. Used in curry powder, and sparingly with some fruits.

Caraway Seeds of European plant related to parsley. Used in cakes and biscuits, and with fish.

Celery seeds Dried seeds of celery plant, generally ground and mixed with salt to make celery salt. Used in pickles, soups and with seafood.

Chervil Related to parsley. Originating in eastern Europe, it needs to be used fresh. May be used with eggs and fish and in hollandaise sauce and salad dressings.

Chillis Hot South American peppers, related to capsicums and pimento. Cayenne pepper is made from ground and dried red chillis or capsicums.

Chives Although usually grown in herb gardens, chives belong to the onion family. They will grow perennially.

Cinnamon Rolled bark of tree from Sri Lanka. Used in cakes, biscuits and pastry. Very good with apples. Used in small quantities with fish.

Cloves Dried flower bud of tree native to Moluccas. Used whole or ground with ham, with apples and in cakes and biscuits.

Coriander Also called Chinese parsley. Can be grown from seeds. Used fresh in salads and soups. Seeds are used in curries, with pork and in pickles and chutney.

Cumin Seeds of Mediterranean plant. Like caraway but stronger. Used in curries and in meat loaves. With chicken sparingly.

Dill

Dill Resembles fennel. Said to aid digestion. Used with potato salad, mayonnaise and as effective decoration on dishes.

Fennel Leaves or seeds of *Foeniculum vulgare*. Aniseed or liquorice flavour. Used sparingly in fish sauces.

Fenugreek Asian plant, seeds of which are used in curry powders and for herb tea.

Garlic Pungent root of a perennial plant of the onion family. Indispensable for cooking. For most purposes a small quantity suffices, but in some dishes and for some tastes a lot is preferred. Roots are usually dried and one or two cloves used at a time.

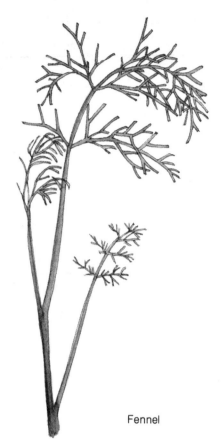

Fennel

paste. English mustard has turmeric added. French has herbs and vinegar. Used with roast beef, steak and in salad dressings and mayonnaise.

Nutmeg Native of Indonesia. May be bought whole or ground. Used with apples, sauces and desserts.

Oregano Wild marjoram, stronger than sweet marjoram. Good with tomatoes, in marinades and stuffings.

Paprika Used extensively in Hungary. Powder blended from ground sweet red peppers. Used in goulash and as sprinkle over egg and cheese dishes.

Parsley One of the best-known herbs. Generally a biennial and several varieties are available now. Used extensively as garnish and finely chopped in soups, sauces, meat dishes and stuffings and salads. Is also fried.

Ginger Root of ginger plant, originally from India. May be green or dried, crushed or ground. Used for curries and chutneys and for pickling. Also in cakes and biscuits and in Chinese fish cookery.

Horseradish Root of European plant, used grated and mixed with whipped cream for sauce served with roast beef.

Lovage South European herb related to angelica. Young leaves used in salads, soups and sauces.

Mace Outside of nutmeg kernel. Sold whole (blade) or ground. Stronger than nutmeg. Ground mace is used in cakes and puddings and in chocolate dishes. Blade mace adds flavour to curries and pickles.

Marjoram Annual herb which may be used fresh or dried. In stuffings for veal and lamb, in omelettes and vegetable dishes.

Mint Native of Europe but grown everywhere. There are different flavours, such as apple, eau-de-cologne, and wild spearmint. Indispensable with roast lamb and with peas.

Mustard Ground seeds of *Brassica* plant which are mixed with water or vinegar to form

Parsley

Pepper Made from grinding seeds of berries grown in South-East Asia. Used extensively in food preparation.

Pepper (black) Dried unripe fruit of Indonesian plant. Loses aroma when ground so should be milled when needed. More pungent than white pepper.

Poppyseed Seeds of poppy flowers. Used to garnish rolls and cakes.

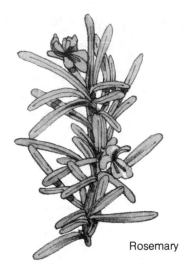
Rosemary

Rosemary Evergreen shrub. Leaves used to flavour lamb, fish and poultry. May be freshly chopped into salads.

Saffron Dried stigmas of a type of crocus. Originally from Asia, saffron is also used as a dye. Must be used sparingly but is indispensable for Italian saffron rice, Spanish paella, French bouillabaisse and other fish soups.

Sage Perennial shrub of which leaves are used fresh or dried with meats such as pork, goose and duck.

Sesame Seeds of annual plant of Asian and Middle Eastern origin. Seeds are used in biscuits and cakes, in halva and in Chinese cooking.

Tarragon Perennial herb which is better used fresh. For flavouring wine vinegar and in salads, stews, omelettes and marinades.

Thyme There are several varieties available, including lemon thyme. Used in soups and stuffings and in a bouquet garni.

Turmeric Related to ginger and originating in Sri Lanka. Used in curry powder and in pickles and sauces.

Vanilla Originally from Mexico but now grown throughout the tropics. Used in flavouring many puddings and cakes.

DAIRY FOODS

Dairy products are a valuable source of protein and, for vegetarians, an important meat substitute. This section includes tips for whipping cream, simple butter recipes, an easy method of yoghurt-making and a guide to the many delicious varieties of cheese available today.

MILK

Milk is one of the most everyday commodities in the kitchen. These days, however, it comes in various forms and serves various purposes.

Most milk sold in Australia is first homogenised then pasteurised. Homogenisation is a process of forcing the milk through a valve under pressure to break up the fat globules and leave them in permanent suspension so that no cream line forms at the top. It is a mechanical process which does not affect the food value of the milk. Pasteurisation is the process pioneered in the 19th Century to which Louis Pasteur gave his name. The most common form of pasteurisation of milk these days is the high temperature short time (HTST) method in which milk is heated to not less than 72°C for 15 seconds and immediately cooled to 4°C. This kills bacteria and increases the keeping quality of the milk.

If your milk is delivered to your home make sure that the milkman does not choose a convenient spot where the milk is in the sun or liable to attacks by birds and animals.

Low-fat milk This usually has a maximum of 2 per cent milk fat and a minimum of 10 per cent solids not fat.

Skim milk Skim, or separated milk, is milk from which the fat has been removed by skimming or mechanical separation. It is not possible in separation to remove all the fat from milk and the average skim milk contains about 0.1 per cent milk fat. Skim milk is not suitable for babies except under doctor's advice because of the change in the chemical composition of the milk during separation.

CREAM

Cream is now generally available as fresh cream and thickened cream. Fresh cream must have a minimum content of butter fat, generally 35 per cent. This is a whipping cream.

Cream is formed by the lighter fat globules rising to the top of milk. Commercial methods hasten the process. In general no foreign substance may be added to cream.

Thickened cream or cream mixture must have a minimum of butter fat but has a small percentage of gelatine, alginate or rennin added as a stabliiser.

Sour cream Sour or cultured cream is pasteurised cream to which a culture of a lactic acid-producing bacteria has been added. Sour cream has a minimum percentage of butter fat, generally 35 per cent, and has the same food value as cream.

TO WHIP CREAM

To do a clean job of whipping cream with an electric beater, cut two small holes in a piece of waxed paper. Slip the stems of the beaters through the holes and attach the beaters to the machine. Then whip away.

If cream will not whip, chill cream, bowl and beater well.

Or, set bowl of cream into a bowl of ice while you're whipping.

Or, add the white of an egg. Chill and then whip.

If cream still does not stiffen, gradually whip in 3 or 4 drops of lemon juice.

Cream whipped ahead of time will not separate if you add a touch of unflavoured gelatine (¼ teaspoon to a cup of cream).

Whipped cream will be lighter and greater in volume if the whisked white of an egg is folded into it. This is not suitable for piping.

Use honey instead of sugar when whipping cream (1 tblspn to a carton).

BUTTER

Butter is a natural product made from pasteurised cream by churning. Standards of content are much the same throughout the world. Butter in general must contain at least 80 per cent milk fat, a maximum of 16 per cent water, 3 per cent salt and 2 per cent solids which are not fat. Much Australian butter has between 1.5 and 2 per cent salt which helps to prolong its life. Butter must contain no additives.

Butter is more easily digested than other fats because of its low melting point and high content of simple fats.

All butter should be stored in the refrigerator. Light spoils the flavour of butter and it absorbs odours from more strongly flavoured foods. The rule is: keep it cold, keep it dark, keep it covered.

Unsalted butter Salt in Australian butter was originally added to make it keep longer in this climate and during export before refrigeration. Today there is strong demand among people of European origin and among fashionable cooks for unsalted butter, which is generally more expensive. Unsalted butter is also sometimes known as Danish or cultured butter.

The cream for unsalted butter is pasteurised, cooled and a special bacteria culture is added. Unsalted butter has the same nutritive value as salted butter.

CLARIFIED BUTTER

Clarified butter is butter that has been melted over low heat and separated from its milky residue so that only butter fat remains. This burns less easily than butter and is ideal for sautés. Heat the butter in a pan over low heat until just melted. Skim froth from the surface. Pour the clear, melted butter into a bowl, leaving the residue behind.

GARLIC BUTTER

Blanch 4 peeled cloves of garlic in boiling water for five minutes, and drain. Crush the garlic and beat into 60g creamed butter with salt and pepper. For red meats and prawns.

LEMON BUTTER

Beat the grated rind of a lemon and a teaspoon of lemon juice into 60g creamed butter. For fish and vegetables.

MAITRE D'HOTEL BUTTER

Beat 2 teaspoons chopped parsley and a teaspoon of lemon juice with salt and pepper to taste into 60g creamed butter. Serve with meat, chicken, fish and vegetables.

YOGHURT

Yoghurt is made from whole or skim milk which has been soured by cultures of the bacteria *Lactobacillus bulgaricus* and *Streptococcus thermophilus*. These produce lactic acid. Yoghurt must have a minimum of 8.5 per cent solids which are not fat.

Yoghurt and other fermented or cultured milks have been known for centuries, particularly in Europe. Their value in preserving the nutrients in the milk and improving its digestibility have been well known. Yoghurt has all the nutrients of the milk from which it is made except that the lactose is used up by the bacteria in making the acid which ferments the milk. Yoghurt should keep in a domestic refrigerator for about three weeks.

MAKING YOGHURT AT HOME

There are two basic ways: you can obtain bacterial cultures and add these to milk, or more simply, you can add some commercial yoghurt to get a similar effect. The following is the latter method.

Use whole or skim milk and dissolve 3 to 4 tablespoons of plain commercial yoghurt at room temperature in 1 litre of milk brought almost to the boil. The milk temperature should be between 28 and 48°C. Stir well, pour into individual dishes, cover and stand for 6 to 8 hours at room temperature, or until yoghurt has set. Refrigerate immediately to stop fermentation. If you can regulate your oven to 45°C, the prepared milk can be put into the oven for 3 to 5 hours (depending on how sour you like your yoghurt). Refrigerate immediately. Your yoghurt won't have the same texture or consistency as commercial varieties, but it will be yoghurt—and you can eat it plain or add honey, nuts or fruit.

CHEESE

The only way to learn about cheese is to eat it. People have been doing just that for more than 4000 years.

The legend is that the world's first cheese was made by an Arabian traveller who stopped in the desert for lunch. This was dates and goat's milk which he carried in a container made of a sheep's stomach. The heat of the desert, the jolting of the pack animal and the small amount of rennet left in the container had, to the delighted surprise of the merchant, changed the milk into curds and whey. He ate the curds and drank the whey and was satisfied. Soon human ingenuity improved on this method of manufacture.

Taste, aroma and texture of the cured cheese are determined by the type of milk used, the curing period, methods of handling and the type of bacterial growth used to ferment the cheese. Some cheeses, whatever their origin, are known, and made, almost world-wide. Others, such as some of the delicious soft cheeses of Europe, are unknown outside their region.

STORING AND USING CHEESE

All cheese, natural, processed or spread, must be refrigerated. The exceptions are hard cheeses such as Parmesan when it is bought in a storage container. Hard cheeses should be wrapped tightly in foil or plastic wrap but should be removed from the refrigerator some time before they are to be eaten to allow flavour to develop. Soft, uncured cheeses, such as cottage or cream cheeses, do not keep well. Soft cheeses may keep longer if you store them in the refrigerator with the carton upside down.

If cream cheese has to be blended with other ingredients for cooking, restore it to room temperature first.

If you are cooking cheese use a gentle heat to stop it becoming stringy. Never let it boil.

To grate cheese without a mess, place a plastic bag over the end of the grater. Insert cheese, grasp through the plastic and grate. Or, grate cheese on a wet plate. The cheese will slip off more easily.

Grate cheese with a vegetable peeler instead of a grater when you need just a little. It is easier to clean.

To cut processed cheese thinly, use a knife dipped in hot water. The knife must be dipped before each slice.

Before storing cheese, dab with a bit of margarine where it has been cut. This helps prevent it going stale.

VARIETIES

Ambrosia Soft, springy texture, butter-yellow with many small oval holes. Tastes mild initially, but has a definite tang.

Bel Paese Soft, smooth sweetish white cheese with creamy texture and appearance.

Blue vein White with blue veins of mould throughout, it is a soft, creamy cheese with a rich piquant flavour.

Bleu Castello A Danish double-cream cheese similar to blue vein. It has a brownish-white surface mould.

Brie Soft, creamy, almost runny consistency inside a felt-like rind of white mould. Choose a wedge-shaped slice from a large one or a small whole round. Best served at its softest and runniest.

Caerphilly Slightly sour, very digestible lemon-coloured cheese. Good with crackers or toasted on bread.

Camembert Similar to Brie, comes usually in a round form.

Cheddar One of the world's best-known cheeses, cheddar originated in Somerset in the 16th Century. A true cheddar is hard, smooth and acidulous. Colour may be white or yellow.

Cheshire Loyal Cheshiremen claim that their specialty cheese can be made only with the milk of local cows, but Australian versions of white Cheshire are available. An all-purpose cheese, mild and flaky.

Cottage cheese Curd-style cottage cheese is a soft uncured cheese made from skim milk. Curd particles vary in size with different brands and may or may not be coated with cream. Dry curd cottage cheese has no added cream. Creamed cottage cheese has a small quantity of cream added in the final stages of making to coat curd particles. This tends to make the cheese look better and be easier to handle.

Cottage cheeses may contain about 18 per cent protein, .5 per cent butter fat and most have much the same nutritive value. They must be stored in the refrigerator and unlike ripened cheese are best eaten when fresh. Cottage cheese may keep for 10–14 days in a household refrigerator.

Double Gloucester Mellow orange cheese of waxy texture.

Edam A mellow, mild-flavoured cheese with a smooth texture displaying a number of small round 'eyes'. Sold in a red waxed ball, or in rectangular unwaxed portions or pre-sliced packs.

Emmenthal A hard Swiss cheese with large holes. Nutty when young with a slight bite, but becomes stronger with age.

Esrom Slightly sour with tiny holes. Flavour intensifies with age. Plain or with caraway, herbs or peppercorns.

Fetta White cheese with a pungent flavour, originally made from goats' or sheeps' milk but now commonly made from cows' milk.

Texture ranges from soft to crumbly and it is often sold in the brine which separates from the cheese. If kept moist, it will keep for about 10 days in the refrigerator.

Gouda Large, flat, round mild Dutch cheese.

Gruyere Hard, flat, pale yellow whole milk Swiss cheese. Taste sharpens with age.

Havarti and cream havarti Pale, creamy cheese with a waxed rind. Firm, not hard, and elastic, with many small holes and slits. Flavour matures with age from mild to very sharp.

Jarlsberg Norway's biggest cheese export. Popular sweet and nutty Swiss-style cheese with random medium to large holes. Firm, buttery texture in a pale yellow rind.

Kasseri Firm, white, slow-melting Greek cheese which is good for any dishes which call for grilling. Like mozzarella, the kasseri curd is dipped into hot water then kneaded into shape.

Leicester Bright gold hard cheese with a slight lemon taste. Melts well.

Mascarpone Velvety textured and as soft, rich, sweet and smooth as cream. Widely used as a dessert cheese flavoured with fresh or dried fruits, chocolate and so on. Use within a day.

Mozzarella Plastic to the touch, often moulded into pear shapes. At its best it should be very white and slightly juicy. However, it is usually sold when it is firmer and drier. Mild with a slight tang. Good for cooking.

Nokkelost Norwegian cheese made partly from skimmed milk. Strong herbal taste to the creamy-textured paste from caraway, cloves and cumin.

Parmesan, or Parmigiano Best for cheese-boards when only slightly matured. Extra hard cheese is used for grating. Full piquant flavour, with a hard, granular texture.

Port Salut Semi-soft, smooth. Tang similar to, but more pronounced than, ambrosia.

Provolone Smooth texture which becomes more granular with maturing. Full, sharp salty flavour.

Quark. Pronounced 'Kvark' Germany's most popular local fresh cheese. Simply made from milk, buttermilk or skimmed milk with varying quantity of cream. Slightly acidic. Made in limited quantities in Australia and generally like a finer, drier version of cottage cheese.

Ricotta White, soft moist cheese sold fresh in tubs or squares of paper. Best eaten within a few days, or its sweetness will deteriorate.

Stilton The gem of English blue cheeses. Off-white paste with green-blue veins and a wrinkled pale brown rind.

FREEZING DAIRY FOODS

Cottage and cream cheese Will freeze for a short period. Can be frozen with other ingredients as dips and spreads.
Cheddar type cheeses Although cheddar cheese will retain its flavour after freezing, it will become crumbly. Grate left-over cheese and freeze for use in cooked dishes.
Blue cheese Wrap in foil and only freeze for short periods. May crumble on thawing.

Dairy food	Storage
Butter, salted and unsalted	6 months
Margarine, cooking and table	6 months
Milk, homogenised	3 weeks
Goats' milk (depending on quality)	1–3 months
Cream	3 months
Sour cream	1 month
Cheese, cream and cottage	1 month
Cheese, cheddar	6 months
Cheese, blue	1 month

PASTA AND RICE

Pasta is the Italian speciality. In its long history it has been the subject of much controversy. 'Our *pasta sciutta*,' declared one Italian intellectual, 'like our rhetoric, suffices merely to fill the mouth.' One supporter of the national dish, the Mayor of Naples, declared that 'the angels in Paradise eat nothing but *vermicelli al pomodore*' to which someone retorted that this confirmed his suspicions about the monotony of life in Paradise.

For centuries rice has fed more than half the world's population. Through much of Asia rice is the staple food. In some parts of China, Malaysia and Indonesia, people eat as much as 100kg each year. By comparison Australians eat only between 2.5kg and 3kg but our consumption is rising and has doubled in the past 30 years. That we are choosing our food from more countries is the chief reason, although increasing interest in vegetarianism may also play a part.

PASTA

Pasta is as varied as the reactions to it. Some makers turn out as many as 52 varieties and in Italy the same shape is known by different names in different regions.

In Australia there is a fascinating variety of pasta shapes and sizes and choice of white, wholemeal or green (coloured with spinach juice). Different shapes are traditionally used for different dishes. Very small ones such as *pastine* or *tubettini* are cooked in clear broths; cut macaroni or shell shapes are used in heartier soups or salads; wide ribbon shapes, such as *lasagne*, and large tubes (*canelloni*) are for casserole use, layered with sauces. *Canelloni* have savoury fillings. Oriental noodles, which are generally finer, are used in soups, or cooked and drained, then mixed with seasonings or fried.

COOKING PASTA
Cook all forms of pasta in plenty of boiling water; 5 litres of water to 500g of pasta is not too much. Use large saucepans and bring water to a fast, rolling boil.

Add pasta gradually so water does not go off the boil, then add salt and a few drops of oil.

When cooking spaghetti hold long strands

at one end and place other ends into the boiling water. The pasta will begin to soften in the hot water and it is then simple to lower strands into saucepan, boiling them neatly inside pan.

Approximate cooking times Spaghetti: 12 to 20 minutes. Vermicelli (resembles very fine spaghetti): 6 to 10 minutes. Macaroni: 12 to 20 minutes. Noodles: 10 to 20 minutes, depending on width. Cooking time of pasta varies according to individual manufacturers and to freshness of the product. Pasta should not be over-cooked; it should be tender but firm (*al dente*).

Start testing at the minimum cooking time given above and, when the pasta is cooked just to your liking, add a cup of cold water to the pan to stop the cooking instantly. Pour pasta into colander, drain well. If you wish, mix a knob of butter or a little oil through the pasta to prevent it sticking together.

Provided sufficient water has been used in cooking, there will be no starch adhering to the pasta, so do not rinse it under cold water; this will cause the tender pasta to harden.

Fresh pasta will cook in about half the time of *pasta sciutta* (dried pasta).

Quantities Spaghetti and macaroni almost double in volume during cooking; noodles remain the same in volume.

FRESH PASTA

Fresh pasta is very fashionable but cynical and experienced Italian cooks do not always rate its superiority over *pasta sciutta* as highly as food-conscious Australians do.

The ingredients for fresh pasta are simple and it requires patience rather than any highly specialised skills.

250g flour
1 teaspoon salt
1 tablespoon olive oil
2½ eggs (see note)
1 tablespoon water
salt
freshly ground black pepper

Sift the flour and salt onto a board or scrubbed, dry bench. Make a well in the centre and add the oil, beaten eggs and water. Using the fingertips, work in the flour gradually. Add more liquid if necessary to make a soft dough. It should not be sticky. Knead well for 5 minutes. Cover with an upturned bowl and leave to stand for 1 hour.

Divide dough in half. Roll each half as thinly as possible on a floured surface. Leave the noodles to dry for about 1 hour or until dough stiffens.

Roll each half loosely and cut crosswise into slices about 1–2cm wide. Unroll the strips onto clean tea towels or kitchen paper and leave to dry for 2 hours.

Note: To measure the half egg, beat 1 whole egg and divide in two.

RICE

Australians now eat rice in Spanish paella, Indonesian nasi goreng, Indian curries, Scottish kedgeree, Malay saki and in many Chinese dishes.

A great advantage of rice is its price. It is one of the cheapest of the carbohydrate energy foods, is easy to prepare and is a good source of easily digested carbohydrate. It also provides protein, vitamins, minerals and fibre.

The two major types of rice are white and brown. Australians still tend to eat more white rice. White rice is produced when the bran layer is removed. Brown rice is more nutritious than white. Enriched rice has had iron and B vitamins added during milling. Parboiled rice is a method of rice production developed in Asia to combat widespread beriberi. The rice is processed before milling so most nutrients are kept.

In spite of its name, wild rice is not rice but the seed of a wild grass. It is much more expensive than rice.

Some health enthusiasts are now eating rice polish. This by-product of milling is high in nutrients. In Australia it is mostly sold as stock feed but it is beginning to appear in health food shops. It is used as an alternative to wheatgerm.

COOKING RICE

When it comes to cooking, length of grain is important. Short and medium grains tend to cling together when cooked. This is pudding rice and for puddings it is exactly what you want. Long grain rice cooks to a fluffy texture and the grains are more likely to stay separate.

Brown rice takes much longer to cook than

white rice. To cut cooking time in half and reduce fuel costs, pre-soak for 12 hours before cooking.

To heat large quantities of pre-cooked rice, spread out in a greased baking or shallow ovenproof dish. Sprinkle with a little milk, dot with butter and cover with foil. Place in a moderate oven, and toss with a fork after about 10 minutes. The heating process takes 15–20 minutes. Smaller amounts of rice can be heated by placing in a colander over simmering water until heated through.

Add a little oil when cooking rice to stop water from boiling over and to aid grain separation.

BREAD, CAKE AND PASTRY

Nothing beats the aroma of bread, cake or home-made pies and tarts baking in the oven. Perhaps this is why many people prefer to make their own, despite the wide variety of excellent commercially-made products available. Included here are common cooking pitfalls and how to avoid them.

BREAD

Bread these days is strictly defined by law and bakers must conform to regulations.

By definition, wholemeal breads are made from 100 per cent wholemeal flour or a mixture of 90 per cent wholemeal flour and 10 per cent white flour. Brown breads must contain at least 50 per cent wholemeal flour and artificial colourings are not allowed. Mixed grain breads have a dietary fibre content about the same as brown breads.

All breads, including white bread, contribute dietary fibre, the proportion being 8.5 per cent for wholemeal breads, 5 per cent for brown and mixed grain type breads and 3 per cent for white bread.

Many people these days are baking their own bread. They find it a satisfying experience, once they gain some expertise.

AN EASY RECIPE
For a quick bread, mix 450g self-raising flour with 1½ level teaspoons salt. Make a well in the centre and pour in 300mL plus 30–45mL (2–3 tbspn) water. Work into a pliable dough and knead lightly. Shape into a round, place on a baking sheet, mark the top with 2–3 cuts and bake in the oven at 220°C for 30–35 minutes. Eat on the same day.

STORING AND USING BREAD
New bread may be cut thinly by dipping the knife into boiling water before using.

Very fresh bread is easier to slice if it is chilled in the refrigerator first.

A frozen sliced loaf of bread can be used for toast without thawing.

You can freeze crusty loaves, but after a week the crust starts to flake.

Make big batches of sandwiches and freeze them. Take one out of the freezer at breakfast and it will be thawed by lunch. Don't put salad and egg fillings in the sandwiches. They don't freeze well.

When making a big quantity of sandwiches, cream the butter in an electric mixer, then combine with the filling. This halves spreading time.

Cut an unsliced loaf lengthways when you are making a lot of sandwiches. This gives the same number of sandwiches but doesn't involve as much spreading.

Prevent soggy sandwiches by putting wet ingredients such as mustard, mayonnaise and tomato between slices of meat and cheese so they don't touch the bread.

Soak stale bread in milk, squeeze out the moisture and add to mince for a looser texture.

To make asparagus rolls, roll the slices of bread with a rolling pin before buttering. The bread rolls around the asparagus easily.

BREAD-MAKING MISTAKES

Many people are put off bread making if their first attempts do not turn out successfully. Use these points to find out what went wrong and you can avoid making the same mistake again.

Loaf lacks volume Insufficient kneading • Poor quality or inactive yeast • Too much salt in recipe • Dough too stiff: more liquid required • Collapse due to excess rising before baking.

Crust too pale Too much yeast: dough proved too quickly • Too much salt • Over-fermented dough (proved too long) • Oven temperature too low.

Crust too dark Too much sugar in recipe • Under-fermented dough • Oven too hot.

Excessive loaf volume Too little salt • Too much proving (over-proved) • Oven temperature too low.

Coarse, open grains inside loaf Dough too wet (also known as 'slack') • Dough over-proved before baking • Oven too cool (or too hot) • Dough moulded too losely.

Crumbly texture inside loaf Too little salt • Dough too stiff (also known as 'tight') • Dough over-mixed • Dough too hot during proving • Dough over-fermented.

Poor crumb colour (usually associated with coarse grain) Too little salt • Dough over-proved (therefore prone to quick staling) • Dough has become chilled due to draughts during proving period.

Crumb-holes inside loaf Too much dusting flour during moulding • Incorrect moulding • Oven too hot (or too cool) • Under-mixed (or grossly over-mixed) • Under- or over-proved dough • Dry skin on dough surface.

BAKING WITH YEAST

Yeast must be fresh. Liquid added to yeast should be lukewarm, as individual recipes specify. If liquid is too cold, it will not have any effect on the yeast (the dough will not rise); if too hot, it will kill the action of the yeast. But liquid of the right temperature will bring the yeast to life.

Handling yeast doughs Dough should be soft but not sticky. If it is too dry, add a little more liquid. If it is too wet, knead a little extra flour into the mixture while it is still in the bowl. Turn it onto a lightly floured surface and knead thoroughly until the dough is smooth and satin-like. If the mixture is still sticky, knead in more flour gradually until dough is easy to handle. It should not be necessary to add additional flour after the first two or three minutes kneading. Recipes should be properly balanced so only a light dusting of flour on the kneading surface is necessary. When kneaded sufficiently dough will spring back if pressed with a finger.

If recipe requires proving in bowl, place kneaded dough into a greased bowl, turn dough to lightly grease top of it (this stops a skin forming). Cover with a clean cloth or a piece of plastic wrap and stand in a warm place away from draughts until dough has doubled in bulk. Then punch down and knead lightly.

Divide and shape as recipe directs, place in pans or on trays. Cover with a clean cloth until dough has doubled in bulk again or reached the required volume. Press gently with a finger: a slight indentation shows dough is ready to bake.

CAKE

Although not a necessity, cake is usually a welcome addition to a school lunch or family picnic, and is perfect with that cup of tea or coffee. Children love making cakes 'the old-fashioned way'.

CAKE-MAKING TIPS

If baking powder with cream of tartar is used, cook the cake as soon as mixed. The baking powder will lose its power once it is moistened. If phosphate is an ingredient of the baking powder, the mixture can stand for a time. Heat will make this type of baking powder work.

Put a long strip of folded kitchen foil across the base of the tin before adding cake mixture. Use the protruding ends of foil on either side to lift the cake out without damage.

A sponge cake is cooked when it shrinks slightly from the sides of the tin; a butter cake will spring back when lightly pressed with fingertips; a fruit cake is done when a fine metal skewer inserted in the centre comes out clean.

There are specific times to remove cakes from pans. Loaf cakes should cool 15–20 minutes and layer cakes 5–10 minutes. If you forget, loosen the sides of cake with a blunt knife and slightly warm the bottom of the pan. The warmth will loosen the paper or soften the bottom crust so cake will come out easily.

COMMON MISTAKES
There is a reason for all cake-making failures. This section suggests ways to prevent them and how to transform some culinary disasters so you do not waste them.

PLAIN BUTTER CAKES
Cake is coarse-textured Insufficient creaming of butter and sugar • Oven not hot enough • Too much raising agent • Insufficient liquid, or insufficient mixing when adding liquid.

Cake is heavy Oven not hot enough • Too much flour, or shortening, or liquid • Over-mixing.

Cake has moist, sticky crust Too much sugar • Insufficient beating to dissolve sugar.

Cake is uneven in texture, with holes in cake Heavy-handed when folding in flour • Insufficient mixing; the flour not evenly distributed • Mixture was put in tin in small quantities. Do not put spoonfuls of mixture into tin, put in as large a quantity as possible. Small quantities trap air bubbles, which result in holes in the finished cake.

Cake falls in centre Too much raising agent, or shortening, or sugar • Oven not hot enough • Oven door opened during early baking and/or cake moved in oven • Insufficient baking.

SPONGE CAKES
Cake is coarse or heavy in texture Insufficient beating of eggs, or eggs and sugar • Insufficient blending of ingredients, or heavy-handed blending • Too much flour • Incorrect oven temperature.

Cake has sticky crust on top Too much sugar • Insufficient beating • Insufficient baking.

Cakes undersized, not risen sufficiently Insufficient beating of eggs and sugar • Overmixed • Incorrect oven temperature • Insufficient cooking • Cakes removed too soon from tins • Tins greased too generously on sides.

FRUIT CAKES
Cake dry in texture Not enough liquid, or shortening, or sugar • Cake baked too long •

Too much raising agent.

Hard crust outside, with damp, uncooked centre Too much liquid • Oven too hot.

Cake sank in middle Too much raising agent • Fruit not thoroughly dried • Cake moved in oven too soon, before mixing has set • Sometimes oven too hot.

Excessive cracking across top Tin too small • Oven too hot • Too much raising agent • Incorrect quantity of liquid.

Cake insufficiently risen Tin too big for quantity of mixture • Not enough liquid • Oven too cool • Mixture not creamed sufficiently.

Cake crumbles when cut Not enough egg to bind ingredients in rich cakes; not enough liquid in plainer cakes • Too much raising agent.

RECOVERING DISASTERS
Spoilt fresh cake can be made into trifle. Or, break it into fine crumbs, add a cupful of coconut and stiffly beaten egg white and use it as a tart topping. Pour the mixture over a pastry base covered with jam and bake the tart in a moderate oven until the topping is cooked, about 20 minutes. Dust with icing sugar.

Crumb broken cakes to make delicious rum balls. Beat 120g cream cheese with ¼ cup sifted icing sugar. Add 2 tablespoons melted dark chocolate, ¼ teaspoon vanilla, ½ teaspoon rum, and the cake crumbs, enough to lightly fill 1½ cups. Refrigerate for two hours then form into balls. Roll in chocolate sprinkles.

To level uneven sponge cakes, place the thicker side of one over the thinner side of the other. After filling the layers, ice the sides and cover with nuts or chocolate sprinkles.

A sunken sponge cake is a good Baked Alaska base. Pile drained canned or fresh fruit in the middle, top with ice cream and cover with stiff meringue. Bake at 230°C for 1–2 minutes and serve immediately.

Cut out the centre of a fruit cake which has sagged in the middle and make a ring cake. Ice and decorate with glace cherries.

A dry fruit cake can be cut into serving-sized slices, wrapped in foil, and steamed to make a plum pudding-style dessert.

The bottom of a fine wire coffee strainer rubbed over a burnt cake will remove charred surfaces without breaking them.

When a cake gets a hump in the middle, an overheated oven could be the cause. Cut the hump off; turn the cake upside down and ice the base.

CAKE DECORATION

To make a simple decoration on a sponge cake put a doyley on top of the cake and dust it with icing sugar.

Dip the spatula in cold water before smoothing icing on a cake so icing doesn't stick to it.

Do not use an aluminium bowl when making royal icing. It can give the icing a greyish look.

Royal icing will be softer if you add 5mL (1 tspn) glycerine to each 450g icing sugar.

Leave royal icing in the refrigerator, covered, overnight to eliminate air bubbles in the mixture.

How to make paper piping bags Cut out a square of greaseproof paper; it must have straight sides and each side must be the same length to give a good-shaped bag for piping. Fold diagonally, cut into two triangles. Hold the apex of one triangle in your left hand with the point of the apex toward you, take the right-hand point in your right hand, curl point of paper over until you have this point and the point of the apex touching; hold these two points with right hand. With left hand and left point of paper, wrap the paper over the top and half-way under the cone so this point meets the other two points exactly. (If you are left-handed, reverse the procedure.) If the triangle is evenly cut, the three points will all touch and the cone shape will not have a hole at the tip.

Secure joins of bag, inside and out, with a piece of sticky tape. Always place the icing or cream used for piping in the bag first, then snip a tiny hole in the tip of the bag and gently push icing down. Fold over ends to prevent icing coming out the top. Enlarge hole with scissors to the required size.

Piping with a paper bag Paper bags can be used for piping whipped cream, royal icing or mock cream style fillings. Drop two heaped teaspoons of mixture into bag. Try to avoid spreading mixture around open end. Gently ease mixture toward point of bag, fold over ends to secure top.

Using sharp scissors, snip 3mm from point of bag, then pipe a trail of icing; if a larger trail is needed, cut a fraction more from bag, then try piping again. In this way, just the right sized trail will be obtained.

When piping, hold the paper bag with right hand so the folded-over section is secure, otherwise the mixture will come out of the top of the bag; use left hand to guide the bag as you pipe. Hold bag at a 45 degree angle, apply a little pressure with right hand for piping. If left-handed, reverse this procedure.

Temperatures for boiling sugar 109°C to 112°C: Thread or very soft-ball stage. The syrup cannot be formed into a ball hard enough to pick up. 112°C to 116°C: Long-thread or soft-ball stage. The syrup can be formed into a soft pliable ball. It can be picked up. 116°C to 120°C: Rather firm ball which will maintain shape when removed from water. 121°C to 124°C: very firm ball which forms into hard-ball mass.

PASTRY

There's more to successful pastry-making than meets the eye, but it's mainly a matter of being aware of the following tips.

RULES FOR PERFECT PASTRY

Keep everything as cold as possible Fat should be firm; liquid should be chilled. If time permits, place mixing bowl in refrigerator for an hour before using.

Use only as much liquid as necessary Too much liquid will result in hard pastry, and will also cause pastry to shrink during baking, as the excess water evaporates in heat of oven. If insufficient liquid is added, dough will be too crumbly for rolling. Add liquid gradually, until just sufficient has been added to make pastry firm enough to handle and roll out without breaking.

Sift the dry ingredients Sift flour and any other dry ingredients well; this helps to incorporate air into pastry mixture, as well as ensuring flour is fine, without lumps.

Fold in as much air as possible With short-crust pastry, lift flour and butter mixture from bowl when rubbing in with fingertips; let it sprinkle back into bowl as you rub.

With puff pastry, air is incorporated through the process of folding and rolling. Roll pastry with short, jerky movements; lift rolling pin after each roll. This allows air to move about in dough. Heavy rolling will destroy air bubbles, resulting in heavy pastry.

Handle pastry lightly Too much handling will make pastry heavy. When handling soft pastries, such as biscuits, roll out between lightly floured sheets of greaseproof paper; this makes them easier to handle and avoids over-working the pastry.

Never stretch pastry — it will shrink back when cooking.

When rolling out pastry on a floured board, use only enough flour to prevent pastry sticking to the surface. Excess flour will upset the balance of ingredients, and could result in tough pastry. For this reason too, never turn pastry over during rolling.

Cook at the correct oven temperature Correct oven heat is as important for pastry as it is for cakes. The richer the pastry, the hotter the oven. Puff pastry, richest of all, cooks in a very hot or hot oven. If moderate heat is used, pastry will not rise; instead of being light and flaky, it will be heavy and sodden.

HOW MUCH PASTRY TO USE

When a recipe calls for 250g pastry it means pastry made with 250g flour (plus the corresponding ingredients).

The exception to this is where packaged pastry is an ingredient; when a recipe calls for 375g or 500g packaged puff pastry, this is the full weight of the completed pastry in its package.

Basic pastry recipes can be reduced or increased if necessary but be sure to reduce or increase all other ingredients in proportion. This guide will help you assess the quantity of pastry you may need.

Tarts 185g pastry will line 18cm pie plate; 250g to 300g pastry will line 20cm or 23cm pie plate.

Double-crust pies 300g pastry will give bottom and top crust for 18cm pie; 375g to 440g pastry will give bottom and top crust for 20cm or 23cm pie.

Small tartlets 250g pastry will make about 24 small tartlet cases. When large tart cases with a filling require a longer cooking time than approximately 25 minutes, a double edge of pastry will prevent edges of tart case from becoming too crisp. Cut long strips of rolled-out pastry, the width of the pie plate edge, and place around edge of pie plate; brush strips lightly with water, then line plate with pastry in usual manner. Press edges together, trim, decorate as desired.

MAIN TYPES OF PASTRY

Shortcrust pastry Probably the most widely used of all pastries, good for pies with sweet or savoury fillings. Basic shortcrust uses half the amount of shortening (butter, margarine) to flour, e.g., shortcrust with 250g flour would use 125g shortening; with 500g flour, 250g shortening, etc. Sweet shortcrust: Add 2 teaspoons castor sugar for every 2 cups flour. Dissolve sugar in the water before adding it to flour, or sift 2 teaspoons icing sugar with dry ingredients.

Puff pastry Used as a topping for savoury pies, for vol-au-vents and sweet pastries. Packaged puff pastry saves a lot of time, but many cooks still prefer to make their own. Full puff pastry uses equal amounts of flour and shortening. Three-quarter puff (using ¾ the amount of shortening to flour) is more generally used. When cooked, it is easier to handle, less liable to break.

Flaky pastry Often used in place of puff pastry; easier to make and delightfully light.

Rough puff pastry Not as rich as puff or flaky and easier to make. Because all the shortening is incorporated into the dough, rough puff pastry should be kneaded very lightly.

Choux pastry Delicate, crisp, light pastry used for many French pastries. It is leavened by steam that builds up in the batter under heat.

Hot water pastry Used mainly for meat or game pies. A firm, strong dough, prepared by adding boiling liquid to flour. Dough used while warm.

Suet pastry Hearty, substantial and filling, suet pastry is used for old-fashioned dishes, both sweet and savoury. One of the few pastries which uses self-raising flour.

TO BAKE BLIND

Often a recipe for a flan or tart requires the pastry to be baked blind. Line the pan with pastry in the usual way and finish edges. Cut a circle of greaseproof paper 5cm larger than the pan, place it over the pastry and press it carefully into the corners. Fill to within 1cm of the top with dry beans or uncooked rice to hold pastry in shape. Bake as directed, or until pastry is set and lightly coloured, then remove paper and beans (beans can be reused in this way). Then either add filling as directed and continue baking, or return pastry shell to oven until golden brown.

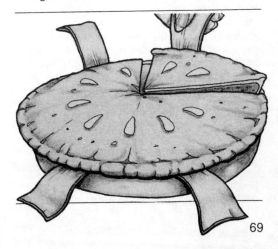

FOLLOWING RECIPES

Most good recipes are easy to follow, but confusion can arise over such things as measurements and English or American terms. Also, most recipe writers assume a basic knowledge of cooking not all beginners possess. The information here should help to clarify such problems.

BASIC METHODS

There are twelve basic methods of cooking, either on top of the stove or in the oven.

Baking Cooking in dry heat in the oven.

Boiling Cooking in a pan of liquid, which must be kept boiling gently all the time.

Braising Almost a combination of stewing and roasting. Meat is placed on a bed of vegetables with a little liquid surrounding, in a covered vessel, and cooked slowly in the oven or on top of the stove.

Casserole Cooking slowly in the oven in a covered casserole dish.

Frying Cooking in a little hot fat in an open pan. Deep frying is cooking by immersion in a deep pan of hot fat or oil.

Grilling Cooking quickly under a red-hot grill; used for small tender pieces of meat, fish, etc.

Poaching Cooking gently in water which is just below boiling point; usually eggs or fish.

Pressure cooking Cooking at enforced pressure so food is cooked much more quickly.

Roasting Cooking with a little fat in oven. Fat from the baking tin usually is poured over the meat or poultry from time to time, using a long-handled spoon: this is known as basting.

Simmering The rate of cooking used for stew: just below boiling point so the liquid bubbles at side of pan.

Steaming Cooking either in a steamer over a pan of boiling water or in a basin standing in (but not covered by) boiling water.

Stewing Cooking slowly until the food is tender. Just enough liquid to cover the food is used; the liquid is served with it and should be rich. Stews can be cooked in the oven or on top of the stove—but always at low temperatures.

OVERSEAS RECIPES

If you have collected recipes from imported magazines, you may have encountered some unfamiliar ingredients. Or perhaps some sounded similar but left room for doubt. Here are terms you are likely to find, with their equivalents.

Australian	American	British
bicarbonate of soda	baking soda	bicarbonate of soda
brown sugar	brown sugar	demerara sugar
capsicum	sweet or bell pepper	green or red pepper
choko	chayote	choko
cornflour	cornstarch	cornflour
cream	light cream	single cream
essence	extract	essence
eggplant	eggplant, aubergine	aubergine
fillet (of meat)	tenderloin	fillet
frying pan	skillet	frying pan
gravy beef	stew beef	gravy beef
grill, griller	broil, broiler	grill, griller
icing sugar	confectioners' sugar	icing sugar
mince/minced (meat)	ground (meat)	mince/minced(meat)
okra	ladies' fingers	okra
papaw, pawpaw	papaya	pawpaw
plain flour	all-purpose flour	plain flour
potato flour	potato starch	potato flour
semolina	farina	semolina
shallots, spring onions	scallions, green onions	spring onions
(to) shell	(to) shuck, hull	(to) shell
sour cream	dairy sour cream	soured cream
sultanas	seedless white raisins	sultanas
thickened cream	heavy cream	double cream
zucchini	zucchini	courgettes

MEASURING

A standard set of measures and the correct technique will avoid costly errors in cooking. You will need:

1 or 2 250mL (1 cup) metric measuring cups for liquids.

1 or 2 500mL (2 cups) metric jugs for liquids.

A set of four metric dry measure cups (¼, ⅓, ½ and 1 cup) for flour, sugar, fats, honey, syrup, nuts and breadcrumbs.

4 metric spoons: 1 tablespoon (20mL), 1 teaspoon (5mL), ½ and ¼ teaspoons.

1 straight-edged spatula for measuring.

HOW TO MEASURE

Flour Lightly spoon sifted or unsifted flour (as specified in the recipe) into a dry measuring cup. Heap it up and level off with a spatula or knife. Do not tap cup.

Sugar Do not sift unless lumpy. Spoon lightly into a dry measuring cup. Level off with spatula and do not tap cup. Brown sugar should be packed firmly into cup.

Liquids Pour into liquid measuring cup on bench or table. Check measuring line at eye level.

Cheese To measure in cup form, cheese should be grated and lightly packed into cup.

CONVERTING OLD RECIPES TO METRIC

Although Australia is officially metric, many cooks still have old and favourite family recipes. Here is an easy way to convert them.

t = teaspoon   T = tablespoon   C = cupful

Ingredient	½oz	1oz	2oz	4oz
Almonds, ground	2T	¼C	½C	1C
Almonds, slivered	2T	¼C	½C	1C
Almonds, whole	2T	¼C	⅓C	⅔C
Apples, dried whole	3T	½C	1C	2C
Apricots, chopped	2T	¼C	½C	1C
Apricots, whole	2T	3T	½C	1C
Arrowroot	1T	2T	⅓C	⅔C
Baking powder	1T	2T	⅓C	⅔C
Barley	1T	2T	¼C	½C
Bicarbonate of soda	1T	2T	⅓C	⅔C

Ingredient	½oz	1oz	2oz	4oz
Breadcrumbs, dry	2T	¼C	½C	¾C
Breadcrumbs, soft	¼C	½C	1C	2C
Biscuit crumbs	2T	¼C	½C	1C
Butter	3t	6t	¼C	½C
Cheese, natural cheddar	6t	¼C	½C	1C
Cheese, processed cheddar	5t	2T	⅓C	1C
Cheese, Parmesan, Romano	6t	¼C	½C	1C
Cherries, glacé, chopped	1T	2T	⅓C	¾C
Cherries, whole	1T	2T	⅓C	⅔C
Cocoa	2T	¼C	½C	1C
Coconut, desiccated	2T	⅓C	⅔C	1¼C
Coconut, shredded	⅓C	⅔C	1¼C	2½C
Coffee, ground	2T	⅓C	⅔C	1⅓C
Coffee, instant	3T	½C	1C	1¾C
Cornflakes	½C	1C	2C	4C
Cornflour	6t	3T	½C	¾C
Cream of tartar	1T	2T	⅓C	⅔C
Currants	1T	2T	⅓C	¾C
Custard powder	6t	3T	½C	¾C
Dates, chopped	1T	2T	⅓C	¾C
Figs, chopped	1T	2T	⅓C	¾C
Flour, plain or self-raising	6t	¼C	½C	1C
Flour, wholemeal	6t	3T	½C	1C
Fruit, mixed	1T	2T	⅓C	¾C
Gelatine	5t	2T	⅓C	¾C
Ginger, crystalised pieces	1T	2T	⅓C	¾C
Ginger, ground	6t	⅓C	½C	1C
Ginger, preserved, heavy syrup	1T	2T	⅓C	⅔C
Glucose, liquid	2t	1T	2T	⅖C
Golden syrup	2t	1T	2T	⅖C
Haricot beans	1T	2T	⅓C	½C
Honey, jam	2t	1T	2T	⅖C
Lentils	1T	2T	⅓C	½C
Milk, powder, full cream	2T	¼C	½C	1C
Milk powder, non fat	2T	⅓C	¾C	1¼C
Nutmeg	6t	3T	½C	¾C
Nuts, chopped	6t	¼C	½C	1C

Ingredient	½oz	1oz	2oz	4oz
Oatmeal	1T	2T	½C	¾C
Olives, sliced	1T	2T	⅓C	¾C
Olives, whole	1T	2T	⅓C	¾C
Pasta, short (e.g. macaroni)	1T	2T	⅓C	¾C
Peaches, chopped	6t	¼C	½C	1C
Peaches, dried and whole	1T	2T	⅓C	¾C
Peanut butter	3T	6t	3T	½C
Peanuts, shelled, raw, whole	1T	2T	⅓C	¾C
Peas, split	1T	2T	⅓C	½C
Peel, mixed	1T	2T	⅓C	⅔C
Potato, flakes	¼C	½C	1C	2C
Potato powder	1T	2T	¼C	½C
Prunes, chopped	1T	2T	⅓C	⅔C
Prunes, whole pitted	1T	2T	⅓C	½C
Raisins	2T	¼C	⅓C	⅔C
Rice, short or long grain, raw	1T	2T	⅓C	½C
Rice bubbles	⅔C	1¼C	2½C	4C
Rolled oats	2T	⅓C	⅔C	1¼C
Sago	2T	¼C	⅓C	¾C
Salt, common	3t	6t	¼C	½C
Semolina	1T	2T	⅓C	¾C
Spices	6t	3T	¼C	½C
Sugar, castor	3t	5t	¼C	½C
Sugar, crystalline 1A	3t	6t	¼C	½C
Sugar, icing	1T	2T	⅓C	⅔C
Sugar, moist brown	1T	2T	⅓C	⅔C
Sultanas	1T	2T	⅓C	⅔C
Tapioca	1T	2T	⅓C	⅔C
Treacle	2t	1T	2T	⅓C
Walnuts, chopped	2T	¼C	½C	1C
Walnuts, halved	2T	⅓C	⅔C	1¼C
Yeast, compressed	3t	6t	3T	½C
Yeast, dried	6t	3T	½C	1C

CONVERTING LIQUID MEASURES

Imperial	Standard Measures	Metric
⅛ fl oz	1 teaspoon	5 mL
¼ fl oz	2 teaspoons	10 mL
½ fl oz	1 tablespoon	20 mL
1 fl oz	1½ tablespoons	30 mL
	2 tablespoons	40 mL
1½ fl oz	2½ tablespoons	50 mL
2 fl oz	3 tablespoons	60 mL
	¼ cup	65 mL
	3½ tablespoons	70 mL
	4 tablespoons	80 mL
	⅓ cup	85 mL
	4½ tablespoons	90 mL
3 fl oz	5 tablespoons	100 mL
4 fl oz	½ cup	125 mL
5 fl oz (¼ pint)	7½ tablespoons	150 mL
	⅔ cup	170 mL
6 fl oz	¾ cup	185 mL
8 fl oz	1 cup	250 mL
10 fl oz (½ pint)	1¼ cups	315 mL
12 fl oz	1½ cups	375 mL
14 fl oz	1¾ cups	435 ml
16 fl oz	2 cups	500 mL
20 fl oz (1 pint)	2½ cups	625 mL
40 fl oz (1 quart)	5 cups	1.25 litres
80 fl oz (½ gallon)	10 cups	2.5 litres
120 fl oz (¾ gallon)	15 cups	3.75 litres
160 fl oz (1 gallon)	20 cups	5.0 litres

CONVERTING OVEN TEMPERATURES

Approximate Thermostat Setting °F (Fahrenheit)		Temperature Descriptions	Gas Mark	Approximate Thermostat Setting C° (Celsius)	
Gas	Electricity			Gas	Electricity
140	140	Plate Warming	0	60	60
175	175	Keep Warm	¼	80	80
210	230	Cool	½	100	110
250	250	Very Slow	1	120	120
300	300	Slow	2	150	150
320	340	Moderately Slow	3	160	170
355	390	Moderate	4	180	200
375	430	Moderately Hot	5	190	220
390	445	Hot	6	200	230
445	480	Very Hot	7–8	230	250

CONVERTING AMERICAN MEASURES

American	Metric
1 tablespoon flour	15 g
1 tablespoon sugar	22 g
1 tablespoon butter	22 g
1 cup flour	135 g
1 cup sugar	210 g
1 cup butter	210 g
1 teaspoon liquid	5 mL
1 tablespoon liquid	15 mL
1 gill liquid	118 mL
1 cup liquid	250 mL
1 pint liquid	528 mL

3

THE BATHROOM

BATHROOMS were once thought of as functional and were almost disregarded from a design and decorating point of view. These days, however, there is a great variety of attractive fittings and accessories available from specialist shops or major stores. The bathroom has come into its own.

Whether you are building or renovating, there are many practical considerations when planning a bathroom. The best advice is to visit showrooms first, and investigate thoroughly what is available and at what price.

En suite bathrooms are often considered these days. Although the *en suite* bathroom is sited next to the bedroom, it should also be placed as close as possible to other plumbing (that is, kitchen or bathroom) to cut costs.

Old houses are often very limited in space. Again, to save costs, the bathroom can adjoin the kitchen or be directly above it in a two-storey house.

SAVING SPACE

The smaller the bathroom the more care needs to be taken with planning. Don't be discouraged by lack of space. Make use of every centimetre and think of all the cleaning saved.

You must allow easy access to toilet, shower and basin. Sliding doors and shower screens will help you to save space.

There are many compact bathroom fittings available, from a fully moulded shower or bath unit to neat basins, cupboards and towel racks which allow you to get maximum use of space.

Modular bathrooms A relatively new solution to your design and space problems may be a modular bathroom made from moulded acrylics and fibreglass with the whole unit virtually in one piece. These are surprisingly easy to install. The whole job may take only two or three days. The makers will install the unit, and the plumber comes and does his part of the job later. No plumbing pipes are exposed and fibreglass, being an insulating material, is warm in winter and cool in summer.

RENOVATE OR REMODEL?

If you want to update your bathroom, you have the choice of renovating or remodelling.

RENOVATING

Renovation is by far the cheaper and easier option. You can introduce new accessories or revive the walls with a new coat of paint or new wallpaper. One step further is fresh tiling and the provision of new shelves and cabinet. With renovation, the key to success is colour. Take a good look at the existing colour scheme and work out how you want to modify or improve it. An *en suite* is generally better in the same tonings as the adjoining bedroom or dressing room. In the main bathroom you can be more adventurous.

REMODELLING

This can involve anything from replacing tiles and fixtures to completely rearranging the space. Remodelling needs to be worked out and costed carefully. Even then you should budget for unexpected difficulties and changes.

A reasonable approach is to draw a floor plan of the existing bathroom and adjoining areas which may be affected by your changes. Make cut-outs of existing fixtures. Move them around on the ground plan until you get the arrangement you want. Place your bathtub first, but, before that, decide if you want a spa, or a square rather than the conventional oblong unit. Handbasins, so often in use, are best away from traffic areas, and perhaps should be near a window. At any rate, it is important to light this area well.

Having made the big decisions, plan your accessories: mirrors, shelves, lighting, and so on. When everything seems in order, check on local building and plumbing codes.

Finally, you are ready to get a quote. This may involve a carpenter and plumber. You may decide it is worth consulting an architect. Make sure that any quotation places liability for unsatisfactory work or damage on the installer.

BATHROOM FITTINGS

It is important, particularly when it comes to cleaning, to know the materials used in bathroom fittings. The main ones are:

Enamelled cast iron These fixtures are very durable and retain heat well, keeping the bath water warmer longer.

Enamelled steel This blend of materials is strong but light, and it is popular for remodelling as it is easy to manoeuvre. The enamel coat is thinner than that of cast iron but can last as long if cleaned carefully with non-abrasive products.

Stainless steel Many industrial basins are stainless steel and small sizes can be used domestically for a modern, high-tech look. Stainless steel needs cleaning more often than porcelain enamel but is very hard wearing.

Vitreous china This is actually a type of glazed porcelain and is most commonly used for toilets, bidets and basins.

Fibreglass-reinforced plastic This is factory moulded, not only into tubs and basins but showers and one-piece tub and shower combinations. Being lighter, it is easier to install than steel or iron but needs care as it is less durable.

Bidets The bidet originated in Europe and there is now a strong demand for them in Australia. A bidet is a sit-down washbasin with hot and cold running water and a douche spray. Australian regulations require a separate water supply. Bidets should be placed next to the toilet. They come in matching colours.

Extractor fans These are very practical, removing steam and odours, and providing better ventilation. Extractor fans can be set into the wall or ceiling, and may be electrically connected so that switching on the bathroom light automatically switches on the fan. Some models are designed to be set into a fixed pane of glass, which could replace an old

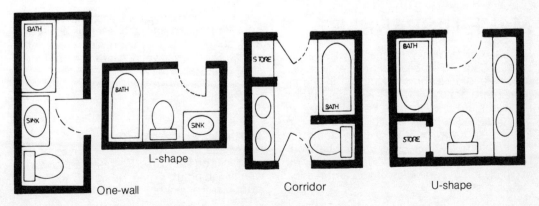

One-wall

L-shape

Corridor

U-shape

window. These may be easier to install than those which need a wall opening.

BASICS

Because of the specialised function of the bathroom, special consideration has to be given to various aspects of the room itself. These include:

Lighting Bathrooms need good clear lighting for both safety and practical purposes. In a small bathroom one overhead fitting may be enough but extra lighting around the mirror helps for applying make-up, or for hair styling. Button fittings or fluorescent strips are practical for confined spaces.

Windows and skylights One of the most delightful things is a bathroom with a view. Unless the bathroom is overlooked, there is no reason for opaque glass. Patterned or stained-glass can be used to provide privacy, when needed, without loss of light. Skylights may be able to bring in light where windows cannot be installed. Some types of skylights are fitted with extractor fans to solve the ventilation problem.

Flooring Flooring needs to be water resistant, durable and easy to clean. Ceramic tiles are traditional but quarry tiles, slate or even marble are other hard floor choices. All these need a solid base. Timber floors may need to be strengthened to support the load without movement. Vinyl tiles or waterproofed cork tiles are also practical.

Timber floors can be attractive when sanded and waterproofed with at least six coats of polyurethane finish. Bathroom carpeting can be used for extra comfort or to cover an unattractive floor but should be loose laid so that it can be removed for cleaning or drying.

MAKE IT SPARKLE

Regular maintenance wins out every time compared to tackling embedded grime and major stains with drastic abrasives and harsh chemicals. There are, however, times when strong measures are unavoidable. You may buy an old house and need to make the best of existing fixtures. You may be absent from home for some time. Make sure you know what your bath and other fittings are made of before you begin cleaning, particularly if you are treating stubborn stains.

VITREOUS/PORCELAIN ENAMEL

Three types of stain are common on enamel baths and washbasins.

• Blue/green drip stains caused by a dripping tap. Rub lightly with a soap pad, or soap-suds with ammonia. Or make careful use of household bleach and water. Get a new washer in the tap.

• Rust stains due to iron in the water. They are usually dark grey. Try the same treatment as for drip stains. Or try lemon juice and salt applied with a sponge.

• Stubborn stains. Rub with a bleach solution. Or apply a paste of cream of tartar and diluted hydrogen peroxide. If necessary, add a couple of drops of ammonia to the paste. Leave for two hours. Or try a paste of borax and lemon juice.

To brighten up a porcelain bath which has yellowed, rub with a solution of salt and turpentine.

For very old porcelain stains, shave a bar of household soap into a bucket of hot water, and add ½ cup of mineralised methylated spirits. Stir to dissolve the soap, then brush on stain vigorously.

In all cases rinse bath or basin well after treatment.

ACRYLIC/FIBREGLASS

Never use harsh abrasives on acrylic or any abrasives on fibreglass. For general stains, rub with washing-up liquid or liquid soap. For stubborn stains gently rub with fine sandpaper until surface is smooth then rub with silver metal polish. Treat scratches and nicks with silver metal polish.

Rinse bath or basin well.

CLEANING TIPS

A low-cost, high-shine way to clean bathroom fixtures is a cloth dipped in paraffin. The smell will remain only for a short time.

A pad of nylon net may be abrasive enough to clean off bathtub rings.

Fine steel wool should remove soap film. Wash surface with a solution of vinegar, ammonia and water.

If you are going away for a long time, prevent marks from a dripping tap by smearing the bath or sink with petroleum jelly.

LAVATORY

To get rid of lavatory rings, flush to wet sides, apply paste of borax and lemon juice. Leave for two hours and then scrub.

Or, pour two tablespoons household bleach into the water for several hours. Do not use this treatment with septic systems.

Rust stains under a lavatory bowl rim can be removed with laundry bleach.

Used solution from sterilising babies' bottles can be poured down the lavatory to help clean and sterilise it.

Never use one type of lavatory cleaner with another. The result may be explosive and/or toxic.

SHOWER CURTAINS

Plastic shower curtains wash down easily with half a cup of household bleach in five litres of water.

Many plastic shower curtains can be laundered in the washing machine with warm water, but only for 3 to 5 minutes of agitator time. Do not put curtains into a drier. Shake off excess water and hang to dry.

Wash nylon shower curtains by hand and drip dry.

Add a teaspoonful of ammonia to the water when washing your plastic shower curtains to dissolve soap residue and stains.

Plastic shower curtains will stay soft after cleaning if you add a few drops of mineral oil to the rinse water.

To prevent mildew on shower curtains soak in a solution of salt water before hanging.

Use a paste of bicarbonate of soda or a mild solution of bleach and water to remove mildew. Rinse.

SHOWER RECESS

A handful of washing soda in half a bucket of hot water will clean the tiles. Wear rubber gloves and use a long-handled brush. Wash off well, using a hose if possible.

A quick alternative is a sponge mop with a liquid organic cleaner.

For extensive stains, make a paste of bicarbonate of soda and bleach. Scrub. Rinse thoroughly.

Before cleaning walls or tiles, run the shower with hot water to loosen dirt.

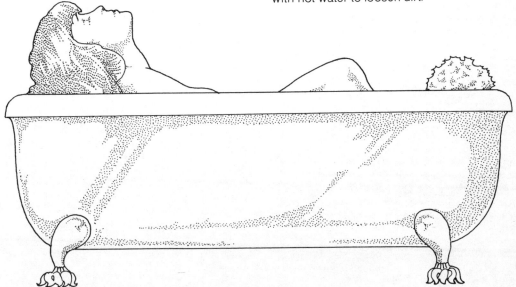

Laundry bleach will remove mildew from grout. Rinse off thoroughly.

To freshen white grout, cover it with white, liquid shoe polish. Any polish that gets on the tiles can be wiped away later.

To clean glass shower doors, sponge with white vinegar.

Furniture polish or wax on clean ceramic tile walls will keep soap film from accumulating. (Don't treat the floors or they will become slippery.)

Moulded fibre shower recesses generally come with instructions not to use abrasive cleaners. Equal parts of brown vinegar and kerosene will clean them.

Clogged shower head Remove head and, if metal, boil in ½ cup of vinegar and 2 litres water for 15 minutes. Plastic shower heads should be soaked in equal amounts of hot vinegar and water. Do not boil.

MIRRORS
A rub with a cloth dipped in glycerine or equal parts glycerine and methylated spirits will help stop a bathroom mirror from fogging up.

Rubbing with soap and then polishing with a clean cloth does the trick too.

Talcum powder will polish up mirrors.

Remove hairspray from mirrors with methylated spirits.

ACCESSORIES
Loofahs and natural sponges tend to become slimy with soap unless they are cleaned regularly. Rinse them under a cold water tap then soak them for an hour in 2 tablespoons of vinegar per litre of water.

Attach a plastic curtain ring to bathroom plugs. The ring will float and saves tugging.

Use a sponge as a soap holder. It will pick up enough soap for a shower or bath and the soap holder won't need cleaning.

A few extra shower curtain hooks hung on the rod can hold a back brush, a net bag for bath toys, or the family wash cloths.

Have a perfumed shower by placing some bath salts in the shower sprinkler. The sprinkler is easily unscrewed, and the salts will dissolve leaving no crystals to clog up the shower head.

Glue small magnets inside the bathroom cabinet to hold nail files, cuticle scissors, clippers and other metal objects.

4

THE LAUNDRY

LAUNDRIES are often neglected when planning and decorating a house. Whether your laundry is tucked away in the passage to the back door or the washing machine is incorporated into the bathroom, or you are lucky enough to have a large utility room, the laundry should be a pleasant, comfortable place in which to work. If you are contemplating a new laundry, or you would just like to reorganise the old one, a little time spent now can save time and trouble in the future.

PLANNING A LAUNDRY

THE LOCATION

When deciding on the location for a new laundry, remember that it is cheaper to keep the laundry close to existing plumbing. Many people like to have an outdoor drying area (although this may not be possible), so keep the laundry close to this to save trekking wet clothes through the house. Avoid unnecessary steps to an outside clothesline as they are hazardous when carrying baskets of washing. Ramps are safer.

Driers are usually necessary for unit dwellers, although you should plan an area where you can dry woollens and other items which cannot be machine-dried. Laundry hung from balconies is rarely allowed under tenancy rules.

WORKABLE PLANS

It is not necessary to allocate a separate room for the laundry. If you are short of space, a laundry area could even be incorporated into a family-room, provided the area is closed off with floor to ceiling doors and the noise of the machines working does not interfere with family activities. Another good spot is the bathroom—a carefully-designed area that takes up minimum space can cope with a family-size wash.

Don't put the laundry in the kitchen. Apart from the unpleasant aspects of mixing dirty washing with cooking, building regulations may not allow plans or renovations in which both activities share the same space. Before

Combined sewing area

beginning any structural renovations to the house itself, check your council's regulations as you may need to submit plans and get council approval.

There are four main activities for which space should be allocated. Sorting clothes, washing (both by hand and machine), drying and ironing. Sorting can be done on the floor, or even as the clothes are dropped into the machine, but it is easier if there is some bench space or separate baskets.

The washing machine needs to be located near the tub so that there is an outlet for dirty water. Tubs with a bypass system are best, as the tub can be used for hand-washing while the machine is also being used. These are necessary for suds-saving machines. In a bathroom with no separate laundry tub, the water will have to drain into the bath or handbasin.

STORAGE SPACE

Every laundry, no matter how small, needs some storage space, if only for washing powders. A lockable cupboard for poisonous cleaners such as bleach, dry cleaning fluid, etc. is essential if you have young children. Dirty clothes need well-ventilated storage such as plastic or wicker baskets or even louvre-door cupboards to keep them out of sight.

Fold-down ironing boards are great space savers and can be concealed in their cupboards when not in use. With a stool, they can double as sorting or mending space. It is a good idea to have some storage space handy for a portable board and any ironing remaining to be done. It is a depressing sight to have an ironing board permanently set up in the living-room.

Bathroom-laundry

DUAL PURPOSE ROOMS

If you are lucky enough to have left-over space in your laundry, there are many uses to which it can be put. A sewing area is the most obvious, with a small table for the machine, shelving and drawers for fabrics and haberdashery, a full-length mirror and a larger table for cutting out. Trestle tables are very handy as they can be de-mounted when not in use.

The laundry can also store larger cleaning equipment such as brooms and vacuum cleaners, sporting equipment, suitcases, handyman's tools and bulk stores of preserved, dry or tinned foods. Linen cupboards right up to the ceiling are not impractical for things needed only occasionally.

EFFECTIVE DECOR

Ideally, lighting should come from several sources: a general fluorescent overhead with additional close lighting for ironing, sewing or hobbies. Track lighting can be useful with several spots angled to light different areas and activities.

Floor and wall finishes should be water resistant to cope with inevitable spills. Suitable coverings range from vinyl, cork and rubber to ceramic and quarry tiles, but make sure tiles are non-slip.

Ceramic or quarry-tiled floors can be cold and hard on the feet; a rubber mat or a washable non-slip rug adds comfort. Gloss or semi-gloss paints or vinyl wallpaper will cheer up dull walls. Timber panelling protected with polyurethane finish adds warmth.

APPLIANCES

Today's washers and driers are all efficient, but some will be more suited to your laundry space than others. Select a brand that is gentle on the clothes and is backed by warranty and good service.

Your choice of appliances will largely depend on the amount of space available and the size of the regular wash. Generally, washing machines fall into three categories: the popular top-loading family washer, the front-loading machine and the twin-tub models.

WASHERS

Top-loading machines Australians have a preference for top-loading machines against front-loading ones. Admittedly, top loaders are the easiest to control: you can adjust the water levels as well as the timing; you can stop the machine in mid-cycle to add the extra pair of socks and you can remove delicate articles before they go into the spin. Some models also have a suds-saving device which enables you to return the water to the machine and re-use it in another load. Because they are generally larger machines than the front-loading type consumers are inclined to think they are stronger and will take more clothes. This is not so—in fact some front-loading machines hold more than some top-loading ones.

Front-loading machines take up little space and are ideal for small areas. Being flat-topped they allow for a stackable drier, a very necessary item if you live in a unit or have small children. But you cannot interrupt the programmes as easily, nor can you be at all forgetful—once the door is closed it cannot be re-opened until the cycle is complete. When front loaders were first introduced flooding occurred if the door was inadvertently opened during the cycle. Machines now have a lock on the door to prevent this, although the programme can be advanced in an emergency.

Twin-tub machines have been around for years and are ideal for the consumer who wants an inexpensive machine that takes up little room. They are light and easy to move about and can be wheeled up to the water supply and disconnected when the washing is finished. These compact machines will wash and spin dry the clothes, but you do have to transfer the load manually from the wash tub to the spin dryer.

Having decided on the type of washer, check on the details of its styling. Does it have sharp corners that can catch on clothes and cut small people who tend to hurtle through laundries? Are the controls child-proof? Does the machine stop if the door is opened during the spin cycle? In the case of a possible malfunction, are the electrical parts protected with an external water overflow? If the motor overheats, will it automatically cut out?

SOME HELPFUL HINTS

Whatever type of machine you choose, read the manufacturer's booklet very carefully before operating.

Those washing cycles are there for a reason. Some clothes can and should be washed in really hot water, the temperature of which would be harmful to others. Certain fabrics must not be spun dry for any length of time and woollens need special care.

Never overload the washing machine or clothes will not be washed thoroughly.

Vary the size of items in each load. A couple of sheets and several small articles will wash cleaner than a load of large items.

When oily clothes have been washed in the washing machine, spray the insides lightly with pre-wash stain remover and wipe with a dry cloth.

A wet bottle-brush is an effective way to clean fluff from your washing machine filter.

To clean the lint trap on a tumble drier use a small, stiff paint brush.

Washing machines standing on hard surfaces often travel when in operation. This can strain plumbing inlets and outlets. Cut squares of soft vinyl or linoleum and place them under the legs of the machine.

DRIERS AND OTHER EQUIPMENT

Tumble driers are increasingly popular and most models are designed to be free-standing, wall-mounted, or stacked on front-loading washers. Make sure you can reach wall-mounted models easily. Fold-out drying racks are handy on rainy days if you don't have a dryer. Laundry trolleys are useful for wheeling loads of wet clothes to an outside drying area.

Portable ironing tables are handy if you like to iron in front of the TV or close to the bedrooms so that clothes can be easily put away. Adjustable height models are best and experiment until you find the height which is most comfortable for you.

WASHING

WASHDAY TIPS

Check that garments are washable. A care guide is usually attached by the manufacturer. If there is no indication of washability, hand-wash a small area to check that colours are fast.

Today's wash contains many different fabrics. Before washing these should be sorted into loads according to the programmes on your machine. Where a garment is a mixture of two or more fabrics, treat as for the most delicate of them.

Items such as sheets, pillowcases, cotton shirts, blouses, tablecloths and table napkins may be washed together. Non-colourfast items should be washed separately.

Fragile fabrics, acetates, rayons and other

delicate synthetics should be separated from heavy fabrics and washed with a mild detergent.

White synthetic materials (such as nylon and Dacron) should not be washed with coloured garments, even pastel shades.

Permanent press and wash-and-wear garments should be washed according to the manufacturers' instructions and the appropriate programmes on your machine.

Wash rugs, blankets, slip covers and curtains separately.

Before washing, close zippers and pre-treat soil and stains. Buttons are best left unfastened. Turn pockets inside out to check for coins, ballpoint pens, tissues etc.

If clothes aren't badly rumpled or dirty an airing will probably do them more good than a wash.

Button cuffs of shirts to the front of the shirt before putting in the washing machine and you will have fewer tangles.

Let the hems of curtains down before washing in case they shrink. Soak in cold water to remove the bulk of the dirt before washing them.

When washing small, delicate items by machine, put them in a pillow-case. This protects them and makes handling several items easier.

A foam-rubber pillow should be washed in its case to prevent fraying.

To prevent nylon from turning yellow, soak in a solution of warm water to which a dessert-spoon of bicarbonate of soda has been added. Then wash as usual. White socks can be restored if they are soaked in the same solution.

When hand-washing, use vinegar in the rinse water. It cuts down on soap and you will need to rinse only once.

Any laundry product is suitable for washing baby clothes, but rinse clothes well to ensure detergent or soap is completely removed to avoid skin irritations.

Some nappy rash creams contain a chemical which, when combined with chlorine (or household) bleach, can cause brown stains. Soak in a normal detergent solution and wash in hot water.

Don't use more laundry detergent or soap than recommended. You will waste money, make an inefficient job of your wash, and you may damage your washing machine.

Dissolve detergent before adding the clothes. Otherwise, the washing cycle will be half over before the detergent starts to do its job.

High temperatures dissolve powders more quickly. Even if you wash in cold water, dissolve the powder or soap flakes in hot first.

Keep laundry powder in a glass jar. This keeps it dry and you can see how much is left—saves being caught short.

If the washing machine overflows with suds, pour in a little fabric softener. The suds will subside.

Pre-wash sprays contain stronger chemicals than ordinary detergents. When using spray on a garment for the first time, test for colour-fastness in an inconspicuous position.

Before soaking anything in a solution using a dry ingredient, dissolve powder completely or colour spotting may occur

RINSING

Fabric softener works in between fibres tangled during washing, separating them and giving them a protective coat. This film makes garments easier to launder in future. It also eliminates static cling. Because separated fibres hold less water than those that are matted,

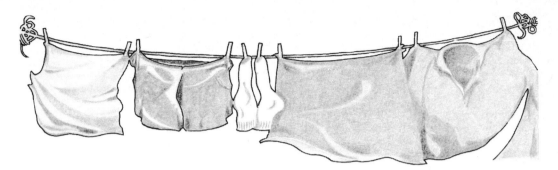

more air is let through and conditioned fabrics dry more quickly. Also, the iron will glide more easily over smooth fibres.

Always use fabric softener in the final rinse or all its advantages will be rinsed out.

For thorough rinsing, add 1 cup white vinegar to the rinse cycle. This helps dissolve the alkalines in soaps and detergents.

A teaspoon of Epsom salts to four litres of rinse water helps keep many materials from fading or running.

Lightly starch slips to stop them clinging to knitted dresses.

Sugar in the rinsing water will stiffen lace, muslin or silk.

DRYING

Never leave wet washing in the laundry basket for any length of time. Dark colours can run into paler ones.

Peg clothes on the line at their strongest part. Peg men's shirts and women's dresses by the hems (or by the shoulders if you are anxious about a garment losing shape); shorts by the waistband; T-shirts and other knit shirts by the shoulders; socks by the toes.

After washing a permanently pleated skirt, gather pleats together tightly and slip a stocking down over the skirt. Hang it up to dry and the pleats will look freshly pressed.

Dark colours, particularly woollens, dry more slowly than pale. In a multi-coloured garment, the pale areas can absorb moisture from the dark areas (and dye with it). To avoid dye pick-up, dry garments quickly.

Use the gentle spin cycle for all heavy garments to avoid creasing and wrinkling.

Take shirts and dresses from the line or drier and put them on hangers immediately to avoid creasing.

When drying patterned quilt covers, hang them on the line inside out to prevent the sun fading them.

To avoid peg marks on skirts after washing, attach large safety pins to the loops on either side and pin them to the washing line. A peg on either side will stop the pins slipping.

Hang out printed T-shirts inside out and, if possible, at night. That way the transfer won't fade.

When drying garments outside on hangers use two hangers with their hooks facing opposite directions on the line. This forms a lock and clothes won't blow away, even in very strong winds.

Articles will dry faster and more evenly if the drier is only half full.

Don't put dark-coloured items with light-coloured towels in a tumble drier as fluff may be transferred.

Use two baskets when collecting washing from the line. Put articles to iron in one, and articles you only need to fold in the other. It makes sorting and selecting clothes easier.

Or, save extra trips by pegging a pillowslip to line and filling it with small items.

For faster clothes sorting, mark underwear and other look-alikes with a different colour marking ink for each member of the family.

Place a small box or basket beside your washing machine. Every time a mateless sock turns up, put it in the box. Eventually you will have a pair.

After washing a length of lace, wrap it around a milk bottle to dry. Lace will dry wrinkle-free and undamaged.

COLOURFASTNESS

To test a fabric for colourfastness, dampen an inconspicuous patch and press with a hot iron between two pieces of white cloth. If there is any staining, wash the item separately.

Always soak an entire article so that any colour change occurs overall.

Use scraps left over from home-made garments to test for colourfastness, shrinkability, drip-drying qualities, iron heat and so on.

FADING

Black lingerie, dresses and shirts tend to look brownish after several washes. To restore colour, add bluing, coffee or strong tea when rinsing.

Prevent black articles getting a faded look by adding a few drops of vinegar to the wash.

If fabric dye runs it is possible to 'salt the dye' to stabilise it. Rinse the garment several times in cold water to which two to three tablespoons of salt have been added.

Rejuvenate a pair of faded jeans by washing them with a pair of jeans that have never been washed. Dye and fabric finish from the new jeans will add colour and body to the old.

To stop colour fading from jeans, soak them for an hour in a solution of two tablespoons of salt to 4½ litres of water before washing. Use cold water for both washing and rinsing.

FLUFF AND LINT

Wash corduroy and dark clothes wrong side out to prevent lint from sticking to them.

Wash dark socks inside an old nylon stocking to keep them free from lint.

To remove fluff from corduroy, wash and dry slowly. While still damp, brush with a clothes brush.

You can eliminate fluff problems by adding 1 cup white vinegar to the final rinse cycle.

Some nylon netting in the clothes drier is a good lint catcher.

HARD WATER

Hard water contains a high concentration of chemicals which, if used over a long period of time with insufficient washing products, can cause a build-up of chemicals, making clothes look dirty. If you live in a hard water area (certain parts of Queensland and South Australia), it is best to use liquid detergent rather than soap, which can form a scum.

If you do have hard water, water conditioner should be added to the wash and rinse waters.

In soft water areas, water conditioner will reduce the amount of detergent you need.

A water softening solution can be made by dissolving 25g washing soda in just over 500mL boiling water. Bottle and add to hard water. Start with 1 tablespoon for each 4½ litres, then add detergent or soap flakes. If the water is still too hard add another tablespoonful of the solution.

A teaspoon of borax to 2 litres of water will also soften water. Glycerine will soften water in

which woollen articles are to be washed.

Here is a traditional method of testing water for hardness: Dissolve 15g of white soap in 2½ cups of rain water. Allow to cool and settle. Mix 30mL of this with 2½ cups of the water to be tested. Soft water will remain clear, but hard water will become milky.

WORK CLOTHES

Treat grease and grime on shirt collars and cuffs by rubbing in a thick coat of chalk. Allow to sit overnight, and launder with a strong solvent detergent.

Here is a lazy but effective way for workers to wash a drip-dry shirt. First treat the collar and cuffs with a spray detergent. Leave it in soapy water in the bath after your shower. When you return home, rinse the shirt. The more it drips as it hangs the better it will keep its shape.

When washing greasy working clothes, add a cupful of ammonia or a handful of washing soda to the water. A cup of salt also works.

For stubborn or industrial dirt, treat area with a pre-wash agent, then apply a paste of washing powder and water. Leave for 30 minutes before washing. If a treated area is a slightly different colour after paste application, it may be necessary to soak the entire garment for even colour.

BEDCLOTHES

Eiderdowns and quilts Machine washing is possible for quilts, eiderdowns and continental quilts with synthetic polyester fillers and covers. The problem can be drying. Choose a day when you can dry outdoors if possible. Few household tumble driers are big enough to handle a large quilt or eiderdown satisfactorily.

Use a mild detergent. Add water softener or borax. Use a warm water cycle. The bath is an ideal place to wash large articles such as quilts and blankets. The bath should be filled with enough warm water to cover the article completely. Detergent or soap flakes should be dissolved in a small quantity of very hot water before being added to the bath. Stir thoroughly before adding the article.

If you can dry in your household drier, set it for the lowest temperature. For drying outdoors, put the quilt across two parallel lines. Keep out of direct sunlight. From time to time work the filler fibre with your fingers to stop it matting.

If your quilt is of real duck feathers,

remember that although ducks take to water they do not take as well to soaps and detergents. Alkaline detergents can have much the same effect on duck feathers as they have on wool—they take out the natural grease. Always use a neutral washing product.

Blankets It's a good idea to wash and moth-proof blankets at the same time. You will need the following:

   3 dessertspoons of eucalyptus oil
   1 large breakfast cup of methylated spirits
   225g best soap flakes

Mix together in a screw-top jar until all are dissolved. Add one tablespoonful of the mixture to every 4½ litres of water and soak blankets until clean. Then put them through the wringer or spin drier. Do not rinse as the eucalyptus oil replaces the oil in the wool. Dry outside on a windy day. The mixture will keep.

A very little olive oil added to the final rinse will keep woollen blankets soft and fluffy. For blankets made with synthetic fabrics, use a fabric softener (which also reduces static).

Drying is the main problem with washing blankets at home. You can do this by tumble drying without heat in a large clothes drier.

The most effective way to rinse blankets (after excess moisture has been removed) is to hang them on the line and hose them. After rinsing, spin on the machine's gentle cycle and hang in shade.

HOUSEHOLD LINEN

To get teatowels and other household linen clean, plunge them dry into boiling water in which you have brought detergent to a good froth. Leave to soak until the water is cold, wring them out and rinse well.

Or, soak in boiling water and cream of tartar. Use two scant tablespoons of cream of tartar to every litre of boiling water.

Add a little borax to the water when washing teatowels. It helps remove grease and dirt and also will disinfect the towels.

Add starch to the water when rinsing teatowels to prevent them leaving lint on glasses.

Wash blue towels, sheets and pillowcases with your white wash to brighten it.

New coloured linen should be washed separately for the first few times.

New bath or kitchen towels will become more absorbent if soaked in a bucket of water with two handfuls of Epsom salts for 24 hours.

To keep face cloths fresh, wash until clear of soap, soak in water containing lemon juice or vinegar, rinse and hang out to dry.

Lightly starch pillowcases to prevent them from becoming stained by cosmetics.

FABRIC GUIDE

Woollens Always wash wool in pure soap flakes or a product which has the Australian Wool Corporation's recommendation. General-purpose detergents contain ingredients for removing dirt from heavily soiled articles which make them alkaline. This can affect the acidic-type dyes used for wool.

Unless a garment is labelled 'Dry Clean Only' or 'Machine Washable' wash by hand. Dissolve the soap flakes or detergent thoroughly in lukewarm water, squeeze suds through garment. Do not rub or twist; this will cause shrinkage. Rinse well in lukewarm water. It is helpful always to wash and rinse wool in water at the same temperature. Roll in a towel to absorb excess moisture. Ease the garment into its shape and size for drying.

For machine-washable wool, use correct cycle (wool or slow). Wash for two minutes, rinse one minute, spin dry to remove excess moisture.

Keep woollen garments soft by adding 5mL (one tablespoon) of glycerine to washing and rinsing water. Or add a capful of creme hair rinse to the final rinse water. This will also help prevent itching skin when the garment is worn.

When washing wool, work under water so the water weight does not strain the wool fibres. To regain fluffiness of angora or mohair, wash as normal for woollen fibres, squeeze well and when almost dry, hang in a windy place.

Hanging some wool garments to dry will pull them out of shape. If in doubt, lie them flat on a towel and turn from time to time to dry evenly. Direct sunlight can have a weakening and discolouring effect on wet wool.

Or lay the garment on a frame so air can circulate all round it.

When drying woollens on a line, thread a nylon stocking through the sleeves and fasten the pegs to this.

To dry a sweater flat more quickly, put a cardboard tube from rolls of kitchen paper or foil into the sleeves.

If cuffs and waist of a woollen sweater have stretched, sponge them with hot water and dry with a hot air drier.

Not much can be done for deep scorches on woollens. However, if the scorch is superficial, brush it lightly with the finest sandpaper.

Soak an accidentally washed woollen item in tepid water to which you have added a good hair shampoo. Sometimes this will soften the wool fibres enough to allow reshaping.

Don't toss out shrunken woollens. Try soaking them for half an hour in 100g of Epsom salts and boiling water. Squeeze and stretch to size.

Keep winter woollens fresh by storing in a cupboard which has been sprinkled with Epsom salts. The Epsom salts also keep pests like silverfish and moths away.

Cashmere Cashmere sweaters and jumpers need careful hand-laundering. Use very cool suds made with a wool washing mixture. Use a tub with a plug so that the water can be released after washing and subsequent rinsings and excess water can be pressed out. Cashmere must not be wrung, but it can be spin dried. Put a towel or other soft clothing into the spin drier to act as a buffer, or roll the wet garment in a large towel and press out water.

Cashmere will stretch with the weight of water so, when wet, it should be lifted in both hands. Dry inside out, pinned to a sheet hung like a hammock between three or four lines, or on a metal jumper drier, or by slipping the legs of old panty hose through the sleeves. If a drier is used, maintain a low setting. Steam press when dry.

Cottons Soak colourfast, close-weave cottons if necessary then wash vigorously in hot water and standard detergent or in cold water and cold water detergent. More delicate cottons may be washed by hand if desired.

Silk Generally it is better to have silk dry cleaned. If the label says colourfast and washable, hand-wash as for wool but the last rinse should be cold. If colourfastness is doubtful, or if silk is multi-coloured, wash in cold water, adding 1 tablespoon of white vinegar to four litres of water. A little white vinegar in the final rinse helps restore sheen to silk, but soak the garment in cold water for at least 10 minutes to remove the vinegar before the next wash.

Drip dry to avoid unnecessary squeezing. Dry silk in the shade. Direct sunlight can cause yellowing.

Iron silk while the garment is still damp, with a moderately hot iron.

Synthetics Wash frequently. Hand or machine wash. If machine washing, use a gentle cycle. Don't spin. Acrylics: warm water, standard detergent powder. Roll in a towel, dry flat, away from heat. Acetate and triacetate: as for acrylic. Nylon: hot water, standard detergent powder. Never boil or use bleach. Rinse well. Drip dry. Terylene: hand-hot water and mild detergent. Drip dry.

Mixtures Wash blended fabrics in the same way as the component fibre which needs the gentlest treatment.

Linen Pure linen is so rare and expensive these days, it should be washed in soap or wool detergent.

Ethnic garments Examples are batik and Indian cotton. If you are uncertain of colourfastness, wash in cold water with two table-spoons of salt and half a cup of vinegar. Do not soak. Let garments drip dry.

Cotton jersey Wash as for wool. May be rolled in a towel to remove some of the moisture. Dry flat, if possible.

Washable velveteen Gently swish in lather of lukewarm water and soap flakes or mild detergent. Rinse well. Drip dry, shaping occasionally while drying.

Flame-resistant fabrics Flame-resistant fabrics are of great importance in families with small children. They need special treatment in the laundry. There are two types of flame-resistant fabrics. There are those which have been made that way by the application of a special finish to cotton fabrics. Some woollen fabrics are also modified by use of a special finish but this is not yet widely used. The other type of flame-resistant fabric is achieved by the modification of the fibre itself. An example is modacrylics or modified acrylics, such as Dynel and Teklan and a viscose fabric, Darelle, which has a flame retardant incorporated in the fibre at the time of manufacture.

Flame-resistant fabrics (modacrylics or fabrics with a flame-resistant finish) must not be bleached or soaked in any washing product.

Normally they must not be washed in soap or soap products as soap can mask the properties of the finish. Flame-resistant cotton should be washed at a temperature of 50°C, that is, hand-hot, and cold rinsed. Flame-resistant wool should be washed at a temperature of 40°C with a cold rinse and normal spin. Modacrylics should be washed at 50°C with a cold rinse and short spin.

DYEING

When dyeing in a washing machine, don't dye more than half the maximum load or less than 1 kg.

Dye dull or faded sheets with hot-water dye in your washing machine.

To clean your machine after using it for dyeing, after thorough rinsing of dyed article remove and fill machine immediately with hot water to the highest water level. Add ½ cup detergent and 1 cup of liquid household bleach and set machine for longest wash. During wash, stop machine and wet a cloth with the solution to wash off any dye splashes on the outside of machine then let cycle complete. Clean the lint filter.

Never try to dye fabrics which have faded unevenly or have scorch marks or noticeable stains.

When dyeing, a new colour will combine with the old rather than cover it. Blue over red will give you purple. Yellow dyed blue turns green.

When dyeing something dark a lighter colour, first take out the original colour with dye remover.

Tint dull nylon underwear with tea. Brew your tea and strain off all leaves. Test on a small piece of cloth, then immerse garment.

Wash dyed articles separately for the first few washes, as dye may run into other garments.

IRONING

Ironing is such a time-consuming job that it's worth doing it as efficiently as possible.

THE IRON

The invention of the electric iron in 1915 made ironing easier.

Know your iron, and take good care of it for longer use.

Read your instruction book carefully.

You can use water out of the tap, except where there is a high mineral content (hard water), when distilled water is necessary.

Never use an iron with a frayed cord or damaged plug.

Avoid ironing over objects such as buttons, zippers, and hooks. They will scratch the plate.

If your steam iron spatters, make sure you have filled it properly, and that it is not overfilled. Switch iron to steam after filling when it has had time to heat. If iron spatters during ironing, stand on the heel rest for a few minutes before resuming.

Store iron on its heel rest in a dry place with the cord wrapped loosely around the handle; never store a steam iron flat on the plate.

Revitalise your iron by rubbing it regularly with a cloth dipped in salt, or moistened with vinegar.

Let a steam iron reach its pre-set temperature before you use it after filling, or it may drip and leave water marks on fabrics.

To remove mineral deposits from the inside of a steam iron, fill it with equal parts of water and white vinegar. Let it steam for several minutes, then disconnect and leave for one hour. Empty, and rinse out with clear water.

Remove brown or burned-on spots on an iron by rubbing with a heated solution of vinegar and salt.

Starch marks on an iron may be removed by rubbing with a cake of soap while the iron is still warm. Polish off with a clean cloth.

Bicarbonate of soda is a good scouring agent when the face of your iron needs cleaning to make it glide smoothly. Apply it dry or with a damp sponge, gently scrubbing the surface until it is clean.

Another method is to rub with candle grease while iron is still warm, then wipe with a clean cloth. Other cleaning methods are running the iron across a piece of aluminium foil or paper sprinkled with salt.

Clogged steam vents can be cleared with a cotton swab or a pipe cleaner and soapy water.

Always empty a steam iron after use or it will fur up and block the vents.

IRONING TIPS

Be comfortable when ironing. Have ironing board at correct height. Stand on foam rubber or rug. In hot weather, iron in a cool part of house or in cross-current of breeze. Listen to the radio or watch television.

If called to the doorbell or telephone when ironing, always turn iron off and pull out cord from electric socket.

If clothes are folded immediately when taken out of the drier or off the line, it will make ironing easier.

For faster ironing, place a strip of heavy-duty aluminium foil over the length of the ironing board and cover with pad. As you iron, heat will reflect to the underside of the garment.

Or, you can starch your ironing board cover.

Cut material on the bias when making a new cover for your ironing board and it will fit perfectly.

To dampen clothes for ironing put them in the drier with the heat off, add a few wet towels, and tumble.

Or, place clothes in a large plastic bag and splash with water. Fasten the bag and leave several hours. Do not leave longer than 24 hours. The clothes might collect mildew, especially in warm weather.

Clothes dampened with hot water will be ready to iron sooner than clothes dampened with cold.

Articles can be dampened and placed in a plastic bag in the refrigerator overnight. This is particularly good for jeans.

If you have dampened ironing that you can't finish, put it in the freezer until you are ready.

A newly-ironed garment will crease again quickly, so avoid wearing or packing it for several hours.

Iron starched items, especially table linen, on the right side to increase resistance to soiling.

To iron a circular cloth, begin at the outside edge, then work in progressively smaller circles towards the centre.

To prevent the toe of the iron from catching in lace, use the iron with a sideways motion.

Iron embroidery face down on a soft towel. The embroidery will stand slightly raised from the fabric.

When ironing newly-knitted garments, use brown paper instead of a damp cloth. It will not flatten the pattern during ironing.

You can press sleeves without leaving creases if you slip in a rolled-up towel.

The shiny look of chintz can be restored by ironing the fabric right side down on waxed paper.

When ironing velvet, put a thick towel on the ironing board so the pile can sink into it while you press the velvet on the wrong side.

Make creases in trousers and pleats in dresses and skirts sharper by spraying with starch on the inside before ironing.

Or, rub a damp cake of soap down the inside of the creases before ironing. Turn to the right side and press through a damp cloth.

If you let down the hem of a garment and the

old crease remains, dip a handkerchief into a bowl of white vinegar, place on crease and press a hot iron on it. Repeat until crease is invisible. Test on an unobtrusive area of the fabric.

Hold pleats in place with paperclips when ironing.

Spread handkerchiefs or table napkins in a pile before ironing, and iron from the top. Halfway through the pile, the job will be done.

Use a ball of nylon netting to remove lint and fluff while ironing.

Keep corduroy clothes looking like new by ironing from the wrong side.

Iron shirt collars from each peak towards the centre of the back of the collar to avoid creases.

Sprays Take care when using pressure pack ironing aids that the spray does not go on vinyl tiles, kitchen vinyl or linoleum, or any surface which may become slippery. The silicone in the ironing aids sets up a polish and it is easy to slip.

If pressure pack ironing aid will not spray, remove nozzle and run through with hot water and replace top. This will remove particles of starch clogging nozzle.

Read instructions carefully on pressure pack ironing aid. This will ensure that starch can be used to end of pressure pack.

IRONING GUIDE

Fabric	Damp or Dry	Heat	Side
Acetate	Slightly damp	Cool	Wrong
Acrylic	Dry	Cool	Wrong
Cotton	Slightly damp	Hot	Right unless dark colour
Corduroy	Nearly dry	Fairly hot	Wrong
Linen	Damp	Hot	Right (shiny) Wrong (dull)
Nylon	Nearly dry	Cool	Either
Polyester	Slightly damp	Cool	Either
Silk*	Slightly damp	Warm	Wrong
Triacetate, tussore	Nearly dry	Cool	Either
Shantung	Dry	Fairly hot	Wrong
Velvet	Dry	Warm to fairly hot (depending on fabric)	Wrong
Viscose*	Slightly damp	Warm	Wrong
Wool**	Nearly dry	Warm	Wrong

* Do not sprinkle as fabric shows water marks
** Do not press ribbing or welts of knitwear

5

SPILLS AND STAINS

THE SECRET of removing most stains is to act quickly, usually removing the offending deposit first. As well as a general stain removal guide, a special section on the treatment of carpet stains has been included.

SAFETY FIRST

Read the labels on bottles and jars. Note what ingredients are in them. Follow instructions to the letter. Observe all warnings and precautions.

Many cleaning agents are toxic and poisonous. Some are explosive. Label all bottles and jars clearly. Don't pour any solvent into another container, particularly not into a soft-drink bottle.

Keep all cleaners out of reach of children.

Do not use a hair drier or heat lamp with flammable fabrics or agents. Do not smoke while you are working. If possible, work near an open window, or better still, work outside. Do not work near fire or flame.

WHAT TO DO

There are generally three situations in which you may have to deal with a stain: on a washable fabric which can be handled (i.e. it is not being used for rigid upholstery); a non-washable fabric which can be treated in the hand or taken to a dry cleaner for advice or treatment; and non-washable or washable fabrics which cannot readily be moved, such as carpets and upholsteries.

Act quickly. Deal with any stain as soon as it happens.

Follow manufacturer's instructions carefully. If the stain is on a garment, read the care label. Keep labels from upholstery and carpets for future reference.

First try to classify the stain. There are basically three types—greasy, non-greasy or combination stains.

Fabrics with special finishes, such as drip dry and easy care, tend to retain greasy stains. With fully washable fabrics, washing in hot water may be all that is needed to remove a stain.

If you are not sure how to treat a stain or are uncertain of the fibre content of the article, take it to a dry cleaner, or, if it involves carpets or heavy pieces of furniture, call one to the house.

What you decide to do about a spill depends on:
• Your experience with that sort of stain.
• Your knowledge of the fabric:
• What you have in hand to treat it with.
• The extent of the stain. You may decide to dab at a few food spots on a printed silk dress, knowing any residual mark might go unnoticed, but not risk a large shadowy ring on a plain fabric.

Above all, what you do depends on the value

of the article you are tackling. You might take a risk with a well-worn tie or scarf but send a new dress straight to the cleaners.

Even the intrepid should hesitate before tackling upholstery and carpets. The behaviour of fabrics in these circumstances is quite different from materials you can handle easily; they may also have had treatments or be attached to backings which make them impossible to clean at home.

If you are baffled by the variety of spot removers on the market, ask your dry cleaner for advice on what is useful and harmless in the house. Ask for details of the properties of any product at the chemist or hardware store before you buy.

It is probably unwise and unnecessary to keep a battery of solvents and other cleaners in the house in case of spills. This could be more expensive, and less satisfactory, than good dry cleaning.

HOW TO WORK

First, remove any solids from the stain area. Use a blunt knife or, if appropriate, paper towels or tissues.

Blot up as much as you can. When you begin work on the stain, dab—don't rub. Begin at the outer edge of the stain and blot toward the centre.

Apply any treatment from the back of the fabric if possible. Otherwise you will only be rubbing the stain further into the fabric.

If possible, put a substantial pad of tissues, paper towels or any clean white paper underneath and mop up as you go along.

Don't work away to get rid of the last traces of a stain. Often you risk spoiling the fabric by applying too much solvent or by rubbing too hard.

The back of a spoon can be a useful way to apply liquids to small areas, enabling you to exert firm pressure without rubbing.

If a cleaner isn't working, don't strengthen the solution. Let the fabric dry out before trying another remedy.

Always rinse or air after treatment.

When you go to the cleaners, tell them what caused the stain and be honest about your home treatments. Pin a note to the garment if you think it is necessary.

CLEANING AGENTS

ABSORBENT POWDERS

These include Fuller's earth, cornflour and cornstarch, French chalk, powdered starch, talcum powder, and cat litter.

All are good grease removers. All are basically harmless but can be difficult to remove from fabrics which are non-washable.

Sprinkle the powder over the damp stain. If the stain has already dried out, sponge it with cold water. Leave to dry, then brush off. If situation warrants, use the vacuum cleaner. Repeat until no more powder can be absorbed. Often a dry cleaning fluid, white spirit or methylated spirits are necessary to remove remnants of stain.

SOLVENTS

These are used to get rid of grease or oil stains. Incorrect use can damage fabric, delustre glossy finishes and remove dyes.

Unbranded solvents include white spirit, surgical spirit, paraffin oil and acetone. Others are sold under brand names in liquid, aerosol or paste form.

NEVER use petrol or benzine in the home for dry cleaning. As soon as petrol is exposed to the air it gives off large quantities of vapour which can ignite in seconds. Don't keep petrol in the house at all. Benzine is highly flammable.

Fat (butter or margarine) will soften tar or oil.

Glycerine will soften some grease and other stains, particularly on non-washable fabrics.

It is sometimes possible to remove grease with an alkali, such as ammonia or washing soda (sodium carbonate). Washing soda dissolved in water can remove grease. Too much can spoil colour of fabrics, shrink woollens and remove their natural oil. But it can work with white cotton or linen.

A borax solution can remove grease and soften water. It can be used for delicate fabrics.

BLEACHES

These are (from strong to weak): chlorine, ammonia, hydrogen peroxide, lemon juice and white vinegar (acetic acid).

There are two kinds of bleach, those which oxidise, removing the stain by adding oxygen to it and those which work by taking the oxygen away. Oxidising bleaches include hydrogen peroxide, and chlorine bleaches, usually containing sodium hypochlorite, which are sold under trade names.

Bleaches which work by taking oxygen away are usually in the hands of professional dry cleaners.

NEVER use metal containers when soaking articles in bleach because metal accelerates the action of the bleach. Use enamel, porcelain, glass or china. For the same reason, never store bleach in metal containers.

A reasonably safe solution of bleach is 10mL of bleach to 800mL cold water. If the fabric can be immersed, a weaker solution of 10mL of bleach to 8 litres of cold water can be made up. Soak the article for about 10 minutes.

Chlorine bleaches can be used only on washable fabrics and should be rinsed off thoroughly.

Chlorine damage may not show up until the garment has been ironed.

A reasonably safe solution of hydrogen peroxide is one part peroxide to eight parts water. Rinse thoroughly before washing. To remove a stain, you can use undiluted in small quantities, but test on fabric first. Do not pour unused hydrogen peroxide back into the bottle. It is susceptible to impurities.

HOUSEHOLD REMEDIES

Common household substances useful for removing stains include:

- Lemon juice or a 5 per cent solution of citric or tartaric acid.
- Acetic acid, from the chemist, or white vinegar. Vinegar must be white. Malt or wine vinegar will leave a stain of their own. It may be used straight from the bottle in some cases.
- Methylated spirits. Highly flammable. Poisonous.
- Household ammonia, an alkali. It may be used straight from the bottle but with care. It can restore colour changed by contact with acids. It is an irritant and attacks skin and eyes. It removes grease and softens water.
- Detergents: Use liquid detergent for spills and stains. Detergent can be applied to the back of the fabric and worked in. Or you can moisten the fingers with detergent and work in that way.

Biological detergents play a role in removing stains from washable fabrics. The enzymes in these need time to work so soaking, for up to 12 hours, is recommended. Very hot water or chlorine bleach will negate any action by the enzymes.

- Turpentine: Flammable, toxic and dries the skin. A balsam made from the pine tree. It will remove some paint stains.
- Oxalic acid, derived from sorrel, is effective on many rust stains. It is, however, poisonous and must be handled with care. Wear gloves, use disposable containers and cloths. Perhaps it is easier to get the job done professionally.

IMPROVISED REMEDIES

How do you cope when you are far from home — say in a restaurant, in a motel room or at a picnic?

If possible, put the article under a cold tap. Or sponge with cold water.

Other useful instant stain treaters:
- Soda water. Pour a little on the spot, let it stand for a minute or so and sponge up thoroughly.
- Shaving cream foam is a good spot remover.
- Lemon juice or even green tomatoes are mild stain removers which can work on some food stains. Rinse off after applications.
- Even in these days of fewer smokers in public places someone may have lighter fluid.

The quickest general remedy for:

Grease: Cover with absorbent powder.

Fruit/wine: Cover with salt.

Other stains: Rinse under cold tap or sponge with cold water.

HELPFUL HINTS

Water may be all that is necessary. It often surprises how many stains are washed away under a cold tap. If the article cannot be put under the tap, the best way to apply water is from a plastic bottle with a nozzle which dispenses a fine spray. This way there is less risk of flooding the area.

Don't apply heat. Heat can fix stains and you will never get them out. Many food stains contain albumen and heat sets it—any heat applied to an egg anywhere, even on a footpath, simply cooks it.

With some stains, such as chewing gum or candle wax, cold, in the form of ice cubes, is far more effective than heat. And with some greasy stains or fat spills, if you can freeze the surface quickly, it may be better than heat as a first measure.

Test any cleaning agent on an inconspicuous part of the article. Always test for colourfastness.

At times—particularly if you are a home dressmaker—you may be able to apply an identical stain to a scrap of the same material and experiment with that first.

Several light applications of solvents are more effective than one large.

After treating, dry the article as quickly as possible. After water or a non-toxic and non-explosive agent, such as vinegar, if the article cannot be dried outside, work with hair drier or heat lamp.

AVOIDING MISTAKES

NEVER soak wool, silk, non-colourfast or flammable fabrics in anything, even cold water.

NEVER pour cleaning fluids directly on to a surface. Dab or sponge.

NEVER flood an area with solvent or any dry cleaning fluid.

NEVER use undiluted bleach. Bleach can harm your skin as well as fabrics.

NEVER use dry cleaning fluid on rainproofed articles.

Acetates Never use acetone. It will remove fabric as well as stain. Never use paint brush cleaner, methylated spirits, white spirit or white vinegar.

Denim Never use bleaches.

Felt Never soak in water.

Linen Never use chlorine bleach. Linen is stained easily by strong bleaches. The iron in hard water can cause rust spots.

Nylon Never use hydrogen peroxide.

Rayon Never use methylated spirits, white spirit, acetone, paint brush cleaner or chlorine bleach. Never boil and never soak for long.

Silk Never use soap, alkalis, ammonia, chlorine bleach, biological detergents. Never rub. Never dry in the sun or artificially.

Wool Never use hydrogen peroxide plus ammonia, or ammonia. Never use alkalis or water-softener. Never soak in chlorine bleach or biological detergents.

STAIN REMOVAL

ACIDS (INCLUDING BATTERY ACID)

Strong acids, such as sulphuric and hydrochloric, may destroy fibres, especially cotton, linen and nylon, before being rinsed out. Weak acids, such as vinegar, normally won't. But both weak and strong acids can change the appearance of dyes.

• Washable articles: Rinse thoroughly under the cold tap. Then sponge with ammonia solution, or baking soda solution (one tablespoon of soda to a cup of water) or a weak borax solution to neutralise remaining acid. If the stain is light or the material spots easily, hold the stain over an open bottle of ammonia. The fumes may neutralise the acid and restore colour.

Watch carefully to make sure the ammonia itself is not damaging the dye. If this happens dab quickly with white vinegar or acetic acid.

After any treatment, rinse thoroughly, then wash as usual.

• Non-washable articles: Dab carefully with ammonia or the borax or baking soda solution suggested for washable articles. Do not use undiluted ammonia on woollen or silk fabrics or wool or silk blends. If the stain is light, try the open ammonia bottle remedy.

After any treatment, sponge carefully with cold water. Do not overwet. Dry quickly.

ADHESIVES

There is a great variety of adhesives. It is difficult in many cases to be sure of treatment. Many have their own special solvents. Ask when you buy. If an emergency arises, ring the manufacturer for advice.

Balsa wood (aeroplane) glue Dab on acetone or non-oily nail polish remover. Use amyl acetate and not acetone on acetates.

Cellulose-based (contact) adhesives Dab with acetone or non-oily nail polish remover. Use amyl acetate and not acetone on acetates.

Cyanoacrylates These are the ones which 'bond in seconds', the fast fixers which have managed to stick fingers and even eyelids together. This type of glue is activated by water and water is the only hope of dissolving it.

Epoxy resin A glue and hardener mixed. Spills can be removed with methylated spirits before they set. Once they have hardened they cannot be removed.

Glue (water soluble; animal or fish origin) This may come out in water.
• Washable articles: Run under cold tap. Then treat with ammonia or soak in biological detergent. Rinse. Wash as usual.
• Non-washable articles: Sponge with cold water. Then treat with household ammonia. Sponge with cold water.

Polyvinyl acetate (PVA, filled PVA)
• Washable articles: Dab with methylated spirits. Rinse. Then wash as usual.
• Non-washable articles: Dab with methylated spirits then sponge off with cold water.

Plastic glue Fresh plastic glue stains on washable articles can be removed by washing in detergent and warm water. Dried stains sometimes respond to the hot vinegar treatment. Immerse the article in a solution of 10 per cent white vinegar and water. Keep at or near boiling point until the stain is removed. It may take 15 minutes. Rinse. Wash as usual.

Adhesive labels, adhesive or sticky tape
• Washable articles: Soak or leave adhesive covered with a wet cloth. Rinse. Wash as usual.
• Non-washable articles: Sponge with methylated spirits or white spirit or eucalyptus oil.

ALCOHOL

Fresh stains may be invisible when dry but can gain colour with age or heat. Alcohol dissolves many finishes, so treat it quickly. Alcohol includes many medicines, skin lotions and perfumes.

Beer
• Washable articles: Rinse under the cold tap. Then treat with white vinegar or soak in biological detergent. Rinse after treatments. Wash as usual. A prompt rinse in cold water and washing at high temperature may be all that is needed. On white fabrics, use bleach or a borax solution.
• Non-washable articles: Mop up as much as you can. Then treat with white vinegar or with hydrogen peroxide. Sponge after treatment with cold water.

Wine Act quickly. There are almost as many popular remedies as there are wine drinkers.
• Washable articles: Take your choice of squirting with soda water, saturating red wine stain with white wine, saturating with white vinegar. Or cover with salt. Rub off when dry. Other remedies are to pour boiling water from a height over the stain, or soak in borax or biological solution, or hold article in milk while it is simmering on the stove.

For stale stains, treat with hydrogen peroxide solution or dip in a solution of one tablespoon household ammonia to two litres water. If residue remains, cover stain with glycerine. Let stand five minutes.

After all treatments, rinse. Wash as usual.
• Non-washable articles: Sponge with cold water. Then sponge with detergent solution or use upholstery cleaner.

Spirits Rinse in or sponge with cold water then treat with methylated spirits or hydrogen peroxide solution.
• Washable articles. After treatment rinse, then wash as usual.
• Non-washable articles: After treatment sponge with water. Dry as quickly as possible.

ALKALIS

Alkalis can damage fabrics and change colours. Silk and wool are particularly vulnerable. Cold water is often enough to rinse out mild alkalis, such as ammonia or washing soda. If the colour has been changed, try to neutralise with white vinegar or lemon juice. Strong alkalis, such as caustic soda, may destroy colour and fabric. Rinse and apply white vinegar or lemon juice immediately.
• Washable articles: After treatment, rinse. Wash as usual.
• Non-washable articles: After treatment sponge with cold water. Dry as quickly as possible.

ANTI-PERSPIRANTS AND DEODORANTS

There are great differences in ingredients and how they react with individual skins and perspiration.

• Washable articles: Wash or sponge with warm water and liquid detergent or, sponge with chlorine bleach solution if fabric is suitable or with hydrogen peroxide solution.

A more drastic measure for old, discoloured stains on fully-washable articles is to make a paste of biological detergent and cold water and rub into the stained areas. Put in a plastic bag and leave for about eight hours. Then wash in very hot water. Rinse. Wash as usual. If any discolouring remains, dab with dry cleaning fluid. Test any coloured article for colour-fastness before trying this.

• Non-washable articles: Sponge carefully with warm water and liquid detergent.

ASPHALT

See Tar.

BALLPOINT INK

See Ink.

BATTERY ACID

See Acids.

BEER

See Alcohol.

BEETROOT

• Washable articles: Rinse under cold water tap as quickly as possible. Then soak in biological detergent or work undiluted liquid detergent into the stain. Rinse. Wash as usual.

• Non-washable articles: Sponge with cold water. If possible, let water run through.

BERRIES

See Fruit and Berries.

BIRD DROPPINGS

Wipe off deposit.

• Washable articles: Soak in warm biological detergent or treat with hydrogen peroxide. Rinse. Wash as usual.

• Non-washable articles: Treat with 60mL

household ammonia to 2 litres of water then with white vinegar. Sponge with cold water. Dry as quickly as possible.

BLOOD

It is hard to remove old or dried bloodstains. A suggested treatment for bloodstains is to cover area with a meat tenderiser mixed with cold water to make a paste. Leave half an hour, sponge off with cold water.

• Washable articles: More conventional treatments are to rinse first or soak in cold, salty water, then sponge with ammonia solution or soak in biological washing powder. For old or stubborn stains, soak in a hydrogen peroxide or ammonia solution or wash in detergent with a few drops of ammonia in it. After any treatment rinse with cold water. Wash in cooler water than usual.

• Non-washable articles: Sponge with cold water. Blot up. Blood on silk or crêpe-de-chine may respond to a paste of starch and water. Cover area thickly. Allow to dry and brush off.

BLUEING

For excess blue on washables, sponge with cold water or soak.

BURNS

See Scorch Marks.

BUTTER

Scrape off as much as you can. Iron with a warm iron between layers of absorbent paper, remembering that an iron may not be hot enough to change the colour of white paper but still hot enough to damage the fabric.

• Washable articles: Rub powdered detergent into the stain with the fingers. Rinse. If stain remains, dab with dry cleaning fluid. If fabric is suitable, a hot wash may be all that is needed.

• Non-washable articles: Try ironing under paper if suitable, followed by putting a pad of cotton wool under the stain, if possible, then dabbing with a pad soaked in dry cleaning fluid. Blot up moisture. Repeat if necessary.

CALAMINE LOTION

• Washable articles: Sponge with water. Sponge with dry cleaning fluid. Keep moist. Repeat as necessary. Wash as usual.

• Non-washable articles: Sponge carefully with water. Sponge with dry cleaning fluid.

CANDLE WAX

Scrape off as much as possible. This will be easier if you can put the article in the freezer in a plastic bag for an hour or two. Otherwise, use a few ice cubes to harden the wax. Then place fabric between sheets of blotting paper, or between several tissues with stronger paper on top, and iron with warm iron. Remove any fragments with methylated spirits or dry cleaning fluid.

• Washable articles: If the fabric is strong, pouring hot water through the fabric from a height may work on the stain.

CANDY AND SWEETS

See also Chocolate/Cocoa.

• Washable articles: Most should wash out in warm water and detergent solution.

• Non-washable articles: Work powdered detergent mixed to a paste with water into stain, from the back if possible. Sponge lightly with warm water then sponge with dry cotton pad. Dry cleaning fluid should get rid of any residue.

CAR POLISH OR WAX

Treat with dry cleaning fluid. Then work liquid detergent into the stain, from the back if possible. Rinse. Wash as usual if washable article. If non-washable, sponge lightly with cold water.

CARAMEL

Rinse with cold water. Treat with liquid detergent. If necessary and possible, treat with solution of half hydrogen peroxide and half water. If washable article, rinse and wash as usual.

If non-washable, sponge lightly with cold water.

CARBON PAPER

• Washable articles: Sponge with methylated spirits or dry cleaning fluid. Or work diluted liquid detergent into the stain from the back. Rinse or sponge with cold water. If stubborn, add a few drops of ammonia to the detergent. Rinse. Repeat the treatment if necessary. Rinse. Wash as usual.

• Non-washable articles: Dab with methylated spirits.

CARROT

See Fruit and Berries.

CELLULOSE TAPE

See Adhesives.

CHEWING GUM

Chill with ice cubes or put in freezer to harden. Scrape off as much as possible. Apply dry cleaning fluid or methylated spirits or white spirit or solvent for cleaning paint brushes. Then rinse with cold water and wash as usual if washable article. If non-washable, sponge with pad to dry quickly.

CHOCOLATE/COCOA

Scrape off solids with a blunt knife.

• Washable articles: Use boiling water poured from a height or use biological detergent and work from the back of stain, mopping up as you sponge. Rinse. Use aerosol grease solvent to get rid of any residue. Wash as usual.

• Non-washable articles: Sponge with warm water. Use aerosol grease solvent.

CHUTNEY

See Jams and Preserves.

COD LIVER OIL

Mop up as much oil as you can.

• Washable articles: Fresh stains should be washed immediately in detergent solution. For dried stains, use dry cleaning fluid or lubricate stains with glycerine. Rinse. Wash as usual.

• Non-washable articles: Sponge with dry cleaning fluid. Woollens: Fresh stains should be sponged immediately with mild detergent solution. Try liquid stain remover on old stains but they may prove difficult.

COFFEE

Mop up as much as you can quickly.

• Washable articles: Soak in a borax or biological detergent solution or treat with liquid detergent. If fabric will stand boiling water, cover stain with borax and pour boiling water over it. Let article stand in borax solution for half an hour. Hydrogen peroxide can be used to remove final traces of stain. Rinse. Wash as usual.

• Non-washable articles: Sponge with borax solution. Mop up with warm water or apply a borax paste. Leave for 30 minutes. Brush off. Repeat if necessary. Glycerine will soften an old stain.

COLA
• Washable articles: Wash immediately.
• Non-washable articles: Sponge with water. Apply glycerine if stain has dried. Blot. Flush with dry cleaning solvent.

COPPER/BRASS
This is the discolouration caused by these metals. Stains will be green or brown. Do not use bleach.
• Washable articles: Wash in soap and water. Apply dry cleaning solvent. Wash as usual.
• Non-washable articles: Apply dry cleaning solvent.

COSMETICS
Remove deposit. Loosen with glycerine if necessary.
• Washable articles: Apply liquid detergent. Rinse. Repeat as long as it is necessary, letting fabric dry between treatments. If necessary, soak in ammonia solution. Rinse. Wash as usual.
• Non-washable articles: Sponge with dry cleaning fluid until cosmetic colour is removed or use upholstery spotting kit or sponge with eucalyptus oil.

CRAYON
Apply liquid detergent. Rub between finger and thumb. Rinse under cold tap if washable article. Sponge with cold water if non-washable article. Repeat if necessary. Dab with dry cleaning fluid or white spirit. If colour residue remains, dab with methylated spirits.
  On walls use a household cleaner. Wallpapers may have to be patched.

CREAM/ICE CREAM
Scrape up or sponge off as much as you can.
• Washable articles: Rinse in cold water. Then soak in biological detergent or borax solution.

When dry use dry cleaning fluid on greasy residue. Rinse. Wash as usual.
• Non-washable articles. Dab with dry cleaning fluid, then dab with methylated spirits to get rid of colour residue.

CREOSOTE
• Washable articles: Dab with eucalyptus oil or lighter fuel. Wash as usual. For old stains, use glycerine first to soften.
• Non-washable articles: Consult a dry cleaner.

CURRY
Scrape off and mop up as much as you can. Turmeric in curry powder is mainly responsible for the vivid yellow stain.
• Washable articles: Soften with glycerine solution then soak in biological detergent or ammonia solution. White fabrics may be bleached. Rinse. Wash as usual.
• Non-washable articles: Use ammonia solution or borax solution. If necessary, consult a dry cleaner.

DEODORANT
See Anti-perspirants.

DYE
Treat immediately with cold water. Hot water will fix many dyes. Old stains will persist forever. Sponge up as much moisture as possible.
• Washable articles: Soak in biological detergent or treat with liquid detergent. If necessary, follow up treatment by dabbing with ammonia or methylated spirits. Rinse. Wash as usual.
• Non-washable articles: Consult a dry cleaner quickly.

EGG
Do not apply heat or hot water. It will cook the egg. Sponge with or soak in cold salted water.
• Washable articles: Soak in a non-metallic container in biological detergent. Use aerosol dry cleaner to get rid of yolk traces. Very stubborn stains on white fabrics may be removed by soaking in hydrogen peroxide with a few drops of ammonia.
• Non-washable articles: Treat with undiluted liquid detergent. Rub in gently. Apply methylated spirits to get rid of detergent traces.

EXCREMENT
Remove deposit.
• Washable articles: Sponge with 1 teaspoon liquid detergent and 1 teaspoon white vinegar in 1 litre warm water. Rinse. Wash as usual.
• Non-washable articles: Sponge carefully with 1 teaspoon liquid detergent and 1 teaspoon white vinegar in 1 litre warm water.

EYE MAKE-UP
See Cosmetics.

EYEBROW PENCIL
See Cosmetics.

FAT
For cold fat first remove deposit.
• Washable articles: Soak in or spray with biological detergent solution and treat remaining grease with grease solvent.
• Non-washable articles: Dab with solvent.

Spills of hot fat from the stove on man-made fibres may be at higher temperatures than the melting point of the fibres, causing them to melt and fuse. In this case, do not use dry cleaning solvent. It may remove the colour. Treat washable and non-washable articles with liquid detergent and rinse or sponge with cold water. Repeat if necessary.

FISH SLIME
Should be treated while still wet if possible. Soak or sponge washable articles in cold salted water. Wash as usual.

FLOWERS
See Grass.

FRUIT/FRUIT JUICE, BERRIES
For fresh stains, sponge or soak at once in cold salted water, soda water or milk. Stains must be removed before the article is washed. Heat and age will set fruit stains and they will stay forever.
• Washable articles: Treat with detergent, rubbing it into the stain with the fingers. If necessary, treat with borax solution or vinegar or hydrogen peroxide solution or ammonia solution. Dried stains should be first loosened with glycerine. Leave for about an hour. Then treat as above. If fabric is suitable for washing at high temperature, cover wet stain with salt, then wash.
• Non-washable articles: Sponge with cold water. When dry use dry cleaning fluid or upholstery spotting kit.

GRASS/FLOWERS/FOLIAGE
• Washable articles: Soak in biological detergent or treat with equal parts of cream of tartar and salt. Remove this after 10 minutes. Or they can be sponged with eucalyptus oil or methylated spirits or treated with glycerine left on for an hour. Rinse and wash as usual. White fabrics may be bleached.
• Non-washable articles: Sponge with liquid

detergent, then with cold water, or treat with methylated spirits.

GRAVY
See Fat.

GREASE
Scrape up deposit.
• Washable articles: Apply several sheets of absorbent paper and iron carefully with a warm iron, changing paper frequently, or sponge with white spirit or dry cleaning fluid. Rinse. Wash in warm soapy water. Non-iron, easy-care or crease-resisting fabrics need more intensive work than fabrics which are un-treated. Old stains may respond to a hydrogen peroxide solution.
• Non-washable articles: Use absorbent paper and a warm iron or apply an absorbent powder. Let dry. Brush off. Repeat if necessary. Or apply dry cleaning fluid. For heavy stains try paint brush stripper.

HAIR DYE
Vegetable dyes such as henna should come out of washable articles. Rinse under cold tap then treat with liquid detergent. If necessary, dab with ammonia, methylated spirits or hydro-gen peroxide. Rinse. Wash as usual.

Vegetable dyes on non-washable articles may respond to dabbing wih liquid detergent on a pad with another pad underneath, if pos-sible. Otherwise, treat with ammonia or methy-lated spirits or hydrogen peroxide. Sponge with cold water.

Hair dyes will not generally come out once they have dried. Most hopeful treatment for dried hair dyes is first with liquid detergent, then with white vinegar and again with liquid detergent.

HAIR OIL
See Grease.

HAIR SPRAY
Marks on clothing from aerosol cans of hair spray can often be removed with liquid deter-gent. A large mark may be treated with amyl acetate then methylated spirits.

HONEY
Remove any deposit with blunt knife.
Rinse washable articles under cold tap. If non-washable, sponge with cold water. Then treat with liquid detergent or, if washable, soak in biological detergent. If necessary, treat the stain with hydrogen peroxide.

ICE CREAM
See Cream.

INDELIBLE PENCIL
Indelible pencil is hard to remove. It may be sponged with dry cleaning solvent then with methylated spirits. Treat stain that remains with liquid detergent with a few drops of ammonia in it. If necessary, treat with hydrogen peroxide. If washable article, rinse. Wash as usual.

INK
There is a great variety of inks on the market. Some respond to treatment with turpentine. Place a pad underneath if possible and sponge from the back of the fabric with turpentine. Change the pads as soon as they absorb ink colour. Then, if washable article, rinse in hot water, then rub with powdered detergent. Rinse. Wash as usual.

Many dried inks need an acid to get rid of stains. Effective ones, such as oxalic acid, are highly poisonous. It may be better to hand the job over to a dry cleaner. Many inks have their own solvents. Read the label on the bottle and follow instructions for getting rid of the stain.
Ballpoint This is one of the most common stains. Act quickly.
• Washable articles: Sponge with or soak area in methylated spirits. Rinse. Or sponge with lukewarm glycerine. Blot frequently. Keep stain moist until it is removed. After any treatment rinse. Wash as usual. Ballpoint stain on poly-ester may respond to spraying with hair spray.
• Non-washable articles: Dab with methylated spirits. Or consult a dry cleaner.
Indian Act quickly.
• Washable articles: Soak in or sponge with cold water. Then wash with liquid detergent. If necessary, soak in or sponge with ammonia solution. If colour of article is affected, sponge with white vinegar.
• Non-washable articles: Work in detergent solution, then sponge with ammonia solution and, if colour is affected, sponge with white vinegar to restore.

IODINE
Act quickly. Iodine makes a brown mark on

most materials. Starch and ironing can alter the colour of the stain. One method of treating is to moisten the stain and put it in the sun or in front of a radiator. Another is to place on absorbent pad and force steam from the iron through it.
• Washable articles: Sponge with or soak immediately in water. Then soak in a detergent solution. Rinse. Wash as usual.
• Non-washable articles: Dab with alcohol. Or, if you are willing to take the risk, place a pad of cotton wool soaked in alcohol over the stain. Keep stain wet with alcohol for several hours. Or sponge with methylated spirits.

IRON MOULD OR IRON RUST
There are many proprietary rust removers. Oxalic acid can be used for rust stains. It is a poison. Ask your chemist how to use it.
• Washable articles: Rub with lemon juice and salt. Dry in the sun and keep damp with lemon juice until the mark fades. Boil fabrics which can be boiled for 10 minutes in a solution of 500mL water to 60mL cream of tartar. After any treatment, rinse thoroughly. Wash as usual.
• Non-washable articles: It is almost impossible to remove iron mould from silk or woollens or from fabrics which must be dry cleaned.

JAM/PRESERVES
Remove deposit with blunt knife. Rinse in or sponge with cold water.
• Washable articles: Soak in biological detergent or in borax solution. If necessary, and possible, use a chlorine bleach.
• Non-washable articles: Use dry cleaning fluid.

LEATHER
These are stains caused by leather rubbing against a fabric. The stain probably comes from the tannin used in tanning leather.
• Washable articles: Moisten with ½ teaspoon biological detergent in ½ cup warm water. Keep wet for 30 minutes. Flush with water. Wash as usual.
• Non-washable articles: Apply glycerine to soften. Dab with water. Use vinegar and water solution.

MARMALADE
See Jam.

MAYONNAISE
See Cream.

MEAT AND MEAT JUICES
Act quickly. They are hard to remove once they have dried. Rinse under cold tap or sponge with cold water.
• Washable articles: Soak in biological detergent, if necessary working a little of the powder into the stain with the fingers. If necessary, apply dry cleaning solvent. Rinse. Wash in cooler water than you would normally use.
• Non-washable articles: Apply dry cleaning solvent.

MEDICINES
Medicines have many bases and many different ingredients. If the stain is on an expensive article, take to a dry cleaner. If medicines are used regularly by children, it is worthwhile asking your chemist their base when you buy or have the prescription made up.
Iron-based See Iron Mould.
Syrup-based Many common medicines have a syrup base.
• Washable articles: Wash in detergent and water or soak the article in biological detergent. Rinse. Wash as usual.
• Non-washable articles: Flush out with detergent and water from the wrong side if possible, keeping a pad underneath to mop up moisture. Treat any remaining stain with diluted household ammonia. If necessary, treat with amyl acetate or methylated spirits.
Oil-based Treat with solvent.
Tar-based Soften with petroleum jelly, lard or white spirit. Then, if washable article, rinse. Wash as usual. If non-washable article, treat with dry cleaning fluid.
Alcohol-based These include many liniments. They can be sponged with methylated spirits. If possible work from the wrong side and keep a pad underneath to mop up moisture.

METAL POLISH
Remove deposit.
• Washable articles: Rinse under running water. Treat with liquid detergent. Rinse. If necessary, treat the stain with methylated spirits. Rinse. Wash as usual.
• Non-washable articles: Dab with white spirit or lighter fluid or dry cleaning fluid.

METALLIC STAINS

Stains caused by metal buckles, buttons and belts rubbing against fabric can usually be dissolved with white vinegar, lemon juice, acetic acid or oxalic acid. Acetic and oxalic acids are stronger and more dangerous to use. Do not use bleach as part of any treatment. It may aggravate the damage.
• Washable articles: Rinse after treatment. Wash as usual.
• Non-washable articles: Sponge carefully with water after treatment of fabric.

MILDEW

Prevention is better than cure. Mildew fungus spores are floating in the air, just waiting.
• Washable articles: Light stains may wash out in the laundry. If not, unless the fabric is drip-dry, easy-care or crease-resisting, soak in diluted bleach. Other methods are rubbing with a cut lemon dipped in salt or dabbing with hydrogen peroxide and leaving in the sun. Keep moist until the spots fade. Rinse thoroughly. Wash as usual.
• Non-washable articles: Heavy mildew spots on articles which may have been stored carelessly should be taken to a dry cleaner.

MILK

• Washable articles: Rinse under cold tap. Then soak in biological detergent or detergent and water with a drop or two of ammonia, in both cases using cooler water than usual. Heat may set the stain. If necessary, use dry cleaning fluid. Rinse. Wash in cooler water than you would normally use.
• Non-washable articles: Sponge with cold water. Dab with dry cleaning fluid or use upholstery spotting kit. If drying quickly, use an electric fan, never a radiator.

MUD

Wait until mud has dried and you may be able to brush most of it off. If there is a large daub of solid matter, lift it off carefully while the mud is still wet. After you have brushed, concentrate the suction pipe of the vacuum cleaner over the area.
• Washable articles: Sponge with detergent solution and warm water. Rinse. Wash as usual.
• Non-washable articles: Dab dried stains with pad moistened with detergent and water solution. Then use dry cleaning fluid.

MUSTARD

Scrape off deposit. If dried, brush.
• Washable articles: Rinse under a cold tap. Then sponge or soak in mild detergent. Use ammonia solution or dry cleaning fluid on remaining stain. If necessary, sponge with hydrogen peroxide solution with a drop of ammonia added. Rinse. Wash as usual.
• Non-washable articles: Sponge with cold water, then use ammonia solution or dry cleaning fluid. If the article ring-marks easily, consult a dry cleaner.

NAIL POLISH

Wipe up deposit. Treat with amyl acetate or acetone, not oily nail polish remover. Flush out with white spirit. Remove colour traces with methylated spirits. If washable article, rinse. Wash as usual.

NAPKIN STAINS

See Urine.

NICOTINE

Dab with eucalyptus oil or methylated spirits. If washable article, soak in biological detergent. Rinse. Wash as usual.

OIL

See Grease.

PAINT

Tackle paint stains while they are fresh. They become impossible to remove once they have hardened. There is a great variety of paints on the market. No single method will work with all. It is worthwhile to ask when you buy the paint what is a suitable solvent, particularly if you are painting rooms already carpeted and a moment's carelessness can mean a disastrous spill.

Read the label on the paint tin to see what is recommended as a thinner. It may be the best chance of getting rid of the stain. There are many paint removers on the market.

Scrape or wipe off deposit. Test any method of removal first on an inconspicuous part of the fabric.

Acrylic paint Rinse under cold tap if washable. If non-washable, sponge with cold water. Then wash in or sponge with detergent and water. Dab with stain-removing solvent or methylated spirits. If washable article, rinse. Wash as usual.

Oil-based paint Sponge with warm detergent and water, then dab with white spirit or turpentine or paint brush cleaner. Sponge with cold water if non-washable article. If washable, wash as usual.

Water-based paint This should be easier to remove than it often proves to be. If it is still wet, it will wash out reasonably well in cold water. If it has hardened, use methylated spirits or paint brush cleaner.

Enamel paint It is vital to catch this when it is fresh. Treat with methylated spirits or a branded paint remover.

Unless alcohol will damage fabric dyes, it can be used to remove turpentine and detergent. Dilute with water if used on acetate.

PARAFFIN
See Candle Wax.

PERFUME
Sponge with cold water at once. Dab with glycerine solution or white spirit. Treat with household ammonia undiluted, testing first on an inconspicuous part of the fabric. If the ammonia does affect the dye, dab quickly with acetic acid or vinegar to neutralise the effect. If washable article, rinse and wash as usual as soon as possible.

PERSPIRATION
Act quickly. Perspiration will weaken fibres and fade dyes. Wash or sponge off as quickly as possible with warm water and detergent.
• Washable articles: Soak in biological or ordinary detergent. White fabrics can be bleached. White linen and cotton can be treated in methylated spirits with a few drops of household ammonia. For old stains use white vinegar or hydrogen peroxide and for fresh stains, ammonia. If an oily residue remains, dab with dry cleaning fluid.

If a yellow underarm discolouration persists, dab with hydrogen peroxide and keep wet with peroxide for 30 minutes. Should odour cling, soak in warm water and salt. Remove stains before ironing. Ironing will weaken fabric.

For nylon, polyester and viscose fabrics, diluted bleach may be used, but never for more than 15 minutes.
• Non-washable articles: Sponge as quickly as possible with warm water and detergent. For silk and wool sponge with hydrogen peroxide and water solution. Keep damp with the solution for several minutes.

If anti-perspirant is combined with perspiration stain, treat with dry cleaning fluid then ammonia.

PET STAINS
See Urine.

PITCH
See Tar.

PLASTIC
Melted plastic—say a button ironed with a too-hot iron—can stain fabrics. Scrape or wipe off deposit. Treat stain with dry cleaning fluid or amyl acetate.
• Washable articles: Rinse. Wash as usual.
• Non-washable articles: Sponge with cold water.

PLASTICINE
Scrape off deposit. Dab with liquid grease solvent.
• Washable articles: Rinse. Wash as usual.
• Non-washable articles: Sponge with cold water.

PUTTY
Remove deposit. Loosen residue with dry cleaning fluid.
• Washable articles: Dab with dry cleaning fluid. Flush with water. Wash as usual.
• Non-washable articles: Dab with dry cleaning fluid.

RUNNING COLOURS
See Dyes.

RUST
See Iron Mould/Rust.

SALAD DRESSINGS
See Cream.

SALAD OIL
See Grease.

SAUCES
See Cream.

SCORCH MARKS
Bad scorch marks will not come out. Scorch marks on some fabrics can become less noticeable if they are rubbed carefully with fine sandpaper.
• Washable articles: Sponge or soak in a borax, hydrogen peroxide or ammonia solution. A more intensive treatment is to sponge area with peroxide, mask off rest of article with a cloth or brown paper and expose the scorch area to sunlight, keeping it damp with peroxide until the brown fades. After treatment, rinse. Wash as usual.
• Non-washable articles: Sponge lightly with glycerine solution. Sponge with warm water. Repeat if necessary.

SEAWATER
Brush dried stain to remove salt. Rinse in warm water. A few drops of vinegar may restore colour.

SHELLAC
Act quickly. Treat with dry cleaning solvent or methylated spirits.
• Washable articles: Rinse. Wash as usual.
• Non-washable articles: Sponge with cold water.

SHOE POLISH
Shoe polishes contain a variety of ingredients. Many polishes are difficult to remove. Scrape off as much as you can.
• Washable articles: Apply white spirit or grease solvent or, if the dyes can stand it, alcohol or turpentine. If turpentine is tried, remove afterward with warm detergent solution or alcohol. Whites can be bleached. After treatment, rinse. Wash as usual.
• Non-washable articles: Use white spirit, grease solvent, turpentine or alcohol, diluting the alcohol for acetates. If turpentine is used, sponge off afterward with warm detergent solution or alcohol.

SOFT DRINKS
See Fruit.

SOOT
Sprinkle a layer of table salt over soot. Leave for a while then vacuum if possible, or brush off.

SOUP
Remove deposit.
• Washable articles: Sponge with cold liquid detergent solution or soak in biological detergent. Rinse. Wash as usual.
• Non-washable articles: Sponge with cold water, then with dry cleaning fluid.

SPIRITS
See Alcohol.

STOVE POLISH
• Washable articles: Rub undiluted liquid detergent on to the stain, if possible from the wrong side of fabric. Rinse. Wash as usual.
• Non-washable articles: Use an absorbent powder then apply dry cleaning fluid.

SYRUP
See Jam.

TAR
Scrape off as much of the deposit as possible. If stain has hardened, soften with salad oil, petroleum jelly or raw linseed oil.
• Washable articles: Apply dry cleaning fluid, eucalyptus oil or white spirit. Rinse. Wash as usual. White fabrics may be bleached to get rid of residual stain.
• Non-washable articles: Dab with dry cleaning fluid, eucalyptus oil or white spirit. If in any doubt, consult a dry cleaner.

TEA
See Coffee.

TOBACCO
See Grass.

TOMATO JUICE
See Fruit.

TREACLE
See Jam.

TURMERIC
See Curry.

URINE
Act quickly. Fresh stains are generally easy to remove.
• Washable articles: Fresh stains—rinse in cold salted water then wash as usual; dried stains—soak in biological detergent. If necessary, use hydrogen peroxide and ammonia solution.
• Non-washable articles: Sponge fresh stains with cold water then with white vinegar solution. If colour has changed, sponge with household ammonia or hold over open ammonia bottle. Do not use ammonia on wool or silk. For dried stains, consult a dry cleaner.

After cleaning up after a cat, rub the spot with a cloth soaked in ammonia. This will stop the cat from doing it in the same place again.

VOMIT
Scrape off deposit. Rinse under cold tap if washable article, or sponge with cold water if non-washable article.
• Washable articles: Soak in biological detergent. Rinse. Wash as usual.

• Non-washable articles: Sponge with warm water with a few drops of ammonia. Do not use ammonia on silk or wool. Sponge with clear water.

STORAGE

Before storing baby clothes, wash and rinse in a vinegar and water solution. Dry in the sun. Do not iron but store between layers of blue tissue paper.

To store wedding dresses or christening robes, wrap them in white acid-free tissue, then place in a box lined with blue tissue. Store in a cool, dry, well ventilated cupboard.

Yellow or brown stains sometimes appear on clothing and house linens which are stored for some time. First wash the article, treat with a mild bleach solution. If something more drastic is needed, treat with oxalic acid. This is a strong poison. Handle with the utmost care.

Brown dots that sometimes appear on stored linens are often caused by hard water used for ironing. Use water softener when preparing house linens or other articles for storage.

Yellowing of silk can sometimes be lightened with white vinegar or hydrogen peroxide, applied carefully with a cloth pad.

CARPET STAINS

Act fast. The faster you act the milder the remedy.
• Blot liquids and wipe up surface deposits.
• The best instant all-purpose remedy is the soda syphon or cold water. Blot up excess.
• Keep the manufacturer's care label handy for reference.
• Test cleaning agent first in inconspicuous place.

- Don't be rash.
- If in doubt, consult a professional.
- After treating an area, shampoo the whole carpet.
- There are some basic differences between animal, vegetable and man-made fibres in carpets. Wool, camel or mohair fibres prefer acids to alkalis. Polyesters prefer acids. Cellulose fibres prefer alkalis to acids, and so, if you have some Indian rugs, do cottons. But it is better to have antique and Oriental rugs, felt carpets, skin rugs and Indian cotton rugs professionally cleaned.

CARPET CAUTION
- Never use acetone, paint brush cleaner, methylated spirits or white spirit on acrylic carpets.
- Never use detergents, washing soda, ammonia, strong alkalis or soap on sisal or rush matting.
- There is a great deal of difference in the amount of water which wool and man-made fibre carpets can absorb. This is an important point when shampooing, and something to remember before you saturate part of a carpet where there has been a spill. One hundred kilograms of wool will absorb between six and seven times as much water as a man-made fibre carpet.
- Do not overwet carpet. Soaking may cause rings and spread the stain further. Do not rub. Rubbing will spread the stain and distort the pile or fabric. Blot up excess moisture with clean towels, tissues or absorbent cloths after treatment and between treatments.
- Don't let dry cleaning fluids touch rubber or latex backed carpets.
- When you do use detergent, it should be neutral.

CARPET TREATMENTS

ALCOHOL
Beer Sponge with a solution of one teaspoon of detergent, one teaspoon of white vinegar and one litre of warm water.
Red wine Use absorbent powder, leave for 12 hours and vacuum the next day. Sponge with warm water. If necessary, carefully dab with dye stripper, testing on an inconspicuous part of the carpet first.

White wine Sponge with a solution of one teaspoon of detergent, one teaspoon of white vinegar and one litre of warm water.

BEETROOT
Sponge with a solution of one teaspoon of detergent, one teaspoon of white vinegar and one litre of warm water.

BLEACH
Sponge with a solution of one teaspoon of detergent, one teaspoon of white vinegar and one litre of warm water.

BLOOD
Sponge with cold water. Blot. Dry. Dab with dye stripper.

BURNS
Dab with a solution of one part hydrogen peroxide to 10 parts of cold water. Do not use on dark or patterned carpet. Sometimes a burn mark can be made less noticeable by rubbing gently with fine sandpaper.

BUTTER
Dab with dry cleaning fluid, lighter fuel or mineral turpentine. Then sponge with a solution of one teaspoon of detergent, one teaspoon of white vinegar and one litre of warm water.

CANDLE WAX
Freeze with ice cubes and carefully remove solid matter with blunt knife. Dab with turpentine, if necessary mixed with equal quantity of dry cleaning fluid.

CHEWING GUM

Freeze with ice cube and carefully remove solid matter with blunt knife. Dab with methylated spirits or white spirit. There are special chewing gum removers on the market.

CHOCOLATE

Sponge with solution of one teaspoon of detergent, one teaspoon of white vinegar and one litre of warm water. Dab with dry cleaning fluid, lighter fuel or turpentine.

COFFEE

Dab with dry cleaning fluid, lighter fuel or turpentine. Sponge with cold water. Sponge with a solution of one teaspoon of detergent, one teaspoon of white vinegar and one litre of warm water.

For black coffee, immediately flushing with a soda syphon may do.

CRAYON

Dab with dry cleaning fluid, lighter fuel or turpentine. Then sponge with a solution of one teaspoon detergent, one teaspoon white vinegar and one litre of warm water.

CREAM

Dab with dry cleaning fluid, lighter fuel or turpentine. Then sponge with a solution of one teaspoon detergent, one teaspoon of white vinegar and one litre of warm water.

EGG

Sponge with a solution of one teaspoon of detergent, one teaspoon of white vinegar and one litre of warm water. Do not apply heat.

FRUIT/FRUIT JUICE

Sponge with warm water, then with a solution of one teaspoon of detergent, one teaspoon of white vinegar and one litre of warm water.

FURNITURE POLISH

Dab with dry cleaning fluid, lighter fuel or turpentine, then sponge with a solution of one teaspoon of detergent, one teaspoon of white vinegar and one litre of warm water.

GRASS

Dab with methylated spirits.

GREASE/OIL

Dab with dry cleaning fluid, lighter fuel or turpentine. Work from edge of stain in a circle so you don't ringmark the carpet.

ICE CREAM

See Cream.

INK

Ballpoint Dab with methylated spirits. Sponge with a solution of one teaspoon of detergent, one teaspoon of white vinegar and one litre of warm water.

METAL POLISH

Dab with dry cleaning fluid, lighter fuel or turpentine. Sponge with a solution of one teaspoon of detergent, one teaspoon of white vinegar and one litre of warm water.

MILDEW

Sponge with a solution of one teaspoon detergent, one teaspoon of white vinegar and one litre of warm water. Dab with a solution of one part hydrogen peroxide to 10 parts of water. Do not use peroxide on dark or patterned carpet.

MILK

Sponge with warm water. Dab with dry cleaning fluid, lighter fuel or turpentine. Then sponge with a solution of one teaspoon of detergent, one teaspoon of white vinegar and one litre of warm water.

NAIL POLISH

Dab with nail polish remover. Do not use acetone on acetates. Use amyl acetate. Then dab with dry cleaning fluid, lighter fuel or turpentine.

OIL

See Grease.

PAINT

Plastic (water-based) Act quickly. Remove deposits then sponge liberally with fresh water. Finally apply mild solution of carpet cleaner. Rinse and pat dry with clean cloths or a piece of towelling.

Oil base Dab with turpentine. If necessary, mix with an equal quantity of dry cleaning fluid. Sponge with a solution of one teaspoon of detergent, one teaspoon of white vinegar and one litre of warm water.

RUST

Dab with dry cleaning fluid, lighter fuel or turpentine. Then sponge with a solution of one teaspoon of detergent, one teaspoon of white vinegar and one litre of warm water. Finally, sponge with a weak solution of white vinegar or lemon juice and cold water.

SALAD DRESSING

See Grease.

SHOE POLISH

Dab with dry cleaning fluid, lighter fuel or turpentine, then sponge with a solution of one teaspoon of detergent, one teaspoon of white vinegar and one litre of warm water.

SOFT DRINKS

Sponge with warm water, then with a solution of one teaspoon of detergent, one teaspoon of white vinegar and one litre of water. Finally, dab with a solution of one part of hydrogen peroxide to 10 parts of water. Do not use peroxide on dark or patterned carpet.

SOOT

Cover with salt. Let stand. Vacuum. Sponge with solution of detergent and warm water.

TEA

See Coffee.

URINE

Sponge with a solution of one teaspoon of detergent, one teaspoon of white vinegar and one litre of warm water.

VOMIT

Remove deposit, then sponge with a solution of one teaspoon detergent, one teaspoon of white vinegar and one litre of warm water.

6

A CLEAN HOUSE

THERE IS no right way to go about household cleaning. It depends on the type of household and the people living there. More importantly, it depends on the attitude and temperament of the person who is doing most of the cleaning.

Some people love the clean sweep. They are happy to let it all lie, then spend a full day doing the lot, even down to cleaning the silver. For a fleeting moment it all looks beautiful and woe betide the first person who mars the effect. But marred it is, and so begins the long slide down again.

Other people like doing a little at a time. They use their time efficiently when tidying the living-room each morning by doing more than emptying ashtrays, removing dishes left by snackers, and plumping up cushions. With a duster always in a handy place (perhaps behind a bookcase) they flick away dust and if needed, vacuum the carpet. When they make the beds they give bedrooms the same once-over treatment. They clean up the kitchen thoroughly after a cooking session. They mop bathroom floors and swish around baths after daily showers. So the house always looks in good shape although not entirely sparkling.

Any approach is fine as long as it suits the household.

CLEANING PRODUCTS

What a waste and a shame is inefficient cleaning, with its endless unnecessary effort! To avoid this you need intelligence and commonsense. Be alert to new and better products and to new and better ways of doing things. That does not mean you should at once invest in a giant-size pack of anything new you see advertised on television. It would be just as foolish, however, to assume that manufacturers are just trying to get at you. Science does find better ways of doing things, so use them.

If you see something that seems to have promise, ask about it before buying. Make sure the tool is the most suitable for the job and that the cleaning agent has the properties needed, that its base or dissolving agent is right. Water will not cut oil. Vinegar cannot cut grease. When you are dealing with oil or tar you will need a solvent such as thinners, turpentine or other petroleum-based cleaner. Ask when you buy. Read the label on the bottle.

If it is a large household you may find it worthwhile to try the tools of the professionals. At least, learn their methods. If you have ever watched a professional window-cleaner at work you will know what that means.

Remember, something like 75 per cent of stain and dirt removal can be done chemically, not by 'elbow grease'.

STOCKING THE CLEANING CUPBOARD

Use a cleaning caddy—a basket, a bag, a child's wagon—to tote all your small-size cleaning supplies around the house.

Floors
Brooms, soft and stiff
Carpet-cleaning fluid
Carpet sweeper
Cleaner/polisher for vinyl floors
Dustpan and brooms
Sponge mop
Vacuum cleaner
Wax polish for wooden floors

Furniture
Aerosol polish for plastic surfaces
Furniture cream for painted furniture
Plenty of good dusters and old towels
Saddle soap for leather furniture
Teak oil
Wax polish

Metals
Brass and copper polish
Silver polish
Stainless steel cleaner/polish

Other
Ammonia
Feather dusters
Methylated spirits
Mirror cleaner
Spray bottles
Squeegees
Window cleaner

FLOORS

Keep hard-surfaced floors well swept even when dust is not visible. Invest in a good-quality mop. It can be most effective.

To wash floors, first remove as much furniture as possible. Prepare 2 buckets, one with hot water and cleaning solution, the other with fresh water for rinsing mop or scrubbing brush.

Remove scuff marks from hard floors with a cloth dipped in white spirit. A pad of fine, dry steel wool will remove them from a waxed floor. On linoleum, vinyl or rubber floors, wash scuff at once with warm soapy water.

Cork tiles Do not use detergent on cork tiles.

Wash with a cotton mop and warm water. Every month or so, add a couple of tablespoons of methylated spirits to the bucket of water. Remove scuff marks by rubbing with a cream cleanser on a sponge. Remove traces of the cleanser with a wet sponge.

Concrete floors To prevent dust gathering on concrete floors, paint them with two coats of a mixture of 1 part PVA adhesive to 5 parts water.

Mosaic tiles Mosaic tiles need only to be wiped with a sponge.

Quarry tiles Treat quarry tiles with a damp mop and an occasional application of a good non-slip wax.

Remove white patches from quarry tiles with a solution of 60mL vinegar in 5 litres water. Leave to dry without rinsing. Repeat if necessary.

Terrazzo To clean terrazzo, use a solution of hot water and washing soda to cut back grime and old polish. Use ½-cup of soda to ⅓-bucket of hot water. Rub stained areas with soaped steel wool. Rinse floors well with clean water. Apply a non-skid polish lightly, but not under mats.

Vinyl floors Keeping them clean is the secret of gleaming non-wax vinyl floors. Dirt and smears wipe off easily and there is no need to wax or polish.

Clean vinyl or rubber floors with a rubber-headed car-washing brush, without its hose, dipped in warm soapy water. The bristles are soft enough to clean without scratching and flexible enough for corners.

Wooden floors Wash wooden floors with as little water as possible, even ones that have a sealer coat or are painted. Never leave pools of water on the floor.

Remove embedded dirt from a varnished floor by rubbing with a mixture of powdered pumice in lubricating oil and wipe with a solvent-saturated cloth to pick up oil, which may collect grit.

WAXING

Waxing helps keep dirt from sticking to surfaces, saves wear and tear, and makes washing easier.

To get rid of old wax or finish, use a commercial wax remover or a solution of water and ammonia. Do as much as you think you can before the solution dries. When the solution on the floor looks creamy it means that the dirt and old wax are coming loose. Squeegee this into a small area, scoop up as much as you can with a dustpan and squeegee then transfer it to an empty bucket. Rinse the mop in clean water and mop the area. You may have to apply the solution more than once in spots where wax has built up. When the floor is dry apply a light coat of wax. When rewaxing, apply only to heavy traffic areas.

To remove wax from a linoleum or tile floor, mop with a solution of 3 parts water to 1 part alcohol.

Electric polisher When using an electric polisher, dust the floor before you begin, or the machine will polish dirt into the floor.

CARPETS

Good carpet is a good investment. If, however, you are in your first home, on a low budget, or with small children, you may have to settle for some other covering or for cheaper carpet the first time around.

Efficient maintenance will keep any carpet looking good longer. You will need to keep dust and dirt from alighting on the carpet, possibly by strategically placed mats. You must also regularly extract as much embedded grit and dirt as possible from the carpet and deal with surface grime by effective shampooing.

Vacuum cleaners Suction-type vacuum cleaners will get rid of surface dirt and bits of litter from your carpet but the noise this type of vacuum makes is no guide to its efficiency. If you want to make sure that embedded grit, which is what generally breaks down the fibres, is regularly removed you will need a beater-brush type of vacuum cleaner.

Soil retardant It is generally a good idea to use a soil retardant. This can be applied to new or old carpet. A good soil retardant will enable carpet to resist damage from both water- and oil-based spills.

Shampooing This is a procedure you have to think carefully about whether or not to do yourself as it can turn into an expensive exercise if things go wrong.

Vacuum the carpet before shampooing. Move furniture from the room, if possible. Protect the legs of the remaining furniture with foil or plastic bags so they won't stain the carpet. Test the cleaner on an inconspicuous area. Blot with a white cloth. If any dye comes out, the carpet is a job for a professional.

Pre-treat spots and traffic areas. Do not saturate the carpet.

Steam cleaning Here are some tips on what is involved in rented equipment for steam cleaning carpet. Basically, hot water and detergent are injected into the carpet by the cleaner which then vacuums or sucks up most of the solution and the dirt with it. This goes into a waste tank. Using suction only you should go back over your work until no water enters the tank. It takes 1 to 2 hours to clean an average room and about 5 hours for the carpet to dry out.

Burnt spot To repair a burn, remove some fuzz from the carpet by shaving or pulling out with tweezers. Roll into the shape of the burn.

Apply cement glue to the backing of the carpet and press the fuzz down into the burned spot. Cover with a tissue and put a book or heavy weight on top, so that the glue dries slowly, giving the best result with the repair job.

Moths For moths in carpets, spread a damp towel on the area and press with a hot iron. The heat will destroy insects and eggs.

Loose thread Do not pull a loose thread in carpet or you may unravel part of it. Snip thread level with pile.

Flattened pile Raise flattened pile on carpets with a steam iron. Build up a good steam and hold the iron over the flattened surfaces. Do not let the iron touch the carpet. Brush briskly.

Carpet squares and rugs A wrinkled carpet square can be straightened by strips of foam-rubber, cut to the width of the carpet and glued underneath.

Throw-rugs will not slip if you put strips of double-faced carpet tape under the corners.

Stop floor rugs curling at the edges by stitching a triangular pocket under each corner and putting a piece of stiff cardboard into each pocket.

Sheepskin rugs and other items can be cleaned by sprinkling with carpet cleaning powder. Work well into the fleece, roll up and put in a plastic bag for 12 hours. Vacuum the powder out or shake well.

WINDOWS

This may not be anybody's favourite household task but there is something very pleasing in having a clear and bright view of the world.

Almost any household cleanser such as detergent or ammonia will do the job, but the secret of success is in your equipment and your technique. For equipment it is worthwhile investing in the sort of brass or stainless steel squeegee which professional cleaners use. These have a blade of around 30cm.

USING A SQUEEGEE

Add only a small quantity of cleaning liquid to your bucket of water as too much will cause streaks and leave residue.

First, lightly wet the window with the cleaning solution. Have ready a damp cloth or chamois to wipe the dry rubber blade of the squeegee. This will give it a smoother action. Tilt the squeegee at an angle, pressing one end against the top of the window pane. Pull the squeegee across the window horizontally. If you make your first move horizontally across the top you should avoid most of the drips which come with working vertically. Wiping the blade again with the damp cloth or chamois, place the blade horizontally in the dry area, above your first wipe, and pull down, lapping over enough into the dry, clean area to avoid any surplus water running in the cleaned part. Using this technique, a window can be cleaned from either side or from the top. Clean off the bottom of the window sill with a damp cloth.

COMMON HOUSEHOLD FORMULAE

Water mixed with vinegar, borax or ammonia; applied and dried with a soft, dry cloth.

A solution of 30mL (two tablespoons) vinegar in a small bucketful of water; applied with a chamois and buffed with crumpled newspaper.

Using crumpled newspapers to wash and then buff windows. They do not leave fluff or lint and the printer's ink should prevent smearing.

Rubbing with glycerine to prevent frosty or steamy windows.

Dam or bore water makes cleaning windows harder. Add ammonia to warm water, then rinse and wipe over. Or use equal parts of methylated spirits, kerosene and water. Mix well and apply with a soft cloth. Polish windows with a soft, clean cloth when they are dry.

SOME HELPFUL HINTS

To avoid drips of water running down your sleeve, turn back the cuffs of your rubber gloves. This should catch most of the drips.

Do not wash windows on sunny days. They will dry too fast and show streaks.

Use the spray bottle attachment that fits on a garden hose to clean the outside of upstairs windows without using a ladder.

Fly screens To wash fly screens, attach a car brush to the hose and wash the screens with the brush.

Darn small holes in fly screens with a piece of fuse wire.

Aluminium frames Aluminium window and door frames will regain their shine if you rub them with a cloth dipped in ammonia.

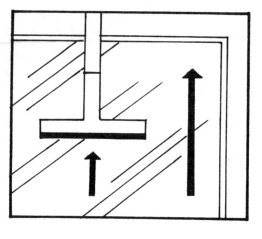
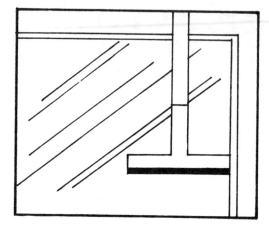
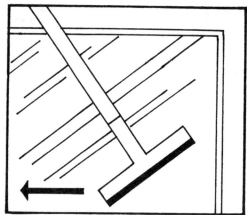
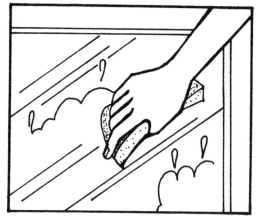

CURTAINS

Net and other light curtains are easier to arrange in pleats and folds if rehung while slightly damp after you have washed them.

If curtains are not to be rehung immediately after cleaning, store them on a clamp-type skirt hanger with the lining facing outward.

If there are more than two curtains on a rod, number them and change the order at intervals so fading is evenly distributed.

Wax curtain rods before sliding curtains on. The curtains will slide on easily and wax will stop rods rusting.

Rusty curtain rings or hooks can look like new if boiled in vinegar aand water for a few minutes. Dry well.

BLINDS

Venetian blinds Two ways to make the chore of cleaning venetian blinds easier: wear an old pair of fabric gloves, dip fingers in warm soapy water and then draw each slat between the fingers; or, soak a cloth in methylated spirits, wrap it around a spatula and run it along the slats.

Use heavy-duty packing tape to repair a broken venetian-blind tape. Apply to the side facing the wall and it will not be visible.

Brighten blind tapes with white shoe polish on a damp sponge.

Holland blinds A soft rubber may remove some stains on holland blinds.

A blind that will not lift easily needs more tension. Remove it, roll it up two or three revolutions and rehang.

A blind with too much tension can be fixed by removing it from the bracket and unrolling it by hand two or three revolutions.

Awnings Occasional washing down with the garden hose keeps awnings fresh. Before taking down awning, brush off dirt or spray with hose.

FURNITURE

Furniture is a large investment. Make sure when you buy that you know what it is made of, what any upholstery fabrics are made of and what finishes have been applied by the manufacturer. You will need to know if the fabrics have been treated with a soil retardant or if the wood has been given a heat- and water-resistant finish.

FURNITURE POLISH

With furniture polishes there are two main points. The first is to select one type of polish and stay with it. Many disappointing results come from switching from one type of polish to another. If polishes are incompatible they will give dulled and streaked finishes. The other point is, do not use too much polish. That only builds up layers on the surface which need more and more hard work to remove.

There are four main classes of wood polishes:

Liquid or paste solvent: hard to apply; low gloss.

Clear oil polish: mineral or vegetable oil, turpentine blend. Used on bare wood and sealed wood. It has a high gloss but leaves a film which collects dust. Warm furniture oil is easier to apply and works in better than cold.

Oil emulsion polish: cream type, much the same as clear oil.

Water or oil wax emulsion (aerosol or spray): good results.

To remove a build-up of old polish: rub with a cloth wrung out in a solution of 1 part vinegar to 8 parts warm water.

Home-made furniture polish Take ⅓ cup each of boiled linseed oil, turpentine and vinegar. Mix and shake well. Apply with a soft cloth and wipe dry. Polish with another soft cloth. Do not try to boil linseed oil yourself: it is not the same process. Buy it at a hardware or paint shop.

Another useful polish can be made with an eggcup each of paraffin oil and vinegar. Put in a screw-top jar and shake well. Put in a duster and when it is saturated, hang it out to dry. Keep the duster in the jar or in a plastic bag. It makes an excellent duster and polisher.

POLISH FOR ANTIQUES

50g beeswax
50g paraffin wax
500mL turpentine
100g pure soap
500mL warm water

Add grated waxes to the turpentine. In a separate container, add grated soap to warm water. Leave both for 24 hours, stirring occasionally. When waxes and soap are dissolved, combine the two liquids and warm gently in a double boiler. Make sure turpentine does not come into contact with a naked flame, as it is highly flammable. Stir mixture vigorously until it forms an emulsion which looks similar to mayonnaise. Cool and store in a screw-top bottle and label. Shake well before use and apply sparingly. Three or four applications will give a lustrous sheen to old wood furniture.

TO FRENCH POLISH

The formula is 125g of shellac to 600mL of methylated spirits. Allow time for the shellac to dissolve. If when dissolved the solution seems too thick, add a little more methylated spirits.

If repolishing an old surface, sandpaper with No. 0 (fine) sandpaper, adding a few drops of raw linseed oil to the paper. Sandpaper with the grain of the wood until smooth. Use fresh sandpaper when the old gets dirty or worn. Always put a few drops of oil on the sandpaper surface, then wipe the surface of the wood clean with a piece of cloth.

To apply the polish, use a pad of cotton wool. Soak the pad in the shellac mixture and squeeze out excess liquid. Cover the pad with old linen and apply polish, polishing with the grain on flat surfaces. Practise polishing on a piece of wood until you get used to using the pad.

Repeat until you have built up a sufficient film of polish. Then sprinkle a little raw linseed oil on surface of both pad and furniture. Rub with the grain and then begin to rub in a circular or number eight motion. This will help smooth the polish and fill in the grain. Repeat the process— but do not sandpaper again—until you have brought the surface up to your requirements. Finish off by polishing with the grain in order to dry out the oil, but keep your pad moistened with shellac mixture.

If you are polishing a new surface, be sure to smooth the surface down with dry sandpaper, finishing off with No. 0 (fine) sandpaper. After polishing as described, allow at least 24 hours to dry. Then sandpaper with No. 0 sandpaper, applying some drops of raw linseed oil to the surface and paper. Sandpaper with the grain until smooth, wipe surface clean with a cloth and repeat the polishing procedure as described.

MINOR SCRATCHES

For minor scratches, try liquid shoe polish in a matching colour. Other remedies are white petroleum jelly or a mixture of vinegar and olive oil. Sometimes just a fresh coat of wax or polish will work wonders. For larger scratches, fill with plastic wood and touch up with matching stain.

When repairing a scratch, rub with the grain of the wood.

Walnut Rub the scratch with the meat of a fresh, unsalted walnut.

Mahogany Rub with a dark-brown crayon or apply brown paste wax.

Red mahogany Apply brown iodine with an artist's brush or cotton bud.

Maple Combine equal amounts of iodine and white spirit. Apply with a brush or cotton bud, then dry, wax and polish.

Ebony Use black shoe polish, black eyebrow pencil or crayon.

Teak Rub gently with very fine steel wool then polish with a mixture of linseed oil and turpentine.

Oak Use a matching shoe polish.

SOME HELPFUL HINTS

To remove white water rings or spots from wood, apply a paste of butter or mayonnaise and cigarette ashes and buff with a slightly damp cloth. Or apply toothpaste on a damp cloth to the spots. If the stains are stubborn add baking soda or bicarbonate of soda to the toothpaste. Table salt mixed with a light oil often works. Remedies from the hardware shop include camphorated oil or gum turpentine. Rub dry and buff. Often, however, your usual furniture polish does the job. The last resort with difficult spots is to strip off the old wax and resurface, using a water-resistant paste polish.

For scorches on wood, rub with fine sandpaper or steel wool to remove charred ash, then bleach out discolouration with laundry bleach.

Rub in linseed or a clear mineral oil to restore the natural oils of the wood. Stain, if needed, to blend with original colour. Then restore the finish, whether lacquer, varnish or rubbing oil. Hand rubbing helps blend in the repaired section with its surrounds.

Small dents in wooden surfaces can be removed by covering them with wet cloth and some thicknesses of newspaper then ironing over the dent until the wood swells back. Extreme care must be taken while ironing.

To remove candle wax from wood, soften wax with a hair drier, wipe with paper towelling and wash down with a solution of vinegar and water.

To remove paper stuck to wood, do not scrape with a knife. Pour any salad oil, a few drops at a time, on the paper. Leave to penetrate then rub with a soft cloth.

Stickers can be removed from wood by painting with white vinegar. Give the vinegar time to soak in, then gently scrape off.

Veneered furniture may crack if standing in sunlight. To prevent this, rub with a silk cloth dipped in warm linseed oil. If old veneers are drying out, paint all surfaces, including the undersides, of furniture.

Renew the finish of unvarnished walnut or teak with linseed oil. Let the oil seep into the grain for an hour or so. Then wipe off excess. Rub the surface with a felt pad to work in the oil, then apply wax polish.

A small clean soft brush dipped in furniture polish or silicone wax will help keep carved furniture looking good.

Plastics Never oil vinyl. Oil makes vinyl hard and it is almost impossible to reverse the process. To clean vinyl, sprinkle vinegar or bicarbonate of soda on a damp cloth and apply. Then wash with a mild liquid soap. Oils from the body will harden vinyl so regular cleaning is necessary.

Burns on plastic laminates can be made less noticeable by light sanding. Usually, however, the surface has to be renewed.

Cane Cane furniture can be renewed by wiping with a solution of equal parts vinegar and water. Rub to a shine with a soft cloth. Routine cleaning can be done with a tablespoon of salt in a litre of water. The saline solution should stop the cane from turning yellow.

To prevent cane drying out, apply lemon oil occasionally.

Never let cane freeze. It will crack and split.

Cane needs moisture, so use a humidifier in winter.

To lighten old dark cane chairs, scrub vigorously with a bleach and water solution. Rinse well and dry.

Tighten a drooping cane chair seat by giving it a hot water bath and placing it in the sunlight to dry. After it has dried thoroughly, apply either lemon or cedar oil to prevent cracking and splitting.

Outdoor furniture At the beginning of summer, scrub down outdoor furniture with a soft brush and detergent, rinse with garden hose and dry with old towels.

Wax the bottoms of legs on wooden patio furniture to keep out moisture.

Apply a coat of liquid wax to cast or wrought iron furniture when new to stop rust. Repeat from time to time.

Rust on metal furniture may be scrubbed off with turpentine.

Glass To clean glass table tops, rub with lemon juice, dry, then polish with crumpled newspaper.

Toothpaste can deal with small scratches on glass, or they can often be removed by rubbing with jeweller's rouge and a drop of methylated spirits. Make a paste and rub gently.

Metal When cleaning brass handles on wood furniture, cut a cardboard collar and put it round the fitting. Brass cleaner can eventually take the colour out of wood.

The shining finish of metal can sometimes be restored with silver or copper cleaning paste and a lot of rubbing, but if the corrosion has pitted the surface, it needs professional help. Protect metal surfaces with a coat of clear lacquer.

LAMPS

Plastic shades can be washed in the bath: use soapy water then rinse. Wipe metal parts carefully. Dry, if possible, in the open. Fabric shades can be cleaned with a dry cleaning spray. Ask your hardware store for advice.

If parchment shades are not too soiled, rub with fine oatmeal dipped in cottonwool pads, replacing cotton as it becomes soiled. Or try a crust of dry bread.

Clean your ruffled or pleated lamp shades with an old shaving brush.

Wipe fluorescent lamp tubes and fixtures regularly with a duster. Replace lamps that flicker on and off or have dark rings at the ends.

To clean chandeliers: filll a bucket with warm water, add a squirt of dish washing liquid, plus ¼ cup of ammonia; put a cotton glove on your hand, dip it in the solution and clean the chandelier section by section.

A strip of luminous paper or paint on electric light switches makes them easy to find in the dark.

Pearl light bulbs will not throw shadows, as clear ones do.

PICTURES

All pictures should be dusted regularly. If the picture is behind glass this should be wiped occasionally with a cloth moistened with methylated spirits, a chamois wrung out in warm water or a brand-name window cleaner. Take care not to let trickles seep inside the glass and damage the picture.

Provided the backing is in good condition, a glass or perspex covered picture should need no further attention. Prints and engravings sometimes develop mildew stains. Removing these is a job for an expert.

Oil paintings sooner or later will get a build-up on the surface no matter how often you dust them. You can buy cleaning materials at artists' supply shops. If, however, the painting is at all valuable or even if it is of some sentimental value, you should get it restored professionally.

Hanging a picture To prevent walls being marked with nail holes from false starts when hanging a picture, make a paper pattern of the picture. After you have found the correct position for the hanger, perforate the paper with a sharp pencil to mark the wall.

Or, a wet fingerprint will mark the right spot for a hanger and dry without a trace.

Two nails placed slightly apart will help a picture to hang straight.

Wind some adhesive tape around the centre of the picture wire. The wire will be less likely to slip.

If picture wire will show, nylon fishing-line makes a strong and almost invisible substitute.

PICTURE FRAMES

Picture frames are now fairly expensive so it pays to restore and re-finish rather than buy new ones; in fact it pays to look around second-hand shops for old frames that could be restored.

As a general rule, never colour a frame lighter than the lightest colour in the painting. The frame colouring should complement the painting rather than overpower it, so try to pick up a minor colour in the painting and use this for the frame colour.

Rubbed finish You will have to strip the frame back to bare wood using a paint stripper (if painted or varnished). If the frame has carved sections or fluting, you may need a stiff brush to get into the crevices. When the paint has been stripped off, wash with warm water and detergent, rinse with clean water and allow to dry thoroughly. A light sanding may be necessary to remove any small spots of paint still clinging and to smooth the wood.

To rub colour into the frame use an oil paint. Take a piece of soft cloth to dip into the paint, dab the excess off on a piece of newspaper, then rub the colour into the wood, along the grain. The result is a soft finish which has the irregular handcrafted look. The depth or strength of the colour depends on the amount of paint used.

Antique finish This is similar to rubbing. The paint is rubbed on in irregular patches and when dry, sanded lightly with wet and dry sandpaper to get a silky finish. Artists' oil paints are best and colours like yellow ochre, chrome yellow, venetian red, burnt sienna, and raw umber can look wonderful. When the colour has dried thoroughly and been sanded, a very thin coat of burnt sienna diluted with turpentine can be brushed over the frame to give it a lovely patina. There are also antique finish paints on the market; follow manufacturer's instructions for them.

Gold leaf First paint the frame with a heavy coat of venetian red then, when dry, apply a coat of bronze paint. When this is dry, rub over with steel wool, so that in places the bronze is rubbed through to expose the red.

FIREPLACES

Vinegar will clean brick tiling around the fireplace. Dip a brush in white vinegar and scrub. Sponge to absorb the moisture.

Heavy discolouration of the bricks may respond to a paste of powdered pumice and concentrated ammonia. Dry, then wash with a cleaning agent, rinse and let dry.

Clean smoke film from fire glass by rubbing with a damp cloth dipped into the ashes from the fire. Shine up with another damp cloth.

METALS

Brass and copper The most frequent threat to copper-based metals, as with silver, is tarnish caused by pollution in the atmosphere or by damp. Corrosion, probably in the form of a powdery green deposit called verdigris, may come with continued neglect. If you have valuable or antique items of brass or copper that have become corroded or stained, it is best to take them to an expert.

A homely method for cleaning brass is by rubbing thoroughly with a cut lemon dipped in salt or a cloth moistened with vinegar and dipped in salt. A small brush dipped in ammonia will clean old polish from engraved or ornate brass. A homely treatment for badly corroded items is spirits of salts rubbed on with a rag tied to the end of a stick. Spirits of salts is poisonous and corrosive, so wear rubber gloves and work in a well ventilated place, out of doors if possible. Rinse article in clean water thoroughly afterwards.

Brass and copper can be protected with clear lacquer. This should be applied in a dry place to avoid sealing in any moisture. When discolouration eventually occurs under the lacquer, the lacquer can be removed with cellulose thinners or nail polish remover.

Bronze Dust bronze regularly. It can be cleaned with soap and water and polished with a cloth with a few drops of oil on it. A light application of dark-brown shoe polish followed by a good buffing will improve its appearance and may ward off the green spots which sometimes show up on bronze.

Very soiled bronze should be washed in hot soapy water or cleaned with turpentine or paraffin and then polished when dry.

Chrome Brighten chrome by rubbing over with plain flour or with a cloth dampened with ammonia. Wash off then polish with a clean cloth.

Nickel Nickel-plated fittings will sparkle if rubbed over with a cloth moistened with methylated spirits.

Pewter Most collectors of pewter like it to have a soft glow rather than a shiny finish. If so, just wash it in soapy water and rub with a soft cloth. If you want a bright surface there are special pewter polishes or you can use any good metal polish.

Neglected pewter develops an oxide scale which tarnishes. This is a job for an expert.

SPECIAL SURFACES

ALABASTER
Alabaster should not be cleaned with water as it is very porous and will absorb any damaging acids contained within the water. To clean alabaster, wipe over with white spirit.

To remove stains, use household bleach, allow to dry thoroughly, then polish with

furniture wax.

To fill holes and chips Mix epoxy resin with whiting to build up the surface. Whiting gives the resin a translucent colour which is a good match for the material.

BONE AND IVORY
Bone, ivory and soapstone are organic materials and become brittle with age. Items such as small carvings, chess pieces, statues and beads often need cleaning and repairing.

Never wash bone and ivory. The material will absorb water and be damaged by it. Use an artist's soft brush or cotton wool and methylated spirits for really dirty pieces.

To whiten If pieces have become yellowed, bleach with a paste made of whiting and 20 per cent hydrogen peroxide. Make the paste stiff and thick or the ivory will absorb too much liquid and swell. Stand the piece in the sun until the paste has dried, then wipe it off quickly with a damp cloth and dry thoroughly.

Polish Use almond oil to give it a good protective finish and a gentle shine.

Ivory piano keys Clean ivory piano keys with a solution of salt and lemon on a damp cloth. Do not let the solution seep between the keys. Wipe dry. Dust the keys frequently with a feather duster. Keys that have yellowed can be removed for professional polishing. It is said that ivory should be exposed to daylight and sunlight as much as possible. So you have to balance leaving the piano lid open for the benefit of ivory keys or keeping it closed so that household dust does not seep into the works.

JAPAN LACQUER
Wipe japanned objects with warm soapy water. Dry. Sprinkle with flour, leave half an hour. Dust then polish.

LEATHER
Old leather-covered furniture, and also leather or leather-covered containers, books, lamp bases and other objects can often be restored to quite good condition. Do not try to restore valuable antique items yourself. Take them to an expert.

To replace leather coverings which have come loose from their base, scrape away the old adhesive and reglue with a synthetic resin adhesive.

To get rid of indentations from lamps or ashtrays on leather table tops, apply lemon oil to the leather twice a day for a week. To maintain the surface, use lemon oil once a month.

Dried-out leather Soften with liberal applications of a brand-name leather dressing. The best place to find such dressings is a saddlery shop where several different ones are available. Saddle soap on its own is not enough for very dry leather. You may have to treat the leather several times over a week because the first few applications will be quickly absorbed.

Powdery leather Treat with a mixture of 2 parts methylated spirits and 3 parts castor oil, allow to dry thoroughly, then treat with pure castor oil.

Dirty leather Should be washed with saddle soap, also available from saddlery shops, and some hardware stores. After washing, allow to dry and treat with leather dressing.

MARBLE
Marble will absorb stains even if it has been well polished, so anything spilled on marble surfaces should be cleaned up as quickly as possible; this includes floors. When marble is cleaned, the patina gained over the years is lost so it is better to take care that it doesn't get stained in general use.

Light cleaning Wash with soap and water and clear ammonia, say ½ cup added to a dish of water. Oil stains can be removed with a paste made from powdered kaolin and turpentine. Acidic solutions should not be used on marble.

Fungus growths Can be bleached out with a mild solution of hydrogen peroxide and water with a drop of ammonia added. Ordinary household bleach diluted down with water may also be suitable. Green algae growth can be cleaned off with a mild solution of household bleach.

Polishing Silicone furniture polish will give marble a good protective finish, particularly if the surface is buffed with a lambswool pad on a power drill between several coats of the polish. The surface should shine to a mirror finish which will last for many years with regular dusting. Never use oil polish or soft waxes on marble as they can discolour it.

MOTHER-OF-PEARL
Wash in warm water. Wipe with damp cloth dry. Do not use ammonia.

ONYX
Onyx should be handled as little as possible since it has a porous surface which readily absorbs marks. Dust regularly and wipe off any surface dirt with a clean damp cloth. Light staining may respond to rubbing with a cloth moistened with methylated spirits. Marks caused by spilt drinks or wet glasses should be quickly wiped clean, otherwise expensive professional re-grinding and polishing becomes necessary.

ORMOLU
Use a weak solution of ammonia and water, then a mild detergent. Wear rubber gloves. Apply cleaning solution with balls of cotton wool or cotton buds for small items. Rinse with warm water.

SHELLAC
Wipe with a soft clean cloth. Polish with a wax polish used very sparingly. Buff with a soft cloth.

TORTOISESHELL
The less done to it the better but if very soiled wipe gently with a damp warm cloth and dry well. Tortoiseshell is apt to warp.

HOUSE PESTS

Make house pests unwelcome. Do not provide anything for them to eat. Wipe up crumbs after meals, keep food covered, wash up as soon as a meal is over, and don't leave pet food around.

Disinfect your garbage bin after it is emptied and keep it covered. Clean drains regularly with disinfectant or bleach, washed down with hot water. Fill cracks or holes in walls and floors. Brush away spider webs from walls and ceilings.

There is any number of insecticides on the market. Choose one which suits your purpose. Read the label carefully and follow instructions to the letter. Take particular care where there are children or animals.

There are simple home remedies. Many people prefer these because they have objections to using poisons at random. Many more people find that the old methods suffice for minor infestations.

Ants Follow their route march until you come to their nest. Destroy it with an insecticide. If you cannot find how they are getting into the house, spray around sinks and windows and along skirting boards. There are ant traps but they should not be used where children could pick them up.

Ants love sweet things and fats and wouldn't come into the house if not tempted.

Bedbugs Bedbugs are not a nice subject, but if you buy an inner-city house you may find it already inhabited. Spray beds and bedding thoroughly, then move on to other likely areas — skirting boards, behind pictures and in cracks in walls and floorboards. If they reappear, go through it all again.

Cockroaches Cockroaches have been around for a very long time, but that does not make them any more popular. Sprinkle pyrethrum powder or use an aerosol spray, but cockroach baits are gaining popularity as an easier and safer way to cope with these pests.

They breed rapidly. If they are out of hand, get professional help.

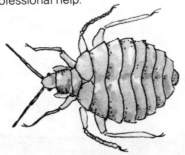

Fleas Fleas love warmth. Vibration is needed for the pupae to hatch. This is why sometimes

houses which have been empty for some time are overrun when new owners move in.

Flea eggs can produce larvae in 2 to 12 days in warm weather but may remain dormant for 2 months or longer if the weather is cool.

Fleas go from one host to the next, leaving their eggs behind. Provided meals of blood are available, a female can live for 500 days and lay up to 500 eggs.

Once you have fleas on pets or in your house, get out the vacuum cleaner. Use it in places where fleas and their eggs may lurk — skirting boards, cushions, upholstery, anything soft and warm. Vacuum regularly and burn the contents of the bag. Wash, burn or throw away the pet's bedding. Substitute something which can be readily disposed of, such as newspaper, until the fleas have gone.

Flies Flies can spread almost 30 different diseases. On the other hand, they do pollinate some food crops.

They are most active in the summer and most active around food and garbage. Slow-release vaporised insect-killers are useful, but it is not a good idea to put them in rooms where babies or old people spend a great deal of time.

Fly-screens are the best protection. Keep them in good condition. Install self-closing screen doors where there is heavy traffic in and out of the house. Wrap up garbage. Keep garbage tins and kitchen bins securely covered.

Mosquitoes Mosquitoes breed in water. Try to get rid of open water near the house, or spray it regularly to keep the population down.

Pyrethrum works well for mosquitoes. Some people prefer coils and others go back to the old-time citronella. Fly-screens are the best way to keep them out.

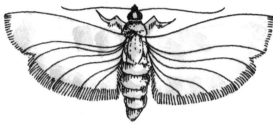

Moths Moths love wool and fur. Man-made fibres are immune, but be careful about blends. It is not the moth but its larvae which do the damage. Before it dies in autumn the moth lays its eggs. When the larvae emerge in the spring, there is a feast waiting for them. Moths are happier if there is dust or dirt about, so dry cleaning before storage offers a fair amount of protection. Clothes stored in polythene bags are usually safe, so long as the bag is well sealed.

Camphor, naphthalene and turpentine are time-tested deterrents for moths. There are also moth-proofing aerosols and other more modern remedies at your chemist.

Rodents One mouse may look a beguiling little fellow, but plagues of mice have been as destructive as flood or fire in country areas. Nobody likes rats.

Rodents will be attracted by food or somewhere dark and cosy to establish a nest. Open garbage tins and garden compost with too much food waste in it will attract them. Stop mice and rats getting into your house by checking for holes and covering any obvious access with aluminium flashing or tin can lids. Mice cannot chew through steel wool so use this to plug their holes.

The mousetrap remains one of the oldest and most effective household products ever devised. Bait with cheese or raw meat. Or mix powdered milk with water to a thick paste and fill the trap, using a blunt knife. Put traps down where you have seen a mouse or rat and leave them out each night until you find them empty.

There are a number of commercially prepared baits. Some are suitable for outside use and others are in solid form to drop into hard-to-reach spots. Generally for mice you should distribute small amounts of bait in several places and for rats, large amounts of bait in one or two places. Continue until bait remains uneaten. As always, do not place baits or traps where children or pets can get at them.

Silverfish Silverfish tend to like cool, damp places but many venture well beyond those. Their diet is mainly sugar and starch and they can work their way steadily through neglected books (particularly the glue on the binding) and starched cotton fabrics. They also eat rayon, which is manufactured from wood pulp.

Spray doors, windows, skirtings and cupboards with household insecticide. You may have to repeat the treatment.

7

ENERGY SAVING

THE IDEAL TIME to save energy is when you are planning your house. However, in these days of scarcer and dearer fuels, there is still a lot you can do in your existing house by more sensible choice of heating and better use of appliances. In most parts of Australia, and in times of drought, saving water is as vital as conserving fuel.

WAYS TO SAVE ENERGY

There are three main areas in which significant energy savings can be made:

By designing a home to take advantage of site and climate to reduce artificial heating and cooling costs to a minimum. This is passive solar design.

By modifying an existing home to make best use of the climate; for example, by installing insulation or planting trees for shade.

By developing energy-efficient habits such as taking brief showers instead of baths, or using the oven fully by cooking several dishes at once; and choosing energy-efficient appliances such as microwave ovens, fans instead of air-conditioners, and solar hot-water heaters.

BUILDING A HOME

Climate varies widely in Australia, so, naturally, design solutions vary. However, the following principles apply anywhere in Australia:

Orientation The main area of windows should be on the north side; sliding glass doors can also be incorporated. Deep eaves, awnings or trees will shade the glass from summer sun.

As there is no direct heat from the sun on the south side, windows should be tall and narrow to minimise heat loss. Keep windows on the east and west sides to a minimum as heat is strong on these sides.

Choice of building materials In cold areas, heavyweight materials such as cavity brick are more effective because although it takes longer for the materials to heat up, more heat is absorbed and the house stays warmer longer.

In hot climates, lightweight materials such as timber are more suitable because, although they heat up more quickly, they also cool down faster.

Slab flooring A concrete slab floor with quarry, slate or vinyl tiles (not cork or carpet, which are insulators) will act as a heat store in winter if the winter sun is allowed to enter through north-facing windows. By evening, the floor is warmed and the heat is gradually given off during the night; heavy curtains should be drawn across the windows to prevent heat loss.

In summer, with effective shading, no direct sun will reach the floor. The floor, in contact with the ground, will stay cool, and the house will feel cooler.

Insulation This can maintain a comfortable temperature indoors, rather than have the house influenced dramatically by outdoor conditions. Insulation should be installed above the ceiling and between cavity walls.

Exterior colour Light-coloured exteriors are best for most climates, except the very cold, as light colours are very effective in reflecting heat in summer.

Ventilation House layouts should be designed to aid cross-ventilation and take advantage of prevailing summer breezes.

During very hot weather, ventilation can be a potential source of heat gain, with hot winds blowing in and increasing the interior temperature. In these conditions, it is better to close windows and curtains and open doors as little as possible. Use an electric fan to keep the air circulating.

If you have an air-conditioner, this will allow it to work efficiently. When the temperature drops or a cool breeze arrives, open all the doors and windows to release the day's heat.

Double glazing This has proved to be an excellent insulator in areas where the winter months are very cold.

A glasshouse or conservatory Incorporated in the design of the house a glasshouse is practical as well as decorative. Such a space, filled with plants, acts as an efficient heat trap during the winter months, naturally radiating back the trapped heat during the night and maintaining a fairly even temperature throughout. Radiation from the sun comes in through the glass and warms up the concrete slab, or rockery, which acts as a heat store. Stored heat is then released during cooler hours.

During summer months, deciduous vines, removable external awnings, internal roller shades and adjustable ventilation can keep the glasshouse shaded and as a cooling space. Although shaded, the glasshouse still heats up

faster than the remainder of the house. The warm air automatically rises, escaping through the opened vents to the outside and at the same time creating a draught of cooler air which is pulled through the house from below.

MODIFYING A HOME

If your home has been built without the above considerations, there are still many things which can be done to improve its energy efficiency and reduce your power bill.

Summer shade Shade north-facing windows from summer sun so that the interior remains as cool as possible.

Extended eaves can block the high summer sun while allowing the lower shining rays of the winter sun in to warm the house.

Pergolas covered with a deciduous vine or deciduous trees, placed for summer shading of northern windows, are also effective as in winter the sun shines through the bare branches.

Planting around the house also affects the internal temperature as plants and lawn remain at a relatively constant temperature, even during hot weather—whereas concreted or paved areas will heat up and pass the heat into the house. For constantly used areas, paving can be interspersed with tough ground cover.

Bare, unshaded walls can also be cooled with suitable vines growing on the wall or on trellises just off the wall. A distance of 200mm is ideal.

Insect screens These are essential in some areas, especially during summer, but, because the air is partly deflected by the surrounding wall, they do obstruct air flow. If windows are sheltered by a veranda, it is more effective to enclose the veranda with insect screens, rather than to screen the windows.

INSULATION

Ceiling insulation is the most cost-effective, accessible and efficient method of reducing heat loss and gain. Check the level of insulation recommended for your climate with the appropriate State authority. Up to 35 per cent of heat losses are via the ceiling.

If your brick house has brick-cavity walls, it is unlikely to be practicable to insulate them.

Before you insulate your house, block all air leaks. These occur mainly at the junctions of walls and floor, electrical outlets, where pipes

enter the house from the outside, and windows and doors. Plugging these leaks with caulking substance or weather proofing will increase your heating/cooling efficiency.

If you insulate your house yourself, check with your hardware store for the best type of insulation for different parts of your house. Always wear face mask and goggles when insulating as fibres and dust may be very harmful.

Wherever fibrous batts are used for insulation, take care they do not touch outer walls—and use a moisture barrier. Most insulation can be done by the home handyman, but more difficult areas of the house to reach—e.g. floors —should be insulated by experienced contractors.

If brick veneer cladding is being added around a weatherboard or fibro house, install insulation foil between the brick and the original wall.

Curtains These also help insulate; curtains should be made of heavy material and have a reflective lining.

An alternative is to have aluminium-backed sheers. These reflect heat away during the summer but keep warm air in during the winter. Solid curtains can be lined normally, thus saving on bulk.

All curtains should be wider than the window and have a pelmet box to stop air movement between glass and curtains.

Close curtains on hot days to reduce the heat penetration through glass; open curtains and windows in the evening for a cooling breeze. Let the sun in during winter days and then close the curtains at night to conserve heat. Reflective window film is also effective in reflecting summer heat away.

Floors Old floorboards can be quite draughty with cracks or gaps, and should be filled. Enclosing the subfloor space, leaving only minimum ventilation, will also slow heat loss from the floor.

Weather stripping Applying this foam tape around doors and windows will reduce heat loss. It is easy to apply, and available from hardware departments and stores.

ENERGY CONSCIOUS

Saving energy is best achieved by changing many of the small, fairly heedless habits which make up daily life for most of us.

You can cut winter energy bills by up to 10 per cent without new appliances or changing life style, just by using what you've got more economically.

HOT WATER SYSTEMS
These use most energy in the average house (35 per cent) so . . .

Fix dripping hot taps; a moderate drip wastes 10 bathtubs of water a month.

Step out of the shower 30 seconds earlier. The average shower takes about 100 litres. The average bath uses more than 140 litres. A bath is economical only when more than one child is bathed in it.

Use the dishwasher only when it is full.

Use cold water to rinse hands, fill the electric jug, etc.

Insulate both your hot water tank and outlet pipes. The latter should be insulated for at least a metre from where they join the hot water system. Check tank does not leak and wet the insulation, thus impairing effectiveness.

Check maintenance requirements of your hot water system with the manufacturer. Check pump, thermostat valve and the element.

Defective thermostats can let water in storage tanks become too hot, even boil. Make sure yours is in good working order.

Try lowering your thermostat setting and see if you still have hot enough water. 60°C is fine. You'll lower your bill and reduce the risk of scalding. You may have to get an electrician to do this for you.

The average hot water heater does not last very long. Heaters more than 10 years old may be so heavily coated on the inside with minerals that they waste a lot of energy.

If you have a long, rambling house it may be more economical to have two heaters, one for the main area and one for bathrooms or a kitchen some distance away.

Turn off the power to your hot water system if you leave your home unoccupied.

ROOM HEATING

This uses about 24 per cent of your energy.

Heat only living areas, not bedrooms.

Close windows, doors and curtains at night.

Stop draughts by blocking cracks in walls, gaps under doors, and around windows. Also stop draughts from unheated rooms. Curtains should be close-fitting and have box pelmets.

On bright days let the sunshine in.

Wear warmer clothes. Keep central heating to 19°C.

Elderly people, people with circulatory problems or those using some types of drugs as well as children may need higher indoor temperatures than do active, healthy adults. Ask your doctor the minimum temperature you should have in your home.

Install insulation.

COOKING

This uses 17 per cent of your energy.

Plan meals. For example, once you have boiled a pan, turn it to simmer. Turn off an electric range a few minutes before food is cooked.

Use the oven for several dishes at once and don't keep opening the door.

Use small appliances for small jobs: the toaster instead of the griller, the frypan not the oven.

Saucepans should have tight-fitting lids and flat bottoms, and should completely cover the element or flame.

Check the seal on the oven door; it should hold a piece of paper in place.

Preheating of gas ovens is unnecessary. Gas heat is instant.

Never boil water in an open pot.

Defrost frozen food before cooking instead of wasting energy doing the job in a saucepan. Move frozen food from the freezer to the refrigerator the day before.

With electric cookers, use bright hotplate reflectors to direct heat where it's needed. Flames on gas hotplates should be kept so that the tips are just below the base of the saucepan.

REFRIGERATORS AND FREEZERS

Don't hold the door open while you decide what you want.

Defrost regularly.

Check that the door seal is functioning effectively.

Make sure your refrigerator/freezer is in a well-ventilated spot so that the heat discharge coils at the back of the unit can operate effectively. Keep excessive dust and fluff off the coils, and ensure the unit is out of direct sunlight.

Because a refrigerator/freezer is operating 24 hours a day, don't buy a unit which is bigger than you need; it will add dollars to your energy bill.

When buying an automatic defrost refrigerator, ask whether it uses waste heat from the unit for evaporating defrosted water, or whether it has additional heating elements. The unit using waste heat is much cheaper to run. A manual defrost uses less energy.

Before buying a new refrigerator, compare the amount of energy used by various models.

Adjust the thermostat to the setting recommended by the manufacturer. Overcooling wastes energy but not having the refrigerator cool enough wastes food.

If you are going away, if possible clean out the refrigerator, leave the door ajar and turn power off.

WASHING MACHINES AND DRIERS

When you buy a new washing machine, compare models for energy-saving features. Soak cycles remove stubborn stains in one wash cycle. Suds-savers let you re-use hot water. If the water level of the machine can be adjusted you can economically do a partial load.

Use cold water and a cold-water detergent when possible.

Never overload the washing machine.

Have a full wash load before using your machine.

Use the clothes line rather than a heated clothes drier. Heated clothes driers use a great deal of energy. Drying on a line generally reduces wear and tear on clothes as well.

Hang clothes carefully on the line and fold them carefully. This saves ironing time.

When you use a heated clothes drier, use it with as many clothes as recommended and not with only one or two items. But do not overload.

Dry clothes in consecutive loads to take advantage of the fact that inside the drier is already warm.

LIGHTING

This uses about 7 per cent of your energy.

Turn off unnecessary lights (including outdoor ones).

Use fluorescent light tubes rather than ordinary bulbs. Fluorescent tubes use one third of the energy and give the same amount of light. They last 10 times as long.

Don't use high wattage lamps unnecessarily. Decide what light is needed. You can generally cut down in laundry, storeroom and garage.

The wattage of a light globe does not measure the amount of light it produces, but rather the amount of energy required to operate it. A single 100-watt globe gives 50 per cent more light than four 25-watt globes

for the same amount of energy.

When you are sewing, reading or working at a table, light only that area and have low-level lighting in the rest of the room to prevent eye-strain.

The best place for a floor or hanging lamp is in the corner of a room where there will be two wall surfaces to reflect light into the room.

Install timers to turn on lights if you don't want to come home to an unlighted house.

SAVING WATER

Garden Garden watering has enormous potential for saving water. Consider that on a hot summer day about 50 per cent of water supplied by water boards is poured onto gardens, much of it running to waste.

A well managed lawn should need a thorough soaking only once a week. Don't pour on water faster than the soil can absorb it, or more than it can absorb.

Don't scalp your lawn. Leaving grass a little longer encourages deeper root growth.

Always water in the early morning or evening to lessen loss by evaporation.

Check hose fittings and taps for leaks and turn off sprinklers securely.

Plant natives that are less sensitive to drought. Mulch, pebbles or bark chips will help reduce evaporation.

Sweep rather than hose the path.

Don't leave the hose running while you wash the car. Rather, sponge it with soapy water from a bucket and rinse clean with a light spray.

Bathroom Inside, this is where you can make the most substantial reduction of water use.

Don't use the toilet to flush away rubbish and check your toilet for leaks. Put a few drops of food colouring in the cistern and see if it leaks into the bowl. Also check the overflow pipe occasionally. (Dual flush toilets now on the market, which provide a small flush or a full flush, are designed to save water.)

Reduce the flow rate when you're in the shower, and run a shallower bath. When washing hands, cleaning teeth, etc., don't leave the water running.

Kitchen Keep a plug in the sink while running the tap. Don't wash dishes or vegetables under running water.

Minimise the use of in-sink waste disposal units. Not only do they use running water but they also put a lot of sometimes undesirable wastes into the sewerage.

Keep a jug of drinking water in the fridge—this saves running water from the tap until it's cold enough to drink.

Dishwashers and washing machines should be used only when full. Use the suds-saver if your washing machine has one.

HEATING YOUR HOME

Few Australian homes are planned for efficient heating. When energy was cheap, insulation was rarely considered. People simply turned up the heat in the winter months. With energy supplies decreasing, it is sensible to think again about your house and the best way to keep snug.

Efficient and economical heating for your home depends on choosing the unit best suited to your needs, then making sure it is located in the most effective position.

No one method is better than another. There are advantages and drawbacks to all heating systems. The design of your home, the area in which you live and whether you own or rent it will all affect your choice.

Insulation can make a big difference to how much your heater has to work. An uninsulated house loses heat much faster than an insulated one.

THERMOSTATS AND TIMERS

Heaters with thermostatic controls will switch off automatically when the room is at the desired temperature, saving power and money. A comfortable daytime temperature is

19°; at bedtime reduce to 15° or turn off. Time switches can be used with some heaters to switch them back on before you wake in the morning.

SPACE HEATERS

Depending on the size of the space heater you choose, you can heat an area of up to about 80sq m fairly evenly without the use of ducting. Heaters can be built into the wall or be mobile. For small families and warmer climates, one or two mobile heaters may be enough. If you have a built-in heater in the living-room, you will probably still need a mobile heater for other rooms.

Space heaters come in a wide range of designs, prices and fuel types.

Electric Oil-filled electric radiators and panel heaters are safe, economical and mobile. Some are fan assisted and some have timers which can be set to warm the house before you wake or when you return from work.

Off-peak heaters may be called thermal storage space heaters or heat banks. They may be controlled or uncontrolled.

During the low-cost, off-peak period, the heaters heat their insulated central core and store the heat. Controlled heaters emit the heat under the control of a thermostat with fan assistance. Uncontrolled heaters have no thermostat.

Under-carpet heating is a heat source woven into a strong fabric which is placed between ordinary carpet and its underfelt. Control is manual or automatic, using time switches, thermostats or a combination of both. Because the heating is spread over a large area there is uniform heat and the actual surface temperature is quite low and it is safe to place heavy furniture on the carpet.

Fan-assisted space heaters may be wall mounted, floor space heaters or electric furnaces. Some may be installed to provide heat to an adjoining room; some require special wiring; others simply plug in and most have thermostatic controls.

Gas All gas heaters have instant ignition systems and most are thermostatically controlled. Before making a final choice, check with the gas authority that it is an approved model, as not all models sold are approved in all States.

Gas wall furnaces are very powerful and ideal for heating large open areas, but must be positioned carefully to allow the warmed air to spread in all directions for effective warmth.

Portable gas heaters are inexpensive and can be moved from room to room and plugged into sockets in the floor. A flexible hose about 2m long allows you to turn the heater to point in any direction.

Gas room heaters are installed on the outside walls, allowing fresh air to be drawn in, warmed and circulated throughout the room, with the warm air being fan-forced out.

Oil Once very popular, with the increased cost of oil it has become less economical. However, for country areas where other forms of heating may be more expensive, it may be a good solution.

Solid fuel Heaters using wood provide excellent warmth and burn economically and safely, and some models may be used for water heating.

CENTRAL HEATING

Central heating includes any system which can heat the whole house and may be divided into four categories: warm air furnaces, hydronic (water) systems, electric floor systems and reverse-cycle air-conditioning.

Your choice of system will depend on the type of house you own which in turn will affect the cost of installation, the availability of fuel and its cost.

Warm air furnaces Using oil, gas or electricity, a central furnace is situated in a convenient place away from the living and sleeping areas. This distance is necessary because the fan which blows the air through the ducts is noisy. An electric wall thermostat is set at the required temperature.

It is possible to add a refrigerant air-conditioner to these systems to provide summer cooling as well.

Hydronic heating This system is commonly used in Europe and provides domestic hot water as well as heating the whole house. A central water boiler heats water to a constant temperature and the water is pumped out of the tank to the heating system.

Electric floor heating This system is installed in the concrete floor slab or under carpet and underlay in a sandwich of grooved pressed hardboard and sheet foil, making it both silent and invisible.

Reverse-cycle air-conditioning Heating the

home in winter and cooling it in summer, it provides the cheapest form of heating with electricity and is ideal for cooler climates where the whole house needs to be heated for comfort.

ELECTRIC RADIATORS

There are few homes without ordinary one or two-bar electric radiators, or small fan-blown radiators. In warmer parts of the country they are all that is needed to take the chill off the air. They are a very expensive way to obtain long-term or large-area heating in your house, but are ideal for instant heat in the bedroom or, as a strip heater safely on the wall, in bathrooms.

NON-ELECTRICAL HEATING

Types of heating which do not involve electricity at any stage are open fireplaces, pot-belly stoves, solid fuel heaters, gas space heaters without fans or timers, kerosene heaters and liquid petroleum gas heaters (they use cylinders of gas).

Any of these would heat only one room at a time. Most methods of transferring the heat into other rooms rely on electrically-powered fans.

Many methods of heating which appear to use power other than electricity (that is, gas central heating), actually depend on electrically-powered fans and timers to control and move the heat through the home.

Fireplaces The appeal of the open fire has never quite disappeared. A large number of free-standing fireplaces are now available. These have the advantage of being easier to install, especially in an existing home where most of the heat disappears up the chimney.

A heat-retaining cover is also available. This is placed over the fire, regulating the amount of air that reaches the fire and converting the unit into a slow-combustion stove which makes fuel last longer.

Open fireplaces need to be screened to prevent sparks flying and young children need to be supervised.

Pot-belly stoves These are enjoying a revival. They have all the advantages of an open fire but have greater heat-giving properties. They will burn any solid fuel including newspapers. Coal is not recommended because it tends to build up too great an intensity of heat. Pot-belly stoves can heat areas from 50 to 180sq m and with extension rings, the range can be expanded. Many models can be fitted with 'wet backs' through which water from a nearby tank is circulated, providing domestic hot water.

SOLAR HEATING

There are two types of solar heating, passive and active.

Passive solar heating Such systems require your home to be specially designed and built to take advantage of the sun's heat.

Most existing homes would require extensive renovations to take full advantage of passive solar heating.

Active solar heating These systems involve constructing specific heat collectors, stores and ducting to distribute the sun's heat throughout your home.

Active solar heating systems need to be designed specifically to suit the house; no standard systems are available.

It is simple to install a solar system to provide hot water, but home heating is complex.

There are two main types of home heating. One involves solar heated water being circulated through the house. In the other, solar heated air is ducted through the house.

8

FIX IT YOURSELF

IT'S EMBARRASSING (and costly) to have to call a plumber every time you need a new tap washer. This section tells you how to mend fuses, change washers, replace fluorescent tubes, and carry out other small but vital repairs— the safe way. In most cases they are easy to fix, once you know how.

SAFETY FIRST

Statistics show that more accidents occur in the home than anywhere else. A large number of these home accidents occur when people are doing home repairs. Here are some safety rules:

Power tools Use only double insulated power tools. Regularly check leads and replace any frayed ones. Make sure drill bits are tight before turning on the drill. When using a power tool, keep the lead behind you. When sawing or drilling, make sure the work in hand is steady and can't slip or tip. When necessary wear goggles to protect your eyes. When using a power tool outdoors, don't let leads lie in pools of water. Have your power tools checked by the makers or their agents once a year.

Clothing Wear clothing which will protect arms and legs from scratches or blows and from getting paint or chemicals on skin. Always wear shoes, not thongs or sandals, both indoors and out.

Easy lifting Lifting heavy objects the wrong way is the sure way to damage your back. If possible, get help. Even when lifting weights within your capacity, do it the right way. Place your legs slightly apart so that the object is between them. Bend at the knees, grip the object firmly and, keeping back straight, straighten your legs slowly, letting leg and thigh muscles, not your back, take the strain.

Light and air Make sure your work area is well lit and ventilated. Install a fire extinguisher. Vapour from chemicals such as rust remover or paint stripper can injure the eyes. Wear protective goggles when working with them for any length of time. In small rooms which don't have good ventilation, use a portable fan to keep air moving. If you begin to feel dizzy, make for the open air.

Storage Keep bottles and cans of solvents or other chemicals on high shelves or locked up away from children. Never use old bottles, particularly soft drink ones, to store chemicals, unless you re-label them carefully and well.

Children Keep children and pets away from the workshop or anywhere you are working. If using power tools in the home, turn off the power and unplug the lead if you have to leave the job for any length of time. Don't leave chemicals or solvents unattended at all.

Roof repairs When scaling the family roof for cracked tiles, slates or leaking iron, a light-weight wooden ladder-like frame is necessary to prevent injury to life and limb. The frame also spreads your weight evenly, lessening danger of further damaging tiles, slates or of slipping on iron.

USING A LADDER

There are right and wrong ways of using a ladder, so follow these simple safety steps.

• When using a step ladder, always make sure the two sets of legs are on even ground; use wide timber chocks to even up the ladder on sloping surfaces and if possible, nail the chock to the floor to prevent it from slipping.

• An extension ladder should never be placed more than a quarter of its extended length from the wall. That means if the ladder is six metres high it should be about 1.5 metres from the wall at the base. Pieces of rubber tubing can be wrapped around the feet and fixed to the legs with flat-headed nails to give the feet greater grip.

• Do not try to carry bulky items like a large paint can or a tool kit up the ladder. It is safer to pull the gear up after you've climbed the ladder. Have a long length of rope you can take up with you, tied around your waist, then pull the gear up. On a step ladder, a very simple attachment can be made which provides a hand-hold at the top of the ladder as well as a trap in which to stand a paint tin, tools and such.

• When at the top of a ladder, keep your body between the uprights and don't be tempted to lean away from the ladder unless you can find a good hand-hold on something other than the ladder itself.

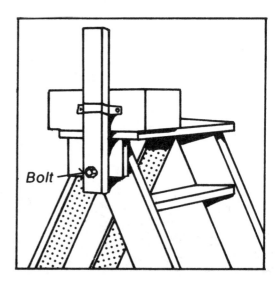

Bolt

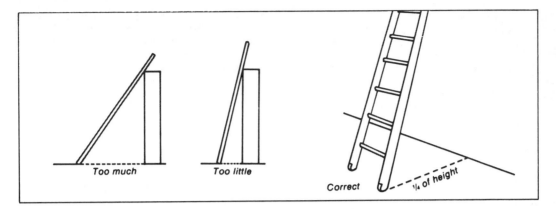

Too much   Too little

Correct   ¼ of height

• Be careful when handling long extension ladders, especially metal ones. When putting the ladder up or taking it down, watch that it won't foul power lines. This kind of mistake could kill you.

ELECTRICAL

MENDING A FUSE

When the power fails, check if the neighbour's lights are still on. If so, arm yourself with the equipment you will need to change a fuse. The basics are 8amp and 15amp fuse wire, a small but sturdy blade screwdriver, pliers or even scissors for wire snippers and a torch if it is dark.

Turn off the master switch in the fuse box to isolate the power and make it safe to carry out repairs. Remove and replace in turn each fuse plug until you find the faulty plug. The blown fuse will have a black scorch mark and a broken wire.

Loosen the screw at the end of each fuse plug and remove the pieces of broken wire. Cut a length of 8amp or 15amp fuse wire, according to what you need for the faulty plug. Plugs are usually placed separately under 'lights' (8amps) and 'power' (15amps).

Insert the wire into the plug and wind each end a few times under the loosened screws. Tighten screws over wire and snip off the ends of the wire. Replace repaired plug in socket and turn the master switch on.

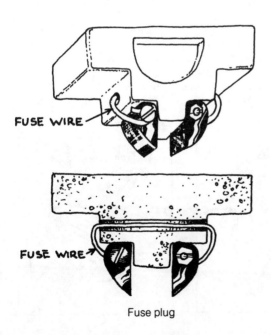

FUSE WIRE

FUSE WIRE

Fuse plug

LIGHTS   POWER

FUSE FUSE FUSE   FUSE FUSE

ON   ON   OFF
OFF

MAIN SWITCH   OFF PEAK HOT WATER SWITCH

Typical fuse box layout

If the fuse blows instantly the power is turned on again, turn off the master switch and call a qualified electrician.

For fast aned efficient repairs, leave lengths of fuse wire, a screwdriver, snippers and a diagram of how to wire a fuse in the fuse box so you are always prepared. Household fuse wire can be bought cheaply from the home repairs section of most stores.

CHANGING A PLUG ON A POWER LEAD

When plugs burn out or the cord becomes frayed where it enters the plug, it is necessary to rewire the plug, an easy job but one that must be done correctly and carefully to avoid serious consequences. Always unplug a lead before working on it.

You will need
Small screwdriver
Electrical insulating tape
Sharp knife
New plug if necessary

To rewire a plug, first remove the cover. On older plugs the cover is removed by taking out the small screws on the face of the plug where the pins are located. It's wise to replace with a modern plug. The modern plugs have a moulded one-piece plastic covering which must be pried off with the screwdriver to expose the terminals.

There are generally three wires in appliance and extension leads. The black wire is negative, the green wire is an earth wire and the red (positive) wire carries the current. On modern leads, colours are blue (negative), brown (positive), and yellow/green (earth).

Some leads may have only two wires, a black and a red. It is wise always to use an extension lead that has an earth wire.

The terminals in the plug should be marked with initials, E for earth, N for negative and P for positive. If there are no marks, use a felt pen to mark the earth and positive terminals **before** you remove the old wires.

When the plastic cover is removed, push it up the cord. Loosen the screws on the terminals and remove the wires. Cut the cord off clean, then pare away the outer plastic to expose the three wires. These are also covered with plastic which must be pared away to expose wire.

Twist each wire with the fingers to bind the strands together and stop fraying, then connect each wire to its correct terminal either by wrapping the wire around the terminal or poking it through a hole in the terminal, whichever system is used for that plug. Tighten the screws, then replace the plug cover.

FIXING A FLUORESCENT TUBE

Fluorescent lighting is efficient, long lasting and more economical than conventional incandescent (ordinary globe) lighting but there are times when a fluorescent tube breaks down, and to the average person, solving the problem of a faulty tube is more of a mystery than simply changing a light globe.

Important Always switch power off at the mains before doing any repairs or cleaning.

When the tube flickers Try turning the switch off then on again, as the trouble could be in the starter. This is a part that can be replaced with a new one. To remove the starter, turn it and allow it to drop into your hand from its socket. To see if the starter is faulty, you could replace it with a starter from another fluorescent fitting, if you have one in the house.

Another reason for flickering tubes could be that the metal pins at each end of the tube have become corroded or bent. If the pins are corroded, clean them by sanding lightly with fine sandpaper. A bent pin can be straightened

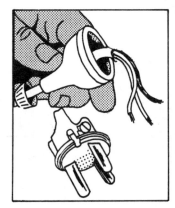
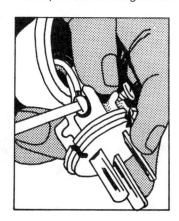

with pliers.

When the tube lights at one end The fault could again be in the starter. Try turning the tube around but be careful it doesn't come out of its socket and fall on the floor. If this fails you can check the starter by inserting a tube from another fixture. If this performs the same way the fault is in the starter. If the trouble persists after replacing the starter, have an electrician check the wiring in the fitting.

Whenever there's a problem with a tube, try a tube from another fitting first. This will tell you straight away whether the tube needs replacing. When changing a fluorescent tube, turn the tube carefully and slip it out of the slotted end first. When putting the tube in, insert the tube into the solid end first, slot the other end into the holder and turn carefully to lock it in. Slots should then be horizontal.

Note Some fluorescent fittings have slots at both ends; in this case either end can be removed or replaced first.

PLUMBING

UNBLOCKING SINKS AND DRAINS

It is often possible, and quite easy, to cope with blocked sinks and drains for yourself. However, if the simple methods shown here are not successful, the blockage could be a major one and will need the experience and equipment of a licensed plumber.

You will need
   Sink plunger
   Steel snake
   Wrench
   Bucket

First try clearing the blocked drain by flushing it with boiling water and ammonia, say a cup of ammonia to a bucket of water. If this doesn't work try the following:

In the case of a sink, place the rubber plunger over the opening tightly (smear some petroleum jelly around the edge of the rubber to get a better seal) and fill the sink with water to cover the plunger. Then pump the plunger up and down several times. If the blockage still remains, look for an obstruction in the S-bend. Put a bucket under the sink and loosen the slip nut with the wrench. This will release the pipe from under the sink. Now push the steel snake down into the pipe, allowing it to follow the bends in the pipe. If there is rubbish in the S-bend the snake will either push it out or catch it so that it can be withdrawn. Most bends have a drainage plug on the underside at the base of the S-bend. If there is a plug, undo this first to drain out any rubbish that may be trapped at the base of the bend, but put a bucket underneath the bend first.

When the bathroom sink is blocked, first check that the basin outlet is not clogged with soap and hair. Use a piece of wire with a hook bent into the end to scrape out the pipe just under the outlet.

Floor drains often become smelly and sometimes block up. If the drain is just smelly, tip a bucket or two of boiling water mixed with ammonia down the drain to flush it out. The plunger can be used to try to unblock a floor drain and if this does not work use the steel snake.

These snakes are flexible spring steel drain cleaners and are sold in various lengths. For average household use, a 3 metre snake would be sufficient. Drains need periodical cleansing and flushing with a proprietary brand of drain cleaner, as most household drains will be affected by a build-up of grease. Regular treatment with hot water and ammonia will also help to prevent clogging.

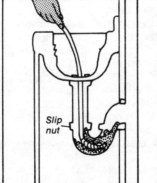
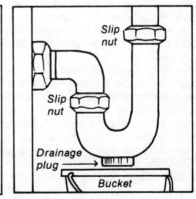

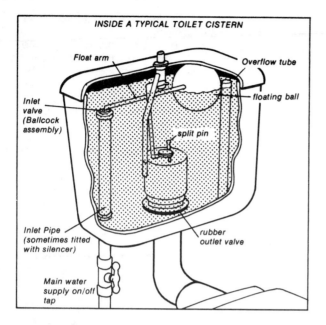

INSIDE A TYPICAL TOILET CISTERN

Float arm

Overflow tube

Inlet
valve
(Ballcock
assembly)

floating ball

split pin

Inlet Pipe
(sometimes fitted
with silencer)

rubber
outlet valve

Main water
supply on/off
tap

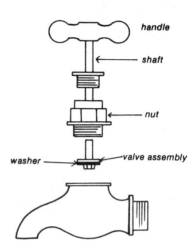

handle

shaft

nut

washer

valve assembly

OUTSIDE DRAINS

Older houses often have outside drain outlets covered with grilles. Keep the grille free of leaves which could block the pipe. Occasionally lift the grille to clean away sludge build-up around the outlet pipe. Wearing rubber gloves, scrape the walls of the pipe with an old piece of plywood or the edge of a flattened can. Pour boiling water and a handful of washing soda into drain to rinse clean. Scrub grille with hot water and washing soda. Replace grille, pour solution of water and disinfectant into drain. Throw out rubber gloves and scraping tool.

STOPPING A CISTERN OVERFLOWING

In most cases the cistern will overflow because the floating ball in the tank has not closed off the valve which stops the flow of water into the tank. This ball is attached to the valve by a lever, and when the water level in the tank reaches a certain height, the ball is raised and operates the lever which seats the valve over the inlet.

Sometimes an overflowing cistern can be fixed by simply bending the ball arm downwards. This will place the ball lower in the tank and therefore it will activate the shut-off valve sooner as the water rises. If this does not work, remove the ball to make sure it is hollow; if there is water inside the ball you will need to buy a new one.

If the cistern keeps running and the tank won't fill This could also be caused by a faulty

ball or the position of the ball in the tank. Try bending the arm again, slightly to the centre of the tank. If this still does not work, check to see whether any of the parts have come loose. If not, some of the parts could be worn and need replacing, especially the rubber washers on the outlet valve lifting mechanism. You can replace this washer by removing the suspension rod which is held by a split pin. Use pliers to remove the split pin then undo the nut holding the washer. If the nut has corroded and cannot be removed, take the part to a hardware store and buy a complete replacement.

Note It is illegal in many areas to attempt to repair any blockages in a toilet system yourself. If a blockage occurs, call a licensed plumber.

CHANGING A TAP WASHER

The illustration is of a conventional tap which is still common outdoors. In modern houses, and particularly in home units, however, there is great variety of taps. Some of these, such as mixer taps, are difficult for the home handyman to handle. There are many kinds of fixtures and replacement parts. It is probably useful to find out who made the taps and what model they are when you buy or build your house.

It is possible to change just the washer in a tap, but it is far easier to buy the valve assembly, which costs a few cents more and comprises the washer and valve in one unit. This is simply dropped into the tap when the old one is removed. Buy valve assemblies with leather washers for cold water taps and composition washers for hot water taps.

You will need
- Wrench
- New valve assembly
- Long-nosed pliers
- Insulating tape

If changing the washer on an indoor, modern tap, you may also need a pair of long-nosed pliers to lift out the old valve unit, as it is deep down and hard to grasp with the fingers.

To change the washers on any tap, first turn off the water at the main or on the hot water supply. In most suburban homes, the mains tap will be at the meter. For hot water tap, also turn off water supply at heating unit and turn off gas supply or electric power switch as well. Next, turn the tap to its fullest on position, then unscrew the nut at the base of the tap. In the case of outdoor taps the nut is located just below the handle shaft; in modern taps the nut is at the base of the tap or you may have to undo the nut at the top of the handle, remove the handle and the covering. When you dismantle the tap the valve assembly will be exposed. Lift it out and replace it with the new one. Then replace the handle assembly and tighten the nut. Turn the water on at the mains.

FIXING A SHOWER HEAD
The two main problems with shower heads are constant dripping and uneven spray, which could be due to poor design but is most likely to be caused by corrosion inside. Both dripping and corrosion can be fixed quite easily.

To fix dripping shower head The problem here is actually in the tap handles which control the shower, not in the head. The solution is to replace the washer, just as you would for an ordinary tap. If the drips after use are hot, it is the hot tap washer that needs replacing; if cold, replace washer of cold tap.

First turn off water supply at the main, or for hot water tap, turn off both water and gas or electricity at the hot water supply. Then replace washer. Remember to turn on water and heat supply afterwards.

To clean shower head
You will need
- A piece of fine wire
- Wrench

Blocked shower heads are a most annoying but common problem in the average household. The blocked holes result from corrosion due to acids in the water. If the shower head can be removed, take it off and wash it out in hot water and detergent. Clean out the holes with the wire. If the head cannot be removed you will have to stand in the shower and poke out the debris with the wire.

RECAULKING AROUND BATHS AND SINKS
When the mortar between tiles and the edge of a bath or sink crumbles and falls out, you can use a caulking compound to seal the joints again. These joints must be sealed to prevent water from getting down behind the wall and causing moisture and wood rot problems.

You will need
- Bathtub caulking compound
- Sharp knife or putty knife
- Turpentine and old, clean paint brush
- Clean rags

First scrape out the crumbly mortar and clean off all grease and dirt. Dip the brush in some mineral turps and brush along the crevice to clean it thoroughly and remove any grease. Dry the crevice well with clean, dry rag wrapped around the point of the knife.

The caulking compound can be applied in various thicknesses by choosing different heads on the tube nozzle. If the gap is a wide one, cut the nozzle off at its wide point; if a thin gap, make the cut to suit the thinner crevice. Generally, the thickness of the bead of caulking material should be slightly greater than the thickness of the gap it has to fill.

Now begin filling the joint, squeezing the caulking compound out in a continuous bead. It helps to have a wet rag handy to push the caulk into the gap. If you keep the rag wet, it will not stick to the compound. Excess compound can be trimmed off later with a razor blade when it dries.

Crevices around taps should be filled with a ceramic tile cement.

REPLACING BROKEN CERAMIC TILES
Cracked, broken or loose ceramic tiles are easily replaced. Be sure to match both tile and grouting colour carefully for a professional finish.

You will need
- An old screwdriver or cold chisel
- Tile adhesive
- Tile grout
- Masking tape
- Replacement tiles

First remove the remains of the old tile, being

careful not to damage the surrounding tiles.

Carefully chisel away the old cement so the new tile can be set into position properly.

Smear tile adhesive on the back of the tile and on the wall and press the tile into place.

Use masking tape in a criss-cross fashion to hold the tile against the wall.

Leave for 24 hours and then remove masking tape.

Now mix a small amount of tile grout and press into the joints around the tile. Clean off excess grout with a damp sponge.

ADHESIVES

There is a vast quantity of adhesives on the market. They have some' main categories. These include:

• Clear adhesives which can cope with many simple household and hobby tasks but may not stand up to tough water and heat conditions.

• Contact adhesives which are often used for joining sheet materials.

• Epoxy resins which give tough joins and good heat and water resistance but don't work well with plastics.

There are also the cyanoacrylate adhesives which bond in seconds.

Many households also make good use of sealants to fill gaps and joins and keep out water, dust and draughts. There is usually some movement between the two surfaces. Sealers either cure to a flexible material which is elastic or remain soft so they can give and take. Curing types usually last longer but are more expensive.

As well, today's hardware shop has an arresting array of substances for special jobs.

If in doubt, explain the job in hand at your hardware store and be guided by the experts.

NUTS AND BOLTS

Coat stubborn nuts and bolts with a little oil or vinegar and leave for a while. They should free more easily.

A simple rule to make it easier to tighten or loosen nuts and bolts or screws from a difficult angle: left is loose, right is tight.

Tighten a cabinet or dresser knob by dipping

its screws in fingernail polish or shellac and reinserting the knob.

Or, wrap strands of steel wool around the screw or push steel wool into the hole. Another method is to dip the screw in nail polish, shellac or coat with putty.

If a tight screw won't loosen, heat the edge of a screwdriver to its hottest point.

Or, put a few drops of peroxide on the screw. Leave to soak in for a few minutes.

Use hot nails in plaster to prevent cracks. Keep the nails warm in a bucket of hot water and use each one as you take it out.

When pulling nails with a claw hammer, protect the wall or board beneath the hammer by slipping a scrap of wood or a spatula under the hammer head.

Hammer decorative furniture tacks without damaging the head by placing a wooden spool on the tack.

Nails are less likely to bend when they are driven into hard wood if they are pushed into a cake of soap first.

Use plasticine or a ball of rubber poster adhesive to hold nail straight when hammering.

HELPFUL HINTS

To stop a door from squeaking, sprinkle talcum powder on hinges.

Or, rub with dry soap or petroleum jelly.

Non-stick vegetable spray will lubricate squeaky hinges, sticky locks and bicycle chains.

Talcum powder in the cracks between floor boards stops squeaks.

To cure dangerous and squeaky loose floor boards, use a hammer and nail punch to drive down fixing nails. If this doesn't work, drill holes next to the nails and fix boards with countersunk head woodscrews.

Set the short leg of a wobbly table or chair on a small amount of plastic wood on waxed paper. Allow to dry. Trim with a sharp knife and smooth with sandpaper.

Wobbly chair legs may be strengthened by wrapping the loose end with a small strip of nylon before applying glue. You can buy wood expanders to achieve the same result.

To silence a drip overnight, tie to the tap a piece of string long enough to reach the drain. Water will run silently down the sink.

Or, wrap a cloth around the tap.

To mend a leaking vase, coat the inside with

a thick layer of paraffin wax and allow to harden. The wax will last indefinitely.

Or, paint over the crack on the inside with clear nail varnish.

Sticking drawers will slide easily again if you rub candle wax or soap on the runner of the side that seems to be stricking.

ONE PAIR OF HANDS

Most jobs are easier when they are shared but there are some tricks to make it easier to do things with one pair of hands.

• To hold one end of a curtain rod, wardrobe rod, moulding and so on while you attach the other end, tape it to the wall with masking tape or suspend it in a loop of string from a nail.

• To hold screws, nuts, brads in awkward positions, stick them in place with modelling clay. Don't use clay on porous surfaces which might absorb oil from the clay.

• If you have no one to hand you tools while you are up a ladder, wear an apron with big pockets which can hold your hammer, tape measure, screwdriver, pencil, nails or whatever.

• To hold a light-weight wall cabinet upright while you screw it to the wall, move a table against the wall then stack books or boxes on it to the right height for the cabinet.

• To keep a door from sagging while you take off the hinges, stand a piece of scrap timber on the floor and clamp it to the door to prop the door up as the hinges come off.

• To keep a sheet of pressed hardboard, or plywood rigid while you saw down the middle, support on two chairs or on whatever you have that will work like sawhorses. Saw between the supports. At about halfway, slip a board under the cut part from chair to chair to keep the sheet from sagging while you finish the job.

STICKY TAPE

You may not feel confident about major repairs about the house but there are some useful things you can do with nothing more complex than a roll of masking tape.

• To hold glued pieces together, wrap the whole object, or the broken part of it, in masking tape until the glue dries.

• To paint a straight line, put two pieces of masking tape across the area and paint between them.

• To keep pictures, posters or groups of pictures hanging straight, put a snip of double-sided foam tape on the back of frames. You can also buy small tabs to do the same job at less cost than a whole roll.

• To stop pipes from sweating wrap in insulating tape which is made with aluminium-covered foam. This will save heat loss.

• To make light switches, bicycles, fire-escape routes glow in the dark, mark with luminous tape.

• To fasten two ends of a cord, rope or electrical wire together without a knot, wrap with electrical tape. There is also a heat-shrink tape that shrinks around the item when you hold a lighted candle or match under it.

• To keep fly-open cupboard doors closed, snip a couple of pieces of magnetic tape and stick them on the door and frame to serve as a magnetic catch for the doors.

• To finish off ugly edges of shelves, press strips of iron-on wood veneer tape with a hot iron, or cover the edges with metallic tape.

• To stick plastic hooks, paper-cup dis-spensers and so on back on the wall, use pieces of double-sided foam tape.

• To put up fake moulding, get some wood-grained plastic tape and apply to walls or furniture.

• To keep rugs and mats from slipping, use a double-faced carpet tape.

DECORATING TIPS

HOME DECORATING can be expensive but it doesn't have to cost the earth, especially if you're prepared to do some of the work yourself. Freshly painted or papered walls and attractive curtains, cushions and loose covers will give a lift to any room.

If funds are limited it's worth haunting secondhand shops and auctions for furniture and knick-knacks. These can be much cheaper than new goods, and often have more charm and character.

PAINTING AND WALLPAPERING

Careful preparation is the secret to successful painting and papering. Unless surfaces are adequately prepared the end results will not last long.

GETTING A PAINTER IN

Major paintwork on your house involves major expenditure. It is useful to know how to deal with a professional painter and how to get a quotation satisfactory to both of you.

Most of the cost in a professional repainting job is labour, and most of that labour must be invested in preparation. On the basis of maintenance costs alone it makes sense to use quality material and save labour costs by extending the life of the paint job. Another argument for high-quality paint is that frequent applications of poor-quality paint become too

heavy a load for the initial coat to bear. Therefore, the old paint system may have to be totally removed. This is time-consuming and expensive.

It is important to agree on all details of the job and have it set down in writing before work begins.

When you have made your decisions, list every surface you want painted, the type and brand of paint you want and the colours you have chosen. This will make it easier for the painter to give you an accurate quotation, allow you to compare prices if you get more than one quotation and give you a permanent record when you want to touch up or repaint

in the future.

When you get your quotation from the painter look for these points:

• Surface preparation and what is involved.

• The paint system, area by area, with details of number of coats, brand, type and colour of paint.

• Special requirements, such as use of fungicidal treatments.

• Price, time for completion and terms of payment.

His quotation should also provide for:

• Ensuring the protection of carpets and furnishings, paths and shrubbery.•

• Removing obstructions to get to the surfaces needing painting.

• Cleaning up after the job.

Some painters ask for a progress payment to cover outgoings while the job is being done. This should be negotiated before the job begins. Also make sure the painter is insured to protect you in case of accident while working on your property. He should also carry liability insurance against damage to your property or that of others.

You might also like to ask each painter from whom you are getting a quotation the names of some recent clients as references.

DOING YOUR OWN PAINTING

PREPARATION

The time you spend in preparation will show in the finished job. It is tedious and hard work, but once it is out of the way, painting is easy. First empty the room. If this isn't possible, pile what can't be removed into the middle and cover. Protect fitted carpet, tiles or polished boards with a dust sheet or polythene taped to the skirting board.

Equipment Vacuum cleaner, brush, detergent, rubber gloves, old sheets or dustcloths, bucket, wire brush, wire wool, various grades of sandpaper, white cellulose filler, putty knife, damp cloth. If necessary, paint stripper and stripping knife.

Cleaning Surfaces can be cleaned by vacuuming, dusting, or scrubbing with detergent. Strip off peeling wallpaper and wire-brush loose plaster and paint. Sand down gloss or semi-gloss paint with an abrasive paper to provide a key for new paint. Test a corner to see that wallpaper pattern does not bleed through the new paintwork. If necessary, seal with primer. Also test that solvents in the paint will not dissolve the old wallpaper glue—you may need to remove it. Paint build-up on old woodwork will have to be stripped off. Use a commercial paint stripper, and make sure your hands and the floor are well protected from the burning caustic. Alternatively, use a blow torch. Do a small area at a time. When the paint begins to blister, scrape off immediately with a stripping knife. Keep flame away from glass, asbestos and plaster.

Cracks Anything larger than a hairline crack should be filled with white cellulose filler. Force mix into crack or hole and smooth over with a putty knife or damp cloth. When dry, smooth with medium-fine sandpaper. Fill larger holes in stages, allowing a few hours drying time between applications. Sand smooth. Rub down metal in good condition with turps to remove grease. Lightly sand a gloss paint finish. Apply a wire brush or wire wool to rusty metal, then paint areas with a rust-inhibiting primer.

New work Plaster, concrete and brick needs three months to dry out before applying gloss paint. You can apply a plastic or emulsion paint as a temporary measure which allows the plaster to breathe. New timber must be sanded and primed before painting. New particle board should be primed and lightly sanded.

PAINTING

There are definite steps to follow when painting. Start with the ceiling, then walls, windows and doors. Always carry a damp rag to wipe away

spatters as they occur. Always wash or clean brushes and rollers immediately you have stopped work.

The paint Water base paints are the easiest to use, but are not always suitable for the job. Stick to a good quality paint—the work will last longer. Cheaper paints tend to be rather thin and need more coats. Mix according to instructions on tin and pour some paint into the painting tray or bucket for easier handling.

Ceilings Always start at the window end of the room. If using a roller, paint the edges and corners first with a 2.5cm brush, then cover the main surface with alternating diagonal strokes, leaving no uncovered patches. Do only a small area at a time, then go back over the work with vertical strokes for a smooth look. If working with a brush, paint in 60cm wide strips. Every metre or so work back over wet paint to eliminate lines.

Walls Try to complete entire wall in one session. Paint in strips about 60cm wide, starting at the top and working downwards. Aim to join up the new paint before the previous strip dries.

Windows There are definite steps to follow when painting windows.

Casements should be painted from the inside mouldings (where the glass touches the frame) then the cross bars, the frame and the architrave (surround). Use masking tape to avoid getting paint on the glass.

Sash windows are a little more difficult. Raise the lower sash as high as it will go and pull the upper sash about halfway down, paint the exposed interior part of the window frame. Next almost close the window and continue painting. Use thin paint for the inside runner

to reduce the risk of sticking. Finally paint the architrave. Do not get paint on the sashcord. Never let windows dry fully shut or they will stick.

Doors Again there is a strict sequence to be observed. Do the job in one session. If panelled, do the panel sections first, then mouldings, the door itself and finally the architrave.

Skirting Mask floorboards with tape to avoid picking up dirt and dust on the paintbrush.

HELPFUL HINTS

To banish paint smells Leave a large dish of water and a tablespoon of ammonia in the room overnight. Or, leave a large cut onion in the pan of water instead of ammonia and it will absorb smells.

To remove paint spatters Nail polish remover will take off paint spatters on windows. Soak for a few moments then rub off with a cloth and wash with warm soapy water.

Or, soften old stains with turpentine or linseed oil and wipe off or scrape with a razor blade. This will also remove putty stains.

For fresh paint stains, a hot vinegar solution works. Or, try steel wool dipped in liquid cleanser.

Baby oil is good for removing paint from the face and hands.

To prevent paint spatters Glue a paper plate under a paint tin so it overlaps the base. This stops drips sticking the tin to the floor.

Prevent drops from landing on your head when painting the ceiling by sticking the paint brush through the centre of a paper plate and taping.

Tie plastic bags around light fixtures to prevent paint marking them.

Coat woodwork with lemon oil before painting walls and paint speckles will rub off easily.

Smear petroleum jelly on hinges, locks and doornobs before painting surrounding areas to eliminate scraping afterwards.

When painting window frames, spread damp strips of newspaper around each window pane, making sure the straight edges of paper fit tightly into corners and edges. The paper will cling until you have finished painting. Peel off the strips—and the paint splashes too.

Softened soap or petroleum jelly rubbed around window panes does the same job, or liquid detergent applied with a paint brush and allowed to dry.

Before beginning a paint job, coat your fingernails with bar soap for a fast clean-up afterwards.

Paint the insides of cupboards first, then tops and sides, doors last to prevent smudging.

Prevent drips when painting drawers by taking the drawers out and painting them standing face up.

When using paint stripper on furniture with legs, put tin cans under each leg to catch drips.

When painting wire screens Spread paint on one side only. Use a dry brush for the other side as enough paint works through the mesh.

Before painting a chair Lightly drive a nail into the bottom of the legs. The chair will rest on the nails and you can paint quite freely.

To clean paint brushes Pour solvent into a plastic bag and insert the brush. Work the solvent through the plastic and your hands will stay clean.

If you need to leave your paint brush for a short while and don't want to clean it, wrap it in foil to keep soft.

Soak a new paint brush in a can of linseed oil before using. It will be easier to clean and last longer.

Simmer very dirty paint brushes in boiling vinegar for half an hour, then wash in strong soap suds.

When cleaning brushes with paint thinner, pour thinner into a lidded tin. After removing brushes, replace lid and leave tin a few days. Paint will settle on the bottom and the clean thinner can be poured off.

Don't let paint brushes rest on their bristles in a tin of solvent. They will bend and lose their shape. Suspend them on a piece of wire slipped through the holes in the handles.

Use fabric softener in the final rinse after cleaning brushes and rollers to help them stay soft and pliable.

Write down the colour and amount of paint used in each room in an inconspicuous place on more-or-less permanent furniture in each room, for example, under the kitchen table or inside a drawer.

Storing paint Oil-based paint will stay fresh if you add 4 tablespoons of mineralised methylated spirits to the top layer of the paint before

storing. Do not stir into the paint until you use it again.

Press a disc of aluminium foil directly on the surface of paint before storing a can of leftover paint to prevent skin forming. Put the can on the foil and draw around it for the right size.

To prevent white paint from yellowing, stir in a drop of black paint. Mix thoroughly.

Before replacing a lid on a paint tin, mark the level on the outside of the tin with a felt pen. You can then tell at a glance if there is enough paint in the tin to complete a job.

Putty Mix putty with the paint that matches the woodwork before puttying around windows.

Putty will not harden if you wrap it in a rag soaked in linseed oil and place it in an airtight jar. Renew the linseed oil occasionally.

If you fill holes in wood with putty instead of powdered filler, gloss paint applied to the surface stays glossy.

To remove coats of paint Use 2½ cups of turpentine mixed with 1 litre of ammonia. Rub on vigorously with a strong, coarse cloth. A brush may be necessary for stubborn patches. If the first application gives spotty results, apply a second coating.

To help cut odours as you paint Mix 2 teaspoons of vanilla essence with each 1.5 litres of paint.

To obtain a better coverage If using only one final coat of paint on an interior wall, tint the white undercoat with a little of the finishing colour.

Painting in cold weather Often this is harder as the paint becomes more difficult to work. Before painting, stand tin in hot water to stir. Don't put tin directly on gas or hotplate.

When paint has bits of skin in it Cut a piece from an old pair of pantyhose and secure loosely over top of can. Dip paint brush into paint through material—skin will be no problem.

Concrete or metal Paint won't peel so readily from concrete floors or metal surfaces if you paint them with vinegar first.

Stairs You can use a stairway while painting it. Paint alternate steps.

Working on wallpaper Slice blisters on wallpaper neatly with a sharp razor blade and spread some paste underneath with a table knife to flatten paper.

Tear wallpaper when you are patching walls and it won't be as noticeable as when it's cut.

WALLPAPERING PREPARATION

Make you first attempts on a wall that has a decent surface and a minimum number of obstacles. Pile furniture in the centre of the room away from work area and cover. For best results—take it slowly. Don't paper new plaster for at least six months as the plaster needs to dry out. New plasterboard can be sealed with primer, then hang lining paper as a backing.

Sanding Lightly sand painted surfaces and wash. Sand gloss paints to a dull finish. If paint is flaking, fill with white cellulose compound, sand and seal. Previously papered surfaces need to be stripped completely first. Soak old paper thoroughly until paste is soft. Scrape off, being careful not to dig into the wall beneath. Wash off old paste. Fill cracks and holes with patching compound then sand lightly.

Size This prevents a wall from absorbing water from the paste too quickly, giving you time to reposition the wallpaper if necessary. Leave it to dry thoroughly and sand lightly. It can be bought at a hardware shop and comes in powder form to be mixed with water. Follow instructions carefully.

Choosing wallpaper Make allowance for patterns when calculating the number of rolls. More wallpaper will be needed if the design requires matching. Check that paper comes from the same batch to ensure colour uniformity; each roll carries matching letters after its design numbers. Check the direction of the pattern carefully before applying each strip. Put a pencil mark at the top of each drop when you cut it to avoid hanging a strip upside down. Beware of wallpapers which must be left with paste soaking on them for long periods: they stretch alarmingly. Thin wallpaper tends to tear and get paste stains. Most wallpaper is sold ready trimmed. If it isn't, get the supplier to do it for you as it is quite a difficult job.

How much wallpaper? Work out how many drops you can get from one roll (usually three from ceiling to floor). Work out how many widths you need per wall, allowing for pattern matching. Have a little left over for future repairs.

Tools Pasting table 180 x 60cm; pasting brush —about 6cm wide (you can use either a roller or a paint brush); large firm sponge for smoothing down wallpaper; roller (optional); paste bucket; plumb line for marking verticals to align edges; easy-trim knife with snap-off

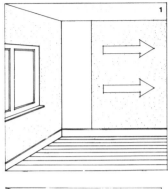 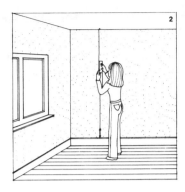 

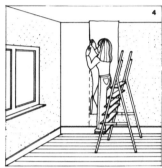  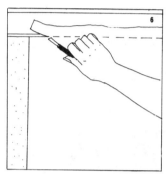

blades and metal straightedge for trimming; pencil; long metal tape measure; sponge and clean cotton rags; scissors; and adhesive. Check with your supplier for the most suitable type.

HANGING WALLPAPER

There are many different wallpapers on the market and some are much easier to hang than others. Pre-pasted wallpapers are the easiest for beginners to use. If you are using wallpaper which must have paste applied, buy adhesive paste which does not stain.

1. It's generally agreed that the best spot to start on is the part of the room that first catches your eye as you walk in, which is usually a chimney breast (if you have one) or next to a window. Ceilings are papered from the window end, as in painting.

2. Drop a plumb line and mark a vertical line on the wall with a pencil—this will give the starting line for the first drop of paper.

3. Cut paper to length of wall with a 10cm allowance each end for trimming. If the paper has a pattern, line up the next sheet with the pattern matching up horizontally and cut to the same length.

Put the bundle of cut lengths on the pasting table, face side down, with the top edge of the wallpaper on your right and the bottom over-lapping. Apply paste evenly down the middle of the strip and then smooth out to the edges. If the paper is longer than the table, pick up the two top corners of the already pasted part and lightly fold back on itself, then pull it along the table and apply paste to the rest of the length. Continue in this way to the end of the paper; when it is fully pasted it will give a concertina effect. It's a good idea to leave one sheet soaking as you hang another.

4. Hold the two top corners and place the paper on the wall next to the pencilled plumb line, with 10cm overlap at the top.

5. Stick the paper to the wall and, using a large sponge, stroke firmly from the centre to the edges.

6. Trim cornices and skirting overlap with the easy-trim knife and lift off excess paper.

7. As you place each additional length of paper on the wall, use the roller to stick the edges firmly down. They should butt up to each other, not overlap.

DIFFICULT AREAS

Corners When you arrive at a corner, cut the sheet narrower so that about 1cm wraps around the corner. Use your plumb line to make sure you get a straight line.

Light switches or ceiling roses Make a series of cuts from centre of switch in a star pattern. Trim and smooth down.

Doors and windows Hang paper so that it overlaps. Gently run down the side of the architrave with the blunt part of the scissors and cut along the line. Smooth back onto wall, pressing the edge of the paper into the angle of the wall and architrave.

READY-PASTED WALLPAPER
Follow the preceding instructions, but in Step 3, cut the paper to size, reroll and place in water trough. Feed the top under the guide wire and draw up slowly, wetting front and back. Heavily embossed paper will need more immersion time to allow the paper to expand fully and become limp in the water trough.

SOFT FURNISHINGS

Perhaps more than anything else, curtains, cushions and covers help to turn a house into a home. Making your own can save you hundreds of dollars.

COVERS

It is inadvisable to undertake loose covers and other furnishings until you are a reasonably experienced sewer. If you make a bad mistake, you may be ruining several hundred dollars worth of fabric. Begin with cushions and throw-over bedspreads and work up to major loose covers. Also, take time and care in selection of fabrics and colours; these are things you will have to live with for several years.

LOOSE COVER FOR CHAIR OR SOFA
Furniture to be covered should be fully uphol-stered with space to tuck loose cover between back and seat and sides and seat. Choose a firm, closely woven fabric. If you are a beginner choose a plain one so that matching does not present too many problems. Velvet is not suit-able for loose covers.

If the chair or sofa has a loose cover, remove and use as pattern. Otherwise cut your pattern from an old sheet. Then make a cutting diagram to estimate the quantity of fabric needed.

Pattern pieces Take a strip of fabric and lay over inside back (1). Cut to fit shape, allow 1.5cm at top and sides, 11cm tuck-in at bottom. Follow same procedure for seat (2), allowing 11cm tuck-in at back and sides, 1.5cm at front. Repeat with inside arms (3), leaving 1.5cm at top and sides, 11cm at

bottom. Measure and cut strip for top and front of arms (arm border 4) allowing 1.5cm on all sides. Measure and cut outside arm (5), then apron (6), top (8), if required, back (9). Pin pieces together on chair as they are cut.

Snip all seam allowances almost to pins, so that when cover is opened out sections can be re-matched at notches for sewing. Remove from chair, unpin and open out. Sew piping to sections, snipping cord about 1.5cm from ends to form flat piping where crossed by a seam.

Using double row of stitching, make up the

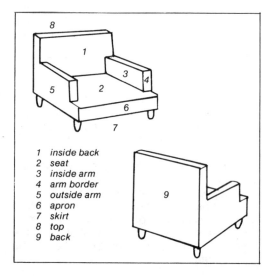

1 inside back
2 seat
3 inside arm
4 arm border
5 outside arm
6 apron
7 skirt
8 top
9 back

cover in sections in the same order as it was cut out. Join back to outside arm on one side, leaving other side free for zipper or velcro tape.

Turn cover right side out and place on chair. **Skirt** (7) should be cut 20.5cm deep (for finished depth of 14cm, plus 1.5cm seam and 5cm for double 2.5cm hem). Length of strip for skirt should be equal to bottom measurement of chair, plus 20cm for each inverted pleat (one at each corner for chair, plus one centre front for sofa). If there are seams they should fall under pleats.

Measure up 13cm from floor on loose cover, mark with chalk and cut off excess. Remove cover and sew piping cord around base. Sew double 2.5cm hem on skirt, sew skirt to bottom edge of cover as for fitted bedspread. See p. 147.

PIPING

One of the ways to add a professional finish to your home accessories is with first-class piping. It may be fine or bold depending on the dimensions of the cord and type of fabric used. It may be attached to straight seams, curves or square corners or used as an insert.

Use a zipper foot. Do all stitching on the underside of a garment. Clip piping seam allowance to 6mm, garment and facing allowances to 6mm.

Making bias strips The first step is to cut bias strips. These are cut on the true bias (see diagrams) which is formed by folding the crosswise grain of the fabric onto the lengthwise grain. The width of the strips should be three times the width of the chosen cording plus 3cm. Join bias strips on the lengthwise grain using 6mm seams (see diagrams); press seams open after sewing.

Sewing corded piping Fold the bias strip around the cord, wrong sides together, and sew close to the cord using a zipper foot and a long stitch.

Piping a straight seam Pin the piping to the edge of the fabric on the right side; line up the previous stitching line with the seamline (usually 1.5cm from the edge) and stitch along this line again, with the zipper foot adjusted to the right side of the needle.

Attach the second seam edge (or facing) over the piping with the right sides together. Stitch between the cord and the previous line of stitching. Press.

UPHOLSTERING A CHAIR

Whether you tackle such a task yourself depends on how much sewing experience you have had. It would be unwise to learn on valuable antiques.

There is great variety in shapes of armchairs but some basic rules of measuring and fitting apply. Fabrics with a repeating pattern or nap (such as velvet) must be cut carefully. Motifs must be centred on the back and seat and match on the arms. Nap must fall the same way or light will reflect unevenly.

First, measure front of chair from top to lower back, brace, pushing tape measure between seat and back of chair. Measure front at widest part of chair.

For the seat, measure from front of seat, between seat and back of chair through to back brace. Then measure from one lower side brace to the other, pushing the tape measure between seat and arms of chair.

Measure from top back of chair to lower back brace and across widest part of back of chair. Remember to add allowance for generous tucks on all measurements, and add the measurements together to determine the quantity of fabric you will need.

If the springs in your chair are sagging, remove back and bottom covers. Replace the webbing, stretching it across the chair as tightly as possible. Slip existing springs underneath and sew in place with strong thread. This will restore the shape of the chair. If there are any loose covers over the original upholstery, remove them.

Treat wood if necessary.

When tacking use a very small hammer and

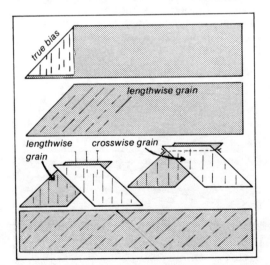

keep material taut. Put an anchoring tack at each end of rows, then fill in tacks between.

Cut fabric for the front and back of the chair. Place together, right sides facing. Tack them across the wooden brace at the top of the back of the chair. Smooth the front section down and push it between the back and seat of the chair pulling to the back evenly and tightly. Tack onto wooden brace. Trim each side of the chair's front cover to the shape of the chair allowing about 3cm to tuck under. Tack in place, easing the fabric evenly around the curves.

Cut fabric for seat. Place fabric face down on the seat, pin. Pin each corner to fit snugly. Cut fabric to fit around arms, allowing generous tuck. Remove fabric from chair and machine darts. Trim off excess. Turn right side out and fit onto chair tautly, securing with tacks. Darts must fit corners neatly.

Push fabric through to back of chair and tack along lower brace. Pull side flaps through, tack along bottom edge.

Place fabric for sides and arms of chair together as for back and front of chair. Tack together along the underside of arms. Cut off excess arm cover, curving to the shape of arm join, leaving plenty of tuck. Pull the arm cover between arm and seat sections, and tack fabric onto the arm brace. Pull the straight side cover down and tack along lower side brace. Tack the front sections of the arms in place.

Cut two narrow pieces to fit the sides of the back of chair. Place the fabric in position wrong side out. Tack in place. Fold the material back, right side out, and tack behind the chair. Bring the back piece of the chair cover down and tack.

Use braid to cover the rows of exposed tacks or make your own from 3cm-wide strips of left-over material. Cut on the bias for the chair's curves.

Lay each strip on an ironing board, face down. Fold the edges together and iron into place. Slip nozzle of glue bottle under each flap and slide down the fabric squeezing gently. Press edges together firmly. Anchor the strips for each section of the chair with a hidden tack. Hold the other end of the strip and squeeze a trail of glue along the underside. Stick to conceal all tacks.

DIVAN COVER
Divan beds make great day-time sofas in teen-agers bedrooms, bed-sitting rooms, or in family-rooms. Fit them with a tailored cover to hide bedding, plus bolsters for back support, and colour match them to other furnishings in the room. If divan is to be left made up with bedding, make it up before measuring to calculate size of cover. Fabric should be of close weave, to withstand use as a sofa.

To calculate fabric

Top of divan: A+2.5cm by B+2.5cm (cut 1).

Boxing strips with attached skirt: A+2.5cm by C+2.5cm (cut 2). B+2.5cm by C+2.5cm (cut 2).

Boxing strips tucked in: A+2.5cm by C+2.5cm+25cm (cut 2). B+2.5cm by C+2.5cm+25cm (cut 2).

Attached skirt with inverted corner pleats: A+2.5cm+40cm by D+6.25cm (cut 2). B+2.5cm+40cm by D+6.25cm (cut 2).

Attached skirt with box pleats all round: 2.5cm+3 x A by D+6.25cm (cut 2). 2.5cm+3 x B by D+6.25cm (cut 2).

Piping (if required) can be added around top of cover, down corner seams of boxing strips, and between boxing strips and attached skirt. Calculate lengths required and make piping. Sew piping to right side of top, raw edges matching.

To make up Pin boxing strips to cover top over piping, right sides together; leave overhang at corners for seam allowance. Pin corner seams of boxing strips, right sides together, inserting a piping strip first if required. Place cover on divan and adjust fit if needed. Sew ends of boxing strips. Sew boxing strip to top of cover over piping cord so that no stitching shows. Stitch piping to bottom edge of boxing strip, right side up, raw edges matching.

Sew strips in one continuous length. Make 2.5cm double hem on one edge. Measure and pin pleats along other edge (10cm folds for inverted corner pleats; box pleats evenly spaced to fit box sides). Stitch tape along pleats, then pin and sew to box sides.

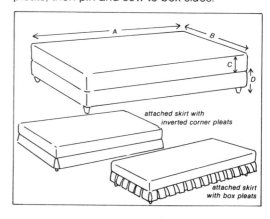

attached skirt with inverted corner pleats

attached skirt with box pleats

THROWOVER BEDSPREAD

To calculate fabric required Make up the bed with sheets, blankets and pillows. Measure length from the bedhead over the pillows, down the bed to the floor. Add 45cm for pillow tuck-in, and 10cm for a 2.5cm double hem top and bottom. (If you want wider hems allow desired width.) Measure width from floor on one side of bed, up and over bed, down to floor on other side. Add hem allowances. Depending on the width of the bed, and of the fabric, you will probably need to join panels of fabric. Divide the width of the chosen fabric into the width of the spread to give you the number of lengths to buy. If the fabric is patterned, allow extra for the pattern repeat.

Joining panels To hang properly the spread should have a central panel with a panel on either side, rather than a central join which will drag. Decide on the finished width for the centre panel, plus seam allowance; cut from one length of fabric. Seams should fall at the edge or just in from the edge of the bed. To calculate width of side panels deduct width of centre panel from the total width required. Cut side panels, allowing for seams. Join the side panels to either side of the centre panel, using open seams if spread is to be lined, french seams if it is to be unlined. Remember to match pattern.

Corners of spread These can be left square or curved to clear the floor. To mark curved corners lay spread on bed and mark corner of mattress (A). Measure from here to floor (B). Remove spread and draw arc as shown; cut off excess, allowing for hem. Turn under and sew a double 2.5cm hem all round; ease at curved corners or mitre squared corners.

Lining Make in the same way as spread, with same size centre panel, but 5cm narrower and 5cm shorter than spread. Slip-stitch lining to spread, wrong sides together, along outer edge of panel seams. Turn under 1.25cm around outer edge, press, slip-stitch to hem of spread.

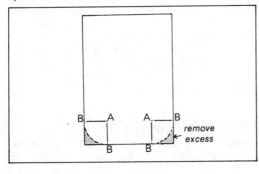

FITTED BEDSPREAD

Calculate fabric for drops as given below. Make a cutting diagram of pattern pieces to calculate amount of fabric; allow for pattern repeat or one-way design.

A reverse sham This can be joined to top of spread to cover and tuck under pillows. Sham should be full width of spread, or at least 30cm wider than top of bed to cover pillows at the side. Measure around pillows, add 2.5cm for seams and at least 20cm for tuck-in. Add this to amount of fabric required. Panel joins, if needed, should match panels of spread.

Reverse sham lining Cut sham and lining same size, panel seams matching. Sew with right sides together, using 1.25cm seams; leave small section open. Turn right side out, slip-stitch opening. Lay sham over top end of spread, wrong sides together, with spread and sham lying away from each other. Sew across overlap, securing ends.

For piped edging Make piping; sew to right side of bedspread top, raw edges matching, before joining drops.

Drops with inverted corner pleats Measure a strip equal to twice length of bed, plus width, plus 80cm for pleats, plus 10cm for hems, **by** height of bed from floor, plus 6.25cm for hem and seam. Cut fabric and join panels as necessary. Pin drop to top of spread, into lower corner. Fold back 10cm and pin, fold drop back to the corner and pin through 3 layers, forming half the inverted pleat. Reverse the process for second half of pleat. Repeat process at other corner. Tack pleats in place, making sure they are even, then sew drop to top panel. Sew double hem around drops and across top of spread. Press pleats.

Gathered drops Measure a strip equal to 4 times length of bed, plus twice width, plus 10cm for hems, **by** height of bed from floor, plus 6.25cm for hem and seam. Cut fabric and join strips as required. Hem one long edge, gather other, and pin to bedspread top, right sides together, easing gathers evenly. Sew with 1.25cm seam. Press.

Lining If required, make in the same manner, attach as for throwover spread.

CONTINENTAL QUILT COVER AND MATCHING SKIRT FOR BED

Fabrics A continental quilt cover for a single bed can be made from one width of 122cm wide fabric; for a double, queen or king size quilt two widths will be required, sewn together in panels, as for a throwover bedspread. You can make a 'wardrobe' of covers to match curtains, in contrasting or matching plain fabric, in smaller or larger print of the same colour, or in a positive/negative combination. Top and bottom of quilt cover can be the same or toning fabric.

Measure and make up Measure the length and width of your quilt and cut two cover pieces, adding 2.5cm to the width for side seams, 6.25cm to the length for top seam and opening at the base. If necessary cut centre and two side panels to match the width, allowing for seams where panels join.

With right sides together sew around two sides and across top of quilt, using 1.25 cm seam. Neaten edges and press seams open. Sew a 5cm seam at either side of bottom edge, leaving 50–70cm centre opening through which to insert the quilt. Neaten raw edges across entire bottom edge of quilt cover, turning under a double handkerchief hem across opening. Turn quilt right side out, press out corners. Sew press studs or velcro tape across opening, insert quilt. No top sheet is required with a continental quilt; bed-making is reduced to smoothing the bottom sheet and fluffing up the quilt.

Skirt If your bed has a sprung base or the legs are unsightly, make a matching flounce to cover the base. Measure the length and width of the bed base, add a 1.25cm seam allowance to sides and bottom and 5cm to top. Cut out in calico and sew 5cm hem across top. For gathered flounce cut and sew together strips of fabric to measure four times the length of the base, plus twice the width, plus 10cm hem allowance, **by** the depth from top of base to floor, adding on 6.25cm for seam and hem. Make a 5cm hem along both short ends and one long side of strip. Gather along remaining long side and fit to sides and bottom of calico cover. With right sides together sew gathered flounce to calico. Neaten raw edges. Position on bed between mattress and base.

SCATTER CUSHIONS

Calico-covered inner cushions These are available in a wide range of sizes from soft-furnishing departments in most stores, but if the shape or size you want is out of stock they are easy to make. Small scatter cushions can be any size, but 30cm, 42.5cm and 45cm round or square are among the most popular.

To make inner cushion Cut two pieces of calico (or any scrap cotton) 5cm larger than the desired size, sew together using a 1.25cm seam, leaving an opening for the filling. Use the filling of your choice—for soft, smooth plump cushions Dacron wadding (from craft shops) is probably the best. Kapok is also good, although it tends to lose bulk after a while.

To make outer cover Cut two pieces of fabric 5mm smaller than you cut the insert—it is best to have the cover a little smaller so the cushion fits snugly. With right sides together sew a 1.25cm seam, leaving one side partly open. Sew a zipper in the opening. Zipper should be only 5 or 10cm shorter than width of cushion to allow cover to be easily removed and replaced.

For a piped edge Pin the piping around the edge of one of the cushion squares on the right side with raw edges matching. Clip piping excess at the corners so it will lie flat. Using zipper foot sew piping to cushion along the stitching line of cover, leaving first 5cm of piping loose. To join piping when you have sewn around the cushion, unpick the first 5cm you left and cut cord from inside. Butt the other end of piping against this cut end and cut off. Turn under the raw edge of the 5cm loose end and fold it over to enclose cut ends of piping. Stitch across the join to secure. Place the two cushion covers together, right sides facing, and finish as before.

For a frilled cushion Cut a strip of matching or contrasting fabric 7cm wide, and long enough to measure twice the outside edge of cushion. Join the 7cm ends, make a narrow hem on one side and gather the other side to fit the cushion. Pin to right side of one cushion cover, raw edges together, sew in place; finish cushion as before.

CURTAINS

Curtain heading tapes, self-lined furnishing fabrics and the multiple styles of curtain rods that come in handyman kits have all made it easy even for beginners to sew their own curtains. Install your curtain rods before measuring for your curtains, check and double-check your measurements as you proceed, and you can confidently sew professional-looking window dressings.

CURTAIN HEADINGS

Box pleats These give a tailored finish. Make them with a deep pleat tape and four-pronged

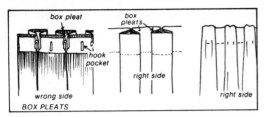

box pleat　box pleats

hook pocket

wrong side　right side　right side

BOX PLEATS

hooks but use only the two middle prongs. When formed, the box pleats are stitched down flat. Fabric 120cm wide pleats down to 81cm.

Triple pinch pleats You need fabric made up in panels to double the width of the finished curtain, plus wide tape and four-pronged hooks. The pleats are formed by the hooks and the heading needs no sewing.

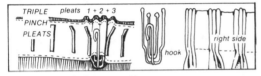

TRIPLE PINCH PLEATS　pleats 1 + 2 + 3

hook　right side

A delicate, pretty heading for voiles and fine nets Use three rows of narrow Terylene tape, gathered. Sew the tape with nylon or synthetic thread. You need 2½ to 3 times the desired finished width for these fabrics.

Cartridge pleats These will give formal elegance to heavy curtains. You'll need deep tape and four-pronged hooks, and three times finished curtain width. Place the second prong of the hook into one of the pockets, miss the next pocket and then insert the third prong into the next one.

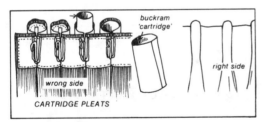

buckram 'cartridge'

right side

wrong side

CARTRIDGE PLEATS

Pencil pleats These give crisp definition to curtain headings. Use special pencil-pleat tape which is stiffened for permanent good looks. Allow 3 times finished curtain width.

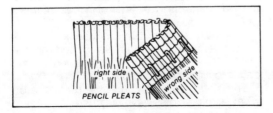

right side　wrong side

PENCIL PLEATS

MEASURING FOR CURTAINS

Once tracks are installed make a diagram of your window.

Width First measure the width of the track (allowing for returns to the wall at either end if required, and centre overlap if curtains are to pull from either side of the window to the centre).

Length Measure from above rod to where the curtains will finish (2cm above sill for sill-height curtains, to bottom of apron below window for apron-length curtains, to 2cm above floor for floor-length curtains). If curtains are to hang under rod, measure from underside of rod. Add hem allowance (10cm for most fabrics) plus 3cm for 1.5cm turnunder at hem and heading. Sheer fabrics should have a double hem for appearance and weight. Allow extra for hem if fabric is not labelled shrinkproof (to be let down after cleaning).

To calculate fabric required Divide the width of the fabric into the total width needed for each window. This will give the number of drops required. Multiply the number of drops by the total length to give the total amount of fabric you must buy. Take your diagram and measurements with you when you buy your fabric so that the sales assistant can help you.

If using patterned fabric you will need to take the pattern repeat into account, and to allow for a complete large motif at the base of the curtain. A cut-off motif looks unprofessional at the hemline.

SEWING CURTAINS

Cut off selvedges so that curtains will hang well. Join panels if required using french seams or overlocking raw edges. Panels of less than one width should be sewn so they occur at the outer edge of the window.

Sew 2.5cm side hems; checking tension so that seams do not pucker. Turn under 1.5cm at top of curtain, press. Pin heading tape in place, following manufacturer's instructions carefully. Sew as directed. Knot cords at one end, pull up to desired width from the opposite end. Do not cut off excess cord, but tie loosely and tuck out of sight. Insert hooks at required distances, and hang curtain.

Leave curtain to hang for about a week before sewing bottom hem.

LINED CURTAINS

Many fabrics have an acrylic self-lining that acts as an insulation as well as giving body to curtains. Sheer curtains can be hung with a

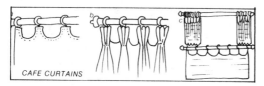

CAFE CURTAINS

separate, gathered lining curtain on a second rod, or you can make the lining with the main curtain. Make it slightly shorter and narrower than the curtain, attaching it under the curtain heading tape so that wrong sides of curtain and lining are facing.

Some colours will fade in too much sunlight. Check with the manufacturer or line them, especially if the window faces west.

CAFE CURTAINS

Fit the rods to the window before measuring for the curtains. The top rod can be fitted to the window frame, but it is often fitted to the wall above the window, projecting slightly beyond it at either end. Fit the second rod on the frame (generally about halfway down the window, or so that the curtain will just cover the sash).

Café curtains can be made in tiers that overlap, or as a single tier with a gathered valance above. They can be made with a simple shirred heading, through which the rod is placed, or with a scalloped heading attached to the rod with clip-on rings. They can also be made with pleated or gathered heading tapes.

Shirred curtains Measure from below rod to desired finished length, add hem allowance (double hem for sheer fabrics). For heading measure depth of rod plus allowance for shirred heading above, double this and add 1.5cm for hem. For width, double width of rod. Join panels if required, and sew side hems. Hem top edge then turn half top heading allowance to wrong side; press. Pin hem and rod channel (1), check that rod will fit easily through channel, sew hem and rod channel. Sew bottom hems or leave a week to drop.

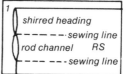
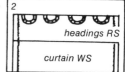

Scalloped curtains You will need twice the width for gathered scallops. For length measure from under the café rings or clips to desired length; add bottom hem allowance; for facing add sufficient depth for scallops plus 5cm. Draw a paper pattern for scallops, using saucer or plate as a template, and adjusting scallops so that they are evenly spaced (2). Sew facing and side hems. Turn facing to wrong side; press. Trace scallops from pattern to fabric; sew, then cut out excess and clip curves. Turn facing to wrong side, slip-stitch to side hems. Hang curtains after sewing bottom hem.

SECONDHAND BUYING

Secondhand shops and auctions are the place to go if you are on a tight budget or want something out of the ordinary.

AUCTIONS

Auctions are more nerve-wracking than pottering around a secondhand shop but you are more likely to do well there. Check newspapers for deceased estate and home clearance auctions. If possible, visit beforehand to see what is for sale, taking a tape measure to make sure that the furniture will fit into your house and a notebook to take down details.

If you are nervous about bidding, ask a member of the auctioneer's staff to help you. Auctioneers know some people don't feel up to bidding themselves. Is it not in their interests to have you too scared to bid.

It is your responsibility to check with the auctioneer when you must pay for and remove goods. Often they must be removed by the day following the auction.

The staff may give you some guidance on what similar lots have fetched at recent auctions but it is impossible to be sure what an item will fetch until it is auctioned. Check whether the auctioneer guarantees goods to be according to their description. Also, note that some lots contain several items. If you bid for one you must take the rest. Unless you are sure you can use or sell the additional items, you may be getting a bad bargain.

Even if you are not bidding, go to the auction yourself. If you can't; the auctioneer may supply you with an absentee bidding card on which you can put your highest bid. If you are at the auction, decide beforehand how much you are prepared to pay. Write the figure down; it will help you to stick to it.

SECONDHAND SHOPS

Before buying at a secondhand shop, inspect the goods carefully. Look inside cupboards and chests of drawers, examine joints, sit on chairs, look for borers, breaks or repairs. Check that electrical appliances are working before you buy and whether they are guaranteed. Don't be too tempted by smart appearance. A piece of furniture in good repair but the wrong colour is better than one which is the right colour but in poor condition.

If you think you have found an antique, seek professional advice before trying to restore it. Amateur restoration can ruin an antique.

10
A STITCH IN TIME

TODAY the homely skills of sewing, knitting and crochet are as valuable as ever, despite the wide range of off-the-peg clothes available. If you make your own clothes they can be tailored specially to fit you, you have an almost unlimited choice of styles and colours, and you don't have to worry about bumping into someone in the identical outfit. General hints and instructions for specific stitches are included for each handcraft.

SEWING

Sewing may be anything from the inevitable mending or making simple clothes for children, to elegant fashions the fit and finish of which is aimed at rivalling Paris.

MEASUREMENTS

Measurements should be taken in usual under-clothes.

Bust (women) Holding the tape measure very slightly up at the back, measure around the fullest part of the bust. Also measure across the back from side seam to side seam.

Chest (men and children) Tape around the fullest part of the chest when the chest is fully expanded.

Underarm to waist From about 2cm below the armpit to the exact waistline.

Armhole From the top of the shoulder-bone straight down to 2cm below the armpit. Do not curve the tape measure.

Hips The fullest part around the hips.

Neck to shoulder From the side of the neck to the top of the shoulder-bone.

Shoulder to waist (front) From the centre of the neck-to-shoulder down across the fullest part of the bust to the waistline.

Shoulder to waist (back) From the top of the spine (prominent neck-bone) to waist.

Arm Unless knitting a tight-fitting sleeve, measure upper arm and forearm loosely. Measure wrist exactly.

Sleeve length From 2cm below armpit down inside of arm to wrist-bone.

Shoulder to shoulder (back) Across shoulders at the broadest part of the back.

Skirt length From exact waistline down side of hip to length desired.

USING A PATTERN

Take time and care in selecting your pattern and in determining your size. Some dress-makers learn by experience that one brand of pattern is more reliable or easier to follow and seems to fit them better than others. They stick to that brand when possible.

No matter how experienced you are, it makes sense to follow the pattern instructions. You may think you know a short cut but sometimes that turns out to be a dead end. You may always have handled a certain aspect of dress-making—setting in a sleeve, fitting a collar—a certain way but the people who design and draught patterns are experts. You will learn more about dressmaking and new and more effective ways to sew from following patterns carefully than you may at some dressmaking schools. Remember, there is always something new in any craft.

Fabric Follow the pattern's suggestions on fabric. Many patterns will not work if the fabric differs in weight, texture or design from those recommended.

Buy the amount of fabric specified on the pattern. If you skimp you may not be able to buy the extra quantity needed when you return to the shop. At the very least there will be frustrating delay in your sewing session. Take the fabric with you when buying buttons, zips and thread, so you get a good colour match. If you cannot match the thread exactly, choose one slightly darker than the fabric. Two spools are enough for the average garment.

Selecting size of pattern Choose your size by bust measurement for a dress and waist measurement for a skirt or slacks. If your hip measurement is larger than that allowed in the pattern, take a size to suit your hips and adjust the waistline accordingly.

PREPARING FABRIC FOR CUTTING

For a garment to hang correctly, pattern pieces must be cut with the grain of the fabric straight. This means that crosswise and lengthwise threads must be at right angles. Some fabrics are pulled off-grain during manufacture or are not cut straight when sold. To straighten a woven fabric pull out a crosswise thread from selvedge to selvedge and cut along the faint line left. Then fold fabric in half, selvedges meeting. Corners should meet. If they don't, pull short corners away from each other until they do. Steam-pressing or damping the fabric can help. Bonded, permanent press and

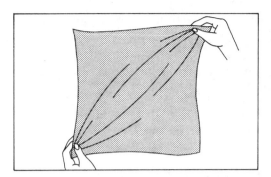

crease resistant fabrics are difficult or impossible to straighten. Check when you buy.

With washable fabric check for shrinkage information on the label or measure then wash and dry a small piece of the fabric. If it has not been pre-shrunk, clip selvedges every 5cm, unfold fabric, soak in warm water and drip dry over something smooth and straight. To shrink zip fasteners, bindings etc., dip in warm water and drip dry.

FABRIC HINTS

Cotton Easy to sew and doesn't normally fray. Be sure cotton is pre-shrunk before cutting.

Linen Easy to handle and tailors superbly. Before cutting out, straighten grain. Cut with long firm strokes using sharp shears. Use pinking shears for heavy linen which tends to fray, and make larger seam allowances.

Silk Varies from soft silks which drape to firm ones with body. Silk is slippery; pin selvedges together before arranging pattern pieces. Keep material flat when cutting. Use very fine pins and needles and silk thread even for tacking. Silk organza is a good mounting material.

Wool In various weights and textures, woollen fabric is generally satisfying to sew. Garments may need to be lined.

Synthetic fabrics Often, synthetics have a selvedge woven tighter than the rest of the material. To prevent puckering while cutting, clip through selvedge about every 10cm before arranging pattern pieces. Use fine needles and pins, synthetic sewing thread. Machine tension may need to be loosened to avoid puckering. Use drip-dry synthetic trims, zips, bindings and lining (when necessary).

Sheer fabric (e.g. voile, chiffon) Use very fine pins, clip selvedge at regular intervals. Use silk thread and small stitches when tacking. Stitch seams over tissue paper and tear away when finished.

Bonded fabric Suitable for tailored garments,

bonded fabric needs no lining and is easy to sew. Seam finishes will not fray.

Napped fabric (e.g. velvet) This requires a one-way layout of pattern.

Linings, facings, interfacings These should never be heavier than the main fabric; match colour. Choose washable linings for washable fabrics.

BASIC STITCHES

There is a variety of basic stitches. Some of these a machine can do. Some must be done by hand and fussy people often prefer to do some by hand even when the machine can help.

Back-stitch A small strong stitch used where machine-stitching is difficult or when sewing in a zip fastener by hand. Make small stitches, beginning each back into the end of the preceding stitch.

Basting or tacking A temporary form of stitching used to hold pieces of fabric together before sewing permanently. The more time you spend basting or tacking, the better fit and finish your garment will have. Some sewing machines have a real tacking-stitch, long and easy to pull out. This must be used only on non-slip fabrics which the needle will not mark.

Hand-tacking Use a single thread and a long needle. Knot one end of thread, make long running-stitches and fasten off with a back-stitch.

Diagonal tacking Used to secure facings, interfacings and lining. Make straight stitches at right angles to the edge of fabric and diagonal stitches will appear.

Slip-tacking Useful for matching seams in stripes and checks and for curved sections. Slip needle through upper fold of fabric then through lower fold.

Hemming With the hemmer-foot of a machine you can stitch narrow hems without tacking or pressing, but hems of good garments are usually finished by hand. Begin with a thread fastened under the hem edge, take stitches diagonally from right to left, through folded edge of hem, picking up a single thread of fabric underneath.

Blind hemming Makes an almost invisible finish by hand or machine. By hand, finish raw edge of hem, then as close to hem as possible, catch a single thread of fabric and carry needle diagonally through hem edge. Do not sew

tightly. Make stitches about 6mm to 9mm apart.

Herringbone Used to finish hems and facings and to keep edges flat. Work from left to right alternating stitches.

Overcasting Prevents raw edges fraying. Use slanting evenly spaced hand-stitches or use machine's blind-stitch zigzag.

Running-stitch Used for easing, gathering, tucking, mending and to secure facings and hems in lined garments. Use a fine needle and small even stitches, weaving needle and thread in and out of the fabric several times before pulling through. Use tiny stitches for seams, 6mm stitches for easing and gathering.

Slip-stitch Used for finishing hems, cuffs, bias bindings, etc. with almost invisible stitches. Bring needle through hem fold, pick up a single thread of fabric. Continue, keeping stitches about 6mm to 9mm apart.

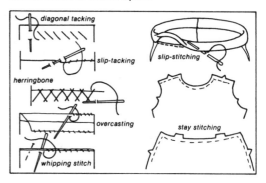

Stay-stitch Used to hold edges of necklines, hiplines, etc. in shape. Use a line of straight, medium machine-stitching on a single layer of fabric before stitching seams. Stay-stitch about 12mm from seam edge in direction of fabric grain.

Top-stitch Done to accent seams. It may be done at all stages of the garment. If top-stitching is a feature of the whole garment it may be done as a first step. Interior seams such as raglan sleeves need to be done at a specific stage. Collars, cuffs and pockets are top-stitched as they are completed and before being attached to the garment. Many machines have an adjustable edge stitcher attachment to help accurate spacing of top-stitching. For when to top-stitch, be guided by the pattern instructions.

Whipping-stitch A tiny stitch useful for joining lace or ribbon to a garment or to hold lining to the back neck-edge of a coat.

SEAMS

Properly stitched and finished seams help give a garment shape and line. Before stitching, sew darts, then pin and tack seams together taking care to match ends, notches and centres.

Plain Place seam under needle with edges to right. Needle should be about 12mm from back edge. Back-stitch to strengthen end, then stitch forward to other end; back-stitch again.

Graded or layered Often necessary to make seams less bulky, it entails trimming each seam allowance at graded distances from the stitching line, e.g. interfacing almost to stitching, facing to 3mm, garment to 6mm.

Curved Use a smaller stitch to make seam stronger and more elastic. To finish seam, clip an inward curve to within 3mm of seamline and at intervals of about 12mm. Notch an outward curve similarly. If turning curved seam to right side (e.g. a collar section) grade seam allowances first. If opening out flat, notch and clip only. Always press a curved seam over a curved surface, such as a tailor's ham.

Bias bound Will completely enclose seam allowance. Machine binding along seam, trim, fold binding over, press, tack, stitch.

Double top-stitched Press seam open, pink edges, then top-stitch.

Eased Used where two seams to be joined are of unequal length. Gather extra fabric, then work from gathered side; pin edges together, matching seam ends and notches. Ease gathering evenly, steam-press to shrink out unwanted fullness. Stitch seam with eased part on top.

Edge-stitched For light to medium-weight fabrics and unlined jackets. Press open plain seam, pink edges. Fold under 6mm, press, machine edges.

French For fine fabrics but not for curved seams. With wrong sides of fabric facing, stitch about 6mm from seamline. Trim to 3mm, press seam open. Turn wrong side out, fold on stitching line, press and stitch on seamline.

Mock french For straight and curved seams. With right sides of fabric facing, stitch along seamline. Trim and press without opening seam. Fold to the inside and stitch.

Herringbone For heavy materials. Press plain seam open; finish edges with herringbone stitch.

Open bound Bind plain seam edges with bias binding.

Overcast Hand-sewn: overcast edges of plain seam with small stitches; avoid puckering. Machine: do plain zigzag stitching near seam edges. Trim close to stitching.

Pinked and stitched Machine-stitch seam allowances 6mm from edge, then pink edges.

SEWING MACHINE

This can be a major expense and it is worthwhile putting in the time to find out what is available and what each machine will do. Before going to the shops, consider well what your requirements are. It is a waste of money buying a very expensive machine which will do lots of complicated things if you do not have the time or skill to utilise it fully. If you are unskilled and plan only to cope with general household sewing and mending, you can manage very well with a modestly priced one. Technology changes rapidly so don't buy a machine for a lifetime. You can put off buying the expensive machine until you are sure you will have sufficient time and skill to use it. Then, with regular use it will pay for itself.

Most modern machines can cope with straight stitching and reversing to bind seams. They have a zigzag attachment to overcast and for use with stretch fabrics, a zipper-foot for easy and effective insertion of zip fasteners and an attachment to make buttonholes.

Having decided roughly what sort of machine you want, tackle the shops. It is sensible to allow yourself time to discuss the machine with the skilled demonstrator and sensible to choose a time when she is less likely to be busy. If you buy, normally she will show you how the machine works until she is sure you can cope. Many companies also have sewing courses on their make of machine. Find out about these.

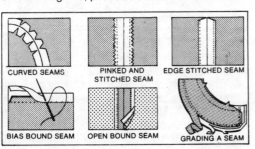

CURVED SEAMS   PINKED AND STITCHED SEAM   EDGE STITCHED SEAM

BIAS BOUND SEAM   OPEN BOUND SEAM   GRADING A SEAM

BIAS-CUT FABRICS

The bias-cutting of fabric is used either to accentuate the drape of a garment or to give a more interesting design to striped or checked fabrics. Most fabrics are suitable for bias-cutting with the exception of stretch fabrics, very loosely woven fabrics and those with a definite nap such as velvets, corduroy, imitation suede.

Preparing fabric for cutting Ensure that the lengthwise and crosswise grains of the fabric are at right angles to each other. If not, gently pull fabric to straighten the grains. Fold fabric along the lengthwise grain, pinning selvedges together and matching raw ends. To find the true bias of the fabric, fold one straight edge onto the selvedge edge. The diagonal fold is the true bias of the fabric and has the maximum stretch.

Cutting bias fabric If using a commercial pattern designed to use the crosswise grain, the straight of grain line will be diagonally across the pattern piece. Match the straight grain line to lengthwise grain of fabric and pattern piece will automatically lie with the bias. If you are adapting a pattern designed to be cut on the straight of grain lay the straight grain lines to the true bias of the fabric. Cut fabric around pattern pieces, allowing an extra 2.5cm around all shapes. Hang the fabric pieces for several hours with the true bias vertical to allow fabric to drop. Repin pattern pieces to fabric and cut out.

Sewing bias-cut fabric To prevent unwanted stretching at neckline, armholes, waistline, etc, sew cotton tape into the seamline or stay-stitch.

Handle garment as little and as gently as possible. Tissue paper in the seam reduces stretching when pinning, tacking and stitching. Remove after machine-stitching. Before hemming bias-cut garment, allow to hang overnight. As the hemline will have probably dropped unevenly, mark the correct hemline, measuring with a ruler from the floor. Trim away excess fabric to leave an even hem allowance. Turn up a narrow hem (no more than 2.5cm), run a gathering stitch close to raw edge, pull up slightly to take in excess fullness in hem allowance. Steam-press then finish hem with bias strip.

Stripes or checks cut on bias Best suited to a pattern with centre opening or front and back seam. Before cutting out pattern pieces, check that stripes or checks match at side, front and back seams. Slip-tack all seams to prevent matched design from slipping out of place when machine-stitched.

STRETCH FABRICS

Patterns designed for stretch fabrics usually include a stretch gauge to help you choose a fabric with the correct extensibility. As a general guide choose a very flexible fabric for underwear, an easily extendible one for clothing such as tops and skirts, and where shape retention is important, for example in a pants suit, choose a double-knit.

Cutting out Check at purchase whether fabric needs to be pre-shrunk. Working on a surface large enough to take the entire fabric, smooth it into position wrong side up. Allow it to rest for a short time as the fabric will have stretched as it was laid out. If using a commercial pattern, select the 'with nap' layout as stretch knits are directional. Pin pattern pieces to wrong side as cut edges curl to right side of fabric. Use fine, sharp pins inserted at right angles to direction of stretch. If fabric is slippery or bulky, cut one layer at a time. Use very sharp scissors to prevent distortion of raw edges.

Thread Always sew stretch fabric with a synthetic thread. Unlike cotton thread, it will stretch with the fabric and prevent split seams.

Stitching If possible use a stitch specially designed for stretch fabric. If not, use a zigzag stitch (narrow width by long stitch length). If machine only stitches straight, gently stretch fabric under presser-foot as you sew.

Needle Always use a ball-point needle which

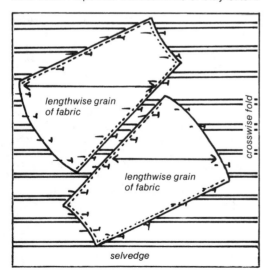

lengthwise grain of fabric

crosswise fold

lengthwise grain of fabric

selvedge

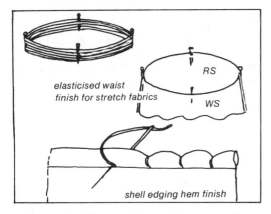

elasticised waist finish for stretch fabrics

RS
WS

shell edging hem finish

pushes the fibres aside unlike an ordinary needle that will cut fibres and cause ladders.

Interfacing There is a flexible interfacing available for use with stretch knits.

Seam allowances Never neaten raw edges as this can distort hang of garment. Stretch knits do not fray. Layer seam allowances of bulky stretch fabrics in collars, facings, etc. Tape seams, e.g. shoulder, where stretch is not desired.

Hem Hang garment for 24 hours before marking hem, measuring with a ruler from the floor. Delicate to medium-weight stretch fabrics should have the smallest hem possible or shell-edge finish.

Fastenings Avoid heavy buttons, interface buttonholes. Use light-weight synthetic zips.

Pressing Many stretch fabrics do not require pressing. Test on scrap of fabric; use a pressing cloth if necessary. Lift and lower iron onto surface: do not slide it over fabric.

Static electricity Many stretch fabrics cling to the body. To minimise this, rinse garment in an anti-static fabric softener after washing. If sewing lingerie tricot, rinse in softener, dry, then sew. This will prevent tricot from clinging to needle and presser-foot.

ALTERATIONS

If you are not a standard size or if you sometimes fall for a bargain that needs alterations it is worth knowing what can or cannot be done easily.

Avoid dropping shoulder-lines, gaping necklines and garments which fit badly across the back and upper chest. These faults are often difficult or impossible to cope with.

Plan your work. If more than one part of the garment needs an alteration consider carefully which one to do first. One alteration may make another unnecessary, e.g. tightening the neckline could pull a poorly fitting shoulder into place. Try on and fit the garment at every stage of the alteration. It is well worth the time and effort.

Hemlines Can be easily shortened either by turning up a new hem or by lifting the skirt at the waistline. Lengthening is harder. You will need a 5cm hem to let down and face. If design and fabric are suitable you can add length by trimming and hem or inserting a band of fabric in the skirt. Do not buy a pleated garment which is too short. If you let it down, the hemline crease will be very difficult to remove. Take care with a coat. You cannot let down the hem if excess fabric under facings has been trimmed at corners.

Sleeves Can be lengthened or shortened in much the same way as hemlines. If you have very long or short arms you must decide whether it is practical to shorten or lengthen long sleeves or if short sleeves would suit the design. Avoid a garment with sleeves which drag across the shoulders when you move.

Hip-line A too-roomy skirt can be taken in at the side seams. If the garment is too tight across the hips you can let it out only if there is room in the side or centre seams. You will still need about 6mm seam allowance. If fabric frays easily do not try to let out seams.

Waistline Can be raised or made smaller, but cannot be lowered satisfactorily, so do not buy a short-waisted dress. If a waistline needs to be let out, check that there is enough fabric in side seams or darts.

Bad fit over abdomen or seat This can alter the position of the seams and make a skirt hang badly. A simple alteration—removing the waistband, pulling up the skirt until the side seams hang straight and then replacing the band—will often solve the problem.

Reshape at side seams Do not tinker with such styling devices as darts just to avoid unstitching a zip: take in and let out as much as possible at the sides.

Trousers Should fit well around the body. Side seams and waistlines can be adjusted for a slightly neater fit and hems can be altered up or down, but changing a baggy or too-tight crutch can spoil the line and be disastrous. Always try sitting, crouching and bending before you buy.

MENDING

Torn neckline Square necks or V-necks of children's dresses, school uniforms and shirts are often ripped at the corners. Remove the facing, reinforce the torn fabric with a lapped patch of interlining fabric or bias tape, then cut a new facing in matching or contrast fabric and apply to right side of garment to conceal the patch.

Torn underarm on magyar sleeve Mark and measure diamond shape for gusset around torn area. Cut a diamond-shaped gusset to fit, adding 12mm all round for seam allowance (one side of diamond on straight grain of fabric). Unpick underarm seam, mark 12mm

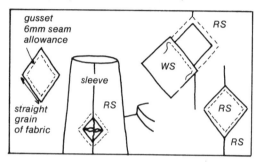

seam allowance inside marked diamond, then trim away excess. Mark seamlines with tacking on garment and gusset. Pin one side of gusset along garment seamline, right sides together, and machine carefully. Fold in and press remaining seam allowances on gusset, then pin and tack gusset to garment. Carefully top-stitch by machine around all four sides of diamond on right side, making neat, angled corners.

Inverted pleats These often rip horizontally across the top. Remove top-stitching (if any), open pleat out, and extend stitching down about 12mm; reinforce seam by stitching in a strip of firm woven tape if necessary. Reposition pleat, press then use matching thread and neat satin-stitch (hand or machine) to mend tear. Replace top-stitching.

Buttons ripped off Mend hole in fabric with a small lapped patch of woven tape then sew on button. If several buttons are missing (e.g. on shirt front) it may be worth removing remainder, inserting a strip of iron-on interfacing, and then replacing all of them.

Broken zip Unpick and remove the zip, taking note of how it was inserted. Press seam allowances in position. Pin, then tack in new zip of same length and weight; machine or hand-stitch around zip. Remove tacking. Stitch ends of tape down or insert them into waistband

and restitch waistband.

Split body seam If fabric is weakened, unpick seam, reinforce both sides with strong woven tape, then restitch along seamline.

Split double seam If seam is frayed, hem each edge closely by hand, darning in any frayed edges as you sew. On a new garment, match the machine-stitch and thread to those of existing seam; pull thread ends to wrong side of garment and back-stitch to finish. Or back-stitch by hand along existing seamlines.

Hole in trouser pocket lining Iron-on patches are easiest. Follow directions on pack. Or buy sew-in ready-made pocket linings.

Torn patch pocket Usually the garment fabric is torn at a top corner. Unpick stitching at corner, reinforce and patch or darn tear, then sew pocket back on.

Hole in trouser knee Depending on size, repair by patching or darning. Alternatively, convert them to shorts and keep the spare fabric for future needs.

Worn seat Reinforce with a patch on outside or a lapped patch on inside (if machine has a free arm).

DARNING

Darning may be almost a lost art but it does survive with socks. It is an ideal television-watching job and needs only rudimentary needle skills. Use wool for woollen socks; and for other textiles, such as cotton, use soft thread to make the darned spot easier to walk on. For the same reason, don't tie a knot in the thread but take several tiny stitches, one on top of another, to secure the end. Put a darning egg —a burnt-out electric light-globe is a good substitute—into the sock and stretch the hole over it. Make one row of small horizontal stitches above the hole. Move down fractionally and take several small stitches on one side of the hole, run your thread over the hole and take several more stitches on the other side. Continue this pattern until the hole is covered with parallel threads. Repeat the sequence vertically but instead of crossing the hole, weave the vertical threads over and under the horizontal threads.

HELPFUL HINTS

When sewing stiff fabric such as denim, hold the pieces together with spring-type clothes pegs.

To sew foam-rubber by machine or hand, rub soap along the foam-rubber and the needle will take to it without trouble.

When sewing shaggy fabric which loops round the sewing machine needle and foot, place tissue paper between the foot and the fabric. Tear if off when you have finished sewing. This works as well for chiffon and other delicate fabrics.

Spray newly-cut edges of hessian or linen with hair spray before sewing to prevent fraying.

For a bolder effect in top-stitching, thread up the sewing machine with double thread on the top.

A quick squirt of hair spray on thread will stiffen it enough to make it easier to thread a needle.

When gathering a long length of material by hand, thread needle and leave thread on reel. The thread will not become tangled and you will not have to estimate the length of thread needed (and maybe fall short).

Zip fasteners To hold a zip for machine-stitching, use transparent tape. After sewing, tear off tape.

To prevent strain on a zip, set the lower end about 6mm below the end of the opening. Stitch across seam firmly by hand.

Hard-to-close zips can be rubbed with a piece of paraffin wax. Talcum powder keeps them working freely.

To re-use a zip, spray with spray starch and it will be firm and efficient.

Hems To remove old hemlines when letting down cotton, woollen and denim clothes, mix 1 cup of hot water, ½ teaspoon of vinegar and ½ teaspoon of borax. Wet a cloth with the solution, wring out and place on wrong side of hemline. Press with a hot iron.

Press a hem fold with a strip of paper between the fabric layers to prevent an impression on the right side of the garment.

Cutting Dip scissors in boiling water to make it easier to cut through nylon and delicate fabrics.

Buttons Touch the centre of a button with colourless nail polish if the threads come loose and you can't repair them at once.

Painting the thread with nail polish after sewing buttons on also makes them stay on much longer. Good for children's clothes.

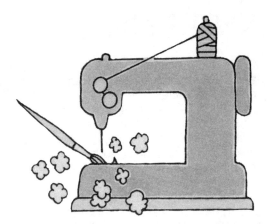

Buttons will stay on longer if you sew each pair of holes separately, breaking the thread and knotting it after sewing each side.

Keep a bit of beeswax in your workbox and when sewing on buttons run the thread along the wax for a secure shank.

To make a straight cut for a buttonhole on heavy fabric, lay buttonhole section over a cake of soap and cut with a razor blade.

Snap fasteners Sew one half of snap fasteners in place, and rub with chalk. Press against the other piece of fabric. You will know where the other side of the fastener should go.

Keep shoulder straps in place with a 3cm piece of ribbon sewn on the shoulder seam with a snap fastener at the other end

Sewing machine Use the finest nozzle of a vacuum cleaner to remove dust and threads from the bobbin case area of your sewing machine.

After oiling the sewing machine, sew through a folded layer of paper towelling several times. This absorbs any excess oil.

Use a damp sponge-mop to pick up sewing threads. This works on carpet as well as on smooth floors.

Save time and energy when sewing by adjusting the ironing board to the height of the sewing machine and setting it up next to the machine.

Keep a small magnet in your sewing machine case to pick up stray pins and needles easily.

You can sharpen a sewing machine needle by stitching through a piece of fine sandpaper.

KNITTING

Knitting is one of the most ancient and basic crafts. There are in reality only two types of fabric: woven and knitted. A hand-knitted fabric will follow much the same principles as a machine-knitted one. Among the most attractive features of knitted fabrics are interest and variety in texture, and flexibility which gives greater fluidity of line for the wearer than woven fabrics can normally achieve.

The difficulty of knitting as opposed to dressmaking is that the garment must be finished or almost finished before you can be sure that it fits and suits the wearer. This means that extra care must be taken with the preliminaries.

You must:

• Measure the person you are knitting for carefully to make sure which size to follow, and mark the size throughout the pattern. Marking can be done with a coloured see-through marker. If later you knit up the same garment in a different size, you can then use a different colour marker for this.

• Be aware that there is a distinct difference in the measurements of the wearer and of the garment. Hand-knitted garments are usually to some degree loose. Sometimes they are distinctly floppy. Most patterns give a Garment Measures measurement. This is usually for bust or chest and will tell you how much larger than the wearer the garment will be.

• Always use the exact yarn specified in the pattern. Buy full quantity of yarn required to complete pattern as dye lots vary.

• Check your knitting tension.

ABBREVIATIONS

alt: alternate

*: (asterisk) repeat the instructions following * as many times as specified, in addition to the original **or** if specified, repeat the instructions preceding *

beg: begin (beginning)

bk st: back-stitch

( ): (brackets) repeat instructions inside brackets, as many times as specified **or** figures inside brackets denote different sizes of pattern and correspondingly different instructions

cc: contrast colour

cont: continue (continuing), that is, work in the same pattern of stitch as before

dec: decrease (decreasing), generally by working 2 stitches together

foll: following

g st: garter stitch, that is, all plain knitting

inc: increase (increasing), that is, knit or purl into front and back of next stitch

incl: inclusive (including)

k: knit

kib: knit into back of stitch

mc: main colour

m st: moss stitch

m1: make one, that is, pick up loop before next stitch, place on left-hand needle and knit or purl it through back of loop

patt: pattern

psso: pass slipped stitch over; used when a stitch has been slipped, next stitch worked either knit or purl; pass left-hand needle through slipped stitch, pass slipped stitch over next stitch and off both needles: thus there will be one fewer stitch on needles.

p2sso: pass 2 slipped stitches over

rem: remain (remaining)

rep: repeat

row: the number of stitches on needle; first row is knitted on the cast-on stitches and is first odd-numbered row; is usually right side of work, unless specified otherwise

tbl: through back of loop, that is, for a knit tbl, right-hand needle is passed through stitch as in purling, point then carried to back of left-hand needle and stitch knitted; for a purl tbl, right-hand needle is placed at back of left-hand needle beyond stitch, turn point and pass through stitch, bring to front of left needle and purl

tog: together

yb: yarn back, that is, take yarn under needle

from purling position into knitting position

y fwd: yarn forward; used in knit row, stitch or stitches before y fwd will be knitted and yarn placed at back of work, yarn is then brought to front between two needles, right-hand needle inserted into next stitch knitways, carry yarn over right-hand needle round point and knit; this strand makes a new stitch

y ft: yarn front, that is, bring yarn under needle from knitting position to purling position

yon: yarn over needle; used after a purl stitch when followed by a knit stitch, yarn is left in purl position; right-hand needle inserted into next stitch knitways, yarn then carried over and round point of right-hand needle and knitted; this forms a new stitch

yrn: yarn round needle; used between two purl stitches, take yarn over right-hand needle and around between two needles back to position to purl next stitch.

BASIC STITCHES AND FABRICS

KNIT STITCH AND PURL STITCH

Keep the stitches on the left-hand needle near to the point and hold the needle with the hand over the needle. The right-hand needle is held like a pencil, with the hand under the needle. The yarn should come over the first finger of the right hand, under the second, over the third and under the fourth. The yarn should pass easily through the fingers, but should be held firmly enough to maintain an even tension.

The knit stitch This is sometimes referred to as plain stitch. Hold the needle containing the cast-on stitches in the left hand. Holding the yarn at the back of the right-hand needle, insert the right-hand needle from left to right through the first loop.

Wrap the yarn clockwise round the point of the right-hand needle, draw a new loop through and retaining this loop on the right-hand needle, slip the first loop off the left-hand needle.

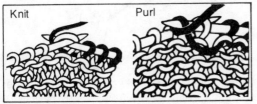
Knit   Purl

The purl stitch Hold the needles as for knit stitch but hold the yarn at the front of the right-hand needle. Insert the right-hand needle from right to left through the first loop, wrap the yarn round the point of the right-hand needle, draw a loop through stitch on to right-hand needle and slip stitch off left-hand needle.

BASIC FABRICS

Garter stitch or knit stitch This is obtained using any number of stitches and knitting every row. Both sides of the fabric look the same and each ridge represents two rows.

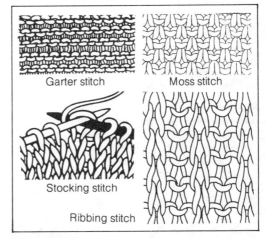
Garter stitch   Moss stitch

Stocking stitch

Ribbing stitch

Stocking stitch Stocking stitch or plain smooth fabric is obtained by knitting 1 row and purling 1 row. This produces a fabric which is smooth on one side and ridged on the other side.

Reverse stocking stitch or purl fabric If the ridged side of stocking stitch fabric is used as the right side of a garment the fabric is generally referred to as 'purl fabric'.

Moss stitch Moss stitch is usually worked over an uneven number of stitches. Moss stitch row: k 1, (p 1, k 1) to end. This row is repeated throughout.

Ribbing K 1, p 1 rib is the closest form of ribbing, usually worked over an even number of stitches. Rib row: (k 1, p 1) to end. This row is repeated throughout.

There are many variations in ribbing built up from the basic k 1, p 1 rib, such as: k 2, p 2 rib — cast on a multiple of 4 stitches. Rib row: (k 2, p 2) to end. This row is repeated throughout; or k 5, p 5 rib — cast on a multiple of 10 stitches. Rib row: (k 5, p 5) to end. This row is repeated throughout.

LEFT-HANDED KNITTING

If you are normally left-handed, there is really very little adjustment to be made in knitting. If you observe your friends knitting, you will find that they use the left hand quite as much as they use the right hand, especially if they knit Continental-style: holding the yarn in the left hand and picking it through with the right hand. The left hand has entire control of the yarn. The fingers of the left hand control the stitches on the needle.

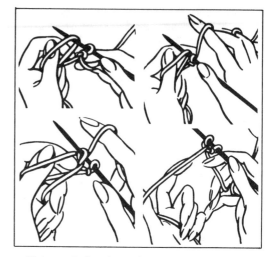

CASTING ON

An even cast-on is essential to good knitting. Avoid casting on too tightly, otherwise edge will break in wearing. Never knit into the back of the cast-on stitches. Use the thumb method for all general purposes.

Casting on: making a loop Wrap yarn around first and second fingers of left hand. Place point of needle under the front loop and draw

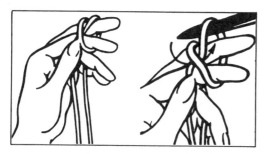

back loop through. Withdraw fingers from loop and draw loop up on needle. Working with length of yarn in left hand, pass this around left thumb.

Casting on: thumb method Sufficient length of yarn must be left for casting on stitches: approximately 12.5cm for every 10 stitches of 4 ply on 2.75 needles.

Place point of needle beneath loop on thumb, drawing loop up slightly. * Hold yarn from ball in right hand ready to pass around point of needle. Wrap yarn from ball around point of needle and draw through loop on thumb. Draw up stitch on needle, pull both ends of yarn firmly and repeat from * until

sufficient stitches have been cast on.

Casting on with two needles Make a loop and hold it on left-hand needle.

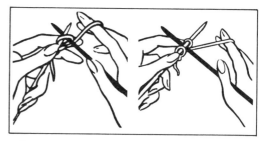

Place point of right-hand needle from left to right through loop on left-hand needle. Holding yarn in right hand, wrap yarn clockwise around point of right-hand needle and draw yarn through loop on left-hand needle, thus forming a second loop. Place this loop on left-hand needle. There are now 2 stitches on the left-hand needle.

Place point of right-hand needle **between** the 2 stitches on left-hand needle. Wrap yarn around point of right-hand needle and draw a loop between the 2 stitches on the left-hand needle. Place this loop on left-hand needle.

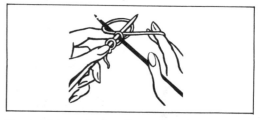

Repeat this action until you have cast on the number of stitches you require, always putting needle between 2 stitches nearest the point of left-hand needle.

Casting on in rib This is a variation of the two-needle method, and is suitable **only** for k 1, p 1 rib.

Casting on for an uneven number of stitches: where the first row reads 'k 2, * p 1, k 1, rep from * to last st, k 1', make a slip loop and place on left-hand needle. Insert right-hand needle in loop knitways, knit a stitch and slip on to left-hand needle. ** Insert right-hand needle purlways between last 2 stitches and purl a stitch (Fig. 1), slip stitch thus made on to left-hand needle (taking care not to twist it), insert right-hand needle knitways between last 2 stitches and knit a stitch (Fig. 2), slip stitch thus made on to left-hand needle, rep from ** for desired number of stitches, finishing with 2 knit stitches.

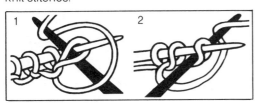

Casting on for an even number of stitches: where the first row reads '* k 1, p 1, rep from * to last 2 sts, k 2', work as for first method but finish with one knit stitch instead of two. Where the first row reads 'k 2, * p 1, rep from * to end of row', make a slip loop and place on left-hand needle. Insert right-hand needle in loop purlways, purl a stitch and slip on to left-hand needle (taking care not to twist it), insert right-hand needle knitways between last 2 stitches and knit a stitch, slip stitch thus made on to left-hand needle, then rep from ** as for first method for desired number of stitches, finishing with 2 knit stitches.

INCREASING AND DECREASING

INCREASING
The usual method of increasing is to knit twice into the same stitch. First knit into the front of the stitch in the usual way then, before slipping the stitch off the left-hand needle, knit into the back loop of the stitch and slip it off the left-hand needle (Fig. 1). When knitting into the back loop, be sure to bring the right-hand

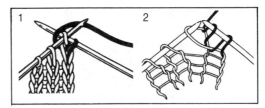

needle out **behind** the front loop (Fig. 2). The same method is used on a purl stitch.

Fashioned increasing This is generally used to form darts or fashioned shaping. With the point of the right-hand needle, pick up the loop which lies between the stitch just worked and the following stitch, place it on the left-hand needle, and then knit into the back of the loop (Fig. 3). The action of knitting into the back of it twists the loop, thus preventing a hole in the fabric.

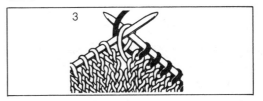

DECREASING
There are two methods of decreasing so that decreasing appears symmetrical on the left and right-hand sides of the fabric.

The usual method of decreasing is to knit 2 stitches together (k 2 tog), that is, slip the point of the right-hand needle from left to right through two stitches instead of one and knit

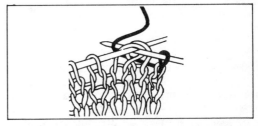

them off in the usual way. The decrease stitches will start to the right. The same procedure is used to purl 2 stitches together, but the needle is inserted from right to left. The abbreviation for this is p 2 tog.

Fashioned decreasing When working fashioned shaping, particularly in raglan armholes, the 'slip 1, k 1, psso' method is used at one end of the needle to give the opposite effect to the 'k 2 tog' at the other end. The decreased stitches will start to the left.

To 'pass slipped stitch over', insert the point of the left-hand needle from left to right, through the front of the slipped stitch (usually the second stitch from the end of the right-hand needle), slip this stitch over the second one and off the right-hand needle.

On the purl side of the work it is necessary to purl 2 stitches together through the backs of the loops (p 2 tog tbl)). Place the right-hand needle at the back of the left-hand needle to the left of the 2 stitches to be worked, inserting

the point through the back of the next 2 stitches on the left-hand needle (the needle will be pointing towards you), bring to front of left-hand needle and purl the 2 stitches together.

CASTING OFF

Knit the first 2 stitches, * insert the point of the left-hand needle from left to right through the first of these 2 stitches, slip this stitch over the second one (and, therefore, off the right-hand needle, thus leaving only one stitch on the latter), knit the next stitch and repeat from * until only one loop remains. Break off the yarn, draw the end through this loop and pull up to fasten tightly.

The edge formed by the cast-off stitches should be as elastic as the remainder of the garment. If you find it difficult to cast off loosely enough, use a needle 1 or 2 sizes larger.

Always cast off in the pattern being worked

(that is, cast off purl fabric purlways, or rib in rib) unless otherwise stated.

When a number of stitches are cast off at the beginning of a row, the stitch left on the right-hand needle after casting off counts as the first stitch of any number of stitches mentioned after the casting off. For example, if instructions read 'cast off 3 stitches, k 2' the stitch on the right-hand needle counts as the first of the 2 stitches, so it will only be necessary to knit one more stitch.

MAKING UP

Tapestry needles with their blunt ends are ideal for sewing up knitted garments. Use the same yarn as that in which you knitted your garment. Divide thick yarns into strands. Certain nubbly yarns are not suitable for sewing up and suitable plain yarn should be used.

Seams should be sewn as specified in the pattern. Do not start with a knot in your yarn when sewing a seam. Run the yarn along the seam edge for about 2.5cm before commencing seam.

Slip-stitch This is the method used for turning up hems or stitching double neckbands in place. Work one stitch into each cast-on or cast-off stitch to be sure that the work will be elastic. Always be sure that the stitches follow up evenly and do not form a crooked line.

Back-stitch This is the method most commonly used for joining knitted garments. The seam should be sewn one full stitch in from the end of each row so that all seams will be even. One stitch should be worked over every row. Darn in all ends of yarn **after** sewing seams.

Running-stitch A running-stitch seam is an easier and quicker method than back-stitch yet it gives the same neat appearance on the right side of garment. It is worked from the right side, making the matching of stripes, fair-isle and fancy patterns quite simple. The stitches should be taken one knitted stitch in from the edge so care must be taken to unroll edges of work as you go along. Place the 2 pieces of knitting side by side with right side uppermost. Leaving an end of about 15cm long (to be finished off later), insert the needle from wrong side to right side between the first and second rows on the left-hand piece of knitting. This is the only stitch which is taken from wrong side. Move to the right-hand piece of knitting, insert needle between cast-on and first row and bring it out between second and third rows, thus picking up 2 cross bars. Return to left-hand piece, insert needle in same space that yarn came out from previous stitch (between first and second rows) and pick up 2 cross bars. Continue working from side to side in this manner. Leave stitches about 1cm wide until you have completed about 2cm of stitching, then pull thread up fairly firmly to close seam. Yarn should be tight enough so that it does not show but loose enough to allow the garment elasticity. Check that pieces are even at the top of the rib and at any horizontal lines in pattern. Finish the top of your seam with 1 or 2 straight stitches over the cast-off edge and run the end along the edge of the fabric down the seam for about 3cm. Thread the end left at the cast-on edge into your needle and finish this off in the same way, taking care that you take the stitches over the cast-on edge and not over the seam. The lower edge of your garment will be perfectly straight with no dip at the seam.

Flat seam This method is sometimes used for knitted garments but more often for crochet garments. A flat seam may be worked from either the right or the wrong side of the work. Place the 2 pieces of fabric evenly together and sew stitch by stitch, always bringing the needle up from underneath to top through the centre of the stitch, then in same manner through corresponding stitch on second piece of fabric.

Note The methods are the same for knitting or crochet. Always keep work elastic: there should be as much stretch in your seam as there is in the rest of your garment.

PRESSING

Do not press your tension square.

Take pieces of work to ironing table and pin out with wrong side up. Pin out to correct width and as near correct length as possible. Dip a fairly thick cloth in a bowl of warm water, wring out tightly then press the iron over it a few times. Place the cloth over the work and bring the iron down to rest on the cloth. Do not glide your iron.

• Never press on the right side.
• Never press ribbed bands or collars.
• Never press without a cloth.
• Use your steam iron on a dry setting as the steam produced can damage the yarn.

HELPFUL HINTS

If you are working with several balls of yarn, put them in a plastic bag with holes in it (such as used for fruit and vegetables). Thread the yarns through the holes and they will stay clean and untangled.

A plastic ice cream container with a small hole in the centre of the lid also keeps yarn clean while you knit.

White talc rubbed on your hands will keep white wool white while you knit.

Knitters sometimes purl more loosely than they knit. You can even out your tension by using needles specified for knit rows and a size smaller needle for the purl rows.

If you must use yarn from different dye lots, knit alternate rows of each lot.

When storing wool scraps, wind them around a mothball.

Joining yarn Always join yarn at the end of a row, knotting it with a slip loop and darning the ends in when the work is completed.

Picking up dropped stitches Dropped stitches can be picked up easily with a crochet hook by working the stitches up from one row to the next. Work on right side of knitting for stocking stitch and from alternate sides for plain knitting (garter stitch). When the stitch is back in place, slip it on to needle and continue work.

SIZES FOR KNITTING NEEDLES AND CROCHET HOOKS

Metric size, that is, millimetres, is given first, followed by the old size.

Needles		Hooks	
12.00	0000	7.00	2
10.00	000	6.00	4
9.00	00	5.50	5
8.00	0	5.00	6
7.50	1	4.50	7
7.00	2	4.00	8
6.50	3	3.50	9
6.00	4	3.00	10/11
5.50	5	2.50	12
5.00	6	2.00	13/14
4.50	7		
4.00	8		
3.75	9		
3.25	10		
3.00	11		
2.75	12		
2.25	13		
2.00	14		

CROCHET

Crochet is altogether a more elegant and amusing craft than knitting. In crochet you can use all yarns from chunky wools to the finest of fine cottons and silks. And with this process you can make anything from fashion garments to children's toys, from massive woollen bedspreads to fine collars and flounces, and magnificent filigree bedspreads which can and should become family heirlooms. Crochet also combines with woven fabrics more easily than knitting. It is useful for edgings and insertions.

Before starting work, consider the following checklist:

• Check your tension carefully using the hook and yarn specified. Vary hook size and make another sample until correct tension is achieved. Measure tension over 10cm as crochet stitches and patterns do not lie as flat as knitting, and need more care.

• If using a yarn other than that specified in pattern, be especially careful in checking tension.

• Buy full quantity of yarn required to complete pattern as dye lots vary.

• Be aware that there is a distinct difference in the measurements of the wearer and of the garment. Most patterns give a Garment Measures measurement. This is usually for bust or chest and will tell you how much larger than the wearer the garment will be.

INSTRUCTIONS AND ABBREVIATIONS

alt: alternate
*: (asterisk), repeat the instructions following * as many times as specified, in addition to the original.
beg: beginning
blk(s): block(s)
cc: contrast colour
ch: chain
crab st: crab stitch, that is, work as for dc but from left to right instead of right to left so that sts are worked backward
dc: double crochet
dec: decrease, that is (yoh, draw up a loop in next st, yoh and draw through first 2 loops on hook) twice, yoh and draw through all loops on hook
dtr: double treble
foll: following
gr(s): group(s)
htr: half treble
inc: increase
lp(s): loop(s)
mc: main colour
p: picot
patt: pattern
pc st: popcorn stitch
rep: repeat
rnd: round
sep: separate(d)

sl-st: slip-stitch
sp: space
st(s): stitch(es)
tog: together
tr: treble
t tr: triple treble
yoh: yarn over hook

BASIC STITCHES FOR RIGHT-HANDERS

Place end of yarn in palm of left hand. Wrap yarn round first and second fingers of left hand.

Place hook under top front loop, draw the back loop through; remove fingers from loop, draw it up.

Take hook and yarn in right hand, hold left hand flat; bring yarn up between little finger and third finger of left hand, wind over little finger, then bring yarn up between third and second fingers and over second and first fingers and grip knot with thumb and first finger. Curl the little finger to give a firmer tension to the yarn—you will discover which is the most comfortable way to hold it.

Hold hook in right hand as you would a pencil (with the hook side facing you), placing your thumb on the flat part of the hook. When working, the thumb and first finger of left hand

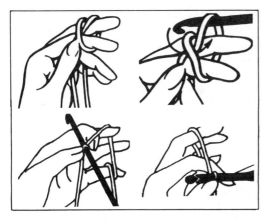

hold work as it is formed, while the second finger is extended so that hook may easily pass under the yarn. From now on, hands are omitted in sketches.

Chain (ch) Beginning of all crochet. Pass hook from left to right under the yarn held in left hand, draw thread through loop on hook.

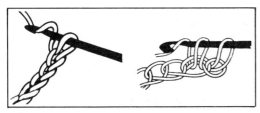

Repeat this action for number of chains required, holding work, as it is formed, quite firmly between thumb and first finger of left hand. When counting your chain, do not count the loop on your hook as a chain.

Double crochet (dc) Miss first chain below hook.

* Put hook from front to back under 2 top loops of next chain, take yarn over hook and draw through (2 loops now on hook), take yarn over hook, draw through both loops on hook (1 loop on hook). Repeat from *.

2nd Row: Make 1 chain (this is called 'turning ch').

* Put hook from front to back under 2 loops forming top of dc of previous row, take yarn over hook and draw through, take yarn over hook and draw through both loops on hook. Repeat from * to end.

Half treble (htr) Make 2 chain (turning ch). * Take yarn over hook, put hook from front to back under 2 loops of dc of previous row, take

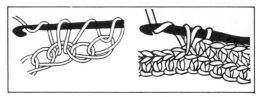

yarn over hook and draw through (3 loops now on hook); take yarn over hook and draw through all 3 loops on hook (1 loop now remains on hook). Repeat from * to end.

Treble (tr) Into first htr of previous row work 1 dc and 1 ch—this forms the turning ch which in treble and any higher stitch counts as one stitch and must be worked into when working the next row.

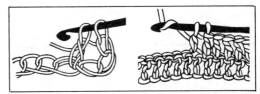

* Take yarn over hook, put hook from front to back under 2 top loops of htr of previous row, take yarn over hook and draw through (3 loops now on hook); take yarn over hook and draw through first 2 loops on hook (2 loops now remain on hook), take yarn over hook and draw through remaining 2 loops (1 loop remains on hook).

Repeat from * to end.

Slip-stitch (sl-st) Used chiefly for shapings. * Put hook from front to back under 2 loops of tr of previous row, take yarn over hook and draw through stitch and also through loop

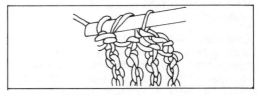

already on hook. Repeat from * three more times. Work 1 double crochet and 1 chain in next tr, then 1 treble in each tr to last 4 sts (which are 3 tr and turning ch), turn.

Fasten off Break off yarn, draw the end through the loop on hook and pull up to fasten.

BASIC STITCHES FOR LEFT-HANDERS

Place end of yarn in palm of right hand. Wrap yarn around first and second fingers of right hand.

Place hook under top front loop and draw the back loop through; remove fingers from loop, draw it up.

Take hook and yarn in left hand, hold right hand flat; bring yarn up between little finger and third finger of right hand, wind over little finger, then bring yarn up between third and second fingers and over second and first fingers and grip knot with thumb and first finger. Curl the little finger to give a firmer tension to the yarn—you will discover which is the most comfortable way to hold it.

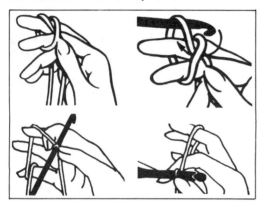

Hold hook in left hand as you would a pencil (with hook side facing you), placing your thumb on flat part of the hook. When working, the thumb and first finger of right hand hold work as it is formed, while second finger is extended so that hook may easily pass under the yarn. From now on, hands are omitted in sketches.

Chain (ch) Beginning of all crochet. Pass hook from right to left under the yarn held in right hand, draw the yarn thread through loop already on hook. Repeat this action for number

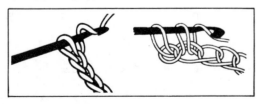

of chains required, holding work, as it is formed, quite firmly between thumb and first finger of right hand. When counting your chain, do not count the loop on your hook as a chain.

Double crochet (dc) Miss first chain below hook.

* Put hook from front to back under 2 top loops of next chain, take yarn over hook and draw through (2 loops now on hook), take yarn over hook, draw through both loops on hook (1 loop on hook). Repeat from * to end.

2nd Row: Make 1 chain (this is called 'turning ch').

* Put hook from front to back under 2 loops forming top of dc of previous row, take yarn over hook and draw through, take yarn over hook and draw through both loops on hook. Repeat from * to end.

Half treble (htr) Make 2 chain (turning ch). * Take yarn over hook, put hook from front to back under 2 loops of dc of previous row, take yarn over hook and draw through (3 loops

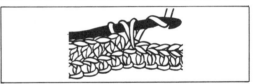

now on hook); take yarn over hook and draw through all 3 loops on hook (1 loop now remains on hook). Repeat from * to end.

Treble (tr) Into first htr of previous row work 1 dc and 1 ch—this forms the turning ch which in treble and any higher stitch counts as one stitch and must be worked into when working the next row. * Take yarn over hook, put hook from front to back under 2 loops of htr of previous row, take yarn over hook and draw

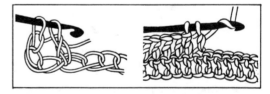

through (3 loops now on hook); take yarn over hook and draw through first 2 loops on hook (2 loops now remain on hook), take yarn over hook and draw through remaining 2 loops

(1 loop now remains on hook). Repeat from * to end.

Slip-stitch (sl-st) This stitch is used chiefly for shapings. Usually no turning ch is worked. * Put hook from front to back under 2 loops of tr of previous row, take yarn over hook and draw

through loop already on hook. Repeat from * three more times. Work 1 double crochet and 1 chain in next tr then 1 treble in each tr to last 4 sts (which are 3 tr and turning ch), turn.

Fasten off Break off yarn, draw the end through the loop on hook and pull up to fasten.

tog in the following way. Work next stitch all but the last movement, leave it on the hook then work the following st all but the last movement, yarn over hook and draw through all 3 loops on hook.

To work 3 sts tog, work all 3 sts all but the last movement, leaving each on hook, yarn over hook and draw through all 4 sts on hook. This applies to double crochet, half treble, or double treble and decreases should lie flat and be hardly noticed when work is complete.

• To increase in plain crochet it is usually possible to work twice into the same stitch.

• When increasing each end of row in plain crochet try to work increases 1 st in from edge of work to keep side edges as even as possible.

• If you have to join a new ball of yarn in the middle of a row, do not knot 2 ends together, but commence the new ball and continue working. Later tie the ends carefully and neatly at back of work and the knots should be almost invisible. Darn ends along at back and trim.

CROCHET HINTS

• Commencing chain should be worked fairly loosely. It is a good idea to use one size larger hook for the chain only.

• Make sure to work last stitch in each row into the turning chain at beginning of previous row. Otherwise work will gradually get narrower, as you will be losing 1 stitch each row.

• Count your stitches often, as it is easy to miss a stitch in plain crochet and size will soon suffer.

• The turning chain at the beginning of each row is counted as the first st, therefore the second stitch is worked into the top of the second last st of previous row.

• Insert hook under both top loops of stitch in all cases unless otherwise stated. Work into top of each stitch, not between sts, unless pattern states otherwise.

• Turn work before making turning ch for next row. This way turning ch will lie flatter and edge will be straighter.

• To give a straighter edge in treble (instead of working 3 ch at beg of row) turn, work 1 dc in top of last st, then 2 ch. This will stand the same height as the usual 3 ch and sit better. The same method can be used for half treble, where you would work 1 dc, 1 ch, or for double treble where you would work 1 dc, 3 ch.

• To decrease in plain crochet, work 2 sts

TRICOT CROCHET

Tricot crochet is worked with a special tricot needle, in two separate steps for each row. In the first step all loops for the row remain on the hook. In the second step the loops are worked off progressively.

Tricot is based on four simple steps:

Crochet chain and first step of first row Make a crochet chain of desired number of sts. Miss first ch, draw up a loop in 2nd ch and in each ch across, retaining all loops on hook. There should be the same number of loops on hook as there were ch sts to begin with.

Second step of first row, working all loops off Yarn over hook and draw through 1 loop, * yoh and draw through 2 loops, rep from * to end of row. One loop remains on hook at end of row.

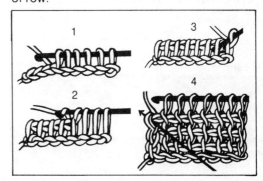

First step of second and subsequent rows
One loop left on hook at end of previous row forms first loop of next row, so miss first vertical st. * Insert hook into next vertical bar st on front of work (formed by loop of previous row) and draw up a loop, rep from * to last vertical bar st.

Making a firm edge Insert hook through last vertical bar and the st directly behind it (see arrow) and draw up a loop. There should again be the same number of loops on hook as there were ch sts to begin with. Rep steps 2, 3 and 4 for patt.

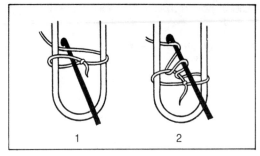

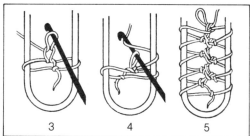

HAIRPIN CROCHET

Hairpin crochet is a traditional craft worked either on a simple loom or, more usually, on a metal 'hairpin' shape, using a crochet hook. Decorative lace strips are produced which can be used for edgings on inserts, or joined together to make table mats, stoles, cushion covers and so on.

To work a strip of hairpin crochet, make a slip-loop at one end of your yarn as for knitting or crochet, and holding the hairpin between thumb and first finger of left hand, with prongs upwards, slip the loop on to left-hand prong of the pin (the slip-loop should be long enough to reach halfway across to opposite prong).

Pass the yarn in front of the right-hand prong, then, holding yarn at back of pin, over fingers of left hand, as for crochet, insert the crochet hook through front of the loop on left-hand prong (1), and draw a loop through, yarn over hook (2), and draw through loop on hook.

(3) * pass crochet hook over top of right-hand prong so that it lies at back, then turn hairpin from right to left so that hook is now in front and the yarn lies over right-hand prong; insert hook under yarn round right-hand prong

(4), and draw through loop on hook, insert hook under front loop on left-hand prong, yarn over hook, draw a loop through, yarn over hook and draw through the two loops on hook, thus working 1 dc into left-hand loop. *

Rep from * to * until you have obtained the number of loops required (5), making certain you have the same number of loops on both sides of the strip; then fasten off as for ordinary crochet.

If you have too many loops on pin for comfortable working, count 51 loops on each side of pin, mark 50th loop with coloured thread, slip all loops off pin, and reinsert prongs in 51st loops. Continue working this way until the required number of loops has been worked.

Note To keep the strip from twisting before completing the number of loops required, try rolling strip as it comes off the prongs in a narrow piece of clean linen and pinning with a safety pin to bottom of prongs.

11

INDOOR PLANTS

ALL HOUSE PLANTS are really only at home outdoors. Many come from dense jungles, often starting life in the deep shade of a foliage canopy, gradually moving upward to claim their share of sunlight. This probably makes some plants adaptable to indoor conditions.

House plants can, however, be grown successfully without recreating a jungle. The key to success is remembering that warmth, moisture and light need to be kept in reasonable ratio. If warmth is decreased, moisture should also be decreased. Where light is poor, warmth and moisture should be reduced also.

Poor light and high temperature are common causes of problems. Blinds or curtains are often drawn during weekdays in working households. Sun on glass or other parts of the building makes the rooms hot. Then, on the days when the household is at home, the rooms are bright and sunny. Plants find it hard to adapt to these changes.

This high temperature, low light condition causes weeping figs, jade and some other plants to drop foliage suddenly and new growth to become weak. In hot and dry situations, tips and edges of leaves will brown and shrivel. Cold conditions and wet soil make many house plants rot, especially snake plant (sanseviera), pedilanthus, desert cacti, ixora and some pileas.

HEALTHY PLANTS

HOW MUCH WATER?

We often hear advice to give of water per week to a plant. This can be unreliable. The amount of water a plant need depends on temperature, humidity and the size of the plant in relation to soil and light. A plant in a warm, well-lit position may use twice as much water as one in cool shade. If a plant is making new growth, its water demands will be much greater than those of a dormant one.

The only answer is to let the surface soil dry out to a stage where it feels dry then give a good soaking.

The main exception to this is ferns, especially maidenhair, and to a lesser extent, flowering house plants.

Water ferns daily unless they are in peaty soil that holds water well. If so, water them when the soil surface is drying out.

Cold water can shock most house plants,

171

retarding growth, stopping flowering and, on plants such as African violets, can cause unattractive marks on foliage.

Use water at room temperature. Fill your watering container after use and leave it indoors until needed again. Or add enough hot water to take the chill off the tap water.

Chlorine can affect many plants. It can cause brown tips on spider plants, dracaenas and can kill Venus fly traps. It also causes brown blotching on leaf margins of dracaenas. This problem can be overcome by using cooled water which has been boiled: what is left in the jug or kettle before refilling.

Fluoride is more difficult. About half a cup of lime water, made by adding a teaspoon of hydrated lime to a litre of water, every three months for each sensitive plant is the best solution. Keep the lime water well corked.

WHEN TO FEED

Regular feeding is not automatic. Food should be given only when light intensity and temperatures are high enough for growth. Applying plant food that cannot be used can damage soil and plant. This can be minimised by leaching the soil before feeding. Soak the pot for 10 to 20 minutes in a container with water at about soil level. Then, as the last of the water is leaving the drainage holes, slowly pour another two litres or so of water through it.

Plant foods applied at about half the strength recommended for normal feeding are sufficient for most house plants. Never feed sick plants. Leave the feeding of newly bought or repotted plants for four to six weeks.

TESTING FOR LIGHT

It is hard to be specific about good or poor light. One rough test for light intensity is to place a white card facing the light source and hold your hand with outstretched fingers about 25cm above it. In theory, if light is 'bright', the hand will throw a definite shadow. If the shadow is faint, light is moderate. This test doesn't work when light is coming in through a wide area or from several directions and is actually coming under the hand. Probably a more reliable test is to say light is bright where room light switched on makes no noticeable difference to the brightness of the position.

Light can be supplemented by artificial lights, especially by fluorescent tubes only half a metre or so above the plants. This works well for foliage plants but to make flower buds, the red rays of incandescent globes are needed. Too many of these too close can create too much heat whereas fluorescent lights are not hot. There are special plant lights on the market.

HELPFUL HUMIDITY

For healthy growth all but desert cacti, succulents and snake plants need relative humidity in the vicinity of 40 to 50 per cent. This will not cause dampness of furnishings but is about the same as we need for healthy, comfortable living.

When air is heated in an enclosed room, the relative humidity drops considerably, in some cases to less than half that of the unheated air. This low humidity occurs in closed rooms

which have sun on large areas of glass, or with room heaters. The result is poor growth, lack of foliage and lustre, brown tips or edges on the leaves. It can affect flowering of African violets or cause flowers to become limp prematurely.

The effects of low humidity can be off set to some extent by keeping your plants well away from heaters and by grouping them together so that evaporation from soil and foliage forms a more humid micro-climate around them. Better still, place moist material below them, or use the old trick of standing them on a tray of pebbles with sufficient water in the base to keep the pebbles damp without it touching the pots.

CHANGES IN ENVIRONMENT

House plants are often affected adversely by change of environment. They have probably come from a nursery greenhouse, then been transported, sometimes in hot trucks, to a different set of conditions in shops. They may be left in a hot, closed car or carried through wind before reaching their new home.

It is good practice to let plants acclimatise for the first three or four weeks with only moderate watering, no feeding, good light and, if necessary, increased humidity.

SPRING CLEAN

Many house plants belong in the tropics. They tend to lose condition in areas with cool winters and are even more unhappy with the changes of temperature brought about by irregular house heating.

When spring comes, they will revive. Some will need repotting but most will respond to care. First trim off dead foliage. Some brownness may be old age but some may be caused by over-dry atmosphere.

If growth is poor and colour bad, a plant may need repotting. Tap the plant from its container. Cover most of the soil with one hand, invert the pot and tap the rim. The soil ball should come free. Untangle roots and transfer the plant to a container two sizes larger. Firm soil around root ball, then put container in a bucket of water for a good soaking. Do not feed for a few weeks when new growth should show.

Many plants with glossy or leathery leaves can be spring cleaned by sponging with soapy water (do not use detergent). This removes dust and can help remove pests. Do not put water on the leaves of African violets, gloxinias and others with downy leaves.

HOLIDAY HELP

Plastic bags are the best inexpensive help for your indoor plants if you have to go on holiday, although there are fold-up miniature plastic tents on the market which are specially planned to house your plants safely.

Before you cover plant and pot with a plastic bag, put a few stakes into the soil so that the plastic bag won't collapse on to the plant.

A plastic covering allows the plant to survive without watering. It traps the moisture that evaporates from the soil or transpires through the leaves. This reduces further evaporation. If you reduce light and temperature generally, this will also help the plant to get by without watering. If necessary, move your plants to a situation with indirect light before covering.

For baskets or pots which can't be covered, the best thing is to give a good watering and cover the surface with soaked sphagnum moss. This holds large quantities of water and imparts it slowly to the soil.

SIGNS TO WATCH

Browning and shrivelling of lower foliage This is natural but can be excessive if a plant is underwatered or underfed. Cut off dead foliage.

Falling of lower foliage This can be a natural seasonal occurrence. If it occurs often with weeping figs or jade, etc, it may be caused by warm but poorly lit situations or a sudden change of environment.

General yellowing and limp foliage This can be due to dryness or overwatering. In the latter case the soil will normally look dark with a slimy or mossy surface and the stem is usually darker. That the symptoms can be the same for both sounds odd, but for healthy functioning, roots need oxygen as well as water. In normal circumstances the oxygen is taken in through the tiny spaces or pores between the soil particles. When soil is continually wet, these spaces are filled with water, preventing oxygen from entering. Then the oxygen-starved or drowned roots are unable to take up water, even though they are in it, and therefore the plant shows much the same symptoms as with excessive dryness.

Dull sandy mottling of foliage This is usually due to attack by red spider mites, seen only in bright light, and more easily with a magnifying glass.

Sponging both sides of the foliage with a soapy cloth is usually effective; also misting with water during dry periods helps to prevent the problem. Spraying the plant in outdoor shade with malathion, Lebaycid or Folimat is an effective chemical cure.

Leaves limp or shrivelling, match-head size or smaller downy white objects in crevices along leaf veins, stems and foliage of ferns This is mealy bug. A common pest of pig-a-back plant, African violets, ferns, it can also attack most plants. When infestation is not extensive, touch each plant with a cotton wool swab moistened with methylated spirits. Otherwise, move to outdoor shade and either sprinkle some Disyston granules on soil below plant or spray with Folimat.

Small green or brownish-grey insects on young shoots, particularly on maidenhair fern These will be aphids. Carefully inverting plant and dunking foliage in soapy water usually removes them. Otherwise, use bioresmethrin or pyrethrum sprays.

PLANT CARE GUIDE

Different plants require varying conditions. The following is a guide to the care of your indoor plants, arranged alphabetically:

Adiantum (maidenhair) See Ferns.

African violet (Saintpaulia) Needs bright light near a window but not direct sunlight through glass, also moderate humidity. Allow soil surface to become just dry between waterings. Use room temperature water. Feed every three to four weeks, when in active growth, with African violet food or half-strength packeted complete soluble food, supplemented by a scant one-quarter teaspoon of superphosphate scattered over potting mix every three months.

Remove runners or suckers from base of plant and occasionally thin out clustered foliage. Propagate from leaves with leaf stem slightly bedded in peaty potting mix or just touching water.

Aglaonema modestum (Chinese evergreen) Long oval then sharply tapering leathery dark green foliage later developing caney base. Suits poor or moderate light, moderate watering. Silver King and others have more slender silver variegated foliage.

Aluminium plant See Pilea.

Anthurium (flamingo flower) Handsome foliage, waxy red-pink or white artist's palette-shaped flowers. Prefers conditions similar to African violets but a little drier when the room is cold.

Aphelandra Caney plant grown for handsome dark glossy variegated foliage. Prefers bright indirect light. Allow soil surface to dry between waterings.

Aralia See Fatsia and Dizygotheca.

Asparagus Numerous varieties all with fern-like foliage. Water as aphelandra. If room is warm, needs bright light, otherwise accepts moderate light.

Aucuba (gold dust shrub) Has large glossy gold-flecked foliage, excellent cold resistance. Grows best with spells in outdoor shade.

Begonia Rex begonias are grown for colourful foliage; need bright to moderate light and soil surface to become just dry between the waterings. Tuberous begonias with camellia or rose-like flowers prefer bright indirect light, moderate to warm, but not high, temperatures and good ventilation. Elatior type, like smaller tuberous begonias, prefer moderate to cool temperatures and high humidity.

Billbergia See Bromeliad.

Brassaia Taller umbrella tree (see Schefflera).

Brassaia arboracola (dwarf umbrella tree) Finer, darker and closer set foliage than its larger counterpart. Best with two or three canes in 20–30cm cm pot and pruned down to about 1.5m. Stands bright to low light, moderate watering.

Bromeliad Includes aechmenas, billbergias, neoregelias, nidulariums, vriesias, etc. Grown for spectacular foliage and either interesting flower spikes or richly coloured plant centres. They grow in poor light but need bright light to flower or colour well. Vase-shaped plant types need water kept in centre of plant. Moderately moist peaty compost is not essential but benefits most types.

Cacti All but strap leaf types stand very dry atmosphere, need moderately cool conditions and soil to dry out between waterings in winter, and nearly so at other times.

Cacti (strap) The epiphyllums and nopalxochia need loose, well-composted soil and regular watering except for a few weeks during January. Zygocactus, ephilopsis, schlumbergera, etc. (crab's claw types) — needs are similar to strap cacti but they flower better with a dry period in early autumn and, if kept dark at night, during March and April.

Caladium Grown for large arrow-shaped, beautifully coloured foliage. Need bright light,

high humidity and watering whenever soil surface dries during warm conditions, then dryness as foliage yellows towards winter. Tubers shoot again during spring.

Calathea (peacock or prayer plant) Beautifully marked oval or elongated foliage. Needs bright light for good colour, water whenever surface dries during warm conditions, keep fairly dry if cold in winter. Low humidity causes leaf edges to brown.

Calceolaria Broad clusters of globular red and yellow marked flowers. Needs moderate water and moderately cool conditions with bright light. Plant naturally dies in summer.

Chinese evergreen See Aglaonema.

Chinese fire fern The attractive bronze foliage falls with sudden changes of environment, poor light and with cool winter conditions. Prefers bright light and moderate water while environment conditions are warm.

Chlorophytum (spider plant) Rosettes of tapering strap-like green and cream foliage. Needs moderate to bright light. Chlorine or fluoride water causes browning of tips and margins.

Cissus antarctica (kangaroo vine) and Cissus rhombifolia with divided foliage Both are handsome twiners needing moderate watering and moderate to bright light, especially in the case of Cissus antarctica.

Cordyline terminalis Rosette of broad strap-like foliage on slender canes.

Crab's claw (zygocactus) See Cacti.

Croton Beautifully coloured slender leathery foliaged shrubs. Need very bright light, even direct sun through glass, plenty of water in heat but allow to nearly dry out and keep further from glass when nights are cold.

Cyclamen Unlike African violets and many other house plants, cyclamen need cool nights because warmth induces dormancy and ends their flowering cycle. In warm rooms it pays to put them out at night or close to glass where outdoor cold is transmitted. An hour or two of direct morning sun improves them further. Water thoroughly whenever surface soil feels dry and feed sparingly, if at all, once flowering commences.

Devil's ivy See Scindapsus.

Dieffenbachia (dumb cane) Canes with large oval cream spotted or marked foliage. Needs bright to moderate light, water when soil surface dries; avoid positions close to glass on chilly nights as it resents extremes of temperature. Over-leggy canes can be cut back in late spring. Avoid eye or mouth contact with the plant's sap.

Dizygotheca (finger aralia) Erect cane surrounded by slender-stemmed large bronze leaves divided into serrated finger-like leaflets. Stands moderately poor to bright light. Water moderately. Size may be reduced as with dieffenbachia.

Dracaena (happy plant) Canes crested with a rosette of strap-like foliage. The handsomely variegated D. deremensis types adapt to low or bright light. Allow surface to dry between waterings. Brown tips and margins due to low humidity, also chlorine or fluoride in water. D. godseffiana has spotted oval leaves on thin pendulous canes.

Dumb cane See Dieffenbachia.

Fatsia (Japanese aralia) Erect cane to 1.5m with handsomely lobed leathery green leaves 30–35cm across. Adapts to outdoor semi-shade or moderate indoor light; cold tolerant, moderate watering.

Ferns The main need, especially of maidenhair, is plenty of water. Keep soil surface damp and feed sparingly, if at all. Avoid draughts and aspects where foliage is dragged by curtains, electric cords, etc. Cut off old outer fronds that die (happens naturally).

Brown or black streaking of foliage is due to leaf nematode (eel worm). Pinch off and burn or for large infestations, spray or water in outdoor shade with Metasystox, observing label precautions carefully.

Most ferns need moderate to bright light. Holly fern (cyrtomium) and, to some extent, fish-bone types adapt to poor light.

Ficus (rubber trees, weeping figs) Large leathery-leaved rubber trees adapt to moderate or moderately low light provided soil surface is allowed to dry between the waterings. Weeping fig (Ficus benjamina) drops foliage in poor light, especially if room is hot and closed up. Low humidity, found in such areas as near heaters during winter, causes browning of leaf margins.

Fittonia (nerve plant) Low bushing oval-leafed plant with contrasting lighter or red veining. Suit low to moderate light, keep fairly damp except when room temperatures are low. Ideal for terrariums as they like high humidity.

Gloxinia Gloxinias provide a fine show of colourful red, blue and white large waxy bell flowers during summer and die back to a dormant corm during winter. They are repotted in fresh potting soil when the new growth begins in spring. Need bright light like African violets, water whenever the soil surface becomes dry and three to four weekly feedings with one-third to half strength complete soluble plant food when in active growth. Withhold feeding and reduce watering when flowers finish.

Hedera (ivy) Many types useful for baskets or other trailing effects. Needs moderate to bright light, only moderate watering. Check occasionally for red spider mite or scale.

Hoya Twiner with exquisite flowers. Needs moderate to bright light and humidity-fibrous compost that nearly dries between waterings. Do not cut old flower spurs as these produce again.

Jade See Portulacaria.

Kangaroo vine See Cissus.

Kentia See Palms.

Maranta Treat as Calathea.

Palms Most palms need bright light and the soil surface to become dry between waterings but not for soil to completely dry. Most losses are due to overwatering or excessive dryness.

The most adaptable to indoor conditions of the taller palms is kentia (howea) which survives in moderate light and, of smaller types, neanthe bella (parlour palm). Majority of others need bright light and moderate humidity.

Brown tips are due to dry atmosphere or, more frequently, over-dry or, occasionally, to over-wet soil. To regain appearance, trim these to retain near-natural leaf shape. Occasional loss of a lower frond is natural; trim it off. Excessive loss indicates poor light or incorrect watering.

Leaf spotting usually indicates soft, downy, palm scale or flat scale. Remove either by sponging foliage on both sides with a soapy cloth—easiest when plant is on side and leaf spread over flat surface. This treatment also checks red spider mite which causes fine mottling or dull sand-blasted appearance, or leaf-stripping caterpillar which lives in leaves it webs together.

Feed only when there is sign of new growth, then at half strength, and leach soil with water first to remove build-up of excess soil salts.

Pedilanthus Plastic-like zig-zagged stems, small leaves, pinkish in good light. Needs soil to be kept fairly dry in cool conditions.

Peperomia Diverse family, those with rosetted growth may rot at base if soil is too frequently damp. If so, remove and re-root plant on drier soil. Otherwise, moderate to bright light is needed except for the variegated types such as Pink Lady that colour better away from bright light.

Philodendron Covers a great variety of plants. The most striking are the trailing or climbing Poxycardium varieties with leathery, heart-shaped, deeply-divided, palm-like leaves eventually reaching nearly one metre across. These grow in open gardens in warm climates, gradually developing a stout trunk but all types adapt to moderate light provided the soil surface is allowed to dry out between waterings.

Pilea cadierii (aluminium plant) Needs bright light, moderate water and to be away from coal, gas or oil fumes. Brown-edged foliage indicates that humidity is too low. P. serpillacea (artillery fern) needs brighter light. Drops foliage in poor light or in closed warm rooms.

Portulacaria afra (jade) Branching growth with small, waxy, jade-like foliage which drops in closed warm rooms, especially when light is poor. Overwatering also causes foliage drop.

Primula obconica Heads of primrose-like flowers in lavender, purple, white or pink. Best raised in outdoor shade and brought into moderate to bright light indoors for flower display which lasts at least six weeks. Water whenever soil surface dries.

Rubber plant See Ficus.

Saintpaulia See African violet.

Sanseviera (snake plant or mother-in-law's tongue) Waxy, erect, strap-like leaves, usually banded and cream margined. Stands poor light, needs to be kept fairly dry, especially so during cold conditions or base rot occurs.

Schefflera (Queensland umbrella tree) Caney stem with umbrella-like cluster of large, bright green, glossy leaves divided into oval leaflets. Needs moderate to bright light to grow well. Over-leggy plants can be cut to preferred size in spring to encourage side shoots. Tip, with foliage removed, can be restarted as a cutting.

Scindapsus (devil's ivy, pothos) Similar to

heart-shaped philodendron with thicker twining or pendulous canes and glossier foliage heavily variegated gold. Makes an attractive basket or totem plant. In warm, humid situations develops large divided adult foliage.

Has a similar adaptability to philodendron but needs moderate to bright light for good colour.

Tolmiea (pig-a-back plant) Common name comes from the formation of plantlets on the long-stemmed, slightly hairy green leaves. This is not a jungle plant, being native to the north-west coast of North America from Alaska to San Francisco. Therefore it is at home in cool conditions provided light is moderate to bright.

Umbrella tree (dwarf) See Brassaia arboa-cola.

Umbrella tree (Queensland) See Schefflera.

Zygocactus See Cacti (strap).

HELPFUL HINTS

Bulbs can be forced, that is, made to flower early, for their first season, but not for the next year. If you grow bulbs indoors, buy new ones each year. Old bulbs can be planted outdoors or, if you don't have a garden, can be given to a friend with the warning that they won't flower until their second season.

To moisten bulb fibre thoroughly punch several holes in the plastic bag and immerse it in a bucket of water until the fibre is soaked. Squeeze it almost dry before using.

Turn plants around regularly to stop them leaning toward the light.

Castor bases are worthwhile for large pots on balconies or terraces. The pots can then be moved about to get the best of the sun.

TERRARIUMS

To prevent fungi or algae in a terrarium, sterilise the soil. This is most easily done by baking in the oven. Use cooled boiled water to dampen the soil at all times.

Position a terrarium in a well-lit position out of direct sun and add a teaspoon or two of water every few months if it is sealed and more often if it is open.

RECIPE FOR POTTING MIX

Combine seven parts of volume of raw com-posted garden loam, three parts moistened peatmoss and two parts coarse river sand. If the garden soil is heavy, add a little more sand. To each 8–10 litre bucket of the mix add one level teaspoon of garden lime or dolomite and one heaped teaspoon of complete plant food.

NO PLACE LIKE HOME FOR PLANTS

What happens to your plants if you move house? Consider these points:

• The Australian Department of Health and the Department of Agriculture prohibit the free movement of plants, fruits etc. between certain areas of Australia.

• Plants are difficult to load with furniture and effects and can cause damage to your valued possessions, or some other customer's valued possessions.

• Plants cannot be stacked to gain maxi-mum loading density. As you pay for cubic space, the freight cost of plants may be more than their value.

• Packing of plants is very expensive and on long journeys, lack of ventilation, water and light may make it hard for them to survive.

• So say goodbye to your plants. Leave them where they belong to be looked after by their new owners.

12

FUR, FIN AND FEATHER

NO ADDITION to the household except a child is likely to make more difference than a pet, particularly if the chosen pet is an active, strong-minded cat or dog. Such an animal will mean disruption to routine but will bring great fun and affection. It will also mean that you will become acquainted with a vet, possibly with a council officer, and, if you are keen about breeding or showing, with other fanciers. These people can be a valuable source of encouragement and information to you.

Visiting a vet is much like visiting a doctor. He will be prepared to listen but he expects you to have your animal prepared and in a fit state to be examined. An animal at the vet is much like a very small child at the doctor—it cannot explain where it hurts or what is wrong with it. You should watch your animal's behaviour and physical changes closely so you can give the vet as many clues as possible. Don't be afraid to discuss fees beforehand. Animals these days are treated with sophisticated drugs and machines which can be expensive.

LIVING WITH PETS

Kittens love to sharpen their claws on the best carpets, and puppies love to chew the furniture. Both cats and dogs tend to shed hairs and fleas round the house. The following hints will help you to look after your pets—and protect your home.

A home-made cat-tree should keep a new kitten from scratching furniture. Nail an ordinary log of firewood, about 50cm long, so that it stands upright on a piece of board about 50cm square. Cover the log with an old piece of carpet and introduce your kitten to it.

A few mothballs in the cushion of a chair will keep cats off it.

A damp sponge will remove animal hair from furniture.

To stop a new puppy chewing the furniture, dab a little oil of cloves on the wood. If the smell does not keep him away the taste will.

Scattering orange peel is a homely old way to keep cats off the garden. There are, however, tablets on the market these days which combine every known harmless cat repellent.

To make an extra hole in an animal's flea collar, heat a steel knitting needle over a flame and push it in.

Reflector tape on your pet's collar will cut down the danger of its being struck by a car at night.

Remove burrs from a pet's coat by working oil into the area or by crushing the burrs with pliers. Crushed burrs lose their grip and can be combed out.

Remove tar from dogs with eucalyptus oil.

Rub in, leave for an hour then shampoo your dog.

Try a creme rinse for dogs whose fur tangles. To cut soap film and wash away strong soap smells, add vinegar or lemon juice to the rinse water.

Put a little laundry blue in the shampoo or rinse water for dogs or cats with pale fur for a whiter, brighter pet.

When your pet is moulting, put a strainer in the drain-hole at bath time to stop pipes clogging.

DOGS

Dogs remain the most popular of all pets. People acquire one to watch, to work or simply for companionship. In a family with young children another reason is often to teach children to think of others and to take responsibility.

The average dog's life is about 15 years. By the time a child is about three he or she is independent enough to cope with a pet, although some large dogs (and a dog can be fully grown at six months) may be physically too much for them. If a dog is acquired as a puppy when the first child in a family is about three, the dog should be around long enough to see the family moving through the last years of childhood.

When — or before — you get a dog you would be wise to choose a vet. It is worth asking friends with pets about their vet experience, although in the average suburb or town there is often little chance to shop around; you might as well settle for the one closest to home. It is also important to ring your local council and find out exact requirements for registration and any other regulations affecting your pet. These vary from State to State.

CHOOSING YOUR DOG

Young or old? A puppy of about six weeks is probably the ideal as a family acquisition. There are the disadvantages that you have to toilet train it, and teething will probably make it an endless chewer of any socks, slippers or such left lying around. Balanced against the wisdom of choosing an older dog which has been trained and has a good medical history is the fact that you will have to work hard to establish good relations and that the dog may not like children particularly and may never come to like them.

Male or female? Desexed females are generally accepted as the most trouble-free and affectionate pets. It is common sense to have any dog, male or female, not intended for breeding desexed. It won't change their nature but it will improve their social acceptability.

The ideal dog If sentiment and impulse did not come into it, every dog owner in Australia would acquire a fairly small, short-haired, dark-coated dog with small upright ears. That would give the dog the best chance of avoiding illnesses and upsets coming from the Australian environment with its heat, ticks and bush. It would also keep the owner's expenditure of cash and time within bounds.

Dogs which bite Among breeds more likely to bite are corgis, cocker spaniels, afghans, cattle dogs, terriers, dalmatians, dobermanns and collies.

How to choose? You will not be an instant expert, but there are a few simple tests you can make and precautions you can follow.

First, it is worth while to check on how many litters the mother has had over the previous few years. Too-frequent litters may have left her bones depleted of calcium and this deficiency may have been passed on to the pups. Also, check on whether she was wormed and vaccinated during gestation.

Once you are satisfied that the breeder knows his or her job, turn your attention to the litter. Although your heart may go out to the small and vulnerable runt, you will be buying yourself trouble later on. Watch the pups playing and look for one which is active with glossy coat and bright eyes. You can weigh him in your hand against others in the litter to make sure his size is right.

CHECKLIST
While looking at the pup, check for the following:

- The coat should be glossy.
- The eyes, including the irises, should be the same colour and the same shape and size in their general outline. Eyes should be bright.
- Smell the ears; a foul smell means an infection inside the ear. This is a fairly common problem which a vet is able to rectify.
- If the dog is shaking its head, this indicates ear mites. However, this is not serious as they can be cleared with ear drops.
- Feel the abdomen for hernia which will show as a lump in the middle part of the stomach around the navel region. Only surgery will rectify the problem.
- Check the tail is not broken and run your fingers down it to make sure it has no kinks.
- Check the dog for fleas and for signs of diarrhoea or vomiting, both of which could indicate trouble.
- Make sure the teeth are in line, the gums a healthy pink, and that upper and lower jaws are the same length.

FIRST NIGHT HOME
This can be emotionally draining for dog and owner. There are a few tricks to make the puppy feel at home. Get a rag or cloth from the breeder and use it in the pup's bed, together with an old jumper from the puppy's new home. These will give it some sense of security.

Place a ticking clock in the bed. This will stop it crying.

Keep the puppy warm and well fed with a drink of warm milk. A hot water bottle can help.

For the first few days give the puppy the same food it has been having.

POPULAR BREEDS

TOY BREEDS
Small dogs, less than 30cm at shoulder, light-boned.

Pug Short-faced, short coat. Gentle and calm. Ideal family pet.

Chihuahua Small, cheap to feed, but inclined to be nervous.
Miniature pinscher Short-haired, excellent temperament, good with children.

TERRIERS
Originally bred to be rodent killers, in general alert and active, at times aggressive.
Australian terrier Rough-coated. Will love the family's children but may be aggressive towards visitors.
Bull terrier Totally devoted to its own family but aggressive to other dogs.

GUN DOGS
Bred to work with hunters, generally gentle and sensible.
Cocker spaniel Medium size and relatively short-haired, although it requires grooming. Gentle and kind.
Labrador retriever Short-haired, very gentle to people and dogs. Considered an ideal family pet.
German short-haired pointer Very pleasant dog although, like the labrador, bigger than recommended for a city dog. Stands about 50–55cm.

HOUNDS
In theory, bred to hunt foxes and hares.
Dachshund Medium-sized dog on very short legs. Lovely temperament and good housedog. Wonderful to family.
Whippet Looks like a small greyhound. Very short-haired, gentle, quiet and easily trained. Affectionate but content by itself when you're busy.
Beagle Will become very attached to its family but tends to go off on expeditions and, although he will always try to come home, this isn't ideal in a city dog.

Basset A biggish dog on short legs. Excellent temperament and short-haired, but long ears and wrinkles can render it prone to skin problems.
Basenji About 35cm tall, very short coat, elegant and easy to care for.

WORKING OR GUARD DOGS
This category includes kelpies and cattle dogs which are too active for city life.
German shepherd Also known as alsation. Big, with undeserved reputation for aggression. As temperamentally sound as any breed. Community prejudice can be a problem.
Collie (rough) and bearded collie Not as energetic as the Australian working dogs so is happy in its own backyard. Good family dog.

NON-SPORTING
Boston terrier Beautifully marked, ideal family dog. Active, intelligent.
Dalmatian Middle-sized, comes with black or brown spots. Excellent temperament.
Miniature poodle Most intelligent little dog which will be lonely by itself. Needs grooming and clipping.
British bulldog Short-haired, good pet but can suffer sunburn in summer because of his flat face. Gentle, but fierce expression.
Boxer A lovely dog, good with its family but aggressive to other dogs.
Dobermann Larger than recommended for city life, good watchdog, aggressive. Needs fair amount of exercise.

TRAINING

HOUSE TRAINING
This should begin the moment the puppy is weaned. Start with a newspaper or dirt tray filled with sand or ashes and put the puppy on to the tray several times a day, particularly after a feed. If this is done regularly, the puppy will soon get the idea.

As the pup grows older it must learn to go to the toilet outside. Gradually move the tray towards the door, finally moving it outside. The pup should be placed on it five or six times a day, always first thing in the morning, last thing at night and after each meal.

While the puppy still needs the tray, it is a good idea to leave a bit of used newspaper or sand behind after cleaning so the pup will

recognise the smell and be stimulated to urinate. Choose a spot in the garden where the earth is reasonably soft so the dog can scratch around in the dirt; also, its smell will remain in that area and it will keep going back.

When your puppy goes to the toilet, praise it. Dogs respond better to praise than punishment. Always reward your dog by telling it it's a good pup. If it makes a mistake, never rub its nose in the puddle or faeces. Take it to the spot, hold it near and say 'no'. Or scold it, saying 'bad dog' several times. Then put it out of the house or take it for a walk. Remember, reward the dog but don't physically punish it. You can teach your dog to do its toilet anywhere you want by giving it a reward whenever it does the job in the right place.

GENERAL BEHAVIOUR
Never allow your dog to worry you or your visitors at mealtimes.

Don't give a dog titbits from the table or feed it sweets or biscuits while you are eating; this encourages it to beg.

Feed your dog at the same time and place every day so that it recognises a regular mealtime.

If your dog is to live indoors, right from the start keep it in one place—on a mat, cushion, basket or in a box. Watch, and if it ventures beyond this domain, push it back and say 'no'.

Emphasise the limits of its territory by slapping a rolled-up newspaper on the floor. This makes a lot of noise, so don't overdo it or you may make the pup nervous. When you feel

you can rely on it to stay in its box or on its cushion, go out of the room for a couple of minutes and watch through a crack in the door. If it attempts to get out of the box, call out 'no'. Eventually you should be able to leave it for a time by itself.

Give it some playthings of its own: a rubber bone or perhaps an old shoe. If it attempts to chew curtains, rugs and so on, scold it and offer it its own toys. Train it not to bite or chew electric plugs or wires.

Stop your puppy from jumping up at you by bending down—it is only trying to get near your face—and saying 'no' in a sharp tone if it gets too close. If it starts developing other bad habits, use the same command situation.

EXERCISE
The size and sex of the dog are important in determining territorial requirements. It is rare to see female dogs roaming far from home. Little dogs need less space and cause fewer problems in public areas.

Most dogs require about half a hectare of land to satisfy their needs but naturally that's impossible in urban areas. Restrictions can upset the dog psychologically and it will show its displeasure in many different ways: excess barking, the destruction of furniture, gaining weight, wandering around schools. Wandering brings the dog into other dogs' territory, often resulting in fights and detention in a pound.

WASHING
Washing should take place about every three weeks.

Any bland soap is suitable or you can use a shampoo. If the dog becomes sensitive or starts scratching after a shampoo, change the brand or go back to a bland soap.

Choose a sunny day and take the dog out

on to the lawn or sit it in a bathtub. Rinse the dog first and then apply soap or shampoo. Leave lather on for five to ten minutes, then rinse.

If you use a flea wash, for dogs between three and seven months it should be diluted to about half the manufacturer's recommended concentration. Always wear gloves.

If your dog loves swimming in the sea, it always must be washed afterwards as the salt water will irritate the skin and may cause dermatitis.

DIET

Up to the age of seven months most of the dog's food intake has been required for growth. But at seven months the dog is fully grown and food intake goes into maintenance.

If your dog is not pregnant, lactating or working, it should only be fed once a day, usually in the evening. In the morning a small drink of milk or a biscuit is sufficient.

In some toy breeds which are finicky eaters you may have to increase the quantity of the feed and perhaps offer food two or three times a day.

Rule number one is never overfeed your dog. An overweight dog is heading for problems. Once the dog is ten months old, supplements are unnecessary unless on a raw meat diet, in which case calcium carbonate should be fed at the rate of one teaspoon per 5kg of body weight.

DIET FOR YOUNG DOGS
Here is a reasonable diet for a dog between the

ages of six weeks and three months, if you do not choose to use commercial food:

In the morning Between 7 and 8am, milk with cereal (Farex, porridge or cornflakes).

Second meal Around 11am, a small portion of finely minced or scraped meat. Any meat such as beef, mutton or kangaroo, either raw or cooked, is suitable.

Afternoon tea Between 2 and 3pm, feed a small portion of milk with a couple of dog biscuits or maybe a soft, boiled piece of bone to keep the pup occupied during the afternoon.

Main meal Between 6 and 7pm, this meal eventually will become the dog's main meal as he grows older. It should consist of meat and supplements such as calcium. The meat can be either finely minced or cut up and ground, whichever the dog prefers. The calcium carbonate should be added at one level teaspoon per 5kg of puppy. You also can add scraps and cooked vegetables or gravy that have been left over from your own meal.

Although only four meals a day are necessary, it is not a bad idea around 9 or 10pm to give it a titbit such as a biscuit. This will make the dog more contented and more likely to sleep through the night.

DOG BISCUITS
3½ cups wholemeal flour
1 cup white flour
125g minced steak
1 dessertspoon salt
water

Put flours, salt in basin and rub in mince. Mix to a stiff dough with water, roll out and put on oven tray. Cut in squares and bake in slow oven. Add 1 tablespoon cod liver oil if biscuits are for a puppy.

THE LAW

Your dog will have to be registered with your local council within a stipulated time of your acquiring it. This time varies between States so check with your council on what you have to do.

Biting 'Beware of the dog' signs carry little weight. A victim may not see it or even understand it. You must keep your dog under restraint if you know it is likely to bite or cause damage. However, if your dog bites a thief or trespasser it is most unlikely you will be fined.

You may not be fined if the victim teased the dog.

Damages Your dog can be destroyed for attacking horses, cattle, sheep, goats or pigs if the owner has no reasonable way of stopping the attacks. Damage suits can be for bodily injury, death, damage to clothing, injury to another animal or damage to a vehicle. If a dog causes the death of a person, the Dog Act provides that the relatives can sue the dog's owner under the Compensation to Relatives Act, just as if the person had been killed in a road accident.

Fines The owner of a dog which attacks or causes injury to a person in a public place can also be fined. Any greyhound owner who does not muzzle the dog effectively can be fined.

Strays Unaccompanied dogs found in a public place or away from their homes can be seized. If they are not collected within a certain time of a notice being sent to the owner, they can be destroyed.

German shepherds These must be kept on a chain, cord or leash, otherwise the owner may be fined.

Bitch on heat No female is allowed at large at any time while on heat. The owner may be fined if this happens.

Fouling the footpath Some States and councils have fines for this offence.

Barking Your continually barking dog not only may irritate the neighbours, in some areas it is illegal. Barking is a dog's natural means of communication and this is part of its usefulness. If it barks continually it could be for many reasons: it is chained allowing insufficient movement for long periods; lack of reasonable exercise; lack of training; no shelter from bad weather; loneliness; unsuitable or insufficient

diet or lack of water; ill health; or competition with other dogs. Most of these causes can and should be eliminated. There are also a few simple ways to subdue barking, such as eliminating direct line-of-sight vision between the dog and children or animals, taking the dog to a recognised animal trainer or insulating the kennel against noise.

COMMON COMPLAINTS

When taking your dog to the vet make sure it has been bathed recently, secure its collar and if it is likely to be savage, have it muzzled. Take the dog around the block first so that it will have emptied its bladder.

If your dog is healthy, the vet is still the best person for advice and action on vaccination, worming, teething and desexing. If it appears to be sick, observe it as carefully as you can. The vet will rely on you for help in diagnosis.

ALLERGIC ECZEMA

One of the most common problems seen by vets, this is certainly the most prevalent skin ailment. The allergic reaction may be caused by fleas, mites or by vegetation.

Allergies to plants cause the worst type of eczema as they flare up every time the pet roams in the garden or may recur at certain times of the year corresponding to the particular plant's growth. The types of vegetation most likely to cause allergies are wandering jew, paspalum, kikuyu and buffalo grass.

The condition is more common among low-slung breeds, such as dachshunds, corgis and cocker spaniels. An acute red rash will appear suddenly on the underbelly, with or without angry pimples, pus or larger infected areas.

Treatment may aim to localise the cause of the allergy.

Dogs which are taken for a run through a park or thick undergrowth often develop a rash that night or the next day. Regular administration of anti-inflammatory drugs may be necessary throughout summer.

BAD BREATH

Raw meat or meat buried too long down at the bottom of the garden can cause bad breath in your pet.

Bad breath can also be caused by infections of the mouth such as: tartar build-up on the teeth leading to inflammation of the gums (gingivitis), ulcers, viral attacks and bacterial infection of tonsils or lymph glands of the mouth.

Most causes of bad breath require veterinary treatment.

CONSTIPATION

This can be defined as infrequent or difficult bowel movement. Causes include slipped discs where there is a weakness in the back legs, paralysis, pelvic fractures, mechanical obstructions, excessive amounts of bone in the diet or painful anal area cuts.

If a dog is prone to constipation do not include bones in the diet. Serve canned food, or at least semi-moist food. Do not feed dry rations.

Give the dog paraffin oil orally at the rate of 5mL twice daily, depending on the consistency of the droppings following each treatment.

Give Dilax or Coloxyl tablets; one tablet twice weekly depending on droppings.

CONVULSIONS

Fits can be caused by epilepsy, insecticidal chemicals, strychnine poisoning, snail killer, distemper infection or low glucose levels in the blood to the brain.

The precise causes of epilepsy are not com-

pletely understood. The earliest occurrence is when the pups cut their teeth at two to six months, particularly if they are heavily infested with worms.

Later, epilepsy can be caused by shock, fear, injury, sexual excitement, pain or stress. Toy breed pups are particularly susceptible to fits. But often medication will help them grow out of it.

As a first-aid measure, when the dog starts to have an epileptic fit, place it in a dark room and keep it quiet. The fit usually lasts only two or three minutes, in which time the dog may urinate, defecate and produce a frothy saliva at the mouth. Then it will be totally exhausted and lie down.

Always contact your vet.

A number of poisons like strychnine and snail bait cause fits. Symptoms include spasms of shivering which progress to collapse and violent spasmodic extension (intensified by noise) of the legs and head. Take the dog to a vet immediately.

Insecticidal rinses, such as those with an over-concentration of malathion, can cause fits. These rinses should *not* be used on

puppies as the insecticide is absorbed through the dog's skin and can cause permanent brain damage.

DIARRHOEA

This has many causes: bacterial and viral infections, worms, gut tumours, hepatitis, distemper, leptospirosis, poisoning, coccidiosis, overeating, food allergies, bad foods, sudden dietary changes, defective pancreatic secretions, chronic liver disease and nervousness.

Diarrhoea may be acute or chronic. Acute diarrhoea is manifested by watery, sometimes bloody stools in a previously healthy animal. If accompanied by fever, depression, failure to eat and abdominal pain, the gastro-intestinal tract is probably inflamed. Eating garbage or other spoiled foods is a common cause.

Diarrhoea in young pups can be caused by cows' milk. Stop the milk for three to four days and give the animal Kaomagma. After a few days' break, return the pup to the cows' milk, broken down 50/50 with water for three to four weeks. Then gradually increase the concentration of the milk.

Worms, particularly roundworms, also may cause diarrhoea in pups.

To rectify the diarrhoea, feed for a short time the following preparation (it is for a normal 12kg dog). It is made by boiling one cup of dried rice in two cups of water, then adding either 115g of cottage cheese or the same quantity of cooked, lean meat. Potatoes may replace the rice and cooked eggs may replace the cottage cheese.

In acute cases of vomiting and diarrhoea, withhold both food and water for 24 hours, then feed small amounts of the above formula every four hours for two to three days.

Where home treatment does not cure the problem within 12 hours, veterinary advice is needed immediately.

DISTEMPER

Distemper is a highly contagious viral disease which is universal in dog populations and is transmitted through contaminated objects or by close contact.

The incubation period is about nine days, the first signs being a high temperature for one to three days. The temperature then returns to normal before a second run of high fever, lasting a week or more. Pus accumulates in the corners of the eyes which squint and redden. Sometimes there is a pus-filled nasal discharge and diarrhoea.

A dog may recover from these symptoms and then succumb to further complications about four weeks later. These consist of convulsive seizures, inability to stand, jerking movements of the head and jaws and padding motions of the legs. Sometimes there is a trembling of the muscles in the temples, just in front of the ears. The dog may wander aimlessly, unaware of its surroundings.

Prevention The pregnant mother should be immunised halfway through the gestation period, giving the puppies an increased immunity at birth. They should be immunised at six weeks and then again at 16 weeks.

Treatment Because it is caused by a viral agent, treatment is not always effective. However, it is always preferable to try to treat the dog because even the most serious cases can sometimes show a remarkable improvement. Treatment consists of anti-canine distemper serum, plus supportive therapy.

EAR INFECTIONS

Infection is indicated either by a foul smell from the ear canal, a discharge from the ear or by the dog shaking or pawing its ear. In very acute cases the dog may carry its head to one side.

Ear infections usually are started by ear mites which are transmitted from mother to puppy. Dogs with floppy, hairy ears are particularly at risk.

Because the canal, even in medium-sized dogs, is small, it is important to eradicate the disease as quickly as possible. Your vet will prescribe ear drops and it is important to give the dog the full treatment. In some chronic cases ear surgery can open up the canal permanently.

HEARTWORM

This has become prominent in the last 10 years. It's not a gastro-intestinal worm but one which lives in the heart. Adult worms are long (12–30cm), slender, resembling very thin strands of spaghetti.

Heartworm is most common in northern Australia. For example, in Darwin nearly every dog is affected.

Symptoms Heartworm can be fatal. In dogs the main effects are mechanical obstruction to circulation, inflammation of blood vessels, lung embolism, chronic heart failure, damage to the liver and a build-up of fluid in the abdomen.

Mosquitoes are carriers, biting one dog and transferring the worms from its bloodstream to the next dog they bite. It is also possible for a pregnant bitch to infect her unborn young with larvae migration through the placenta.

Treatment This is a major problem. Once the worms are destroyed they break up or dislodge from the heart into the circulatory system and so may cause artery blockages in vital parts of the dog's body. Treatment requires careful monitoring of these side-effects.

On rare occasions embolisms from the breaking-up dead worms may occur from five to 30 days after treatment, causing high temperatures, increased rate of breathing, coughing, lethargy and failure to eat. The dog should be taken immediately to a vet.

Prevention of heartworm DEC, or diethylcarbamazine, should be given at a daily rate of 12mg per kilogram weight of the dog. The drug is given orally, beginning when the dog is certified free of heartworm and continuing throughout the mosquito season and up to 80 days afterwards.

In endemic areas, such as north Queensland and the Northern Territory, it is almost mandatory to start lifetime daily DEC therapy when pups are between eight and ten weeks old. Blood tests are advisable every six months, the dog should be housed in a mosquito-proof kennel at night and treated with suitable repellents.

VOMITING

Vomiting is controlled by a centre in the brain which can be stimulated by disagreeable odours, tastes, smells, toxins, drugs and poisons.

Vomiting is very weakening for the dog. A list of possible causes follows:
• Indigestion, overeating, bad food (particularly if the dog is likely to dig up bones or old meat), poisons, constipation.
• Acute abdominal problems such as pancreatitis or peritonitis; swallowing a bone; a deep internal wound; a ruptured organ after a car accident.
• Diseases such as distemper, hepatitis, pyometra, septic kidney.
• In young puppies it can be due to a dilation of the food pipe between the throat and the stomach. This condition can be rectified to a point by making the dog stand on its hind legs to eat and giving it small quantities at a time.
• Ticks. One of the initial signs of tick poisoning is vomiting and salivation.
• Drugs. Digitalis or heart tablets given in excess cause vomiting. Stop the tablets for a day and then commence at half the recommended dosage. Certain antibiotics and morphine can cause vomiting. In any such case cease medication and phone your vet.
• Nervous problems, such as car or motion sickness or lesions within the brain.

When you take a vomiting dog to your vet it is important to know whether the vomiting is related to eating, how many times a day it vomits and whether the food is digested or not. The colour also is important and if possible take a sample of the vomit along with you.

Where the dog appears healthy but vomits occasionally, there is generally no need for concern. Dogs tend to vomit about once a week or once every 10 days. This is perfectly normal.

CATS

Cat-lovers generally do not have to be encouraged to acquire a pet but may have to be restrained from acquiring too many. Cats make wonderful, and sensible, pets. They are intelligent, independent, courageous and inquisitive. As pets they are clean and fastidious and need little exercise. They like lying around and noticing what is going on and they need only a small living space for this.

CHOOSING YOUR CAT

Cats, unless you choose a rare breed, are relatively cheap to acquire, and cheap to feed and medicate.

You will have some essential veterinary expenses: cats have to be vaccinated and desexed and your pet may get into the odd fight.

Young or old? Raising a kitten takes a lot of work. It has to be fed four or five times a day and be toilet trained. Most kittens are ready to leave their mother at six weeks of age; by this time they should be able to eat and drink of their own accord. Weaning should start at four weeks. If you work and are only looking for a hunter, a mature cat is more sensible.

Male or female? Both sexes have busy love lives. Female cats can be given contraceptive tablets or be desexed. Male cats are ready to mate at any time and will spend much of their time on the prowl. Unless you intend breeding, desexing is sensible for both. It will not alter their disposition and will make life easier all round.

Long or short hair? Short-haired cats in Australia are more sensible, because of climate and such things as ticks and fleas. Long-haired cats are usually more docile but require a great deal of grooming. This is not only for appearance; if neglected, dermatitis and other skin complaints will occur. Short-haired cats are better ratters and need less grooming.

Pedigree or tabby? Your ordinary alley cat makes an excellent house pet and is unbeaten at rat and mouse extermination. It has hybrid vigour, is less susceptible to disease than better bred animals and has virtually no hereditary or congenital abnormalities. Pedigree cats, such as creams and chinchillas, have many upper respiratory tract problems. Siamese and

burmese breeds are susceptible to cat flu. Other points: blue-eyed white cats usually are congenitally deaf; tortoiseshell cats usually are females or, if male, sterile; white cats are subject to sunburn.

Life span Cats do not have nine lives but with good care and food, a cat may live twelve years or more. These days some live longer, even reaching the early twenties. Females tend to age more slowly than males.

Where to buy? Many breeders or owners of cats which have just had litters advertise in the local paper. Such owners may be just as fussy that the kittens are going to a good home as you are about acquiring a healthy cat. Pet shops are often cheaper, but sometimes this is because they acquire the less desirable members of a litter.

When buying a pedigree cat, be sure to get the pedigree papers. In the case of a cat which is already registered, get a transfer form signed by the breeder.

Regardless of where you buy the kitten, if possible ask for a fortnight trial period so that, if the animal is incubating a disease, it can be readily returned.

How to choose? When you buy from a breeder or cattery it is useful to find out how many litters the mother has had. If she has had two or three in 12 months her bones may be depleted of vitamins and minerals and the weakness may be passed on to the kittens. She should have been wormed before pregnancy and been given calcium and vitamin supplements during gestation.

Don't buy on appearance. Look carefully at the whole litter. A very shy kitten may not be able to cope with family life. Look for a kitten which is lively and robust with a glossy coat. When you have selected one, take it in your hand and compare weight with others in the litter.

CHECKLIST

With the kitten in your hand, check for the following:
• The coat should be soft and glossy.
• There should be no patches of scuffed dry skin, lice or fleas.
• Look for diarrhoea or matted faeces attached to the hair around and under the tail.
• The gums should be a healthy pink.
• It must not have a cleft palate (opening in the roof of the mouth).
• Push the eyelids back to expose the mucous membrane which should be a healthy pink. Watch for kittens which have matter in the corners of their eyes or a watery discharge; these conditions can be associated with cat flu or some other serious infection. Blindness can be checked by darting the fingers towards the eyes – the kitten should blink.
• Check for any smell or discharge from the ears. Tell-tale signs of infection are the kitten shaking its head or pawing its ears. Ear infections can be cured but you should allow for veterinary expenses.
• Hernias show up as a small bubble in the centre of the abdomen. They can be repaired surgically.
• Count the number of toes on each foot – there should be five on the front feet and four on the hind legs.
• Determine the sex of the kitten.
• Watch for bad legs which may be the result of a nutritional deficiency.

FIRST NIGHT HOME

Leaving mother and siblings can be traumatic for a kitten. Make sure it is warm, well fed and has company; a ticking clock in the blankets is fine.

Cats tend to like sleeping above floor level but young kittens are happy in baskets or boxes on the floor.

Keep the kitten on its usual diet for at least four or five days. Watch for diarrhoea after feeding cows' milk. If so, milk should be stopped. It can be re-introduced gradually over four or five weeks.

Cats like toys: a ball or a spool with a length of wool attached will keep a kitten happy.

THE IDEAL HOUSE

Cats can be housed in or outdoors as long as the area is warm and draught-free. They like to be elevated so that they can observe the surrounding activity and still be safe from dogs and small children.

The ideal is to fit a special cat door to the area the cat considers his lair – the kitchen or an insulated outhouse. The door is merely a flap on a two-way hinge (so that the cat can go in and out), just big enough for it to fit through. It is a good idea to fit a bolt to the flap so you can confine the cat in the case of illness or that of a female being on heat.

The best bedding for a cat is newspaper; it is cheap and disposable which means that it is hygienic. Fleas, lice and worms can be thrown out with the paper and burned regularly. Paper is also very warm.

If a cat has to be kept inside for a lengthy period, a litter box made from a waterproof tray about 30 x 38cm lined with newspaper and filled with soil or sawdust is essential. The litter should be changed daily and the tray washed out with non-irritant detergent. Some antiseptics, soaps and disinfectants are poisonous to cats (check the label) and other strongly-smelling substances may deter the cat from using the tray.

Food and drink bowls should be solid with flat bottoms. Saucers are not ideal as they tip over easily.

HOUSE TRAINING

Cats are naturally clean and most kittens will have been taught by their mothers where to go to the toilet. This can be in a litter tray or in the garden. You must clean out litter trays several times a day or the kitten will look elsewhere for a clean place.

To avoid confusing the cat do not use the same litter in the tray and the sleeping box. For example, if you use shredded paper in the sleeping box, use shavings, sawdust, soil or commercial cat litter in the sanitary tray.

Initially, place the tray near the sleeping box; after a few days move it a short distance. If you want the cat to use the garden, gradually move the tray outdoors. Once it is used to the idea of going to the toilet outside, train it to use the garden. Place a small portion of soiled litter in the spot you want it to use then take the cat to this place after feeding.

If the odd toilet accident happens in the house, don't slap the kitten or rub its nose in the mess. Instead, chastise it with your voice and put the kitten either in its tray or outside in the garden. Cats learn quickly.

DIET

Cats have some unique nutritional requirements. They are fussy eaters and easily become addicted to a particular diet or type of food, so it is important to expose your kitten to a variety of food. The complex nutritional requirements of cats, especially in the growing stage, can most easily and economically be met by using well-made commercially-prepared cat foods.

These commercial rations can be mixed together or with other foods to satisfy the cat's taste. Supplementary meat, eggs, table scraps, gravy and so on can be added but should not exceed twenty-five per cent of the total diet, otherwise the nutritional balance will be lost.

Where a home preparation is preferred, supplement with calcium carbonate 0.5gm (½tspn per 100gm of meat).

Meat-fed cats should have calcium carbonate and an egg (at least the yolk) and some milk (if tolerated) to improve the diet.

Meat should be cooked. If fed raw, it should be deep frozen for at least fourteen days to prevent the transmission of parasites.

Whole eggs should be cooked, as uncooked egg white is indigestible and contains more than half the protein content of the egg.

How often should you feed? From six weeks to three months the kitten should be fed three or four times a day. When nearly six months old, feeds should be reduced to twice a day. Obesity is uncommon in cats and when it occurs is usually due to overfeeding of relatively confined or inactive cats.

Protein Cats need nearly double the dietary protein of dogs and several times that of human beings. So important is this requirement to a cat that it will refuse to eat food which has less than around twenty per cent protein in it and protein offered must be high grade and easily digestible. A nutritionally induced blindness has been recorded in cats fed a protein-deficient diet.

COMMON COMPLAINTS

When taking your cat to the veterinary surgeon you must have it in a secure cage. If you do not have one, a pillowslip or sack is suitable. At the surgery the presence of other animals will make it nervous, so do not release it until you are in the consulting room.

Have the animal ready for examination. Where possible have it reasonably clean and remember that the vet depends on you for a history of the complaint. Do not clean up dermatitis or discharge as the vet wants to see the whole complaint.

ABSCESS

This is perhaps one of the most common problems encountered by the urban cat. Some people blame possums and dogs, but an abscess usually results from a scrap with another cat.

These encounters usually take place in darkness and it is more common for cats which have not been desexed to be involved.

The yowls of the brawl are usually clearly heard, and if puss returns home the loser he is usually pretty sorry for himself in the morning. Within 24 hours soreness invariably develops around the bite area. As the abscess gets bigger, he starts to reject his food.

A quick trip to the vet to lance the abscess, plus some antibiotics, usually does the trick.

CAT FLU

This is a highly contagious viral upper respiratory tract infection which causes a similar syndrome to human flu. The cat has watery eyes, a fever, sneezes profusely and may lose its appetite.

Siamese and burmese cats are especially vulnerable and they suffer the most. Sometimes there may be fatalities, especially in young kittens or older cats. Young kittens, especially, may be left a legacy of chronic conjunctivitis, ulcers of the eyes and even blindness. In the ordinary tabby cat the disease passes without great incident over a 10-day period.

If any cat with this syndrome is off its food or fails to drink, veterinary attention is essential to prevent dehydration and to give supportive care.

Because the disease is so prevalent and so serious, a vaccine has been produced and is now available. Booster shots each six months are necessary to keep up the immunity.

CONSTIPATION

This is a common problem in cats. The main cause is too small a pelvis, due to a nutritional calcium deficiency while growing or to fractures of the pelvis as a result of accidents.

Unfortunately, the problem is usually serious by the time it is noticed. The cat is usually poised over the sand-tray or in the garden for prolonged periods. An immediate trip to the vet is best.

Where the condition is noticed early, lubricants such as paraffin oil (one or two teaspoons daily) or faecal softeners (tablets or liquid) will do the job. For long-term control alter the diet. Don't give more than ten per cent of the diet as bones. Feed liver or kidney several times per week. Some cats' faeces will soften if milk is given. Vegetables in the diet will also soften the faeces.

Cats with severe narrowing of the pelvis can have surgery.

ACCIDENTS

Cats' natural curiosity increases their risk potential as it often places them in perilous situations. Here is a list of some common accidents.

• Falls from windows or rooftops.
• Car accidents.
• Scalds in the kitchen.
• Imprisonment in boxes, drawers or cupboards.
• Poisoning by owners washing their cat with insecticidal rinses, then not rinsing them off properly, i.e., several times with clean water. Cats also are poisoned by licking paint cans and by eating rodent and insect poisons.
• Electrocution by live wires, overturning floor lamps or biting an electric lead.

- Strangulation by ribbons or collars. The best collars are those with an elastic piece in them so if it catches on a branch or twig it will slip off over the animal's head.
- Being stranded up trees, telegraph poles or on rooftops. Cats can climb very easily but often find it rather more difficult to get down.
- Drowning.
- Fights. These are probably the most common cause of injury and usually happen because the animal's territorial requirements are much larger than the average urban block.
- Snake bite, insect bite and tick infestation.

BAD BREATH
Cats are pampered pets. Unfortunately, many owners are guilty of allowing their beloved cats to dictate just what food they eat. This usually means liver, kidney, soft tinned food, sardines, pilchards, tuna, minced steak, boned fish and even cleaned, shelled prawns! However, all these soft foods allow dental decay and tartar to build up on teeth. In turn, gingivitis (gum disease) develops. The cat usually dribbles and is sometimes reluctant to eat because of sore, decaying teeth.

Encourage the cat to eat some dry food and to strip meat from shanks of bones. The cat will not appreciate this change in its diet and may not eat for a day or two — but don't give in.

BALDNESS
The most common areas are over the back, at the base of the tail and down the back of both hind legs. The former is usually caused by fleas, so check this out by back-combing the area and searching for the tell-tale black spots of flea dirt or the fleas themselves.

Unfortunately, if the baldness is due to flea allergy it will be some time before puss has a new thick coat, but often the vet can help out with some hormone pills that will hasten the process.

Baldness down the back of both hind legs usually indicates a hormonal deficiency. The cat often loses its hair with no evidence of irritation or dermatitis.

Hormone tablets are the answer and new hair begins to grow back within a month. The hormone therapy is a supplement, not a cure. If it works, tablets will be needed at intervals for the rest of the cat's life.

COUGHING
The cough reflex is stimulated by something tickling the throat or the windpipe. A most prevalent cause is the lungworm. The cat gets lungworm by eating lizards and insects from the garden. The young, immature worm wanders through the cat's lungs, stimulating the cough reflex. The cat becomes thin and the coat rough, but it maintains a healthy appetite.

Ordinary worm tablets are useless against this worm. Special tablets called levamisole are effective.

DEAFNESS
The cat depends heavily on the hearing sense for survival. Deafness, therefore, is rare in the cat except in blue-eyed white cats which have a hereditary deafness. Nothing can be done to return their hearing to a normal level.

Sometimes, severe ear infections (canker) may impair hearing. These infections are usually caused by ear mites.

Proper veterinary treatment and cleansing of the ear canal will usually resolve the problem.

DIARRHOEA
This is very common in young kittens fed cows' milk. Some kittens, particularly siamese, do not produce lactase, an enzyme for breaking down lactose in the milk. The unbroken lactose causes scouring. This problem is quickly resolved by eliminating milk from the diet. Lactose-free milks, available from the chemist, may be substituted.

Worms, especially roundworms, cause diarrhoea. Kittens should be wormed each month until six months of age, then each three months. Coccidiosis, a microscopic parasite, is common in young kittens, especially those bought from pet shops.

In adult cats, diarrhoea can be caused by any of the above.

Diet should always be examined in cases of diarrhoea. Liver, high carbohydrate diets, milk and vegetables can all cause diarrhoea. Once the causative agent has been eliminated, feed a diet of starchy foods such as boiled milk, cooked rice or cottage cheese.

If it persists for more than 24 hours, or contains blood or is foul-smelling, the cat will need veterinary treatment immediately.

DRINKING

Cats normally do not drink very much. Their kidneys have a great capacity for concentrating their urine, so they have less need to pass out waste products in the form of urine.

Perhaps it is this activity which eventually takes its toll on the feline kidney, for this is the first organ of the cat to collapse in the aging process.

This condition is called nephritis and is evidenced by an increased thirst, loss of weight and, in the later stages, loss of appetite. The cat begins consuming so much water that it is found sitting over garden pools, shower recesses or its water bowl almost continuously.

Prompt action by the owner is important if treatment is to be effective. Where possible, a urine sample (30mL) and the cat should be taken to the vet.

Other causes of increased thirst are fever, vomiting, diarrhoea, infected wounds, cortisone therapy and diabetes.

Dry foods can also make the cat more thirsty. When transferring a cat from tinned food (85 per cent moisture) to dry food (10 per cent moisture) it is best to teach the cat to drink more water. This can be done by moistening the dry food and adding a small quantity of salt.

EAR CANCER

This condition is especially prevalent in white cats, but can affect any light-coloured animal. The solar radiation causes severe sunburn of the ear-lobes, resulting in itchiness and scab formation.

In severe cases the ear-lobes have to be removed by cautery. If the condition is noticed early it is best to always feed the cat at 9am and keep it indoors until 5pm. In addition, human 'block-out' sunburn preparations can be applied to the ear-lobe, or others such as zinc cream. In early cases the ears can have a tattoo to impregnate the ear with black dye.

EAR INFECTION

Shaking the head is the first indication of an ear infection. Other symptoms include scratching at the ear with the paw or holding the head to one side.

The majority of cases begin with an ear mite infestation — usually caught by a kitten from the mother. The tiny mites multiply rapidly and irritate the lining of the ear canal, allowing bacteria to establish an infection known as 'canker'.

Cats' ears, unlike some dogs' ears, are short, upright and relatively hairless. This enables most infections to be cleared up effectively with ear drops.

FLEAS

Warm, humid weather can herald a flea infestation and problems for your cat. Cats, dogs and humans all have their own separate species of fleas, but the fleas don't mind which host they are on when they are thirsty. All fleas live on blood, and with frequent blood meals they may live for up to a year. Newly-emerged fleas can live for many weeks before feeding.

The flea is also the intermediate host for the common tapeworm, and therefore proper flea control is important in eradicating tapeworms.

Why do fleas cause a problem? Basically the flea saliva irritates the skin, causing an allergic dermatitis. Constant scratching and rubbing leaves the cat with an unkempt coat and an irritated skin. Severe flea infestations can even cause anaemia, resulting in the death of young kittens.

When cats with severe flea infestation are washed, the water may be coloured bright red by the dried blood in the fleas' faeces.

Control of fleas in cats is difficult because cats are very sensitive to insecticides and death may result unless great care is taken. In young kittens good results are obtained by leaving a current flea collar buried under clothing in the sleeping box. Adult cats (those more than six months) can be dipped or sprayed with 0.5–1 per cent malathion solution or by dusting with 4 per cent malathion powder at weekly intervals.

As fleas breed in dust and debris, cleaning and vacuuming sheltered areas will help. Spray these areas with 5 per cent DDT at the rate of 5 litres per 400 square metres.

The skin condition of the cat affected by fleas should be treated under veterinary supervision.

HAIR BALLS

Much fuss is made about hair balls by some owners and most breeders but most cats cope with this natural problem. Long-haired cats in particular groom themselves and accumulate hair in the stomach which forms into a 'hair ball'.

In most cases the cat will regurgitate (vomit) the hair mass in the form of a long sausage of hair and mucus. Others will pass the hair on through the intestinal tract. If you feel it necessary, the latter may be helped by the administration of a teaspoon of paraffin oil twice weekly.

N.S.H. (Nutritional Secondary Hyperparathyroidism)

Cats normally are fed a meat diet because they like it. The problem with such a diet is that, although table scraps or commercial foods are added, the diet is still calcium-deficient.

If fed only on beef heart for four to seven weeks, a kitten starts showing behavioural changes, incoordination and marked demineralisation of the skeleton. This is because cats mature so quickly (they are sexually mature at six months) and with such rapid growth it is essential they have a balanced diet.

Nutritional Secondary Hyperparathyroidism is seen most often in healthy-looking, well-grown kittens of about four to six months. The cat looks well because the high protein content and kilojoule value of meat produces initial rapid growth but, as this continues, the animal outstrips the calcium reserves in its body.

OBESITY

This is one of the recent health problems for our pets. With commercial pet foods providing well-balanced nutrition and most owners overfeeding their pets, they enter a vicious cycle.

The more overweight they become the less exercise they do to burn up the excess energy, which is then laid down as fat.

It is very difficult to take your cat for a run on a lead so the only option you have is to reduce its food intake.

Change the diet to one which is nutritious, but relatively unpalatable to the cat. Usually overweight cats have been on either mum's home cooking of best steak, oysters, seasoned chicken, prawns, fish or one of the commercial tinned foods, such as pilchards in aspic.

Generally, dry foods tend to be less palatable than fresh meat or tinned foods. Select one that is the least tasty and feed only once daily.

URINATING INDOORS

This habit must be stopped quickly. There are various causes, the most common being attention seeking due to the introduction of another cat, a new baby or the absence of the cat's favourite owner.

Sometimes cats with bladder infections (cystitis) are caught short and this requires veterinary treatment. Here are a few hints for dealing with the problem.
• Make an extra effort to be affectionate to the cat—nurse it while watching the television or reading.
• Spray a very smelly disinfectant in trouble spots.
• If you catch the cat in the act, raise your voice and scold with words.
• Put the cat outside for 24 hours.
• If all else fails the vet can help with some hormone treatment which tends to return cats to normal behaviour.

URINE BLOCKAGE

Sandy crystals form in the urine and cause a blockage in male cats. It only occurs in male cats because the urethra (or passage from the bladder to the outside) is much smaller in diameter than in the female.

This condition was originally blamed on feeding dry foods, but has recently been shown to be more complex. Some cats, because of laziness, obesity or a reluctance to get their feet wet in damp weather, hold onto urine. This stale urine allows the crystals to clog up the urethra.

This is a very serious problem which requires urgent veterinary attention. The cat is noticed crouching as it tries to urinate and may lick its penis in an effort to clear the blockage. The bladder becomes distended and back pressure into the kidneys can cause serious damage.

Encourage cats to be active. If necessary, reduce their weight and, if prescribed, feed urine acidifiers to prevent crystal formation. Feed your animals with low-magnesium commercial cat food. See your vet.

WORMS
Cats are not as severely affected as dogs by worms. The most common worms in cats are roundworms or tapeworms.

All kittens have some worms and it is important to begin a worming programme early. Begin at three weeks of age with a syrup containing piperazine as the active ingredient. Repeat the treatment each three weeks until the kitten is six months then three times per year.

FISH

Fish, unlike other pets, will not mess up your house, bite the postman, get lost, keep the neighbours awake, require registration or exercise. However, although they are easy to care for, certain requirements must be met if they are to be healthy and contented.

AQUARIUMS

Aquariums are available in a great variety of shapes and sizes from modest goldfish bowls to titanic oceanariums. An aquarium in the house can involve all the family, giving children a stimulus to read and learn in a practical rather than a theoretical situation. It offers a relaxing, miniature natural world to watch. The calming effects of aquariums have been recognised by doctors and psychiatrists.

Types of fish More than half aquariums are for goldfish. Goldfish, the most popular of which are comets and shubunkins, are quite hardy, require less equipment than tropicals (no heaters) and are cheap to buy and feed.

About thirty per cent of aquariums are for tropical fish. These offer a variety of beautiful colours and shapes but you need expert help before you begin with these.

About five per cent of aquariums are for marine fish. These are not suitable for beginners and need the owner to be knowledgable about keeping aquariums and the salt water quality needed to keep the fish healthy.

Which aquarium to buy? Buy the largest you can afford. Larger aquariums are easier to maintain and offer more scope. It is easier and cheaper to buy the right-sized aquarium in the beginning rather than trading in later. When

comparing prices, note that package deals often include only the bare essentials. Buy from a store which will offer a guarantee and the recommendation of the dealer.

Tanks and bowls The water surface of a bowl or tank dictates its holding capacity: 2.5 to 5cm of fish per bread-and-butter to dinner plate sized area of water is a good guide, depending on whether the fish is fully grown.

Large tanks generally need a filter (to clean

195

the water) and an air pump (to oxygenate the water) but goldfish bowls are often run without these.

EQUIPMENT

Filters A filter or combination of filters should be capable of pumping the contents of a tank twice each hour; for example, a 225 litre tank should have a total filter turnover capacity of 450 litres per hour.

Air-operated filters Under-gravel filters and bubble filters are connected to, and powered by, air from the air pump.

Under-gravel filters trap detritus in the gravel. They are inexpensive, easy to set up (if installed initially) and to maintain. For greatest efficiency in a large tank, use with a power filter.

Bubble filters sit in a corner of the aquarium; they contain filter wool to trap detritus. They're inexpensive but need frequent cleaning, are hard to hide and are less efficient than power filters.

Power filters These have their own water pump, and do not need to be connected to the air pump, so they are more efficient and easier to maintain than air-operated filters. However, they are more expensive. The cannister-style is the best; these sit below the tank. Others clip on to the side.

Air pumps Air pumps circulate air to oxygenate the aquarium and power under-gravel filters, bubble filters, aerating ornaments and airstones. This water circulation is very important for your fish, because, if it is left undisturbed, deoxygenated (toxic) water accumulates at the bottom of a stagnant aquarium. This forces fish closer to the surface, where there is oxygen exchange, eventually overcoming them. Air pumps also provide bubble displays.

Lights These enable you to see your aquarium better, illuminate it at night and benefit plant growth. Ten hours illumination per day is usually sufficient.

Heaters Heaters are necessary for tropical fish only. Externally adjustable heaters are the most effective heater because setting the temperature is easy. Tanks 22.5–135 litres should have a 150 watt heater; 135–225 litres should have a 200 watt heater; 225–450 litres should have 2 x 200 watt heaters. Aquariums exposed to unusually low room temperatures should have stronger or more heaters.

CARE OF FISH

A tank should be sited away from strong natural light which will cause excessive plant growth. It should not be too close to electrical appliances or above them. This refers especially to stereos, videos or TV. Site your tank away from the kitchen as cooking fats may drift over the tank or into the air pump. It must be placed near a power outlet if electrical equipment is to be fitted. The best place is against a wall that is not a main traffic area. This allows the fish to become used to people but not be too close to them.

Over a period of time, organic material can build up in the aquarium and form carbonic acids, lowering the pH level (acidity to alkalinity) of the water. A pH test kit is simple to use, and will tell you the pH of your water, allowing you to adjust it to the correct level.

When adding new fish to your tank, float the fish bags, still sealed, in the tank for 15 minutes to equalise temperature. Add ½ cup of water from the aquarium to each bag every five minutes for 20 minutes. After adding water to the bags for 15 minutes, feed the fish already in the aquarium. Release the new fish after the 20 minutes. This procedure allows you gradually to acclimatise new fish to the temperature and water conditions in your tank, minimising stress.

Never stress your fish by adding cold water to the aquarium; match the temperature of new water to the temperature of the aquarium water.

Position the air pump above the tank or use one-way valves to prevent water from siphoning down to the pump during power failures.

Do not expose hot, or connected heaters above water levels. This can happen when changing water.

Do not use steel wool or cleaning agents on anything inside the tank.

Do not allow pesticides to contaminate the aquarium, or enter through the air pump.

Try to avoid placing your hands inside the tank too often. Skin-borne contaminants can affect your fish.

Never rapidly change any part of the fish's environment. Frequent small water changes are better than rare large ones. When adjusting a pH balance in the water, adjust no more than .05 at a time, and then no more than .5 during a day.

Algae can become very thick in your tank. This will not harm your fish but it will make the tank unsightly. This may be caused by too much light, too much food, too infrequent changes of water, or perhaps by a combination of these three.

Chemical filtration media, such as activated charcoal, activated carbon, chemipure, and others purify the water. These will remove medications in the water and should be removed or turned off when medicating the tank.

When changing water, siphon water from the bottom of the tank, taking the opportunity to vacuum up any detritus on the aquarium floor. A garden hose makes a good siphon. It gives more control so you don't siphon up fish or plants as well.

Use a water ager or conditioner when adding new water to the aquarium. These preparations remove toxic chlorine from water. The better quality products also protect fish against stress, help to clear and soften the water, encourage plant growth, and provide a tonic for fish.

When changing filter wool from filters, return some of the dirty wool to the filter with the new wool. This seeds the new wool with beneficial bacteria.

An airstone placed close to a heater will more effectively circulate warm water in the aquarium. This is useful if your aquarium is very large or is located in a cold room.

Try to avoid using rain water in your tank. Often, rain water can contain too much acid for fish. Check with a local aquarium supplier about your water.

COMMON MISTAKES

Overfeeding Most new aquarists overfeed their fish. When feeding flake food, feed twice a day, as much as they will eat in five minutes then clean uneaten food from tank. Fish lose appetite only if they are sick and, if encouraged, they will eat until they burst.

Overcrowding Get an experienced hobbyist or reputable dealer to guide you. Tell him the size tank, the types of fish you want to keep and the amount of time you can spend every week maintaining your aquarium. He will give you an idea of compatible fish and suitable equipment.

Impatience After buying an aquarium, your impulse is to fill it. Don't add more than ten per cent of fish capacity during the first week or two. Get hardy occupants first. Run your tank for 24 hours before adding any fish. This allows dangerous chlorine to dissipate and lets filters clear the water.

COMMON COMPLAINTS

Fish kept in a well-maintained, well-equipped tank rarely become sick. If, however, the fish do become ill, they probably have contracted either white spot or fungus. If fish are ill, first check that your equipment is functioning correctly, also check the pH balance of the water. Change one-third of the water to reduce the potency of the disease in the water.

White spot This disease is capable of multiplying rapidly. It is caused by either a diseased fish in the tank or may occur spontaneously, due to stress, or new arrivals. Symptoms include small, white spots the size of grains of salt on the body and fins. Early signs include clamped fins, flicking and scratching, lethargy, loss of colour, leading to increased respiration.

This disease is cured if the tank is treated with a good quality cure. Consult your aquarium supplier. Treatment should be continued for two to three days after spots disappear.

Fungus Usual causes are overfeeding, inadequate filtration, overcrowding, incorrect pH, or poor maintenance routine. Symptoms include clamped fins, lethargy, increased respiration, white patches, often with a cotton-wool appearance or frayed fins.

BIRDS

Birds are one of the few forms of wildlife to thrive in cities. They can be kept as pets in the smallest of units or houses, or encouraged to visit the smallest of gardens.

CAGED BIRDS

Keeping a caged bird is perhaps the easiest way for a child to begin to learn to look after pets. Birds also make ideal pets for elderly people.

HOUSING YOUR BIRD

Even if you are only intending to keep a budgie for company or a canary for its song, you must first pay careful attention to how it should be housed.

Cages Only budgerigars or canaries should be kept in cages. All other birds need flight for exercise and health. For a pair of budgies, the cage should be a minimum of 60cm long, 30cm wide and 45cm high. Budgies in particular enjoy extra exercise, so if you are sure all the doors and windows are shut (and the cat is locked out), allow your budgie the run of the room on occasion.

Aviaries If space permits, a small aviary offers a better environment than even a large cage.

· A backyard aviary is ideal: it should be sited to face north or north-east, away from rain and prevailing winds. It should be at least 2 metres high, 1.5m wide and as long as possible—a minimum of 3 metres. A fibreglass or corrugated iron roof will provide some shelter from strong sunlight, and it should have walls on three sides to give shelter from the cold.

Two types of construction are recommended, depending on local conditions.

A raised aviary should be 30cm or more above ground level, supported on brick piers and with a galvanised iron floor tray to make cleaning easier.

A ground-level aviary should be protected from rats and mice by sinking galvanised iron to a depth of 30cm on all sides. Ground-level aviaries offer the opportunity of growing shrubs, grasses and trees, providing shelter, nesting material and extra food for many cage birds.

WATER

Birds use a lot of water, and should always have a generous supply to hand (or beak). It is best to have two water containers: a shallow dish for bathing and a spill-proof drinking container designed to avoid waste or fouling.

The easiest way to provide a 'demand' water supply is to attach the top from a salt shaker to a clear glass container about the size of a cough syrup bottle. Simply attach the bottle upside down to the side of the cage; your bird will soon learn to nibble at the opening for water.

FOOD

As far as the pet-owner is concerned, birds can be divided into three groups: the hardbills, which eat grain and seed; the softbills, which eat insects; and the nectar-feeders. It should be remembered, though, that the distinctions between these groups are blurred. Seed-eaters such as parrots will eat insects and green plant material, while nectar-feeders enjoy fruit and insects.

Because they are easy to house, feed and breed, most people prefer seed-eaters as pets. If you are interested in keeping insect-eaters or nectar-feeders, consult your State avicultural association.

Though seed-eaters will live for a while on seed mixtures alone, their proper health requires variety in diet—even to the extent of providing such exotic treats as hard-boiled egg or cheese.

Minerals Some minerals are essential for maintaining good health in cage and aviary birds. Calcium is perhaps the most important, and is usually supplied by cuttlefish bone, available at pet stores. It is usually hung up for birds to peck at, but a better plan is to pulverise it with a hammer and either mix it with seed or supply in a separate container. Salt in small amount is also beneficial, especially rock salt. Many pet shops also sell prepared mineral salts, which contain a balanced amount of essential minerals, to be sprinkled on seed.

Grit While not strictly food, grit is important as an aid to digestion; add some to the sand on the bottom of the bird's cage, or mix a small amount into the seed at regular intervals. It is usually sold as shell-grit.

Green food Consisting of the leaves of plants and their green or half-ripened seeds, green food is as important as clean, properly mixed seed. The amount of green food a cage bird will eat is surprising. It should comprise a mixture of leaves, green seed and flowers. The most popular are chickweed, groundsel, milk thistle, lettuce, dandelion, millet, the young leaves of hibiscus, privet, strawberry leaves. In fact, any plants you see being eaten by sparrows are safe for a cage bird.

Insect food This should be available occasionally, though many cage birds will take some time to notice it. Maggots, mealworms and especially termites are favourites.

Seed Not to be forgotten as a ready supply of clean, well-mixed seed forms the basis of cage birds' health. Prepared mixtures, such as canary or budgie mix, should be kept in a well-lidded container to discourage weevils (though most birds will quickly eat weevil larvae).

Add grit and minerals to the feed when you refill the bird's seed container; an occasional helping of oil-rich sesame or sunflower seeds is a bonus.

COMMON COMPLAINTS

Unfortunately, most bird-owners tend to dis-regard symptoms of ill health in their pets; while they would not hesitate to take an 'off-colour' cat or dog to a vet, they assume a sick bird cannot be treated. This is rarely the case: in fact, some bird illnesses respond quickly to simple home treatment. If, however, you are concerned by your bird's health or if it is injured, immediately take it—in its cage or in a shoebox—to your vet.

Apoplexy Often the cause of sudden death. The bird becomes dizzy and falls to the ground with convulsed limbs: if you can reach it before it dies, plunge its head into a dish of water. If this is successful, the bird should be caged on its own and kept quiet for a few days.

Broken legs and wings Broken limbs are difficult for an amateur to treat successfully. If you suspect your bird has a broken leg or wing, capture it gently and take it to your vet.

Bronchitis An inflammation of the bronchial tubes. The bird shows signs of weakness and laboured breathing, with wheezing or rasping. Consult your vet.

Coccidiosis A parasitic disease, which leads to death in two or three days. Signs are restlessness, fluffed-out plumage and sometimes blood in droppings. See your vet for the appropriate antibiotic and clean the cage very thoroughly with strong disinfectant.

Constipation Common among cage birds which do not have enough green food. Two drops of medicinal paraffin administered into the beak and warmth for a few hours will relieve the trouble in a short period.

Colds Cage birds are particularly susceptible to draughts; always make sure the cage is protected, especially at night. Symptoms of a cold are shivering wings, puffed-out plumage, and occasionally a watery discharge from the nostrils. Your vet will supply antibiotics; keep the bird warm during treatment.

Diarrhoea There are many causes of diarrhoea or enteritis, which can be mild or even fatal if left untreated. Treatment by antibiotics is best, and your vet can advise you about maintaining cleanliness and a healthy diet.

Feather conditions 'French moult' is the most common feather problem, especially in budgerigars. Young birds may not grow flight (long wing) feathers or tail feathers, or these may be few in number, twisted and have soft shafts. If placed in an aviary and given plenty of natural food, this may be cured.

Other feather conditions are usually caused by mites (in particular, red mites) and show up in ragged, dull plumage. Dust the bird with derris powder, thoroughly clean the cage and dust any woodwork where mites may hide.

WILD BIRDS

Birds will add as much beauty and vitality to your garden as flowers. They will also do an important job controlling the vast insect population, both parasites and predators, and acting as scavengers, clearing away the debris left by others. The problem is to lure the birds you admire and want while keeping less desirable ones to a minimum.

A few pieces of bread or a scattering of grain will get you as many sparrows, pigeons and mynahs as you want. Beyond that, things are a little more complicated. Australian native birds will need a well planted environment where they can enjoy some seclusion as well as a natural balance of insect life.

It will also help if you provide water or a bird bath, and, to some extent, honey-bearing flowers. These flowers are often regarded as all-important but they are a particular attraction only to spinebills and wattle-birds and even these birds are also insect-eaters.

It is not essential that native shrubs be grown. Wattle-birds and other honey-eaters love banksias, grevilleas, bottlebrushes and melaleucas. They will, however, visit the flowers of many exotics, including abutilons, hibiscus, camellias, justicia, tecoma, bigononias, fuchsias and many others. Similarly, Australia's smaller insect-eaters, such as wrens, brown fantails, silver eyes and pardalotes carry out their aphid-hunting drives in citrus, camellias, roses and other exotics as busily as they do in natives. Wrens, silver eyes and firetails build their nests as happily in a wisteria or rambling rose thicket as they do in native shrubbery.

Most important, spray with care, using low-residual insecticides such as pyrethrum where possible. Otherwise, insects poisoned by potent chemicals can also poison the birds which eat them.

Nearly all birds love a bath. A wide container with only 5–10cm of water serves better than deep water. Clear an area around it so that cats are less likely to stalk the bird while it is bathing.

FEEDING STATION
Feeding stations will attract honey or nectar feeding birds, depending on the type of food used. For the former there are inverted jar-type feeders that allow the honey and water mixture to ooze through a wick-like fabric. Small grain, such as canary seed, attracts finches, sparrows and redheads or firetails, which appeal even though they're not particularly useful in the garden.

Any feeding station should be out of reach of cats.

It can be suspended about half a metre from a branch or on a slim bracket about the same length from a railing or up a wall. A feeding platform can be made by suspending a length of board with nylon cord, swing fashion, from a tree. The swing feed is supposed to be attractive to native birds but not to exotics.

Do not let birds become dependent on handouts. Use the feeding station for a few weeks to encourage them. Otherwise, confine feeding to long wet or drought periods.

13
TAKING THE PLUNGE

THESE DAYS there is almost as much choice between pools, saunas, spas and tubs as there is between styles and prices of houses. The basic rule with any sort of waterworks on your property is to be slow and thorough in investigating what is available and what you are getting.

A pool represents a large expenditure. When you decide to install one you will soon feel you are treading a minefield between stories of shonky companies which go broke when the work is half done, headlines about pool deaths and grumbles from owners about the endless work involved in maintenance. You are bound to meet someone who comes out with the standard, 'The best days for a pool are the day it is installed and the day it is filled in'. In spite of this, most people who get a pool seem to find that their leisure and their family life are transformed.

Above-ground or in-ground? This is almost entirely a question of cost. Above-ground pools are much cheaper. On some sites they may also be possible where an in-ground pool is a near impossibility. There is one point, though. Many people do not care for the look of an above-ground pool. Excavation and landscaping to make it more aesthetic add to the cost. Also weighed against the cheaper initial cost and cheaper installation is the relative fragility of the above-ground pool in the face of the elements, and its shorter life generally.

IN-GROUND POOLS

The first consideration is what is possible on your land. On most suburban blocks the choice of site is severely limited. Once you have determined where you want the pool to go, get in touch with your local water board or similar authority for a plan of sewerage and water pipes on your land, or, if the site is not sewered, for sullage drains and position of septic tank. You cannot excavate in these areas.

Next check with your local council on its regulations. These may relate to fencing and screening from the street. Most councils like pools to be sited behind the house but if your fencing is adequate, they may allow it in the front. At this stage it is a good idea to talk to as many people as you know who have pools. Listen to their comments and criticisms of their pool builders and the end product.

You may then get in touch with your State's pool building association for the names of some local pool builders. If there are particular difficulties you may get an engineer to design and give specifications for a pool which builders will quote on. What seems the extra expense of an engineer may save you money in the long run. An engineer has no commercial interest so he will not be pushing one product above others. Sometimes pool builders are over-cautious and may specify work which is not necessary. An engineer can advise on all aspects of the pool, supervise the work and maintain quality control.

It is sensible to get two or three quotes from builders for comparisons but too many quotes may only confuse. Pool builders' quotations are not standard so make comparisons between them carefully. If one quote is significantly lower than the others it is possible that what one builder regards as standard is being treated as extras by the pool builder who offers the low price.

One safeguard which has now evolved for consumers is the contract drawn up by the Standards Association of Australia. The contract is not inflexible but does cover schedule of payments, cancellation of contract, many matters relating to the job itself and to completion and hand-over. If possible, use the Standards Association contract. At least, if your builder does not use it, find out why and compare his contract with the Association's.

POOL MAINTENANCE

Once the pool and the pleasure it brings are a reality, work begins. As with any maintenance around the home a regular and efficient routine is far better than sporadic bursts of work. If a pool is neglected you will notice it far quicker than if you neglect to vacuum the living-room carpet.

It is possible to have your pool entirely maintained by a professional. If you are a skilled handyman you can look after it yourself. Most people choose something in between. This generally means that the owner looks after cleaning the pool and leaves the maintenance of filter, pump and motor to someone else.

It is useful, however, to have an idea of how the pool system works. A pool is a standing body of water which will quickly become unpleasant if not treated. A swimming pool has a filter which does the job of turning over the water in the pool regularly. If you have a large pool you will need a large filter. A small pool will need only a small filter. The filter will remove solid dirt particles from the water. It is supplemented by a skimmer box at surface level which can remove floating debris.

A pump, with motor, drives all the water in the pool into the filter and back into the pool by return lines. The efficiency with which your pool is cleaned depends on proper relation between filter and pump. Makers design specific capacity filters to work with specific pumps. It is sensible to be guided by them. Don't mix and match filters and pumps.

There are three basic types of filter: cartridge, which is removable and replaceable; diato-

maceous earth, whereby the water is filtered through a white, powder-like substance; and sand. Each has a different method of maintenance. Get a demonstration when your pool is installed.

CHEMICALS

Even the most efficient filter will not give you sparkling water in your pool. That is achieved by chemicals. There is no final agreement on the best way to treat pools with chemicals efficiently. The best idea is to find a formula which works for you and keep to it.

Balance This is the balance between acid and alkaline, the pH level which runs on a scale from 0 to 14. Seven is neutral, above it is alkaline, below, acidic. The ideal pH level for pool water is between 7.2 and 7.4 because chlorine, used to kill bacteria, is most efficient at this level. Water too acid will irritate skin and eyes and may corrode metal fittings. Water too alkaline will reduce the effectiveness of chlorine. Rainwater and reticulated water are generally slightly alkaline. Everything that goes into a pool, including people, can alter the pH level.

There are many test kits on the market. Choose one of good reputation. To raise the pH level of water which is too acid, sodium bicarbonate or soda ash is added, and to lower too alkaline water, hydrochloric acid is used. Test the water at least once a week. Public pools are often tested every few hours.

Bacteria The job of the filter is to remove as much bacterial food material as possible. Chlorine is the most widely used disinfectant to deal with the rest. Chlorine is affected by sunlight so it is better to add it at night and let it get to work then. Generally chlorine is screened from sunlight by a stabiliser such as cyanuric acid. You can used stabilised chlorine, or use conventional chlorine adding a stabiliser at the beginning of summer, or you can add stabiliser only when necessary.

One thing you must not do is store conventional and stabilised chlorine together. When wet they will explode. Store all chemicals in a cool, dry place out of reach of children.

Always add chlorine to water, never water to chlorine.

Air and light diminish the effectiveness of chlorine. If you buy in bulk it is sensible to decant it into small, sealed containers and use each in turn.

Salt chlorination is rapidly becoming popular. It is claimed that this water treatment is better for asthmatics and people with skin allergies. Automatic salt chlorinators do most of the job of caring for the pool themselves.

Algaecides are useful when long-term protection of your pool is needed, during winter or when the family is away. After the initial dose, top up every three to four weeks with smaller doses.

Content The third aspect of the chemistry of your pool is total alkalinity. This is a measure of the amount of carbonates or bicarbonates in

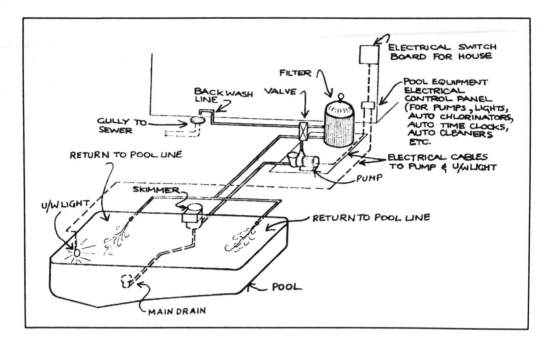

the water. It indicates the amount of carbonate or bicarbonate available to ionise when some of the existing bicarbonate ions are removed by the effect of acid. In simpler terms, total alkalinity is the amount of alkalinity needed to get the right pH level. Most pool testing kits contain a test for total alkalinity. The test should be made regularly. If alkalinity falls below the desired level the pool should be treated with sodium bicarbonate, often called buffer powder.

When filling a test kit, take the water from well below the pool surface. Water taken from the very top may contain impurities which could give a false reading.

An excess of chlorine is often blamed for sore eyes. More often than not, eye irritation is caused by wrong Ph level.

Do not add concentrated chemicals through the skimmer box. The best method is to add the required amount of chemical to a bucket of water and disperse it around the pool.

STARTING UP FOR SUMMER
• Check your water test kit. Buy new bottles of liquid reagents. They last only a season.
• Switch on the pump. If it clanks and rattles, get it overhauled.
• Check your filter.

Sand type: Open carefully and inspect the sand for mud balls or channelling. Sand should be replaced every three to five years.

Diatomaceous earth: Inspect the pads for splits and tears. Mix one part hydrochloric acid with seven parts water in a plastic bucket, with care. Wear rubber gloves. Immerse pads for six to eight hours. Hose down pads and refit.

Cartridge filters: Check for holes and tears. Very small holes can be sealed off with PVC glue. Discard old cartridges. Regular cartridge cleaning is a good idea. Check with the pool shop on what to use for your filter. Some paper-type cartridges can be damaged by too-strong chemicals.
• Chemicals: Discard empty packs. Rinse out the remnants of products under the tap before putting containers in the rubbish tin. Do not reuse container. In the tidying-up process do not tip a part of this into a part jar of that. Mixing chemicals is a fire or explosion hazard.

Liquid chlorine left from last season will have lost potency. Increase dosage.

HEATING

In many parts of Australia heating can extend pool use to all except the coldest days. In temperate areas an unheated pool is generally in use only from three to five months. There are, however, several months in which the air temperature is warm enough for a swim but the water is too cold.

You have the choice of gas, electricity or solar.

Gas and electricity heaters These are about the same price. The critical cost factor is installation. Unless gas is already connected to the pool area, installing gas lines may be expensive. The average domestic single-phase electricity supply may be inadequate to heat your pool and three-phase power may have to be installed.

Solar heating Pool solar heating has gone beyond the novelty stage but it is an area in which you should be cautious and ask plenty of questions. The first problem is finding a reliable, knowledgeable and experienced dealer in an area in which there have been one or two fly-by-nights.

The obvious attraction of solar is that, after installation, running costs are free. However, a sequence of cloudy days will mean the water temperature will fall so most makers of solar heaters recommend a gas or electricity booster.

There are two ways of using the sun to warm your pool: transparent covers to reduce heat loss, or the water can be heated by passing it through solar collectors sited outside the pool.

Pool covers are not enough in themselves to extend the swimming season dramatically but they can be used in conjunction with other methods of heating.

Pool solar heaters generally work on the principle that pool water is pumped into a collector where it is heated by the sun and then flows back into the pool. The faster the flow rate the more efficient the heater. Automatic switches can cut off the flow of water to the collectors on wet or overcast days.

FENCING

Pool fencing is primarily a safety measure to protect children. If you have no children, your responsibility is the same. The Standards Association of Australia has established specifications for swimming pool fences. Some councils are even stricter than these—calling for a height of 1.5m against the Association's 1.2m. Some councils demand that the pool be completely surrounded while others allow the house to be considered a boundary. Yet again, some councils demand that only the pool be enclosed, so barbecues and so on must be outside its bounds.

Check detailed requirements with your council before you decide on your fence.

If your pool is in the planning stages it may be useful to use existing fences as boundaries. This avoids the ugly double-fence look and you may be able to make use of existing shrubs for landscaping.

Fencing is available in brush, timber, steel, aluminium, brick, asbestos cement or glass. One final safety point, it is useless having an efficient fence if the entry gate is not child-proof.

Most manufacturers install their fences but some are do-it-yourself. Choice of fence depends in part on the style of house and pool. A brick fence around a pool near a brick house begins to look like a barracks. Natural material pools blend better with brush or timber but a fairly formal setting and a traditional-style house nearby may take quite elaborate wrought iron.

SURROUNDS

Ideally, you should think about fencing and surrounds when you are planning your pool and get a clear idea of what you want the whole area to look like.

Appearance is not the only factor with pool-side paving, however. It should be safe—made of non-slip material and not too hot or hard on tender feet. It should not attract growth of algae. It should also be hard wearing and need little or no maintenance.

As with other aspects of design, you are looking for harmony without monotony. Too many finishes—a brick house and barbecue with timber patio, steel fence and slate pool surrounds promise only a complete mess.

There are a couple of other minor safety points. Railway sleepers combine well with brick or sandstone. The sleepers are combined with brick for steps and retaining walls. Use new sleepers. Old ones are full of splinters. Some very dark slates can be impossible to walk on in summer. Variegated slate should not be used near the pool itself as the brown and orange streaks are ferrous compounds. Grass near the pool creates the problem of both grass clippings and soil getting into the water. Some bricks absorb a lot of water, become covered with algae and then become slippery. The best and generally cheapest paving for the home handyman is cement pavers. They are easy to work with and generally look pleasant around the pool.

With landscaping generally, trees create shade, which is highly desirable, but they also tend to create leaf problems. The *Weekly*'s Allan Seale suggests that it may at times be easier to cope with one grand leaf fall in autumn than the year-round shedding of natives. These are points to keep in mind when landscaping.

POOL SAFETY TIPS

Pools have been a mixed blessing in Australian households—a source of great pleasure and of some danger.

Here are some rules:
• Keep out uninvited guests.
• Keep the deep end clear for diving, if the pool is deep enough, and keep small children to the shallow end.
• Ban skylarking and running jumps as pool surrounds soon get wet and dangerous.
• Ban horseplay and rough behaviour in the pool.
• Keep pets out of the pool. They are a health hazard.
• There are legal requirements on fencing pools and providing locking gates. The Standards Association of Australia has established standards for these. For your safety comply with them.
• Do not allow non-swimmers to use the pool unless they are supervised.
• Never let anyone swim alone.
• Do not allow diving if swimmers are near or under the diving-board.
• Discourage feet-first diving. It is bad for sinuses and can cause other ear, nose and throat problems.
• Install a diving-board only if the deep end is at least 3m deep and 10m long.

• Do not encourage drinking and swimming.
• Buy unbreakable plates and glasses—keep glassware and glass bottles well away from the pool.
• Do not leave floating objects in a pool—they attract small children.
• Do not leave objects near pool fences for children to climb.
• Do not do deep breathing exercises before entering the water. It can cause loss of consciousness while swimming.
• Perimeter pool lighting should be provided to prevent people accidentally falling into the pool at night.
• Pool lights should be low voltage (12 volts). If not, make sure an earth leakage device is fitted to your home's electrical supply.
• Mains-operated appliances, such as TVs, radios, record-players and food-preparation equipment, should be kept to dry areas at least 3m from the pool. Bare feet, minimum clothing and wet skin effectively lower the body's resistance to electricity, so the effects of a shock on anyone near a pool are likely to be more serious than elsewhere.
• In above-ground pools, remove the ladder if the pool is not in use.
• No safety regulations can substitute for proper supervision by adults. Teach children to swim at the earliest possible age and keep them in practice.
Chemicals These should never be mixed together, stored in large quantities, changed from one container to another or be returned to a container after being spilt on the ground. Put spillages straight in the pool.
Liability Where death or injury occurs at a pool, a legal liability may fall on the owner, even if there is a safety fence or cover installed.

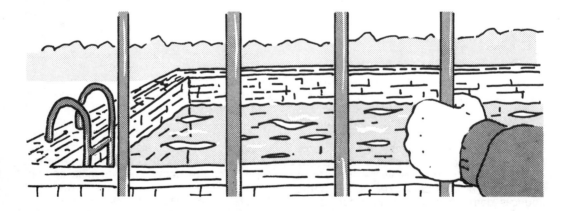

ABOVE-GROUND POOLS

Most people who buy above-ground pools install them themselves. There is little of the excavation and construction which goes with an in-ground pool. As long as you have a sufficiently large, level site with a sand topping an above-ground pool is simple.

Most above-ground pools are sold in a package which includes filter, ladder, test kit, manual cleaning equipment and so on. There is variation in price but generally that is related to the type of filter.

An above-ground pool is not the most attractive addition to the garden, but for many people the cost saving is worth it. Skilful landscaping can help it to fit in better.

Because of the vulnerability of the pool to damage, it is wise to be very clear about guarantees offered in the purchase contract.

Check with your council on any require-ments, particularly regarding safety fencing or screening from the street.

Maintenance This should not be as extensive as it is for in-ground pools but the need to keep water clean is the same. You will have to test water for pH and for total alkalinity, clear the pool regularly of debris and maintain an efficient filter. Unless you thoroughly understand your pool, regular inspection by a professional could be worth while.

Safety Remove the ladder when the pool is not in use.

SAUNAS

The sauna in Australia had to live down a certain amount of prejudice: that it was 'dangerous', 'bad for the heart' and so on. It is none of those things and, properly understood, is a splendid way to calm nerves and refresh tired bodies.

You do not take a sauna. You enter one. Sauna is the Finnish word for the wood-lined, insulated room in which you take a steam bath. The sauna is a long-standing Finnish tradition and has remained unchanged in essentials for perhaps 2000 years.

BENEFITS
It will not help you lose weight. In a sauna you will lose fluid in the form of perspiration but this should be replaced by drinking water or other liquid as soon as you leave the sauna.

The heat stimulates the skin to enable it to carry off body wastes. After only four minutes the skin temperature will rise to 40°C but that degree of heat does not affect internal organs. The warmth will increase the flow to the blood vessels of the skin. The blood is then pumped back into the body so that body temperature rises. This causes exidation of wastes and kidneys are relieved when the skin carries these wastes off.

The heart will beat more rapidly, pumping more blood per second. This does not cause strain in normal hearts but people with serious heart diseases, severe diabetes, tuberculosis or epilepsy should talk to their doctor before trying a sauna bath.

The most sensible way to take a sauna bath is lying down so that the heat is evenly dispersed through the body. If the head is higher than the feet it may become uncomfortable.

In Australia the Finnish custom of whisking the skin with birch twigs to stimulate circulation has often been translated into doing the same thing with fragrant eucalyptus twigs.

PLANNING A SAUNA
Most saunas are built of western red cedar, a hard timber which absorbs moisture and

radiates heat. They may be built indoors or out and can be heated by wood, electricity or oil. An essential is plenty of stones, generally granite or peridotite, heaped on the heater. Water poured on the hot stones is converted into heat that flows into the sauna. This instant heat, which the Finns call 'loyly', is what sauna addicts look for.

The temperature must be uniform so a good heating unit is essential.

Air humidity should be adequate. If the air is too dry it can can be uncomfortable and irritate the throat.

Ventilation should allow stale air to escape and fresh air to come in. An efficient ventilation system will also circulate the heat evenly around the room.

The heating unit is the core of the sauna. It is cheaper to buy a heating system which needs to be on full capacity only when the sauna is heating up and which can then be turned down for the time you are in the sauna. The surface temperature of the heating unit should be low, for safety reasons. Metal parts or nails may give nasty burns when the sauna is hot.

COST AND TYPE

There is great variation in price depending on what you ask for but the general phrase in the industry is that you can get a sauna for the price of a second-hand car. Saunas are available custom-designed, prefabricated and in low-cost do-it-yourself models. Most are available in western red cedar, Californian redwood or baltic pine. Some local suppliers make their own heaters. Most saunas are rectangular but you can get them in octagonal or trapezoid shape. If you want something slightly more elaborate, you can buy a two-roomed cabana for indoors or outdoors consisting of sauna and washing/changing room.

MAINTENANCE

As the essence of a sauna is steam, it is largely self-cleaning. There are, however, a couple of things you can do to keep your sauna working efficiently. About twice a year you should remove benches and duckboards and lightly sandpaper them. It is not necessary to sandpaper the walls except perhaps spots where people rest their head. Sandpapering of benches and duckboards is to remove stains caused by contact with bodies. Do not apply oil or paint to any timber in your sauna. Natural timber is the only effective finish.

The other maintenance job is to annually remove the rocks from the top of your stove. Dust them and the area. More particularly, remove any small ones. The rocks gain tremendous heat, then have cold water poured on them, so in time they crack and shatter. Too many small rocks will slow down the flow of hot air and make your sauna less efficient. From time to time you will have to buy new rocks to top up your supply.

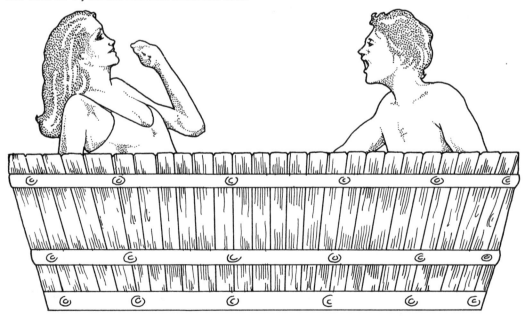

SPAS AND TUBS

Australians had just begun to take the backyard pool and the sauna for granted when they had to face the possibility that they might like a spa or hot tub. The spa, in the form of taking the waters, goes back a long way in history, at least to the Greeks and Romans. The Japanese discovered the pleasure of the hot tub early.

Spas and tubs operate on the same principle. Water is pumped through a heater and circulated to jets which release millions of swirling, massaging bubbles. Pressure is regulated by a valve which delivers a mixture of air and water from the jets. The supply of bubbles is generally increased by an aerator or air blower.

The choice of spa or tub is one of personal preference. The cost is about the same, both for initial purchase and running.

BENEFITS

A tub or spa cannot promise more than a general feeling of relaxation and well-being. They help some rheumatism and arthritis sufferers to greater ease of movement, at least temporarily. They are used to relieve sporting injuries and therapists sometimes make use of them for people with physical disabilities.

SPAS

Spas are generally made from moulded acrylic or fibreglass although some, as adjuncts to pools, may be of concrete or steel. Spas come in a variety of shapes, sizes and colours.

Sizes vary from a spa for one or two people, which is generally emptied after use like a bath, to spa pools for six or seven people. These are generally kept filled like a swimming pool. There are even portable spas on the market which don't need building or council approval.

Outdoor spas are generally installed in the ground. They have their own filtration. The water is retained and must be treated with chemicals to keep it clean.

Spa baths are installed indoors. They are about the size of a bathtub and some manufacturers think they will eventually replace the conventional tub. The spa bath, like the spa pool and hot tub, operates on a pump system which sucks water out of the bath and recirculates it through powerful jets. The water in a spa bath is replaced after each bath so you can add oils, perfumes and salts.

TUBS

Tubs are made of timber, usually redwood or cedar, and generally retain something of the look of a traditional tub. They come in a variety of sizes, up to ones large enough for family and friends. They are usually above-ground and are often outdoors although they may be placed indoors.

Both spas and tubs may be used year round, being heated to around 38°C to 40°C in winter and providing a burst of cool bubbles in summer.

COST AND CHOICE

As with a sauna, the average price is generally given as around the cost of a second-hand car. One Melbourne person, however, paid $15,000 for a custom-built spa. You may save a few hundred dollars by installing your spa or tub yourself but there are some risks with this unless you are an expert tradesman.

It is easy to say 'shop around' when talking about something on the supermarket shelves. Shopping around for a spa or tub is more difficult. Probably you should first talk to anybody you know who owns or uses one regularly. Once you have chosen between spa and tub, visit the local newsagent for any magazines with articles or advertisements for spa or tub. There are also one or two special books on the subject.

You will find then that not all the makers have addresses in each State and that most have only one or two showrooms. You can write for leaflets and study these, but you may decide it is wise to make a special trip to inspect the spa or tub you want.

The makers should be able to give you information about any building or council regulations and inspections entailed with the spa or tub of your choice, but if you have any doubts, do your own check before buying.

MAINTENANCE

Australians are used to a high standard of hygiene in their bathrooms and will find that the spa or tub will be just one more thing to look after. A few disgruntled buyers have complained that the only thing that thrived in the spa was bacteria and there have been reports of skin rashes. All this can be avoided by following the manufacturers' instructions and by realising that a spa or tub must be cleaned as regularly and thoroughly as any bath.

The smaller the tub or spa the more careful you must be to keep water fresh and clean. The filter should be as large as that on a standard size pool although the water capacity is much smaller. It is important to control chemical additives to maintain a correct balance.

This is even more important with hot tubs than with spas. Use of the wrong type of chemical in a tub can pulp the timber surface. Hot tubs generally leak for the first week or so after installation as the timber adjusts to the water content. If the tub is indoors, the maker should ensure waterproofing, at an additional cost. Many tubs leach tannin from the wood for a time. This is harmless.

14

MOVING HOUSE

FOR MOST PEOPLE buying a new house is dependent upon selling their old house. Both ventures involve major financial considerations and can be the source of much worry and tension. This section is intended to help minimise such problems. It gives advice on buying and selling, as well as tips for a smooth move.

BUYING A HOUSE

Buying a house or home unit is a big investment and requires a great deal of careful planning. First, list your requirements and priorities. Know what location you want, the number of bedrooms, the general size of the property and what price you are prepared (and able) to pay. Check the prices of similar properties in your buying area.

INSPECTING A HOUSE
Ask agents for details of advertised properties over the phone. You may save yourself a wasted trip.

When you inspect a property, take a list of things to check. It is unlikely that you will remember everything when you are there.

If you are inexperienced or unsure about inspecting a property, go with someone who knows more.

When you are inspecting a house, take a tape to measure the rooms. Draw a plan of the premises for later reflection.

You can call a building consultant, licensed builder or independent architect to examine a property for you before contracts are ex-

changed. They will be able to indicate possible defects and recommend any necessary repairs. Inform the consultant of any areas which may need additional inspection: electrical wiring, plumbing or pest problems.

Check out the property and the environs by calling the local planning department. They may provide vital information which agents decline to tell you.

Never say yes to an agent immediately. Take time to think it over. If possible, talk to someone else about your plans.

INSPECTION CHECKLIST
• Check paintwork, inside and outside the house. Note condition of plaster and wallpaper. Examine walls for any cracks. Check for dampness in bricks, around window sills and in ceilings.
• Look at the condition of the roof covering, gutters and downpipes.
• See that floors are level and sound.
• Make sure windows and doors close properly.
• Find out if the house is insulated.
• Check whether there is good natural lighting and ventilation in all rooms.

211

- Note the number and position of power points.
- Turn on all the taps to test water pressure. See if the water drains away quickly.
- Ask if the telephone is connected.
- Check the condition of paths and fences. If there is a swimming pool, see if the fencing complies with safety regulations.
- Note if there is a garage or carport.
- Consider actually living in the house. Are there adequate storage facilities? Will it be easy to maintain? Is there room for extension?
- Find out exactly what is included in the price: are floor coverings, curtains, the washing machine, light fittings?
- Measure doorways to see if your furniture will fit into the house.

Bathroom
- Check ventilation.
- Note condition of shower and/or bath.
- See if there are towel rails, cupboards and a mirror.
- Make sure the hot water is connected.

Kitchen
- Check that there is enough cupboard space and bench space.
- Measure to see if the refrigerator will fit and if there is room for a dishwasher.
- Note lighting and ventilation.
- Make sure the hot water is connected.

COSTS
When buying a house, there are costs you will face in addition to the price of the property. These should be taken into account when calculating how much you have to spend.

Loan application or establishment fee Charged by a lending body when a formal loan application is made. It reimburses the lending body for costs involved in investigating the application.

Valuation fee The property has to be professionally valued for lending purposes. Banks usually include the valuation fee in the establishment charge. Building societies will charge a fee based either on purchase price or valuation.

Share capital When you borrow from a building society, a share has to be held in a savings account for the duration of the loan.

Mortgage insurance This is required when the buyer is borrowing more than 70–75 per cent of valuation. It protects the lender in case the borrower defaults. The premium is a once-only payment and is sometimes added to the loan.

Legal fees The fees charged for conveyancing are determined by three factors: the purchase price, the size of the loan and the type of title involved. You will also have to pay expenses your solicitor will incur on your behalf, including title search and fees of government departments for certificates that have to be obtained.

Stamp duty Duty on the contract is calculated on the purchase price. Stamp duty is also payable on loans.

Insurance Lending bodies require the buyer to insure the new property from the date of exchange on contracts.

Survey Most lending bodies require an up-to-date survey showing where the house is in relation to the boundaries.

Pest inspection Required by most lending bodies.

Pre-purchase inspection This is optional but recommended. It is a structural inspection of the house by a qualified person such as an architect or builder who can point out any visible defects.

AUCTIONS
If you plan to buy at an auction, keep in mind the following points.
- Inspect the house carefully before the auction. Make sure it is what you want.
- Study the contract of sale which is available before the auction.
- Get approval for a loan before attending the auction.
- Be prepared to immediately pay a 10 per cent deposit. Personal cheques are accepted.
- Know your own limit and do not bid over it.
- Bid by nodding or raising your hand: indicate the amount by using one finger for $1000, two for $2000 and so on.

HOME UNITS
Buying a home unit can be a fairly complicated process, so it is wise to get a solicitor to help you. Do not engage the same solicitor as the seller of the unit.

Inspection of the books and records of the body corporate is essential before you buy. Never presume that your solicitor will automatically do this. Ask for it to be done for you before contracts are exchanged.

Make sure that appropriate and usual warranties and protections are included in the contract. Do not be put off by the legal language of the contract: ask your solicitor to explain anything you do not understand.

SELLING A HOUSE

When engaging an agent to sell your house, you must reach agreement on several points.
• The period of the agent's appointment, fee structure for the agent's services and when the fee is due and payable.
• Whether the agent is to spend any money marketing or promoting the property.
• Arrangement of set inspection times rather than random visits by prospective buyers.
• The selling price for your house: often best obtained from a qualified valuer but also can be gauged by finding out what prices have recently been obtained for other houses in the street or general area.
• Items to be sold: specify if light fittings and carpets are to be included in the price.
• If the house is to be auctioned you will have to pay an additional sum on top of the agent's commission for advertising signs and so on.

VACATING BEFORE SELLING

If it is necessary to move out of your house before a buyer has been found, there are several matters to attend to.

The house and garden area must be kept clean and neat. Professional cleaners are worth the expense as stains and damage marks show up far more once furniture has been removed. If the house is empty for some time, ensure that the interior is dusted and cleaned regularly. Lawns should be mowed and the garden kept in the best possible condition. Repainting rooms may not be a good idea as the new owners may not like the colours. Bathroom and kitchen, however, could be painted in a neutral tone if they look too shabby.

Your insurance company should be contacted before you leave your home. All insurance companies regard an empty property as a higher risk and an additional premium will be required to cover it until it is sold. The new premium will vary according to the location of the house (some areas are more prone to burglaries or vandalism), what materials it is made of and how long it will be unoccupied. Most companies allow a period of grace when a property becomes vacant, usually between 30 and 60 days, but it is preferable to act before this time.

MOVING

Moving house is a very busy time with a seemingly endless list of things to remember and chores to do. The following advice may help make your moving easier.

CHANGE OF ADDRESS

Notify your change of address to:
the post office, for mail redirection
your bank, to transfer your account
the Electoral Registrar
the Department of Motor Transport for car licences and registration papers
the Taxation Department
your hire purchase company
your insurance company, to transfer your household insurance
your life assurance company
your car insurance company
your health insurance fund
the principal of your children's school (and ask for a letter from him regarding the status of your children in school)
the local municipal authority, for rates
lodges, benefit and other societies
club membership secretaries
publications to which you subscribe
stores where you have accounts
relatives, friends and regular correspondents
government departments, advising them where to send child endowment or other payments
pistol or gun licence authorities
your solicitors
your church
your laundry service.

FINAL CHORES

Defrost your refrigerator and make sure all appliances are ready for removal. Check correct method of preparation for storage with manufacturers of refrigerator, washing machine, and other appliances.

Turn off and drain the water heater.

Have your outside television aerial taken down and dismantled professionally.

Arrange for electricity or gas companies to disconnect any fittings from the supply.

Clean out the bathroom cabinet and dispose of old medicine bottles.

Dispose of your unwanted furniture by auction or otherwise.

Put aside bits and pieces you don't want to take (there is no point in paying to move them).

· Return any garden tools, books and records you have borrowed.

Ask your doctor and dentist to recommend someone in the town or area to which you are moving.

Make sure you have discontinued these services: milk delivery, bread delivery, newspaper delivery, telephone, gas and electricity, water, fuel oil, freezer supply.

Make sure you have collected clothes from the dry cleaners, shoes from the bootmaker, clothes and sporting goods from lockers at clubs and schools.

One last look Have you left anything behind? Check the attic, garden, garage and under the house.

Check that you have not left any taps running or light switches or gas taps on.

Lock all windows and doors and surrender house keys.

It is a good idea to get your new home cleaned before the furniture arrives. It's a lot easier when the house is still empty.

15

LAW AND FINANCE

CAN I GET my money back? How should I approach my M.P.? Where can I get a loan? What sort of insurance should I have? This section gives the answers to these and many similarly important legal and financial questions which arise in everyday life.

LAWYERS

The legal profession is divided into barristers and solicitors in New South Wales and Queensland. In Victoria the profession is theoretically united but lawyers tend to practise as either a barrister or a solicitor. In the other States, all lawyers are both barristers and solicitors.

A solicitor is the one the client consults first, and most legal problems are handled by solicitors. Barristers are court specialists. Solicitors are entitled to argue your case before the court and many do this kind of work. If your solicitor wants to brief a barrister, make sure you are satisfied with the reasons for doing so, because barristers can be very expensive.

If you are dissatisfied with your lawyer or have any complaints, first try to sort out the problem personally with him or her. Demand explanations. Many complaints about lawyers result simply from the fact that they do not always tell their clients what they are doing, why they are doing it, or the reason for delays. If a discussion with your lawyer fails to sort out the problem, write to, or visit, the Law Society or Law Institute with your complaint.

Finding a lawyer While many lawyers do tend to specialise in particular areas of law, they are not specialists in any formal sense. Their expertise develops as a result of their own preferences and experience rather than any formal qualifications they may have. Lawyers are not allowed to advertise the areas of law in which they prefer to practise or in which they have particular expertise, so finding a lawyer to deal with your particular problem can be difficult.

If you need a lawyer and do not know one, try asking among your friends first. Alternatively, you can find one in the phone book, ring

the Law Society in your State (Law Institute in Victoria) for a list of solicitors in your area, or ask at a local community information centre.

If you are concerned about whether or not you actually need a solicitor's help, get advice from a Legal Aid Office, Chamber Magistrate or legal referral centre first, particularly if you are worried about the expense.

COSTS

The cost of employing a lawyer will vary according to what your problem is. For some kinds of legal work (such as conveyancing or probate) there is a set scale of solicitors' fees. However, a solicitor can charge more than this amount if the client agrees beforehand. There are no set fees for barristers so make sure you know beforehand what your barrister is likely to charge. Bring up the subject of costs with your solicitor at the first meeting to get at least a rough estimate.

Try to avoid changing solicitors in the middle of your case. This can cause long delays and more expense.

When the work is done you are entitled to an itemised account. Make sure you insist on this so you will have some idea how the money was actually spent.

Legal Aid The fact that it is cheaper (or sometimes free) does not mean it is second-rate legal representation. Although Legal Aid lawyers are on a salary and have no financial stake in the outcome of a case, they still care about their reputations within the profession and will do their best for you. In fact, because they are on a salary they are free to spend as much time and effort on each case as they think fit. While many Legal Aid lawyers are young and inexperienced, they have the back-up support of the more senior lawyers within their organisation.

To qualify for Legal Aid you must pass a means test. Go to a Legal Aid office or ask your solicitor for an application form. It will be processed and you will be informed whether you are successful and whether or not you will be asked to contribute towards any costs.

MEMBERS OF PARLIAMENT

If you want to approach your M.P. or a minister for whatever reason, some methods are more effective than others. A telegram is far more likely to be read by a minister than a letter. If it is delivered to the Parliamentary office when the House is in session, it could receive more attention. Do not bother with a registered letter. The minister will not open it personally in case it is a bomb. If you can get access to a telex machine, use it.

Letter writing campaigns can be effective. In terms of a member's electorate, there is strength in numbers. Do not ignore the local electorate office, particularly the secretary of your M.P. who often has a great deal of influence over who or what issue is exposed to the member.

Your local member is your representative in Parliament and so has some responsibility to see to your interests.

THE OMBUDSMAN

The Ombudsman is an independent and impartial official appointed by the Governor-General (Commonwealth) or Governor (State) to investigate complaints against government departments, authorities, boards, commissions and committees. Any individual can make a complaint to the Ombudsman as can companies, organisations and associations. There is no charge for the service. Complaints about administrative actions of a government department or authority, particular decisions made (or not made) and delays can be investigated by the Ombudsman.

It is worth trying to solve your problem first by directly contacting the relevant department or authority. If this is unsuccessful then write to the Ombudsman. You can telephone the office if you need advice on how to draft the complaint or if there are any other questions you want answered. It is advisable to call anyway as your case could be solved quickly and informally without the need for a written complaint.

The Ombudsman has the power while investigating, to enter the premises of government authorities and inspect files and records held. Your complaint will be handled confidentially and with complete privacy. You will be sent progress reports where appropriate. If the Ombudsman decides you are in the right, the head of the department or authority, or possibly the responsible minister, will receive a report recommending specific action be taken. If the Ombudsman finds that the recommendations have not been carried out, a report can be prepared for presentation to Parliament.

There are certain matters which the Ombudsman will not investigate. Sometimes there may be a better way of dealing with the problem; on other occasions the complaint may be regarded as frivolous, vexatious, trivial or made about conduct that occurred at too remote a time.

Complaints about the police force are investigated by the internal divisions of the forces themselves. However, the Ombudsman can consider the results of these inquiries and in some cases, conduct additional investigations.

As well as the Commonwealth Ombudsman, New South Wales, Victoria, South Australia, Tasmania and the Northern Territory each has an Ombudsman to handle complaints against State Government departments and authorities, and local government bodies. In Queensland and Western Australia there is a Parliamentary Commissioner for Administrative Investigations who offers the same service. Contact numbers are listed in the State Government section in the front of the telephone book.

DISPUTES WITH NEIGHBOURS

Such disputes can be distressing and disturbing. Always attempt to discuss the problem with your neighbour. Often he or she may not know the difficulties you are experiencing. The following guidelines cover the most common disputes.

Boundaries Disputes about the actual boundaries may be settled by consulting the survey of the land.

An owner or tenant has the right to refuse permission to anyone wanting to enter the property unless there has been a long-standing right-of-way agreement. So it is worth asking the owner before you enter the property to retrieve a football or animal.

Driveways If adjoining owners share a common driveway, usually one person owns it and the other has the right to use. No one, including the owner, has the right to block the driveway either with a parked car or some other obstacle.

Fences The cost of replacing a fence or repairing one must be shared by adjoining owners unless the title deeds state otherwise. If you want to build or repair a fence, first discuss it with your neighbour. If there is no agreement write a letter explaining details of the type of fence, where it will be placed and how much it will cost. If this fails you can take the matter to court. If you want an expensive or unusual fence you may have to pay the entire cost yourself. If the fence has been damaged because of neglect or the direct action of one of the owners, that owner must pay for all repairs.

Overhanging trees You may cut any branches from a neighbour's tree which overhang your property. However, any fruit on the branches must be returned to the owner of the tree. Check with your local council first about any restrictions on the cutting of trees.

NOISE

If you are bothered by noise which you find too loud or which is disturbing you at unreasonable hours, there are steps you can take to have your peace restored. Constant noise such as from a building site or factory can be restricted. In fact the hours during which building operations may be conducted are prescribed by law. The noise or pollution control commission in your State can act on your complaint. In addition, your local council and the police have powers to order that excessive noise cease.

Neighbours who frequently have loud parties or play music late at night should be approached first. You may find that they did not realise how easily the noise carried at night and didn't know that you were being disturbed. If your approach fails to improve the situation, call the police. They can direct that noise be stopped between certain hours.

Coping with traffic noise Some noise such as that of traffic is not so easily dealt with, but the disturbance can be reduced.

Consider rearranging the use of the rooms in your house. Move the bedrooms towards the back, away from the street. The walls in between will act as buffers and keep the noise level down.

A wall or fence between your house and the road will also reduce noise. It should be as tall as possible, preferably higher than the front windows, and built either close to the street or close to the house. It must be solid to be effective: ornamental fences such as wrought-iron are inadequate, and for the same reason, trees or shrubs are not much use.

Make sure front windows are closed; you

can even have them reduced in size. Double glazing will increase the thickness of windows and help keep out the noise.

CONSUMER RIGHTS

When you purchase goods you can expect that they will be free of defects (unless you knew about these beforehand) and be the same as the sample or description you were offered before you bought them. You are also entitled to expect that spare parts and repair facilities will be reasonably available (again unless you were told otherwise before the purchase was made).

If you are engaging the services of a tradesperson you should not be misled or deceived in any way and the service should be carried out with reasonable care and skill using suitable materials.

The protection of these expectations, your rights, is contained in the Commonwealth Trade Practices Act. It applies to you even if you have signed a written contract and is in addition to any written guarantee you get with goods or services.

COMPLAINTS

If you have a problem with any goods or services you have bought, the first thing to do is complain to the seller or serviceperson. Do so in person and/or in writing. If this prompts no reaction the next step is to contact your

Consumer Affairs Department or Bureau. They will advise you over the phone about how to make a complaint which they can act upon. They will generally contact the shop or company and try to reach some agreement. They will also advise you on who to contact if your complaint could be better handled by another authority, for example the Health Department or the police.

For your own protection, keep in mind the following points when you shop.
• Carefully examine goods before you buy.
• If you are unsure that goods will be suitable for a particular use, check with the salesperson.
• If you buy goods on the basis of a sample or description make sure that the goods you get match that sample or description.
• Make sure that the goods or services are adequately described in contracts and receipts.
• Keep all contracts, receipts and other papers. You may need them later.

TRADESPEOPLE

Dealing with tradespeople does not have to be as difficult a task as it often is. Your best approach is to be businesslike and alert; after all, you have contracted someone to carry out some work in your house so you must ensure that the contract is fulfilled. Most tradespeople are hard-working and honest. There are some, however, who are not so interested in getting the job done quickly and efficiently. Keep the following points in mind.
• Is the tradesperson licensed (if required) or a member of a reputable firm or trade association? Check credentials and prices by phoning the consumers affairs authority.
• Ask for a written quote, noting all work to be carried out, alterations made. Make sure the tradesperson signs it.
• Arrange for a friend or neighbour to be at your home if you cannot be there while the work is done, to satisfy any doubts about aspects of the job.
• If it is a building or painting job, cover your carpets and furniture, remove curtains and put down runners in the work area. It will also help the tradesperson who is obliged to clean up.
• Ask for identification before admitting a tradesperson into your home.
• Offer tea or light refreshments only if you are not paying for the time by the hour.
• Inspect the work on completion of the job and before making the final payment. If pos-

sible ask a friend or colleague who is familiar with such work. Local building inspectors will check large jobs.

• Justifiable complaints should be discussed with the tradesperson but if there is no progress call the consumer affairs authority.

Electricity, gas and water Tradespeople from electricity, gas and water-supply authorities provide emergency services and can advise you on safety measures. They wear uniforms and carry identity cards.

If your water supply develops a fault, if you receive electric shocks from light switches or if you smell gas in your house and do not know where it is coming from, contact the relevant authority. They will provide service for these and other related problems.

DOOR-TO-DOOR SELLING

While many reputable companies carry out door-to-door selling, there are also a number of unscrupulous salespeople who will pressure you and take advantage of you to make a sale. You must be prepared if they visit you.

Always ask the name of the company they claim to represent. If they have a business card or brochure, keep one as it may help in identifying them later. Do not tell them any personal details of yourself or your family and do not give the names of neighbours or other people. Be wary of the sales pitch: home repairers who just happen to see some problems around your house, students who claim to be working their way through university and tell you that your purchase will help them, anyone who offers to take you to the bank to withdraw money.

Before you decide to buy, consider whether you really need the goods and whether you can afford to pay. Do not pay cash until the goods are delivered and you have inspected them.

Never sign a contract if you do not understand it. Ask for a copy and seek advice from someone else. The salesperson can always call back.

Remember, you have a 10-day 'cooling off' period from the date of transaction. You are legally entitled to cancel the agreement within 10 days if the salesperson was uninvited, if it is a credit purchase where you pay for the goods by instalments, or if the goods cost less than $5000. If you decide to cancel, the seller must refund all your money within 7 days and you must return the goods to the seller.

CAR SERVICE

Having your car serviced can be very expensive and it is not necessarily always because of over-servicing or over-charging by the mechanic. Car owners often do not specify exactly what they want done. Even if your knowledge of your car is nil you must try to provide adequate instructions. If you really have no idea talk it over with the mechanic first. If major problems are possible, insist that you be contacted before the work is done or you may find yourself up for hundreds of dollars more than you planned.

Basic services for cars every few thousand kilometres generally have set recommended labour prices put forward by the dealers. On top of this there will be oil and grease at least. Ask the basic cost, and if you have other things you want done (e.g. headlight blown, door handle loose) make a list and keep a copy for yourself.

If the mechanic finds a serious problem and calls you, take down all the details (even if they do not make sense to you) including the price quoted for repairs. With this information you can phone the motoring organisation in your State and inquire about how much would be reasonable for the kind of work that has to be done.

If you have a complaint about the work, your motoring organisation will usually try to negotiate with the mechanic. If this fails, contact the consumer affairs authority.

BUYING A CAR

Before you set out to buy a car you should first determine how much you can afford to pay, what size and type of car you are interested in and whether you will buy a new or used vehicle. A note on costs: as well as the stated price, take into account credit charges (if you have to borrow or buy on hire purchase), insurance, stamp duty, registration and any extras you may choose, such as a radio and cassette player or rust proofing.

Study pamphlets on buying cars and your statutory warranty entitlements before going to the car yards.

Insist on a test drive over different types of road surfaces: hilly, bumpy, curved and straight. Remember that even new cars may be faulty.

Make sure you fully understand the order form, which is the basis of contract of purchase. The dealer can increase the price of the car, delay the delivery or force a change in your financial arrangements with your written consent unless you are mindful of every clause.

USED CARS

When buying a used car the first thing to do is not to let anyone rush you at the car yard. Take your time and check cars out thoroughly. Make sure the car is the year and model the seller claims it to be. Observe the general appearance of the car: if it is dented or rusty, possibly the mechanical parts have also been neglected. Never shop at night or on a wet day when you cannot see the duco properly. Duco shines lustrously at night, and rain helps cover blemishes and corrosion.

Check the tyres. Unevenly worn tyres could be caused by faulty brakes, suspension or steering. If the steering wheel is too free or it knocks, parts could be worn.

See that the engine starts easily without too much revving and idles evenly without too much choke. Check the exhaust for excessive smoke when the engine is revved. Look for oil or petrol leaks.

A heavy knock in the engine may mean worn bearings.

Gears that disengage when the car is in motion indicate excessive wear. A whine or howl in the gearbox or differential means expensive repair bills.

Loud thumps from the suspension when driving over rough roads usually means worn suspension parts.

The motoring organisation in your State will inspect a car for you, for a fee. You can pay a holding deposit or 'option to purchase' on a car, which is subject to this inspection being satisfactory to you. If it is not satisfactory you are entitled to get your money back. The inspection will also tell you what repairs are likely to be needed in the near future and the approximate cost.

Watch for 'ghost advertising'. A car that was advertised to lure buyers may not even exist in the car yard, or have faults that were not noticeable in the advertising picture. The dealer may be using an obviously bad car to steer you to a 'better deal'. Do not be fooled by 'demo' cars. In most cases it is the sales rep's car, registered in his or the dealer's name, and does not carry a new car warranty. Be wary,

too, about used cars offered for prices below the minimum statutory price at which a warranty must be offered by the dealer. If defects occur in these cars after purchase you may find it difficult to obtain redress from the dealer.

Before you sign any contract, read it thoroughly. Check the registration papers and make sure the engine and chassis numbers are the same on the car and in the papers. If it is a private sale, ensure that the seller actually owns the car and does not owe money to a financier. Take particular note of warranty conditions.

MOTOR ACCIDENT PROCEDURE

If you are the driver of a car involved in an accident, you are obliged, by law, to do the following:
• Stop.
• Assist anyone who is injured.
• Produce your driving licence.
• Give your name and address, the name and address of the owner of the car, and the car registration number to anyone involved in the accident, and to the police if they have been called.
• Police should be called if someone is killed or injured, or if more than $500 damage has been caused. If it is impossible to call from the scene of the accident, you must report to the police as soon as possible.
• Answer police questions about the accident, but not if they incriminate you. Do not admit the accident was your fault, even if you believe it was, as this could complicate insurance claims. It is advisable to seek legal advice to clarify your position on claiming compensation from an insurance company.
• You must take a breath test when requested by the police.
• You are expected to remove the vehicle or vehicles after an accident, if you are able to do so. Also you should clear any broken glass or other debris off the road.
• Take names and addresses of witnesses— you may need them later.

For the safety aspect of accidents see MOTOR ACCIDENT p. 266.

BORROWING MONEY

When borrowing money, for whatever purpose, it is essential to find out two things before you sign any agreement: first, the effective interest rate, and secondly, what conditions apply to the loan.

Credit rating Your personal credit rating is determined by information provided by you when you apply for credit. You will be required to give details about what work you do and where you live. These details, filled out on a form, will be the basis of your credit rating.

WHERE YOU CAN BORROW MONEY

Banks Two types of loans are offered by banks. An overdraft means the bank will meet cheques drawn up to a certain sum for a period of time even if you have no money in the account. Interest is payable on the amount overdrawn but the rate decreases as you pay the money back. The second type offered is a personal loan which has to be repaid over an agreed period of time at a specified rate.

Finance companies Less security is required than with a bank loan. Interest rates are usually higher.

Credit unions Loans to members are often made at lower rates than those charged by finance companies. A limit to the amount which can be borrowed generally applies.

Money lenders Usually very high interest rates are charged. Details of the loan should be examined carefully before committing yourself.

HIRE PURCHASE

Hire purchase is another form of credit. If you buy goods on hire purchase you pay for them by instalment. Although you take possession of the goods immediately, you do not own them until the final payment is made. Goods will cost you more because you have to pay interest as well as the retail price.

All hire purchase agreements must be made in writing and signed by all parties to the agreement. Do not sign unless or until you understand all of your obligations under the agreement: the full cost you must pay, including cash price of the goods, interest and credit charges. Never sign a blank or incomplete contract.

The owner can insist that goods bought on hire purchase are insured but cannot make you insure with a particular company.

If you want to pay off earlier than originally agreed, notify the owner. However, you may not get the interest fully refunded.

If you have to cancel the agreement because you cannot keep up the payments (or for any other reason), you must return the goods to the owner. You will not get a refund of any payments you have already made and the owner may demand payment of additional costs which you must comply with.

If you fall behind with payments the owner may repossess the goods after giving 21 days notice. This gives you time to pay the money owing. If you want the goods back after they have been repossessed, you have 21 days before the owner is allowed to resell them. You will have to pay the owner any amount due as well as costs which may have been incurred by the owner in repossession.

DEBT

If you get into debt, first talk to your creditor and try to come to an arrangement which is mutually satisfactory, such as payment by instalment. Remember that creditors are essentially interested in receiving the money owed so they will try to work out a solution with you.

If you have fallen behind with payments you will usually receive a letter of demand from the creditor or a debt collection agency. If you get such a letter, write to the creditor requesting a detailed statement of how much is owed and what charges have been added. Keep a copy of your letter. When you have this statement, check it with your own records. If it does not tally, write and demand clarification. If the statement appears correct you should now try to come to an agreement with your creditor. Work out how much you can afford to pay each week and offer this.

If your creditor issues a summons against you to recover the debt you must act on it. It is wise at this stage to seek legal advice as you will be required to answer the summons in court. If you ignore the summons the court will not know of your circumstances and can decide the issue without your being there. If the court decides in favour of the creditor, the amount you are ordered to pay is known as a judgment debt. The creditor can enforce this debt by obtaining a writ of execution which authorises a bailiff to seize your goods and sell them unless the debt is paid. The bailiff can only take property owned by you personally and only furniture and goods up to the value of the amount stated in the warrant. When the bailiff comes you can offer to pay some of the money you owe but it is perhaps more advisable (and not too late) to go to the court and obtain an instalment order. Tell the bailiff if you intend to do this and he might not then take your possessions. To avoid the bailiff's visit, answer the original summons by seeking an order from the court which allows you to pay by instalments. Do not hesitate to seek legal advice at any stage. It will save you a lot of hardship and money.

INSURANCE

An insurance policy is a contract. The insurer promises to pay the insured a sum of money if a certain event happens or a certain situation arises. In return for this promise you (the insured) pay a premium.

The details about when the insurer is obliged to pay are set down in the policy. These are the terms and conditions. You should ask to see the standard policy form for the type of insurance you are applying for before you pay the premium or send in the proposal form. Make sure you understand all the terms and conditions. Once your proposal has been accepted, the contract becomes binding. If you break any of the promises which you have made in the contract the insurer can treat the contract as if it never had existed.

Buying a policy The application form for insurance is called a proposal. When filling in the proposal form answer all questions truthfully and completely. If you forget something

or try to hide any facts, the insurance company may not pay when you make a claim.

Shop around for policies. The cheapest premium is not necessarily the best as it may not offer the benefits and conditions you want. Obtain copies of policies from various companies and compare them to determine which one suits your needs.

Renewal Usually insurance companies send out renewal notices before your policy expires. However, there may be delays for some reason, so it is wise to keep a note for yourself of when your premiums are due. If you allow your policy to expire before you pay the renewal you will not be covered.

Check your policy each year when you renew it. If your circumstances have changed at all — new car, expensive furniture purchases — your policy may have to be altered to include these items. Inform the insurance company which will be able to work out any changes.

Claims Contact the insurance company as soon as possible when you have to make a claim. They will generally provide you with a claim form to fill in and return. If you disagree with the insurance company about a claim, either because it refuses to pay at all or offers less than you feel you are entitled to, seek legal advice or help from a consumer organisation.

TYPES OF POLICIES
There are three types of policies.

Indemnity policy When you make a claim the insurance company has to pay only the value of what the property was worth when it was lost or damaged, even if it was insured for a higher amount.

Replacement policy The insurer has to pay you the full value of lost or damaged property. This means you will be able to replace the goods but you will have to pay much higher premiums.

Agreed value policy Under this policy your property is insured for a value agreed upon between you and the insurance company. It is important with this type of policy that you keep the agreed value up to date so you can recover the full cost of replacing your property if it is lost, stolen or destroyed.

WHAT TO INSURE
Life assurance This is, as it sounds, insurance on your life. There are two basic types of life policies. The first, term assurance, pays out only on death. It covers your family (or some

other beneficiary) for a specific period of years; for example, during your estimated working life. If you die during this time the assurance company will pay out, but if you outlive this period and your beneficiaries, you will get nothing. The second type of cover is whole-of-life assurance. Under this type of policy the assurer agrees to pay out a certain sum when the assured dies. There is no fixed period of assurance under this policy. The premiums are therefore higher.

Household insurance You may have separate policies to cover the actual house itself and its contents. If you have a mortgage the lending body will insist on a policy covering the building. To determine the value of the contents of your house, make a list detailing items. It will be more comprehensive and almost always a higher amount than you would estimate by just glancing around your furnishings and other possessions. Remember, you are insuring to cover replacement of all your goods, so a little time taken in making a list is worthwhile.

Medical insurance Whatever national health scheme is in operation there are many health needs which will only be fully covered by private insurance. Find out what you are covered for now and take extra protection if necessary.

Personal accident insurance This policy covers members of your family who are not covered by workers' compensation. It is useful for self-employed people too. It will pay compensation in the event of death, injury by accident or disablement due to illness.

Personal liability If someone is injured or their property damaged while they are on your property you could be required to pay medical bills and damages. Your household insurance may cover this but make sure that the cover is adequate.

Motor insurance Third-party insurance is compulsory and is paid with your registration. This protects you, as the driver, for personal injury to passengers or people outside your vehicle. It does not cover you as a driver, or any property damaged in an accident, including your own car. There are various policies which would pay for damages to your vehicle and others, as well as insurance for theft. Although you may not think your own car worth insuring, you could be up for high costs if you hit another car.

Travel insurance You can insure for personal accident, medical and hospital expenses (which can often be very expensive overseas), loss of or damage to luggage and unexpected cancellations of trips. You can take out this insurance yourself or arrange it through your travel agent but make sure you check the conditions of the policy before you leave.

Workers' compensation insurance This is compulsory for all employers including anyone who employs domestic help. This covers the employer for injury to a worker either at work or travelling to and from work. It also applies to illness which results from a work situation.

WILLS

Anyone over 18 years of age can make a will. There is no legal requirement that a solicitor must draw up the will and you can buy your own form at a newsagent. However, it is advisable to get legal assistance as generally it will not cost much and ensures that your will is valid and expresses your wishes legally and clearly. When the will is drawn up it has to be signed by you (the testator) and witnessed by two people. The witnesses should not be beneficiaries. You will need to appoint someone to administer your estate—an executor. The executor must be over 18 and should be someone you trust.

Once your will is made it should be kept in a safe place. Generally it is wise to tell a relative or close friend or two where you have put it.

A will can be changed. Any changes must be witnessed by two people (not necessarily the original witnesses). If the alterations are small, you can make a codicil. This is a supplementary document which adds or changes a part or parts of a will. If the changes are significant it is better to draw up a new will which states that all earlier wills are revoked. As soon as you draw up a new will the old one is nullified and should be destroyed as it may cause confusion later.

Remember to keep your will up to date. Marriage, divorce, the death of a friend or relative: these circumstances may require that a new will be made in accordance with your intentions.

If someone dies without leaving a valid will (intestate) the property will be distributed to those people entitled by law to a share.

GLOSSARY OF TERMS
Testator Person who makes a valid will.
Intestate A person who dies without having made a valid will.

Estate All property owned by, or owed to the testator when he or she dies.

Administration of an estate All steps necessary to carry out the terms of the will or divide the property under the intestacy rules.

Executor Person appointed in the will to administer the estate.

Administrator Person appointed by the court to administer the estate when there is no valid will or the will does not appoint an executor.

Trustee Person who holds property and takes care of it for someone else's benefit. The executor or administrator is also a trustee until all the property is distributed.

Beneficiary Person for whose benefit the trustee holds the property; a person to whom property is left in the will.

Probate The court order which makes the executor the trustee of the estate.

FUNERALS

Funerals are not generally the subject of conversation but you are likely to have to deal with them at some time and it is best to know beforehand what is involved.

Funeral costs can be broken down into three parts: service charges, payment to cemetery or crematorium, and the cost of the coffin or casket. The service charge is paid to the funeral director. It covers the hearse, arrangements at the crematorium or cemetery, arranging things with the clergy, discussions with relatives and dealing with the death certificate. The charges can vary from one funeral director to another. If cost matters do not feel self-conscious about asking for the lowest possible quotes. Inquire about the cost of extras: embalming, additional mourning or floral coaches and conducting the funeral outside normal business hours.

The casket or coffin will make up a large proportion of the total account; prices vary enormously so compare costs and choose carefully.

If you want to arrange your own funeral make your wishes about cremation or burial known well in advance. Make a clear will, gather together birth, marriage and insurance documents in one place and let someone responsible know where they are. You can buy a burial site or cremation deed in advance and also arrange insurance which will cover funeral costs. This action is not strange or even unusual and it will spare your relatives a great deal of worry later.

16

KEEPING TO A BUDGET

THE EASIEST way to appreciate the benefits of budgeting is to imagine life without any budgets at all. If nobody bothered to budget, the Federal Government, State governments and local governments would virtually be unable to operate because of financial chaos. Businesses—from big corporations to small private companies—would be similarly affected as would the average person.

HOW TO BUDGET

Budgeting should start with a commonsense—and truthful—assessment of your financial position. An annual estimate of income and expenditure should be made, with any money left over becoming savings.

In order to arrive at a close calculation, two lots of expenses will have to be taken into account. The best way to describe them is bills or expenses that are faced once a year (periodic expenses) and those that crop up monthly, weekly or daily (frequent expenses).

PERIODIC EXPENSES

Rates The two most expensive are council and water. Levied once a year they apply only to home owners and landholders and not to people who are paying rent. These bills can now be so large that some people feel more comfortable paying them off in quarterly instalments. A choice is usually available. If you're forgetful, don't opt for quarterly repayments which means paying four bills instead of one. Place the money you set aside for these annual expenses (and all others) in a higher interest account with a bank, credit union or building society where the money is earning interest for you and delve into it *only* when the need arises to pay major bills.

Insurance This is one bill that a lot of people may prefer to duck, but don't dare.

A house is the biggest purchase most of us make in life. If it was suddenly burnt to the ground and its contents destroyed, very few of us would be able to muster up a spare $50,000 or $100,000 to build another.

An annual insurance bill should be tallied for the house and its contents plus any other policies such as health, accident or life insurance.

House maintenance Large bills likely to be faced during the year should be taken into account. Brick homes are dearer than timber homes to build, but timber homes require more maintenance—once every three years is the general rule for a re-paint to keep them shipshape. If you're handy and can do a thorough job yourself it will take time but save you money. If you need a professional painter, make provision for a quote in your annual expenses. Do the same for any other areas needing attention: a kitchen or bathroom renovations, a new side fence, a home extension.

225

House furnishings These consume large amounts from time to time—a new refrigerator, washing machine, dining or lounge suite. Years may go by before these items have to be replaced. When they do, add their price into the annual budget.

Power, gas, phone Most such bills arrive quarterly (with higher fuel bills in winter).

Heating bills for other fuels such as oil, briquettes, kerosene and wood should also be considered.

The old practice of maintaining a money box for telephone calls can be dismissed. Money boxes these days would rarely accommodate the amount needed for phone bills. It makes far better sense to withdraw the often large amounts needed for the bills twice a year from an account earning high interest.

School Other annual expenses that should be looked at are those related to education: school fees, equipment, uniforms, sporting fees. A wise parent does not necessarily buy new uniforms but sees what can be made at home or obtained from the school clothing pool at vastly reduced prices.

Medical Assess what you are likely to pay the doctor, chemist and dentist during the year. The dentist's bill could escalate sharply if there are young children in the family undergoing orthodontic treatment.

Other How much do you pay each year to belong to social clubs, sporting clubs, a union or professional association and what donations do you make to your church or to charities? Jot them down as an annual outgoing.

What would you normally allocate for spending on gifts for Christmas and birthdays? Mark it up as an annual calculation.

Holidays The final expense for a family or single wage earner is that amount of money given over to a holiday. Holidays often depend on how much money you have left over as savings after all other expenses have been taken care of.

FREQUENT EXPENSES

Housing Mortgage repayments, rent or board are major considerations.

Food The food bill for many people becomes a recurring nightmare: how to make ends meet, how to vary the bill of fare, and so on. The best answer is to look after the basics first (meat, poultry, fish, groceries, fruit and vegetables) and any money left over can be expended on treats and extras.

Making your plot of earth work for you is one area where food costs can be cut.

This means a swing away from ornamental back gardens to productive gardens with fruit trees, fences used for passionfruit vines and beans, trellises for grapes and kiwi fruit, and the exit of flowering annuals in favour of tomatoes, cabbages and spinach. There's no expense for fertilisers when compost from the household (everything from vegetable scraps to tea leaves), lawn cuttings and leaf mould are used.

Even in smaller homes (town houses or units) there can be room for growing strawberries, tomatoes or herbs in tubs and containers.

Cigarettes There's not much change these days out of $2 for a packet of cigarettes. If you're a packet-a-day person, multiply that by 365 and you won't have much change left out of $1000 when the figure is tallied annually.

Alcohol Calculate how long a bottle of spirits or a cask of wine lasts, how often you buy bottles of beer or wine, and in what quantities.

Clothing and grooming On the frequent expenses list, minor items of clothing should be considered (pantyhose, underclothing, socks) and also cosmetics, toiletries and the regular trip to the hairdressers.

Transport Bus, train fares and an allowance for taxis should be assessed, as well as those costs related to running a car.

Credit repayments Bankcard, personal loan, credit card repayments and any lay-bys on goods.

Entertainment How much do you allow for 'nightlife', seeing films, hiring videos, eating out? It is hard to assess this figure annually and easier to look at it in the context of a month.

Newspapers and magazines The bill for newspapers and magazines often catches people unawares if it is allowed to mount up. Add this bill to the list of frequent expenses and look at it on a monthly or weekly basis.

Gambling To what extent do you gamble? Don't discount gambling as an item for the budget. If you try your luck at Lotto or Pools, if you are an on-course gambler or a Saturday afternoon TAB punter, estimate how much you spend (or **should** comfortably spend) and make a rule to stick to that estimate.

RUNNING A CAR

Cars—the purchase of them and the maintenance of them—become major considerations in any budget. People without cars are perhaps a rare breed but they are to be found, certainly in big cities where (normally) efficient public transport suffices for work and taxis for social occasions. These people usually have fatter bank balances because they do not run cars and thereby save thousands of dollars a year. It is, however, a method of saving and a sacrifice that most people are unable to make.

Any car owner can expect two sets of costs with a vehicle. These are fixed costs and running costs.

Fixed costs Those items which are paid for whether the vehicle is used or not. These vary according to vehicle size or type and are essentially outside the control of the vehicle owner.

Included are registration and insurance, purchase costs (if a vehicle is bought new at 25 per cent deposit and the remaining 75 per cent paid for by a loan over a few years) and depreciation, which is the loss of capital value of a vehicle in the course of time. Various factors can affect the actual depreciated value. These include the condition of the vehicle, vehicle popularity, movements in new car prices and market forces. All will vary according to the particular vehicle at a particular time.

Running costs These are incurred in the day-to-day operation of the vehicle and are directly related to the distances travelled. A tally for fuel will have to be taken into account, the cost of tyres and any service and repair charges.

The actual costs of running a car will depend on the circumstances of purchase, the use to which it is put and how well it is maintained.

Total weekly costs The following guide prepared by the N.S.W. motoring organisation (N.R.M.A.) may be of help in assessing weekly car costs for a range of vehicles.

The detailed survey (findings released in 1984) shows the overall weekly cost (i.e. both fixed and running costs) in $/km based on 15,000km travelled annually.

Small cars: Suzuki Hatch — $58.93, Diahatsu CX Charade — $67.81.

Low-medium car: Holden Gemini SLX sedan — $80.88.

Medium car: Holden Camira SLX sedan — $86.54.

Upper-medium car: Holden Commodore SLX sedan — $115.18.

Luxury car: Ford LTD sedan — $222.90.

All the above figures are based on cars being run privately and not used for business.

SUMMING UP

By the time you add up your larger annual expenses (periodic expenses) and the monthly, weekly or daily expenses (frequent expenses) you'll have a fairly accurate picture of your annual outgoings.

	$
• Annual salary/wages	
• Allowances (family, car etc.) +	
• Dividends/interest +	
• Other income +	
Sub-total	
• Less: taxation per annum −	
• Total — net annual income	
• Less: annual expenses −	
• = annual savings	
• Divide by 52 = weekly savings	

If it looks as if your expenditure will exceed your income, then some savage pruning is needed. There will be areas such as rates and repayments where cuts are impossible. The answer is to make cuts in the areas where you have a choice available and opt for a less lavish lifestyle.

Most people are not affected this way. With budget planning they are able to keep their expenditure below their total income so that savings result.

Budget cuts and sound planning in the short term can result in a better lifestyle in the long term. Beach and holiday houses or flats, caravans and boats and overseas holidays are frequently the results of concerted efforts to save.

Once a pattern is established for handling finances, most people soon fall into the swing of things. They are alert for the quarterly bills, the monthly repayments, the big annual slugs. They are aware of how much each bill is likely to be and which months the water and council rates are due to arrive.

For those starting off budgeting, an annual calendar may be a help. It should be kept specifically as a reminder of payments.

17
FITNESS AND DIET

IN THE last few decades medical science has given us a longer life span. Those of us interested in enjoying a long, healthy life should follow a daily routine that will keep us as fit as possible for our age and way of life.

GOOD HEALTH

Good health is maintained through a regime of good nutrition, physical fitness and a positive outlook.

If you are looking for some simple guide to good health for yourself and your family then what you need is some common sense. You need to eat well, sleep well, take regular exercise and avoid situations that cause you anxiety and stress.

Sleep A necessary part of every day. We should make it regular and take as much as we need. Sleep is a time to 'recharge the batteries'. If we suffer from a chronic shortage of sleep we may lack energy and be irritable. And the way to good health is not through a bottle of sleeping pills.

Exercise We should exercise to maintain strength, stamina, co-ordination, flexibility and a sense of well-being. To develop healthy hearts and lungs and reduce the risk of having a heart attack, the exercise needs to be regular and sustained. Exercising only once a week is more dangerous to your heart than taking none at all: 3 times a week is the minimum, 4–5 times is better.

Diet We all eat too much and we eat the wrong things. What we need is a balanced diet. Protein is made up of amino acids and we need a variety of these to build up or replace our body tissues. Carbohydrates are useful as a readily absorbed and quickly available source of energy although if we have too much we store it as fat. Vitamins act as catalysts or chemicals that enable other chemical reactions to occur. Fibre allows proper functioning of the bowel.

A high level of fat in the blood is one of the factors leading to coronary artery disease. This blood fat is made up of triglycerides and cholesterol. To reduce the level of triglycerides we should cut down on sugar and beer. To reduce cholesterol, cut down on the amount of animal fat in your diet.

Relaxation Stress initiates the release of hormones which increase heart rate and blood pressure. Many heart attack victims are rushed, over-ambitious and easily agitated.

If you can't relax, you should learn to do so. Relaxation is like any other skill it can be learned. And like any other skill, to be good at it requires constant practice.

A FITNESS PLAN

If you begin your fitness training by accepting that you will need a system which suits your own personal requirements then you will discover that no system works so well as the one you design for yourself.

Begin by setting your goals and relating them to your lifestyle and capabilities rather than your dreams, which may be unrealisable. Do some basic self-assessment. Write down as many personal details as possible, including name, age, height, weight, occupation, date when you first decided to begin this lifetime training programme, resting heart rates, subjective feelings of fitness and well-being, capacity for work and play, and anything else about your present state of health. This will allow comparison in future, particularly when you begin to become bored or unmotivated and you'll be surprised how much such a diary can help. It will show you just how far you have progressed.

The first 6–12 weeks are always the most difficult of any training programme, especially if you haven't done any regular training before. It will take that time merely to establish or re-establish the exercise habit as a part of your daily routine.

Once you have established a basic routine, make time in your day for a regular swim, run or bike ride. It's really not that difficult. Most people have the beach or a pool nearby and many pools are heated during the winter months. Running is easy, costs nothing and can be done anywhere. Again, gradually build up the distance and when you get tired, slow down and walk for a while. Cycling is wonderful for heart and lungs (like swimming and running) and for the legs. If you are anxious about the traffic, set out early in the morning, a most beautiful way to start the day.

The business of getting fit can be a very involved one. However, remember that the only thing which counts in any fitness programme is its benefit to you.

Fitness never has and probably never will guarantee longevity. What it does offer is more enjoyment of life.

BASIC EXERCISE
The best way to become fit is to plan a programme where you work up to a regular exercise routine each day. Don't do too much too soon. You shouldn't get stiff. Obviously once your routine gets easy you can make it harder for yourself by increasing the number of repetitions and decreasing the time in which to do them. Remember, always slow down if it's a real struggle.

Here are a series of simple, universal exercises that you can fit into your routine. Increase the repetitions over a period of, say, a month. Start with 10 side bends, 10 waist bends, 10 leg stretches, 5 curl-ups, 5 scissors, 5 half sit-ups, 5 side leg-raises, 5 basic press-ups, 5 leg-raises.

Scissors Lie with legs raised to 30 degrees with hands under buttocks. Criss-cross legs like scissors. Work to ultimate goal of 50.

Side leg-raises Lie on side with hand on floor to balance and support body. Support your head on the other hand. Raise your leg as high as you can, keeping it straight. Alternate each leg.

Half sit-ups Place hands on thighs, bend knees slightly. Sit up to angle of 45 degrees and without moving legs and hips too much, bring head to chest.

Leg stretches Sit on floor with legs as wide as possible. Place right hand on left knee. Touch left toes with left hand and point your nose at your knee. Change sides.

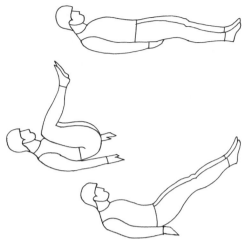

Curl-ups Lie with hands under buttocks, head a little off ground. Bring knees up under chin, straighten legs out to 45 degrees angle and lower.

Leg-raises Lie with hands under buttocks, palms down. Keep head off floor, legs straight, toes pointed. Raise legs to angle of not more than 45 degrees, lower. Aim at 20 repetitions as ultimate goal.

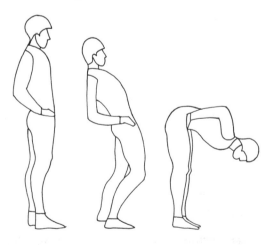

Waist bends Place feet wide and knees slightly bent. Bend forward keeping hips as still as possible. Straighten up and arch back.

Side bends Place feet wide and knees slightly bent. Keeping hips as still as possible, bend to the right, straighten up, bend to the left and straighten.

Basic press-ups Stand with straight back, buttocks tucked in to make a straight line of your body. Rest hands on table, lower yourself on to the table. Push body up until arms are straight again and keep repeating.

EATING WELL

The typical Australian diet contributes not only to heart disease but also to many other health problems including obesity, high blood pressure, breast and colon cancer, tooth decay, diabetes, gallstones, constipation and alcohol-related diseases.

GUIDELINES
Eat a variety of foods Different types of food are necessary each day to supply the main nutrients required for good health. No single food contains all these.

Prevent and control obesity Obesity is one of Australia's major health problems. It increases the risk of heart disease, high blood pressure and diabetes. Reducing excess fats, alcohol and sugar and increasing physical activity will help to bring down your weight. Eat less, rather than cutting out whole categories of food.

Eat less fat Excess fats in the diet may contribute to obesity, high blood cholesterol levels, heart disease and certain cancers. Choose lean meats, low-fat dairy products and use low-fat cooking methods. Use butter, margarine, cream and oils sparingly.

Eat less sugar High sugar intake is associated with obesity and tooth decay. Australians average around 50kg of sugar per head per year. Sugars, whether white, brown, raw or glucose, are solely an energy source and their nutrient content is negligible.

Limit alcohol intake Excessive alcohol contributes to the health, social and nutritional problems of many Australians. Low nutritional status results when habitual drinking interferes with good eating habits.

Eat more fibre-rich foods Constipation, diverticular disease and other constipation-related ailments are linked with lack of dietary fibre (found only in plant foods). Bread, wholegrain cereals, fruit and vegetables provide necessary dietary fibre and a variety of nutrients. They are best for replacing foods high in fat and sugar.

Eat less salt Sodium from excessive use of table salt and salty processed foods may contribute to high blood pressure. Reducing excess sodium intake from an early age may help to control hypertension. Salt should not be added to food prepared for infants.

Enjoy water Australians drink large amounts of soft drinks and alcohol, which may contribute to obesity and/or dental caries. Where possible, quench your thirst with water. Use water rather than sweetened syrups and beverages for infants and children.

VITAMINS

Vitamins are organic substances that occur only in living things. With a few exceptions, vitamins are substances your body cannot make for itself, they have to be taken in the foods you eat. They play a vital and often underestimated role in keeping you well, youthful-looking and emotionally balanced.

Vitamin A (retinol) Helps vision; essential through the menopause. Found in liver, whole milk products, fish, oils, oranges, coloured fruits and vegetables. Toxic if taken in excess.

Vitamin B_1 (thiamin) Used in the metabolism of carbohydrates and in the nervous system. Found in wholegrain cereals, nuts, yeast, liver, meats, Vegemite.

Vitamin B_2 (riboflavin) Used in the metabolism of protein and in skin growth. Found in milk and milk products, yeast, eggs, wholegrain cereals, Vegemite.

Vitamin B_6 (pyridoxine) Used in the metabolism of protein and in conversion of tryptophane (a naturally occurring human amino acid essential for metabolism) to niacin. Found in liver, meat, eggs, nuts, yeast.

Vitamin B_{12} (cyano-cobalamin) Required to make red blood cells. Found in offal, meat, seafood, milk products, legumes.

Vitamin C (ascorbic acid) Promotes healing and iron absorption. Found in citrus fruits and green and other vegetables.

Vitamin D (cholecalciferol) Necessary for proper use of calcium and phosphorus in bone. Can be made by the body when exposed to the sun. Found in fish, oils, milk, butter. Toxic in excess.

Vitamin E Known to protect cell walls and some say it has incredible powers. Found in vegetable oils, wheatgerm, wholegrain cereals.

Vitamin K Used in the formation of blood clots and the prevention of haemorrhaging. Made in the human intestine. Found also in green vegetables, eggs, soya products.

Niacin Used in the release of energy from foods. Found in animal flesh, legumes, wholegrain cereals.

Folic acid Required to make red blood cells. Found in green leafy vegetables, yeast, liver, Vegemite, red peppers.

DIETARY FIBRE

It has become generally accepted that a daily intake of dietary fibre helps promote and maintain good health. But although many of us may think only of bran and 'stringy' foods in relation to fibre, it is found in other forms.

Most people are aware that plenty of fibre in the diet means that you won't need laxatives. But we know that dietary fibre does much more than just prevent constipation. It is intimately involved with the body's biochemistry and is far more important for health than was previously recognised.

Just as many vitamins are found in a variety of foods, each having separate functions, so there are different types of dietary fibre. And for good health, you should try to include foods

Type of fibre	Where to find it	What it does for your health
Pectin	Citrus fruits, other fruits, including the skins where appropriate. Fruits can be fresh, dried or canned. Pectin is perhaps most familiar as the setting agent in jams.	Pectin and saponin are known to reduce levels of cholesterol in the blood. (Perhaps this is why an apple a day keeps the doctor away?) Pectin may help to prevent gallstones, while saponin may slow down the rate at which some sugars are absorbed.
Saponin	Soya beans, chick peas, lentils, peanuts, spinach, eggplant, mung beans, sunflower seeds.	
Cellulose	Bran, legumes; some in all foods of vegetable origin	Cellulose and hemi-cellulose absorb water. Foods containing these types of fibre are filling and should prevent over-eating, provide bulk and prevent constipation. They help prevent various intestinal disorders.
Hemi-cellulose	Cereals (especially coarse bran, oats), legumes, lentils, breads (especially wholemeal and high fibre varieties), wholemeal pasta, brown rice, bulgar, buckwheat	
Lignin	Bran, potatoes, carrots, other root vegetables.	Lignin is the 'tough guy' of the fibre family, and the least understood at present. It is the least digestible, but its exact benefit is not yet known.
Gum, mucilages	Legumes, oats. (Small quantities are also used as thickeners in many processed foods, such as instant puddings, mayonnaise, etc.)	Gums and mucilages from oats and legumes have an effect on the body's blood glucose levels. Large quantities have proved successful in controlling diabetes.

containing different types in the daily menu—preferably in place of fatty or highly refined foods.

DIETING TRICKS

You're on a diet but no-one else is. Everyone around you—your family, friends, co-workers, everyone in the restaurant, people at the party — are packing away food as if there were no such thing as a kilojoule. How can you possibly stay on your diet without locking yourself in your bedroom?

Two simple rules will help you to stick with your diet and lose weight, in the midst of your world of non-dieters: know your kilojoules and plan ahead.

Knowing your kilojoules is simple. Buy a good kilojoule counter. You can pick one up at most bookstores. When you realise that 125g of grilled fish contains 800 kilojoules and 125g of grilled lean steak contains 1360, you're on your way to making intelligent choices.

Knowing your kilojoules will help you to plan ahead, and planning ahead will help you resist temptation in whatever situation you find yourself. Plan for what you can have. There are goodies the dieter can enjoy. Know what they are and indulge in them.

Many dieting women face the problem of being the only one in the family on a diet. Tackle it by enlisting the family's aid. Suggest that if they must snack on sweets and junk foods, they do it out of the house and out of your sight. Promise them interesting, tasty, nourishing meals while you're dieting.

Get rid of all the high-joule, highly processed mixes and extenders on your shelves, and banish flour, sugar, cornflour and other such thickeners from your cooking. Sauté, cook in bouillon or tomato juice. Use pan spray or lined pans rather than cooking with butter, margarine or shortening. Remove fats from meats and skin from poultry. Grill meats instead of frying. Serve more fish, poultry and veal; less pork, ham and beef. Try flavouring vegetables with herbs and spices rather than with butter or cream sauces. Remove your own portion from the family salad bowl before adding their dressing, and toss yours with diet dressing.

Another trick is to make an extra portion when cooking a low-joule dish. Freeze it and heat it up for yourself when the rest of the household are sure they can't live another day without pasta.

If dining out with friends, suggest a seafood restaurant. Choose grilled fish or grilled scallops. Order your salad dry and sprinkle with a wedge of lemon. Pass up the chocolate mousse and cheesecake and have the fruit for dessert.

The cocktail party doesn't have to be your downfall. Nibble those lovely pink prawns (with lemon juice, please, not sauce) and turn your back on the chips and dips. Have a good conversation with someone you love to talk with — far away from the buffet table.

Yes, you can sip a glass of white wine (half a cup of chablis is about 360 kilojoules, depending on the brand) or iced mineral water with a twist of lemon, a very 'in' drink with no kilojoules.

THE AUSTRALIAN WOMEN'S WEEKLY BEST-EVER DIET

This tried and true diet is certainly effective. If you exercise self-control you should lose up to 9kg in 14 days. You must, however, follow rules. Alcohol is not allowed. If this is not observed, the diet is useless. Do not eat what is not in the diet. Replace sugar with substitute. Eat the full allowance, do not skip a meal. Eat all vegetables without butter, salad without oil or mayonnaise, meat lean and grilled, coffee black, tea clear. Stick to quantities where stipulated. Drink plenty of water. Once you have reached your weight loss target, don't make the mistake of resuming bad eating habits. Eat wisely and well.

Monday Breakfast: 1 whole grapefruit, 2 eggs (boiled or poached), coffee. Lunch: fruit salad — eat as much as you like, and include all kinds of fruit without restriction. Dinner: 2 eggs, mixed salad (own choice), 1 piece thin dry toast, 1 whole grapefruit, coffee.

Tuesday Breakfast: 1 whole grapefruit, 2 eggs (boiled or poached), coffee. Lunch: cold chicken (a big helping: drumstick and thigh, or whole breast and wing), 500g tomatoes, 1 whole grapefruit. Dinner: 250g lean grilled steak, tomatoes, lettuce, celery, cucumber (any quantity), coffee.

Wednesday Breakfast: 1 whole grapefruit, 2 eggs (boiled or poached), coffee. Lunch: 2 eggs (these may be made into an omelette, or scrambled — use a non-stick pan), tomatoes (any quantity), coffee. Dinner: 2 grilled lamb chops, celery, cucumber, tomatoes (any quantity), coffee.

Thursday Breakfast: 1 whole grapefruit, 2 eggs (boiled or poached), coffee. Lunch: fruit salad — as much as you like, all kinds of fruit without restriction. Dinner: 2 eggs, mixed salad (own choice), 1 piece thin dry toast, 1 whole grapefruit, coffee.

Friday Breakfast: 1 whole grapefruit, 2 eggs (boiled or poached), coffee. Lunch: 2 eggs, spinach (any quantity), coffee. Dinner: large helping fish (grilled, steamed, or poached) OR chicken, lettuce (any quantity), tomatoes (any quantity), 1 slice thin dry toast, 1 whole grapefruit, coffee.

Saturday Breakfast: 1 whole grapefruit, 2 eggs (boiled or poached), coffee. Lunch: 2 eggs (these may be made into an omelette, or scrambled — use a non-stick pan), spinach (any quantity), coffee. Dinner: 250g steak, celery, cucumber, tomatoes (all in any quantity), coffee.

Sunday Breakfast: 1 whole grapefruit, 2 eggs (boiled or poached), coffee. Lunch: fruit salad — as much as you like, all kinds of fruit without restriction. Dinner: large helping chicken, carrots, cooked cabbage, tomatoes (all in any quantity), 1 whole grapefruit, coffee.

18

ETIQUETTE

KNOWING which fork to use first, the correct way to perform introductions, or what to wear to a funeral can present problems to many people. These and other points of etiquette are discussed here.

INTRODUCTIONS

Many people feel flustered when they have to introduce other people and do it poorly or, worse, not at all. This is probably an area where it is best to keep to the conventions. They make the whole process simpler and smoother.

Most people have two names and should be introduced with both. It is worth while fighting a rearguard action against the multitudes who use only first or given names. There are still people who don't automatically expect to be addressed by their first name.

The convention is that a man is introduced to a woman. For example: 'Margaret, I would like you to meet Peter Jones. Peter, this is Margaret Smith.' And the conventional response is still: 'How do you do?' A younger woman is always presented to an older one: 'Mrs Burton, I would like you to meet Sarah Black. Sarah, this is Mrs Burton.' You should perhaps use 'Mrs Freda Burton' if you feel it is likely they will be on first-name terms. A more formal introduction is 'Mrs Burton, may I present Mr Jones?'

Rules are varied when you are dealing with a man of higher rank. Then the woman is presented to the man. For example: 'Mr Prime Minister, I would like to present Mrs Burton'.

The old rule about shaking hands on introduction was that men did always, but women rarely. Convention dictated that a man should not offer his hand to a woman first and that if you were meeting someone of higher rank, both men and women should wait for that person to extend his or her hand first. The number of women in business has made this rule more flexible. What is rude is to ignore an extended hand, no matter what the circumstances.

Introductions when entertaining Deciding when to perform introductions can be tricky. One might think they should be performed as often as possible, so that people can get to know each other. But if you are entertaining, after about the first dozen people, it is foolish and unnecessary to interrupt the whole gathering to introduce the new arrivals all round. If you keep this up, it will be a complete dampener on the party. It is more sensible to make sure as you move around the room that people are getting to know each other, and to keep new people moving into established groups, although again, discreetly.

FORMS OF ADDRESS

Honorifics can be horrific! It is almost impossible at times to work out how to address people. The answer is that you address them the way they want to be addressed. In the extreme, you can ask them what they want you to call them. But it is not for you to impose your ideas on other people. You may think Ms is a fool of a prefix, but if someone prefers it to Miss, then you should use it. Similarly, if a woman likes to be called Miss it's not your business to call her Ms to fit in with your views.

If a woman wishes to keep her own name after marriage, you should issue invitations in both names, cumbersome as it may be. And if a couple are living together, you should use both names. The general rule is to respect people's feelings and not impose your notions of behaviour or morality on them.

FORMAL INVITATIONS

Formal invitations are rarely sent these days. Notable exceptions are for weddings, engagement parties and twenty-first birthday parties.

It is polite and reasonable to give three or four weeks notice of a party.

You should never refuse an invitation. If you can't go, or if you have any reason for not wanting to go, accept the invitation but regret

that you cannot attend.

Dress It is an old convention that guidance on the formality of an occasion is indicated by what men wear. As women's fashions vary more, that does not seem unreasonable. Some women no longer accept this. When the Federal Government gave a reception at the end of a women's conference and stipulated 'lounge suits', several women, to show what they thought of this, wore just that.

More formal invitations may state 'black tie' which means a dinner jacket. 'White tie' which means tails—and for most men these days a trip to a dress hire firm—is rare today. However, any stipulation about dress on an invitation is strictly to indicate what the host and hostess will be wearing, not to decree what guests should wear.

VISITING

Dropping in on friends unannounced is common enough but many people don't like it. If your friends have a telephone, there is no excuse for an unheralded visit. If they have no phone, it is, of course, almost impossible to think far enough ahead to let them know by mail although you should be organised enough to do this if you are visiting an area distant from your home. If for some reason you do drop in without warning, it is up to you to gauge what your friends are thinking and feeling rather than expecting them to be 'polite' to you. If they are clearly busy, keep the visit short; however in some circumstances you may be able to fit into whatever activity is absorbing them.

If you take children with you to another person's house, you are responsible for their behaviour. Do not thrust them on your hosts. And do not let them play near the good crystal or jump on the velvet-covered sofa. In your house, you are entitled to set ground rules as to where and how visiting children will play.

For weekend or longer visits, there are more formal rules, simply because every household is run differently. The ideal house guest fits smoothly into the household routine. And the ideal hostess lets guests know what the routine is: what time the family eats breakfast; whether the bathroom should be left free early in the morning until someone is ready to leave for work; or when quiet in the evening is necessary.

It is usual to take a small gift when you visit and to write a thank-you note a few days after you leave. The small gift may be varied with a visit to a restaurant for which you pay.

One question which comes up more often now is whether couples living together should be invited to share a room. The answer is yes.

TABLE MANNERS

The first rule is to eat quietly and keep your mouth shut when chewing. Do not talk with your mouth full. Eat at a moderate pace.

Wait until everyone is served before eating unless there is reason to expect their food won't be served for another twenty minutes (as sometimes happens with some dishes in a restaurant). If you are the one with an empty plate it is sensible to suggest to the others that they go ahead, particularly if food is hot.

Elbows on the table are acceptable providing you are not eating at the same time. Even the famous etiquette writer Emily Post admitted that in leaning forward to hear someone across a table, 'a woman's figure makes a more graceful outline supported over her elbows than doubled forward over her hands in her lap as though in pain'.

Good smoking manners are important at the dinner table. At official functions, you do not smoke before the loyal toast. Never smoke while others at the table are eating, and ask permission before lighting a cigarette.

If as a guest you are served food you do not like or for some reason cannot eat, simply leave it on your plate. If you are pressed by

your hostess you may quietly explain the situation and it is up to her to decide what to do. If your reasons for not eating the food are religious or health, it is sensible to explain when you accept the invitation. Otherwise you accept the food offered in the same way that you accept the hospitality.

DINNER PARTIES

INVITATIONS

State clearly what time people are expected: '7.30pm for 8pm' makes it quite clear what time they are expected to arrive and at what time everyone is expected to be ready to sit down to dinner.

When you have chronic latecomers on your list, ask them to arrive at a time which is half an hour earlier than that given to everyone else.

Although you can be very specific about what time people are expected, telling them as specifically what time you want them to leave seems rather too cold an approach. It is probably better to rely on gradually winding-down the party so that the last stragglers will be gone before you collapse on your feet.

WINES

With wines you are really free to serve what you wish but the traditional rule is: sherry with soup; dry white with fish or shellfish; red with rich, seasoned meat; lighter red with other meats; a light red, dry white or rosé with white meat; red or port with cheese; and sweet white or champagne with dessert.

SETTING AND USING IMPLEMENTS

At a formal dinner, guests have separate glasses for each wine and a water goblet. Forks are laid on the left with the tines upward and knives on the right with the blade turned inward. A bread knife is furthest right. You start with the implements on the outside and work towards the centre, course by course.

The dessert spoon and fork can be placed above the setting, but this is less formal. At a very formal dinner, the dessert implements will be brought in with the dessert. Napkins are folded on the left. When you are seated at the table, unfold your napkin and put it on your lap.

Your index finger should not touch the blade of the knife and you shouldn't hold your knife and fork like pencils. If you wish to use your fork tines upward, put your knife down first then eat as you would at a buffet. Cut up your food as you want to eat it. Break bread rolls open with your hands, don't cut them. Butter bread one mouthful at a time from the portion of butter you have placed on your bread and butter plate.

When resting implements during a meal, for instance when you are talking, place them at angles on your plate. Do not rest the handle of a knife or fork on the table. When you are finished, rest your knife and fork side by side with the fork tines upward and knife blade turned inward. Leave your plate in front of you and your napkin, unfolded, by your plate.

Serving   Food is always served from the left and plates removed from the right. No plates should be removed until everyone has finished eating. Then, all plates, used glasses and salt and pepper shakers should be cleared away before dessert and cheese are served. At a formal dinner, don't pass your plates to the hostess or waiter. They are never stacked at the table, but taken out two at a time.

It is polite to say thank you when something is served to you, not necessary when a plate is removed.

HOW TO EAT SPECIFIC FOODS

Asparagus   Use your fingers. Pick up the stalks at the base, dip head into the sauce and bite off the tip.

Cheese   Cut off and eat a small piece at a time.

Corn on the cob   There is no elegant way to eat corn. Just gnaw the corn off and enjoy it.

Fish   Should be eaten with a fish knife and fork. To turn a whole fish over place your knife on top of the fish and your fork underneath.

Mussels and oysters   Usually removed from the shell with a fork.

Paté   Cut off a portion and spread it on toast or biscuit. Eat each piece as it is prepared.

Poultry   The bones are not picked on formal occasions. If you must pick them up hold them in your left hand.

Salad   Usually eaten with a fork, but you can use a knife if necessary.

Snails   Grip the shell with tongs and pick the snail from the shell with a fork.

Soup   Take soup from the far edge of the bowl. When you are nearly finished, tip the bowl away from you to scoop up what is left.

ANNIVERSARIES

These are the traditional wedding anniversary gifts:
First Anniversary – Paper
Second – Cotton
Third – Leather or Linen
Fourth – Flowers and Silk
Fifth – Wooden
Sixth – Iron
Seventh – Copper or Wool
Eighth – Bronze
Ninth – Pottery
Tenth – Tin or Aluminium
Eleventh – Steel
Twelfth – Linen
Thirteenth – Lace
Fourteenth – Ivory
Fifteenth – Crystal
Twentieth – China
Twenty-fifth – Silver
Thirtieth – Pearl
Thirty-fifth – Coral or Jade
Fortieth – Ruby
Forty-fifth – Sapphire
Fiftieth – Gold
Fifty-fifth – Emerald
Sixtieth – Diamond

DEATH

When someone in your family dies, arrangements should be made for his or her friends and business colleagues to be notified. Upon hearing of the death of a friend, a note expressing sympathy should be sent to the family at once.

Any announcement in a newspaper can be brief and followed by a funeral notice when arrangements have been made. If the funeral is private or the family requests no flowers be sent, respect these wishes. Some people now have a private burial or cremation followed by a public memorial service.

Flowers should be sent to the undertaker's or house of the bereaved the afternoon before the funeral. The flowers are a tribute to the dead and the card should say something like 'in loving memory' and not 'with sympathy'. It is appropriate to send flowers with a message to the family after the funeral.

You don't have to wear black for a funeral but dress is usually sombre. What you say in a sympathy letter depends on how you feel and how well you know the person involved. Sympathy letters should be answered as soon as possible.

19

YOU AND YOUR CHILDREN

THERE'S PROBABLY no such thing as a perfect parent—everyone gets tired, impatient and angry at times. But as long as you're able to give your child love, security and—most of the time—understanding, you won't go far wrong.

For the treatment of common childhood ailments, infectious diseases and behavioural problems see MEDICAL GUIDE pp. 243–259.

FROM INFANCY TO SCHOOL

A guide to typical child development, from birth to five years, and tips on helping your child to make the transition from home to school life are included here.

A NEW BABY

Your local health sister and doctor will give you all the information you need for looking after your baby, but what about you?

Your tiny offspring will make enormous changes in your life. Overnight you seem to have lost all freedom, and the endless round of feeds and nappy changes is bound to get you down at times, especially if you're short on sleep. Remember that it's quite natural and understandable to feel depressed at times in these circumstances—no matter how much you love your baby.

It's a good idea to try and keep in touch with friends from the hospital, or to befriend another mother at the clinic. There's nothing like being able to discuss things with someone in the same position!

LIFE AFTER BABY

Here are some further suggestions to help you through the early months.

Buy a sling to cuddle your baby while you walk, read or do housework.

You will be feeling very tired so ignore the household chores and sleep when your baby is asleep—at least until baby is sleeping through the night.

Keep a diary. Some mothers start in hospital. It provides interesting reading later and is an excellent record of your baby's progress and achievements.

Get out of the house for a while every day; it gives a point and direction to what can be a hazy, disorganised time during which all you seem to do is look after the baby and forget about how the rest of the world is getting along.

Remember that your local doctor and baby health sister will come to see you if you can't get out to them.

New-born babies sometimes present tedious feeding and sleeping problems. Ask for advice and don't be content with instructions to go home and relax. The situation can be improved. Should you ever feel that you just cannot cope and might harm your infant through tiredness or exasperation, call for help straight away. Parents' groups, clinics, local hospital or the unit where your baby was born will come to your assistance.

On a lighter note, keep up your outside interests. Plan outings with other children or family members. Once your baby is out of hospital he is ready for family life and will enjoy all of the new experiences.

Make a point of enjoying a regular night out, without your baby. Join a babysitting club (or start one yourself), or leave your baby in the care of friends or relatives for the evening.

Lean heavily on others for support. You are already a supermum: you don't need to prove a thing!

CHILD DEVELOPMENT

BIRTH TO ONE YEAR
First month The baby sleeps about 15 hours a day. A further 6 hours is devoted to cuddling and feeding. He can see and focus but is short-sighted.

Second month He can pull his arms together, straighten legs. Baby becomes more sociable.

Third month He begins using his limbs to communicate, can hold a rattle and can roll over.

Fourth month Baby could have two or three regular wakeful sessions a day. Baby begins to reach. He is fascinated by his own body, studies hands at length and tastes them.

Fifth month He explores his feet. Baby can transfer an object from one hand to the other. He is using all four limbs rhythmically.

Sixth month He loses the sucking reflex and begins to enjoy solid foods. He may now have incisor lower teeth. He can sit unsupported.

Seventh month Baby begins to assert himself. He will cling to toys, interrupt conversations and yell for attention. His constant babbling includes first syllables including Mama and Dada.

Eighth month He loves company. He has learned to drop things and practises this new skill with passion.

Ninth month Baby can pull himself upright in cot. He crawls quite quickly.

Tenth month He may begin to walk. He has mastered the art of sitting back down. He is gaining control of his bowels.

Eleventh month His communication system is more sophisticated than just crying. Upper and lower incisor teeth are growing.

Twelfth month He may be walking. He is anxious to be with people. He talks non-stop in his own language.

ONE TO TWO YEARS
First quarter Baby can make decisions. He recognises the words 'yes' and 'no'. Hand and eye co-ordination is developing well. He is becoming constructive and may design a tower of two blocks or more. Walking needs less concentrated effort and he discovers that he can turn around yet keep his balance.

Second quarter Baby now can easily build a tower of two blocks and he also begins to link words in a kind of oral shorthand. His vocabulary increases dramatically.

Third quarter He has learned to dress himself. He is an avid explorer: chairs, cupboards and stairs are fair game.

Final quarter By now he can point to various parts of his body and name them. He also knows the names for food and drink and starts to label his emotion. Potty training should be taken along slowly. He can kick a ball now, is sociable and keen for company from other children.

TWO TO THREE YEARS
First quarter Baby has begun to comprehend what you are telling him. Encourage his development of language through reading picture books together. Watch out for stories that might promote nightmares. He may tell fibs. Though he is quite guileless, fantasy and reality get their wires crossed.

Second quarter He may have graduated to a child's jigsaw puzzle, will enjoy climbing, swinging, sliding. He can balance briefly on either foot, jump and is learning to walk down stairs. He may revert to crawling in times of stress.

Third quarter Imagination is still linked with reality and nightmares are particularly terrifying. He likes company more but he also begins to take Mum's little absences more sanguinely.

Final quarter You asked for it: here come

the questions, in a torrent, about almost anything. He is getting about well and can climb easily over a cot rail, low fences and such. With other children, play becomes mutual, rather than side-by-side. The child has learned to walk, talk, laugh, play, think, reason, make small decisions and assert himself.

THREE TO FOUR YEARS
Children now, especially quite strong-willed ones, can become frustrated at not being able to realise some activity that's beyond their capabilities. Try to ignore resultant outbursts and leave nature to take its course. A temper tantrum every now and again may be irritating, wearing, even distressing but it is neither here nor there. There are plateaux where the child seems to be making little progress. Be prepared to get, and control, this impression after any rather spectacular period of advancement.

Bladder control is normally mastered in this year but, even when a child is dry during the day, he may continue to have wet beds for some time. Once a child is managing the potty, try him on the lavatory.

The child gradually becomes more adept at spearing food with a fork, but don't bustle him into trying to co-ordinate it with using a knife too soon. He should have a toybox and be learning to put his things away.

FOUR TO FIVE YEARS
At this age, the preschooler tends to be a dawdler, especially when dressing. He is so easily distracted and that imagination is most active. Way-out stories keep cropping up and, in reporting, you would be wise to allow for some exaggeration. Another tricky situation is the occasional use of 'rude' words.

He is beginning to grasp some understanding of time. He continues to cultivate his basic skills while starting to realise others: logic, more rationalised emotions, social relationships. He has become more adept at doing various everyday things for himself.

Events which break up his accustomed routine can have an unsettling effect. A preschooler who is having regular nightmares might benefit from being 'babied' for a while.

STARTING SCHOOL

Your child's first day at school is a day of reckoning. It may be one of happiness, expectation and joy or it may be filled with tears, unhappy faces and trauma. Whatever the events of this occasion—and most people will carry the memory with them into old age—everything usually works out in the long run. Those who find the day one of long-suffering misery are often the ones who discover later that school opens new vistas, new delights.

First-day traumas are not confined to children; many parents suffer too. Do not sit idly by and wait for the big day to arrive. There is plenty of parental homework to be done and the earlier you embark on this, the better.

It is a good idea to visit the school before the first day arrives. Drive or walk past often and refer to it as 'Johnny's school'. Try to pass when the children are at play, to give your child some insight into what to expect. This can be done for the 18 to 24 months before he sets foot inside the grounds.

Whenever the opportunity arises, talk about school in a positive way.

Make sure your child understands that school is a daily affair.

Many children will have attended a pre-school kindergarten or been in a day-care situation where they have become accustomed to attending half days or two or three days a week. Many expect school to be similar and it may come as a rude shock when they realise they must attend for more lengthy periods.

Dress By school age most children have learned how to dress themselves properly. If they have not, hurry up and teach them, for it may reflect poor or inadequate training on the part of the parent. It is essential that your child can put on his shoes and do up the laces. Those who cannot simply walk around with laces dragging and this can cause serious accidents. Many children find it hard to differentiate between left and right shoes. Solve the problem by placing the letters 'L' and 'R' inside the respective shoes or a bix X on the left one. Stick to an easy-to-remember method.

It is an excellent idea to label each item of clothing clearly, particularly the ones that may be removed during the day. Ideally, add the home phone number too, in case something is lost.

Toilet training Of course, your child will be well versed in the toilet business before he or she starts school. But here are a few tips to make his lot easier. Try to get him into the

habit of having a bowel action before leaving for school each day. (This should be started well before school looms on the horizon.) It is much easier for children to move their bowels in familiar surroundings and does not take much encouragement to establish this as part of their daily routine.

Some children in their early days of school wet their underclothing, either through nervousness or being too timid to ask to be excused. Pack a spare pair of pants in the child's bag and make sure he knows where these are and what to do if a problem arises. Explain to him that it is no crime to want to visit the toilet during classes. Rather than have an accident, he simply has to raise his hand for attention, ask for permission to be excused and all is well.

Immunisation Do not wait until the last day of holidays before deciding to take your child for any immunisation booster shot. (This will be given to cover diphtheria and tetanus—a 'must' for sensible families.) Have this done at least a month before school begins to allow for any reaction that may occur (occasionally with a booster the child may have a sore, hot, red arm at the injection site for a few days).

MEDICAL GUIDE

Parents should be able to recognise and act quickly on any of a host of medical problems that may befall a child. There is considerable difference between the effects of an illness on a child and on an adult. Sometimes an illness is serious in childhood and minor in an adult, but in some cases, such as mumps, the reverse is often the case.

This guide is an informative source of reference, but is not intended to replace medical attention. When a child shows obvious distress or when symptoms persist the doctor should be consulted. Illnesses have been grouped in categories, but here is an alphabetical index to help you find what you want in a hurry:

INDEX

COMMON AILMENTS

At some time, most babies and children suffer from a wide variety of common complaints, from coughs and colds to tummy aches. It should be remembered that all illnesses, no matter how commonplace, should be taken seriously, particularly in young babies.

THE COMMON COLD

Caused by a virus. Antibiotics have no effect on viruses but may be used to treat secondary infection caused by other germs—sinusitis, ear infections and pneumonia, for instance. The virus is transmitted by droplet infection.

Incubation period: 2–7 days. The child may be feverish, have watery red eyes, a dry cough, mild swelling and tenderness of lymph nodes in neck, nose stuffiness, mild pain in the ears. A cold usually lasts 3–10 days. Colds are more serious for babies than for adults because sucking is difficult if they can't breathe through the nose. Keep away from anyone with colds, spread by coughing and sneezing.

Treatment: Aspirin for fever; rest, nose drops, cough medicines. Make sure child takes plenty of fluids. Keep away from others, especially elderly and babies. Chest rubs may help. If the cold worsens or secondary infection occurs, see your doctor. If your baby seems ill and has gone off food, even when there is no temperature, see your doctor.

COUGHS

A reaction to irritation, particularly mucus dripping down the back of the nose into the throat. A cough syrup may help the child sleep at night. Persistent coughing should be investigated.

INFLUENZA

A viral infection of the respiratory tract. Transmitted by coughing and sneezing. It starts like a common cold. Symptoms include headache, sore throat, cough, fever, pains in the back and the arms and legs, some gastric upset and sore eyes.

Incubation period: 1–3 days. Contagious for 7 days before symptoms appear.

Treatment: Bed rest. Keep away from others, particularly elderly and babies; aspirin for fever and pains, cough medicine if cough preventing sleep. Give plenty of fluids. Antibiotics don't help except in the case of secondary infection.

Seek medical advice if the disease worsens or complications set in.

SINUSITIS

An inflammation or infection of the sinuses, the air-filled cavities in the face that connect with the nasal passages. The bacterial infection may follow a cold or an allergy or a foreign body in the nose. Symptoms include fever, pain, stuffy nose and cough, headache, discharge from nose.

Treatment: Nose drops, inhalations, aspirin for pain. Your doctor may prescribe antibiotics. Persistent sinusitis should be investigated by your doctor.

BREATHING DIFFICULTIES

These may be caused by asthma, bronchitis, colds, croup, hay fever, pneumonia.

Croup A virus infection, common in children aged between three months and three years. It is an infection of the vocal chords and larynx (voice box). Choking on an aspirated (breathed-in) object, such as a peanut, may resemble croup. The child has a dry, tight, barking cough, hoarseness and difficulty in breathing.

Treatment: Place child in moist air. You can use a steam inhalation or sit with the child in the bathroom of your home with a hot shower running and the door closed. If the noisy breathing worsens or the child's condition does not improve, see your doctor. With a different kind of croup, caused by bacteria, the child becomes ill rapidly over a period of a few hours. Seek medical help immediately.

Asthma An allergic reaction which causes severe spasms of the bronchial tubes which are oversensitive and react by spasm and secreting excessive amounts of mucus. Attacks of wheezing may be triggered by allergy, emotion, physical exertion, upper respiratory infections or irritants.

Treatment: First or second attack of wheezing may not be due to asthma but to wheezy bronchitis. Asthma attacks will persist. Your doctor will advise treatment. Drugs which open up the tubes relieve attacks. Physiotherapy may be ordered. Prescribed medications should be given promptly at the onset of the attack when they are more effective. Preventative medicines are also now available.

Desensitisation by injections of increasing amounts of the offending substances which cause allergic reactions can help occasionally.

If emotional stress plays a part in attacks, attempt to minimise stress.

Bronchitis An infection of the windpipe and bronchial tubes which may follow a cold or chest infection. Symptoms may include wheezy breathing, scratchy throat, sneezing, tightness in the chest, watery eyes and loss of appetite. Fever may be present also.

Treatment: Rest, aspirin for fever, nose drops, moist air treatment (as for croup). Physiotherapy may be ordered. Your doctor may prescribe drugs. Feed extra fluids and a light diet. If the bronchitis recurs, an underlying allergy may require investigation.

Pneumonia An infection of one or more areas of the lungs, caused by bacteria or a virus. Symptoms: rapid breathing, cough, vomiting and diarrhoea, sometimes a high temperature, chills, chest pain.

Treatment: See your doctor who will prescribe drugs. Keep propped up in bed if breathing is distressed. Give plenty of fluids to drink. May need physiotherapy. Keep away from baby, as pneumonia can kill infants. Pneumonia is often treated in hospital.

Hay fever An allergic reaction of the lining of the nose and sinuses to inhaled substances. It may be seasonal, due to pollens or caused by dander from a pet or house dust, house mites, feathers, moulds and so on. Symptoms are nasal congestion, sneezing, clear nasal discharge and itching of the nose. The eyes may also itch. The ears may feel obstructed and bluish bags appear under eyes. The child may feel tired and snore.

Treatment: See your doctor who will suggest medication. Reduce the child's exposure to the offending substances, if possible. The child's bedding may have to be modified. Avoid using nose drops constantly, as this can worsen congestion.

HEADACHES

Common in childhood. Most are caused by a fever, infectious disease or emotions such as fear, anxiety, excitement and worry. Other causes of headache may include sinusitis, epilepsy, emotional problems, head injuries (including concussion), tumours and infection of the brain, eye strain, migraine.

Migraine There is usually a strong family history. It is common in high achievers and perfectionists and sometimes starts with an aura (seeing flashing lights or double vision), is often one-sided and the child is usually nauseated and vomits. The attack lasts for hours and aspirin rarely helps.

Treatment: Your doctor will prescribe special medication.

Sinusitis The child has a stuffy nose and possibly pain over sinuses.

Treatment: Seek medical advice. Your doctor may order nose drops, antibiotics.

Eye strain The child suffers headaches after television or reading.

Treatment: Seek medical advice. Prescription glasses or other treatment may be necessary.

Emotional problems There may be other signs of stress, such as naughty behaviour.

Treatment: Seek medical advice. Try to discover and then eliminate cause of stress.

Head injuries, infections and tumours Headaches worsen and occur more frequently. There may be vomiting, stiff neck, problems with sight, loss of balance, disorientation, fever.

Treatment: If the symptoms are severe, seek medical help immediately. Take child to casualty department of hospital if doctor not available. Frequent or severe headaches should be fully investigated.

SORE THROATS

Caused by a virus or bacteria. Often accompanies other infectious diseases. Symptoms include difficulty in swallowing, swollen glands, a cold.

Treatment: Gargle with warm salted water. Drink extra fluids. An easy-to-eat diet. Aspirin for pain or fever. Keep child away from others. Seek medical advice if the child does not improve or has swollen, tender neck glands, difficulty in swallowing not helped by aspirin, tenderness over the sinuses, difficulty in breathing, chest pain, a rash or has continual vomiting. A sore throat caused by a streptococcus germ is treated with a course of antibiotics.

Tonsillitis Infection of the tonsils which may be caused by bacteria or viruses. Tonsils and adenoids, as part of the lymphatic system, help defend the body against infection. Signs and symptoms: enlarged, inflamed tonsils can be seen in the throat; swollen lymph glands can be felt in the neck; headache, vomiting, temperature, pain on swallowing.

Treatment: As for the common cold or sore throat. See your doctor who will usually prescribe antibiotics.

Tonsils are normally only removed if they become chronically infected or so large that they interfere with speech or breathing. Enlarged adenoids may be removed if they interfere with breathing or cause recurrent ear infections.

EARACHE
Earache can result from a variety of causes, and should always be taken seriously.

See SEEING AND HEARING p. 254.

Treatment: See a doctor if pain persists.

TUMMY ACHE
Most tummy aches are caused by emotional stress but they can also be due to constipation, gastroenteritis, a dietary indiscretion, infections, appendicitis, intussusception, colic or other illnesses.

A child may say he has a tummy ache when he means he does not feel well. He may call a pain elsewhere a tummy ache. It is difficult to decide if he is ill but there will probably be other symptoms, such as high temperature, vomiting, diarrhoea, frequent passing of urine.

Treatment: Do not give a laxative. Try to relieve stress if emotional tension may be involved – the child is not 'putting it on' if the cause is emotional; he really feels the pain. Aspirin, warmth, comfort may help. Try to discover the cause. Do not neglect pain. If the child seems very ill or if you are particularly worried, call the doctor.

APPENDICITIS
Inflammation of the appendix due to infection. The appendix is a small, hollow tube at the spot where the small intestine joins the large intestine.

Acute appendicitis starts with a sudden attack of pain. It may start near the navel, then move to the right side of the abdomen, or it may stay near the navel. The pain is worse on moving. Nausea, vomiting, diarrhoea and fever can result.

Treatment: Persistent stomach ache should be treated immediately by your doctor. An infected appendix can burst within 24 hours or less, causing peritonitis – widespread infection through the abdomen.

Never give a laxative, as this could cause the appendix to burst. Do not feed the child; give clear drinks or chips of ice only. Do not give pain killers. Where appendicitis is acute, an immediate operation is necessary, so see your doctor straight away.

GASTROENTERITIS
A highly contagious infection of the digestive tract, usually caused by a virus but sometimes by bacteria. Incubation time: one to four days. Symptoms: vomiting, diarrhoea, abdominal pain, possibly fever. Stools may be watery and greenish and have blood and mucus in them. It generally only lasts a few days and is not serious, except in babies and young children, who may become dehydrated.

Treatment: Give small drinks such as glucose and water, fruit juice or lemonade frequently, until illness improves. Wash hands before going from a sick child to baby. Keep sick child away from other children. Watch for signs of dehydration, such as dry mouth and sunken eyes. If the child does not improve or becomes dehydrated, see your doctor at once. Hospitalisation may be necessary for intravenous feeding.

COLIC
Spasms of cramplike abdominal pain in babies. Colic usually lasts 3–6 months. Baby may scream for hours, goes red in the face, draws up the legs, clenches fists and sometimes turns blue. As one spasm passes, the scream is reduced to sobs and baby may drop off to sleep until another spasm comes. Air is passed at either end.

Mothers can be greatly distressed by a colicky baby, especially when nothing seems to help. Colic has been blamed on feeding problems, air swallowing, mother's tension, milk mixture being disagreeable. Hunger or illnesses, wet or dirty nappy, nappy rash, constipation or diarrhoea and other causes of discomfort have been considered. Check these.

Treatment: Feed baby with baby health centre nurse present to see if simple amendments help. Additional feeds or a bottle of warm, boiled water may help. You could try a dummy. Make feeding a quiet, calm time for both of you. Check that nipples are not bleeding, as swallowed blood can cause cramps. Burp baby after feeding. Cuddle. Make sure baby is not swallowing wind. If condition persists, see your doctor.

INTUSSUSCEPTION
Part of the intestine telescopes into the part immediately in front, causing the bowel to become obstructed.

This usually affects babies between three and twelve months of age. Severe pain comes

in bouts, every few minutes. Baby screams, often draws up his legs, becomes very pale and may vomit. He may then sleep from exhaustion until the next bout of pain.

Treatment: See your doctor immediately. A barium enema confirms the diagnosis and can cure the condition. Urgent surgery often is needed to correct intussusception before the intestine becomes gangrenous.

DIARRHOEA
This refers to bowel movements which are looser and more fluid than usual.

A baby's bowels are easily upset and frequent greenish motions can occur when he has a cold, is teething or when new foods are introduced into the diet. They soon return to normal. Some loose motions are quite normal. Other causes: gastroenteritis, respiratory viruses, intolerance of certain foods, emotional disturbance.

Treatment: With mild diarrhoea, eliminate foods with roughage. If more severe, stop food and milk and encourage child to drink extra clear fluids. Watch for signs of dehydration—dry mouth, glazed eyes, apathy. Seek medical attention if baby or infant has vomiting and diarrhoea or either in a severe form. For one or two weeks after a severe attack of diarrhoea, the child will not be able to absorb milk or milk

products. Doctor will prescribe a special milk substance which baby can absorb. See Gastroenteritis.

CONSTIPATION
Bowel movements which cause discomfort or pain. It is the hardness of the stool which matters, not how often the child opens his bowels. Some children have bowel movements several times a day; others every few days. It is an individual thing and either pattern is normal. Illness may contribute to constipation. The child may eat or drink less, vomit or sweat a lot due to fever, exercise less, put off using the lavatory.

Treatment: Do not use laxatives which may upset normal bowel habits. Rigid toilet training makes the child anxious and can lead to constipation. Encourage the child to visit the lavatory promptly when bowels want to open. Delaying—perhaps because the child is too shy to ask permission at school—can lead to constipation. Encourage the child to open his bowels after breakfast each day.

Give more roughage in the diet—fresh fruit, fruit juice, foods with fibre. A dessertspoon of unprocessed bran sprinkled on cereal, in gravy, yoghurt, fruit juice is good for the whole family. Milk of magnesia will soften stools.

Constipation in babies rarely needs treatment. You could give a teaspoon of brown sugar in the bottle, or a little extra orange juice or prune juice in their diet.

Soiling Chronic constipation can lead to soiling, as semi-fluid stools leak out from behind hard stools in the rectum. Excessive family concern over bowel movements can lead to a child holding on and becoming constipated. Soiling may result.

Treatment: Treat condition. Reassure the child that it is not his fault.

KIDNEY AND BLADDER INFECTIONS
Infections are usually caused by bacteria but may be due to a spread of infection from the vagina, foreign bodies in the bladder or ureter (the tube that connects the kidneys to the bladder), congenital abnormalities. They are more common in girls than they are in boys.

Symptoms may include recurrent high temperature, pain on passing urine, frequent trips to the lavatory, dribbling of urine, bedwetting, cloudy or smelly urine, abdominal or back pain, vomiting. Some children have few symptoms. Recurrent fever for no apparent reason and failure to grow may give the clues.

If an infection of the kidneys is not treated, permanent damage may result and cause high blood pressure or kidney failure.

Treatment: See your doctor who will investigate. He may prescribe antibiotics. If the infection does not clear up, the child should have a complete investigation of the urinary system which may necessitate a stay in the hospital.

Nephritis An inflammation of the kidneys, commonly after a throat or skin infection caused by the streptococcus germ. Symptoms are passing reduced amounts of urine, urine that is smoky in colour (denoting blood), a puffy face. If severe, there may be fever, headache, vomiting, high blood pressure, convulsions. The illness usually lasts two to three weeks.

Treatment: Your doctor will prescribe treatment and regularly check urine, blood pressure and bodyweight until they return to normal. Bed rest is necessary during the acute phase of this condition. Severe cases are usually treated in hospital. Most cases of nephritis recover completely.

VOMITING

Most infants vomit at times. If the child is gaining weight, it is not usually harmful, but frequent vomiting will cause dehydration and need intravenous hospital feeding. Causes of vomiting range from minor to major and include infections, emotional problems, dietary indiscretions, appendicitis, head injury, brain disease, motion sickness, surgical problems such as pyloric stenosis and obstruction of the bowel.

Treatment: Frequent small drinks of clear fluids such as lemonade, water, fruit juice. Chips of ice to suck. No food until vomiting stops. Watch for signs of dehydration. If vomiting persists, see your doctor. Danger signs are pain, distension of the abdomen and constipation.

NOSEBLEEDS

Common in children. A bump or small blow can injure the small blood vessels in the nose. Sneezing, blowing and rubbing the nose can also start a bleed.

Treatment: The child should sit up with head bent forward so he or she doesn't swallow the blood. The child should firmly pinch the lower part of the nostrils between thumb and fingers until the bleeding stops. Hot weather can dry out the nasal membranes and leave the blood vessels exposed so that bleeding occurs. To prevent this, apply petroleum jelly inside the nose night and morning. If bleeding persists, visit your doctor.

INFECTIOUS DISEASES

Few children reach their teens without having at least one of the common childhood infectious diseases. However, widespread immunisation has made a tremendous difference to the incidence and severity of most—especially those which were mass killers. Diphtheria and poliomyelitis are prime examples.

Each disease has a period in which the child is sickening but the symptoms are not clear-cut. This is called the incubation period and can vary from days to weeks.

If a child looks sick, is pale, off his food, has a dry tongue, scaly lips, droopy eyes or can't concentrate on television for more than a few minutes, he may be sickening from an infectious disease. It is wise to keep him away from other children until the diagnosis becomes clear.

CHICKEN POX

Incubation period: about 13–17 days. A highly contagious viral infection, spread by airborne droplets from nose and throat. Chicken pox is usually a mild disease with one attack giving lifelong immunity.

It may start with a mild cold but the rash is often the first sign. This resembles insect bites but develops small, clear blisters which break and become scabs. Some children develop only a few spots, others have them all over the body and in the mouth, nose, ears and on the scalp.

Chicken pox is contagious from 24 hours before the rash appears until all blisters have dried. The virus causing it may be the same as causes shingles (herpes zoster).

Treatment: Rest. Cut fingernails to minimise scratching. Doctors may prescribe antihistamines to help control itching. Bathe child in lukewarm water, then apply calamine lotion to skin. Pat dry to avoid breaking blisters. Aspirin can reduce temperature.

With babies, change nappies often so that

spots don't become infected. When possible, leave the nappy undone to expose skin to air.

The disease is particularly dangerous to young babies and patients on steroid or immunosuppressant drugs (those which suppress the body's ability to fight disease). Keep child away from others until 7 days after the last spots appear.

ENCEPHALITIS
An inflammation of the brain, usually caused by a virus, sometimes as a complication of infectious diseases such as measles or whooping cough. Signs and symptoms include fever, headache, vomiting, drowsiness, a stiff neck. Neck stiffness means that the child cannot touch his chin to his neck with his mouth closed and is a clear sign of brain inflammation. See Meningitis.
Treatment: Seek out medical help immediately.

GERMAN MEASLES (RUBELLA)
Incubation period about 18 days. This disease has nothing to do with measles. It is caused by a virus, spread by droplet infection, is less infectious and much milder.

It usually begins with a fever, runny nose, slightly sore throat and headache. Your child may feel a little unwell for a day or two before the rash appears. Glands in the back of the neck and behind the ears swell, sometimes remain swollen for weeks. The rash usually lasts only a couple of days. It is a pink spotty rash which starts behind the ears and on the forehead, then spreads to rest of body. One attack usually confers lifelong immunity.
Treatment: Keep a sick child away from pregnant women during their first four months, as the disease can cause damage to the developing foetus. For this reason, all girls who have not had the disease should be immunised at about thirteen years. Any woman exposed to German measles early in pregnancy should immediately discuss the problem with her doctor.

Keep the child at home, away from others, for 7 days after appearance of the rash.

MEASLES
Incubation period about 10–12 days. It starts with a cold: sneezing, runny nose, watery red eyes and a dry cough. Measles is a highly contagious disease caused by a virus but can be controlled by immunisation.

The rash appears about 4 days after the symptoms and lasts about 4–6 days. The fever reaches its height just before the rash appears. It consists of red blotches and spots which start on the forehead and face and spread over the rest of the body to the feet before the fever breaks.

One child in twelve suffers complications, such as bronchopneumonia and middle ear infection. One in a thousand suffers encephalitis (inflammation of the brain). The infection is spread by airborne droplets from sneezing and coughing.
Treatment: Rest. Aspirin, in suitable doses for age (not to children under one), for temperature. Bright light may bother child's eyes (but will not injure them); keep lights dim. Child may need extra fluids. Watch for earache which could be a sign of middle ear infection. Keep child away from other children for 5 days after appearance of rash.

MENINGITIS
A bacterial infection of the meninges, the layers of tissue that cover and protect the brain and spinal cord. Sometimes caused by a virus. The incubation period is 1–7 days.

Meningitis is usually spread by direct contact with or airborne infection from a healthy carrier of the disease. Signs and symptoms are the same as for encephalitis. Complications include deafness, learning problems and brain damage.
Treatment: Seek medical help immediately. With prompt treatment, most children recover completely.

MUMPS
Incubation period 14–21 days. This is a moderately contagious viral infection which affects the salivary glands. Glands in the neck and jaw swell. The child may complain of soreness just below and in front of one or both ears, in the cheek and down the neck. He may be cranky, lose his appetite, have a high temperature and headache, particularly before the glands begin to swell. The disease is spread by airborne droplets. One attack usually confers lifelong immunity on the sufferer, though it can hit again.
Treatment: Rest. Aspirin, in appropriate doses, for pain and temperature; simple, easy-to-eat diet and plenty of fluids. Keep away from other children for ten days from onset of the

swelling. Keeping older children away is very important if they have not been immunised or had mumps. Mumps can involve ovaries and testicles in older children and result in sterility. Rare complications: encephalitis, permanent deafness.

WHOOPING COUGH

Incubation period 7–14 days. A highly contagious infection of the respiratory tract, caused by bacteria. Spread by airborne droplets from sneezing and coughing.

This can be a serious illness, especially in babies under one who inherit no immunity to it from their mothers. So, it is important to immunise baby early (see Immunise for Safety's Sake). Keep baby away from anyone with whooping cough. It can also seriously affect older children whose health has been affected for some reason.

The disease often begins with a runny nose, slight temperature and a dry cough, something like bronchitis, which lasts a week or two before the cough changes to a typical 'whooping cough'. Several short, rapid coughs without breath in between are followed by a 'whoop' as air is drawn rapidly into the lungs.

Babies usually do not have the 'whoop'. The cough normally lasts several weeks but may return with a fresh cold. Complications: exhaustion, from constant coughing; pneumonia.
Treatment: Rest. Frequent small meals. If vomiting is severe, clear fluids only. Antibiotics may be prescribed by your doctor. Keep the child at home, away from others, for 3 weeks from onset of whoop—less if the doctor gives a medical certificate that child is free of infection. Other children who attend preschool and have been in contact with the patient should stay at home 21 days if they've not had whooping cough or immunisation.

IMMUNISE FOR SAFETY'S SAKE

Immunisation is a simple, safe way of protecting your child against dangerous diseases. Authorities say it is the most significant contribution to improved child health in the Twentieth Century.

Grandmothers and older mothers will remember from their childhood how schoolmates and neighbours died from polio, diphtheria and scarlet fever. Polio victims often had to be treated in iron lungs; some were crippled for life. Measles could lead to encephalitis (inflammation of the brain), leaving the afflicted child mentally retarded.

Today, outbreaks of such serious diseases are rare but they can still flare up in a community where the level of immunity drops because not enough children have been immunised. Some parents in this safer society have become careless, not realising they are jeopardising their children's health.

A child should be properly immunised against diphtheria, tetanus, whooping cough, poliomyelitis and measles.

Tetanus, an often-fatal disease, is now rare in Australia but the germ is still present in the soil. It is common in many overseas countries. Injuries such as puncture wounds, cuts and scratches may provide these germs access to your system. Even a tiny scratch or thorn prick can lead to tetanus if the person is not immune.

Tetanus—or 'lockjaw'—results in painful muscular contractions, mainly of the neck and jaw muscles. Later, muscles of the trunk also become affected—causing breathing difficulty. Generalised convulsions and death may follow. It takes between 5 and 20 days before symptoms develop. The first stage may be restlessness and headache.

If your child receives a wound—especially while in the garden, on the road, from an animal bite or a severe burn—contact your doctor. If 2 years have passed since the immunisation programme was completed or since a routine booster shot, he will recommend an injection. Following a child's course of triple antigen (the three-in-one vaccine against diphtheria, tetanus, whooping cough), booster tetanus vaccinations should be given every 10 years or this immunity might lapse.

Because immunisation is so important, all parents should keep up-to-date, accurate record books. You can obtain copies from State health authorities.

THE RECOMMENDED IMMUNISATION SCHEDULE

Two months—triple antigen and Sabin oral vaccine.
Four months—triple antigen, Sabin oral vaccine.
Six months—triple antigen, Sabin.
Twelve months—measles and mumps vaccine.
Eighteen months—combined diphtheria and tetanus (CDT).

At preschool or school entry—CDT and Sabin oral vaccine. Sabin vaccine protects against poliomyelitis.

Girls in high school, up to the age of 15 years, are immunised against German measles (rubella) to eliminate the risk of catching the disease during any subsequent pregnancy, with possible damage to the foetus.

Interruption of schedule If the immunisation programme is interrupted, there's no need to start again with a full course—simply resume the programme as soon as possible where it was interrupted. The preceding schedule is only a guide to the best time for immunisation. See your doctor if your child has missed an immunisation. And do keep that accurate record.

HOW IMMUNISATION IS CARRIED OUT

Sabin vaccine is given by mouth, a few drops of pleasant-tasting mixture on a spoon. Combined vaccine (triple antigen) is injected, as are measles and mumps vaccines.

Where to go for immunisation Your doctor, local council or State health authority.

Precautions If a child is sick—for instance, has a sore throat, cold or diarrhoea—wait until he is well again before going for immunisation. If your baby was premature, small or sick at birth, check with your doctor about the age at which baby should begin the course.

What to tell your doctor If a child has an illness or allergy; if he has had fits, an illness of the nervous system or if members of the family have them; if he has had a severe reaction to an immunisation, has had another immunisation within the past 3 weeks, has had a blood transfusion or a gamma globulin injection during the past 3 months.

POSSIBLE REACTIONS TO IMMUNISATIONS

To triple antigen Sometimes mild redness, tenderness and swelling at the injection site. Slight fretfulness, high fever. If baby screams a lot or has a convulsion within hours or a few days of immunisation, see your doctor without delay.

To measles Possible fever, rash, stuffy nose about 5–12 days after injection. Symptoms last a couple of days, and usually do not need any treatment by a doctor.

To Sabin oral vaccine If a child vomits within half an hour of taking Sabin vaccine, the dose should be repeated.

If you have not started the whooping cough (triple antigen) immunisation course when baby is two months old, you can do so when he is older. The reason for the early start is that whooping cough is most serious in young babies. After the age of two years, the risk of serious effects is much reduced.

SKIN CONDITIONS

Although few skin conditions are serious, they can cause a great deal of misery unless properly treated.

INFANT COMPLAINTS

Some of the following complaints also occur in toddlers and older children, but are most common among babies.

Cradle cap Scaly, crusted patches on the scalp, often near or over the anterior fontanelle ('soft spot'), may extend to the forehead and behind the ears. Affects babies and children up to the age of five years. It is due to excessive oily secretions from the scalp.

Treatment: Daily shampooing with soap and water. Apply baby oil later.

Heat rash Prickly heat is common during hot, muggy weather. Hundreds of small, pink or red pimples surrounded by pink blotches or tiny water blisters erupt on neck, shoulders, skin creases and the nappy area. The rash is moderately itchy.

Treatment: Sponging with lukewarm water may help. Make certain you have dried the skin—especially creases and under armpits—properly and applied bath powder. In hot weather, babies are often best left simply in singlet and nappy in a cool part of the house.

Bubble baths, water softeners and oily preparations may aggravate the rash. Do not put wool or synthetic next to baby's skin. Do not overdress.

Nappy rash A red, slightly rough, sometimes scaly rash over the nappy area. It is often due to dermatitis caused by ammonia. You may notice a strong smell of ammonia when you change the nappy.

The problem occurs when nappies are not changed often enough; germs in the stool affect the urine in the wet nappy. The ammonia is very irritating to baby's delicate skin. Nappy rash can also be caused by thrush.

Prevention: Change wet or dirty nappies as soon as possible. Use mild baby soap and wash off all soap after bathing baby. Petroleum jelly, zinc and castor oil or other ointments put a barrier between skin and nappies. If it looks sore, clean baby's skin gently with oil or baby lotion.

Avoid putting baby in plastic or rubber pants over nappies. Soft nappy liners inside the nappy help keep area dry. Leave nappy off at times, to let air at the skin.

If doing your own washing, use a non-irritating soap or detergent. Give nappies a final soak in a nappy rinse. Some doctors advise boiling nappies. Dry them in sunshine if possible.

Thrush A mild fungus infection in the mouth, common in babies immediately after birth, in infants and toddlers. It may be caused by incompletely sterilised teats and bottles or during birth, if the mother has vaginal thrush. It can also follow antibiotic treatment, chronic illness and poor nutrition.

Thrush looks like white, flaky patches similar to milk curds stuck to the tongue, inside the cheeks or on the roof of the mouth. It can spread to baby's bottom, causing nappy rash.
Treatment: Doctor probably will prescribe Nystatin, a solution put into baby's mouth with a dropper. Nystatin cream is available to use on baby's bottom if the rash breaks out there. Sterilise objects placed in baby's mouth. Nursing mothers may have to use Nystatin cream on breasts to avoid reinfecting baby. Vaginal thrush in the mother will need to be treated.

ALLERGIC CONDITIONS

Hives Red, itchy, raised welts which are an allergic reaction of the skin. Hives come and go and they change size hourly. Possible allergens (substances which produce allergy) include food, drinks, medication, insect bites and stings, inhalants.
Treatment: Cold applications, calamine lotion. Antihistamines may help. If the child has a temperature or his breathing is affected by swelling, see your doctor immediately.
Other treatment: desensitisation to the offending substances—after investigation—may be carried out by a doctor with regular injections.

Infantile eczema A common, non-contagious rash which does not usually start before the age of two or three months. Many rashes which are dry, slightly scaly, pink and itchy look like eczema but turn out to be something else. The eczema rash often becomes red from rubbing and scratching and may bleed. Infantile

eczema has a tendency to run in families and allergy to food, drugs or materials such as wool may be involved.
Treatment: Seek medical advice. Eczema can be a recurring problem and need medical supervision for years. It may be necessary to avoid washing baby with soap or to use a special mild soap. Use the same measures for washing nappies as with nappy rash.

PLAYGROUND INFECTIONS

Head lice (pediculosis) Common in children, especially once they have started school. Lice and nits (eggs of lice) are found in the scalp. Nits, which take about a week to hatch, look like tiny white specks stuck to the hair. Head lice cause intense itching and scratch marks may become infected and glands in the neck swell.
Treatment: Various commercial preparations are available from chemists. Comb out dead lice and nits with a steel, fine-tooth comb. Wash and store infected linen. Do not let children wear each others' hats or scarves or use others' combs. Check heads of other family members. Keep affected children away from preschool or school until the hair is completely clear.

Impetigo A highly contagious skin infection caused by bacteria. It is common on the face and around the mouth, starting with little red spots which turn into blisters containing thin, yellow pus. These break, leaving weeping sores and crusts. Impetigo often starts as a complication of eczema or scabies or after an injury. It is transmitted by direct contact with an infected person, their clothes, towels or toys. The incubation period is 2–5 days.
Treatment: Wash clothes, towels and bed linen. Soften crust with soap and water. Apply ointment. Take the child to your doctor who will probably prescribe antibiotics. Cover the area with gauze, to stop disease spreading, discourage scratching.

Watch other members of the family for possible infection. Keep child away from school or preschool until sores have fully healed. The child may be allowed to return provided sores on exposed areas are properly covered with dressings.

Ringworm A skin infection of the scalp or body, caused by a fungus. It may be caught from dogs, cats or from other infected children, combs, bedding and clothes.

A child with ringworm of the scalp has one or more small, scaly, bald patches with broken

stumps of hair. Ringworm of the body produces round or oval, red, scaly patches which enlarge while they heal.

Treatment: Your doctor will prescribe special ointment to kill fungus. At times, antibiotics are prescribed. Wash linen, brushes and combs and keep separate. Watch other members of the family for signs of infection. Treatment takes three weeks.

Ringworm of the scalp Keep home from school until doctor gives certificate saying child is free of infection. He may also be allowed to return provided he wears a hat or cap with detachable, washable lining.

Ringworm of the body Keep home at least 7 days after start of treatment or until the doctor certifies that child is not infectious. Sometimes he is allowed to return provided patches are covered with dressings.

Ringworm of the feet (athlete's foot) A form often picked up where people walk barefoot indoors in bathrooms and near swimming pools. Sweaty shoes and socks help it gain a hold. The skin between the toes is soft, white, sodden and itches. Underneath, the skin is red and sore.

Treatment: Keep linen separate. Stop child walking barefoot in the house. Wash and dry feet thoroughly every day. Apply anti-ringworm ointment between toes. Put dusting powder in shoes and socks. Continue treatment for at least a week after signs of infection have gone.

Scabies A skin infection caused by a mite, a tiny insect which burrows under the skin. It causes severe itching, worse at night. Scratch marks can become infected. The incubation period is several days to a week.

Scabies is very infectious and spread by direct human contact. Mites under the skin lay eggs which hatch quickly. The offspring tunnel until they mature. Small red dots on the skin mark the openings to insects' burrows and grey or black lines mark their tunnels.

Treatment: Medical lotion or ointment. One

or, at the most, two applications—more may cause allergy. All family members should be treated.

Destroy mites on undergarments, bedding and towels by washing and drying in sunshine. Keep an affected child home from school or preschool until all sign of the disease has disappeared or until the doctor certifies that it is no longer infectious.

OTHER CONDITIONS

Boils A boil is an infection caused by a germ beneath the skin. It spreads down a hair follicle and causes a local abscess.

A boil starts as a small, red lump which feels tender. It comes to a point and bursts, letting out pus which is very infectious and can spread boils to other areas and other people. A large boil with several heads is called a carbuncle; a boil on the edge of the eyelid is a stye. See Seeing and Hearing.

Children who have been ill or feeling below par are more likely to contract boils because their resistance to disease is lowered.

Treatment: Bathe with hot water to which a little Epsom salts has been added. Once boil breaks, cover with sterile dressing. Clean surrounding skin often with soap and water. Use medicated ointments. Keep towels and linen separate.

Never squeeze a boil, especially one that is on the face—you can spread the infection. Treat all small wounds and insect bites promptly to reduce the risk of boils developing. If they do so in an awkward place (the ear, for instance) or if one does not clear up or recurs, see your doctor. Red streaks running from the area of the boil and tender glands mean that the infection has spread to a serious degree. See a doctor for medical advice.

Chilblains Painful, itching, red or purple swelling of fingers, toes, tips of ears or nose. Poor circulation and cold weather are thought to be involved. The exact cause is unknown.

Treatment: Ointment to reduce itching. Keep child's hands and feet warm during cold weather—woollen gloves and warm socks help. Make sure he dries affected areas thoroughly after washing.

Cold sores (herpes simplex) The incubation period is about 14 days from first infection. Sores are caused by the action of a highly contagious virus. Sore areas and blisters appear on the lips, around the mouth and nose, sometimes with a crust on top.

Cold sores are transmitted by contact and

by using handkerchiefs, towels and washers an infected person has used. The first attack, usually affecting babies and toddlers, can cause very painful ulcers inside the mouth and cheeks, on tongue and lips. Gums become red, swollen and painful. Glands in the neck may become swollen. Temperature may rise.

An attack of herpes simplex usually lasts 7–10 days. The cold sores disappear but, after healing, the virus remains for months or even years. It can break out when the child has a fever, suffers emotional stress or becomes exhausted.
Treatment: Relieve pain, use cold sore preparations from chemist . Give soothing, bland foods. Do not touch face or kiss child.
Moles Usually harmless tumours of the skin. Many children are born with small brown or blackish moles. As a rule, nothing has to be done unless they are disfiguring — when they may be removed by surgery. Moles occasionally become malignant (cancerous). Those which bleed, change colour, grow rapidly or have been partly removed by accident should be seen immediately by a doctor. Do not attempt home treatment.
Warts Small, rough, raised growths on the skin, caused by a virus. They are most common on hands and legs. On the soles of the feet, they are called plantar warts and usually require treatment by a doctor because they make walking painful. On the face and eyelids, they are usually removed for cosmetic reasons.
Treatment: Most warts can be left alone because they disappear. If any bleed or become infected, see your doctor. Unsightly warts can be removed surgically, by a doctor, or a caustic ointment will help.

WORMS

THREADWORMS
These look like moving white threads. They live in the large intestine and come out at night when the child is warm in bed, to lay their tiny eggs around the anus (back passage).

The worms cause irritation in the area, restlessness, possible bedwetting, unexplained naughtiness. They live only in humans.

The child scratches and the eggs stay under the nails. He then puts his hands in his mouth and reinfests himself by swallowing some of the eggs. He can also pass on the infection to other people.

Treatment: Your doctor will prescribe worm medicine. All members of the family should be treated, as members can reinfect each other.

Cut and scrub the child's fingernails to remove eggs. Wash underwear, bed linen, towels separately to destroy eggs. Reassure the child that having worms is nothing of which to be ashamed.

ROUNDWORMS
These live in the small intestine and are passed in the child's stools or vomited out.
Treatment: As for threadworms.

HOOKWORMS
The eggs are passed in the stools and develop into larvae in the soil from where they tunnel into the skin of bare feet.

These are not common in Australia but if taking your child on holiday to countries where the worms are prevalent do not let him walk barefoot.
Treatment: See your doctor.

TAPEWORMS
The result of eating undercooked pork, they can cause stomach and bowel trouble.
Treatment: See your doctor.

SEEING AND HEARING

EYESIGHT
Many eye problems develop during childhood. Some of the signs and symptoms are blinking more than usual, frequent headaches, squinting when looking at distant or close objects, frowning a lot, complaining that eyes itch or hurt, not being able to see clearly what is written on a blackboard or in books, sitting very close to the television set, red and encrusted or swollen eyelids, recurrent sties, inflamed or watery eyes, constant stumbling over things, brushing or rubbing eyes.

Defects in the shape of the eyeball sometimes cause difficulty in focussing and blurring of vision.

If your child has any of these problems seek medical advice straight away. He may need prescription spectacles or other treatment.
Accidents With burns and puncture wounds,

cover the eye immediately and take the child to hospital.

If small foreign bodies are not washed out by tears, try to wash out with cold water. Do not put anything in the eye — a damp handkerchief end or damp piece of cotton wool, say, to remove the foreign body.

With chemical burns, such as acid, dilute and wash out the eyes with lots of running water. Seek immediate medical attention.

Acute conjunctivitis The incubation period varies, depending on the type of germ causing the infection. It is highly contagious. The conjunctiva is the transparent membrane lining the inside of the eyelids and the white of the eye. Conjunctivitis is an inflammation of the conjunctiva causing bloodshot eyes. It can also be due to an irritant substance.

There is redness of the white part of the eye and inside the lids, swollen eyelids, a burning sensation in the eye and discharge which may be watery, mucus or pus.

Treatment: Check for any foreign body in the eye and remove. Warm bathing. Your doctor will probably prescribe antibiotic eyedrops or ointment. Treat both eyes, even if only one seems involved. Continue treatment for 24 hours after the eyes appear normal.

Check other members of the family for symptoms. Report to your doctor any disturbance of vision. Keep children home until all discharge has ceased. Avoid over-the-counter eyedrops which treat symptoms but do not cure.

Crossed eyes (squint) The eyes do not move together. One may turn in (crossed eyes) or out, or move up or down. The problem is that one eye muscle pulls harder than the other, so that the eye is pulled too far in one direction. Eyes are then not focussed on the same object. Crossed eyes should be investigated as soon as possible; otherwise the child may lose clear vision in one eye.

Treatment: See your doctor. A specialist may decide that a baby's good eye should be blanked off with a pad. The small child may be prescribed glasses with one lens blacked out — this forces the child to use the weaker eye, which becomes more efficient. Eye exercises may also be prescribed.

Sometimes an operation is carried out to lengthen or shorten one of the eye muscles.

A squint can also start when a child has either short or long sight or astigmatism (a defect in the surface of the eye lens, so that the child sees things as slightly crooked).

Sties A sty is an infection in the hair follicle of an eyelash. It looks like a small boil. The area at the edge of the eyelid becomes red, painful, tender and swollen. The sty comes to a head and usually breaks, drains and heals. Sties sometimes occur in crops.

Treatment: Apply heat to increase blood supply to area and help infection clear more quickly. A good way is to wrap a lint bandage round a wooden spoon, soak in moderately hot salted water and hold it against the sty for a few minutes at a time.

Keep washers and towels separate from rest of family. If sties recur, see your doctor.

DEAFNESS
Hearing problems may range from inability to hear certain types of sound to almost complete deafness. It is important to recognise trouble early because a child's speech learning may be damaged otherwise.

If you suspect hearing loss, ask the nursing sister at your baby health clinic to check. Your doctor or a child health centre can also check.

Babies with a hearing problem may not respond to noises, Later, you may notice that the child can't catch various sounds and may also be slow to learn to talk.

Indications of possible hearing problems are: a baby of three months who ignores sounds; an infant over a year who does not speak at all; a child over two years who uses only isolated words, rather than sentences.

Damage, disease or malfunction of ear structures can cause slight, severe or total hearing loss in one or both ears.

Causes include impacted wax or a foreign body in the canal, swimmer's ear (irritation or infection of the outer ear canal), glue ear (catarrh of the middle ear), abscessed ear, obstructed eustachian tube (that which connects nose and middle ear), congenital deafness, damage from illness or even certain medications.

Treatment: Eardrops to help remove wax, nose drops for head colds, testing at a special clinic for suspected hearing loss, antibiotics for infections. There are special education programmes for deaf children.

Earache May be mild or very painful. A child may have fever, signs of a head cold, hearing loss. Babies will cry, have the snuffles, perhaps pull on the aching ear.

Causes include blocked eustachian tube, nasal allergy, head colds, infected adenoids, swimming, impacted wax, a foreign body in the eardrum, toothache.

Complications: infected middle ear (otitis media); if not treated promptly, the eardrum can rupture; boils may develop in ear canal from scratching.

Treatment: Do not let children with colds and stuffy noses swim or fly. Treat head colds and nasal allergies early with nose drops. See doctor if earache persists. Don't try to clean wax from the ear with a match or bobbypin.

Glue ear A persistent accumulation of thick fluid in the middle ear. It causes repeated earaches, does not respond to antibiotics and can cause hearing loss. The child may have intermittent earaches, display naughty behaviour.

Treatment: A doctor can usually tell by looking at the eardrum if the problem is glue ear. If hearing loss is suspected, he will arrange tests by an audiogram.

DENTAL CARE

A good nourishing diet, effective brushing and regular visits to the dentist are the foundation of dental health.

TEETHING

There are 20 first (baby) teeth but 32 permanent ones, 12 of which come in behind the first teeth as the jaw grows longer. The first permanent teeth to appear are 'six-year' molars.

Many babies have no trouble when teeth come through the gum. Others may have difficulty sleeping, become irritable, lose their appetite or fuss over food, suffer from sore, swollen gums, dribble a lot. Any child will be teething on and off for 3 years.

Treatment: Baby seems to find some comfort from teething rings. Teething jellies may also help. Give aspirin only on doctor's recommendation. Also give reassurance.

Are first teeth important? Some parents think it does not matter if a child loses a first one before time. They are wrong: it is important to keep first teeth as long as possible, as they enable the child to chew and to talk properly.

A child who loses his upper front teeth from decay early will find it difficult to pronounce certain sounds. He gets into the habit of thrusting out his tongue and permanent teeth can then come through out of position. Speech development can also be adversely affected.

Baby teeth hold the space for permanent teeth. If they are lost early, the remaining teeth tend to drift, spaces for permanent teeth close and they can come through crowded.

PREVENTING THE LOSS OF FIRST TEETH

Beware of decay and try to prevent accidents. If a front tooth is knocked out, you may be able to save it. Pick up the tooth, wash thoroughly under a tap and pop it straight back into position, pushing it in firmly. Get the child to the dentist immediately. The bone around the tooth may be damaged and your dentist will want to check it.

TOOTHACHE

Causes are injury, infection between gum and teeth or an abscess at root of a tooth.

The gum is red, swollen and tender. Tapping very gently with the handle of a spoon will cause sharp pain in the tooth responsible. Do not neglect an aching tooth—it may abscess and lead to complications.

For treatment, try aspirin (child's dose) or an icepack on the jaw but, most important, get the child to the dentist as soon as possible. The best methods of prevention are regular visits to the dentist, fluoride and a healthy diet.

GUM BOILS

Abscesses that break through the gum at the site of a decayed tooth. They usually occur only with baby teeth. Sometimes they are painful and the tooth may be tender or slightly loose.

Aspirin or similar painkillers can help to give relief. Bathe with warm water with a half teaspoon of salt added. Contact your dentist who will decide treatment.

WHEN TO VISIT THE DENTIST

If the child has any discoloured area on the front teeth, take him to the dentist. He or she will usually have a quick look when the child is about two to three, to make sure the back teeth have come through without trouble.

To prepare a child, be honest. Tell him the dentist will have a look at his teeth with a mirror and show him a handbag mirror to demonstrate. Parents should not use a threat of a visit to the dentist as a punishment.

It is safer—and cheaper in the long run—to take your child to the dentist every 6 months.

The dentist applies a concentrated fluoride solution to make teeth more resistant to decay. Any decay can be caught and then remedied early.

FLUORIDE
Many water supplies now are fluoridated. In areas with low fluoride supply, pregnant women may need to take fluoride tablets and children may need to take them daily up to the age of fifteen years.

Fluoride has attracted controversy but dentists say that for the tablets to cause mottling is rare—they can remove any slight mottling by polishing. They use a concentrated fluoride solution on teeth during check-up visits. In between, a fluoridised toothpaste is generally recommended.

GENITALS

CIRCUMCISION
Surgical removal of the foreskin which covers the tip of the penis. Much controversy has surrounded circumcision. Many doctors feel that the disadvantages outweigh the advantages.

Disadvantages include possible infection, bleeding, accidental injury to glans (tip of penis) and, later on, reduced sensitivity of the glans during intercourse.

Circumcision is not necessary for proper cleanliness, and circumcised babies are more likely to develop sores at the opening of the penis. The foreskin protects the tip of the penis from irritation of wet nappies and reduces the chance of infection.

Circumcision is still done for religious reasons, for narrowing of the opening of the foreskin and for repeated infection under the foreskin. It should not be done unnecessarily and not just after the baby is born because risks are greater in the newborn.

Some doctors think circumcision may lessen the chance of cancer of the cervix (opening of the womb) of the sexual partner. This cancer is practically unknown in those Jewish women whose husbands have been circumcised.

A tight foreskin for babies is normal. Separation from the top of the penis occurs gradually, usually by the age of four years.

Do not try to force the foreskin back; you could tear the skin which may scar. This could cause permanent joining of the foreskin to the tip of the penis which will then require circumcision to correct.

Care of the foreskin Leave it alone until the child is about four, at which stage try to push it back gently. Do not persist if it does not go back easily. Once it does, gently pull back during washing to clean. It is important that the boy learns to keep himself clean because lack of hygiene in uncircumcised men could increase the risk to their partners of contracting cancer of the cervix.

If tight foreskin persists past six, the child may need circumcision.

Care of the infant after circumcision A gauze dressing covers the end of the penis. Continue washing the baby. Leave the dressing in place until it falls off. Tell your doctor of any sign of infection or continued bleeding.

HERNIAS
A hernia, or rupture, is a protrusion of any part of the internal organs through the structures enclosing them. The most common organ involved is the intestine.

INGUINAL HERNIA
A bulge in the groin which may extend into the scrotum. The swelling often disappears when the child lies down because the intestine recedes into the abdomen.
Treatment: An inguinal hernia which does not disappear when the child is relaxed should be seen straight away by a doctor who may advise an operation.

These hernias can be dangerous because they can 'strangulate'. A loop of bowel is caught up in the hernia and becomes obstructed. Strangulation causes severe pain, sometimes vomiting and nausea and requires immediate surgery.

UMBILICAL HERNIA
A dome-shaped bulge over the umbilicus (navel) with intestine behind it. This usually rights itself, without treatment, before the age of five years.

The belly button or umbilicus is where the cord from the placenta joins the baby in the uterus. Blood vessels bring nourishment through the cord to the baby. After birth, the cord shrivels and falls off. The umbilicus closes and is covered with skin but it is a potential site for a defect which may at some stage form a hernia.

HYDROCOELE
A sac of fluid around the testicle which makes it look and feel larger than normal. This is often present at birth. No treatment is required. The fluid usually disappears on its own. It persists on rare occasions and an operation may be needed when the child is about four years old. Some doctors operate when he is younger.

UNDESCENDED TESTICLE (TESTIS)
Before birth, the testicles—which develop in the abdomen—move into the scrotum. With premature babies, they may descend soon after birth.

Many small boys have the testicles 're-tracted'—temporarily pulled up into the groin by a band of muscle along the spermatic cord. This is no cause for alarm. If an undescended testicle is not down by the time the child is five years old, the doctor will operate.

Treatment: If a testicle appears to be missing from the scrotum, check periodically while bathing the child to see if it descends of its own accord. Don't worry the child by discussing it. If a testicle is not down by the age of one, see your doctor.

It is important for the testicles to develop normally during childhood. An operation will ensure the boy has the best testicle function as an adult. A hernia may also exist with an undescended testicle.

Possible complication is when an undescended testicle becomes twisted, injured or malignant. If this is not corrected, it may be damaged and lose its ability to produce sperm.

PROBLEM BEHAVIOUR

Many of the following behavioural problems cause parents a lot of worry and stress. Try and remember that such behaviour is quite common, and will not go on for ever. Usually, a cuddle will work better than a scolding.

BEDWETTING
If your child is still wetting the bed by the age of about six years or if he starts wetting again after being dry, seek medical advice.

Most bedwetters do not have an underlying physical problem, though a few may be suffering from diabetes or a structural defect of the urinary tract which can be corrected surgically. Emotional problems can play a part.

There is quite often a family history of bed-wetting.

Treatment: Don't make the child feel guilty. Don't fuss. He is not doing it deliberately. Do not blame yourself. There may be unavoidable stresses in his life at that time.

Put a plastic or rubber sheet over the mattress. Toilet training may help. Take him to the lavatory every two hours and just before bed. Restrict fluids at bedtime. And small rewards for keeping dry may help. Some doctors recommend an alarm system whereby a signal is triggered at the first sign of dampness during the night.

If the child wants to stay with friends or go to camp and is embarrassed, doctors can prescribe a tablet which helps suppress bedwetting.

Stress—such as starting preschool, a new baby in the family or a trip to hospital—can trigger off bedwetting. Extra attention may help, if the child feels neglected. It helps mothers to know that the child will eventually become dry.

BREATH-HOLDING
The child—usually a toddler—takes a deep breath, as if to scream, but holds it in and no sound comes out. His face usually goes dark red, then blue. This is quite harmless but, if he holds breath too long, he could have an attack from lack of oxygen.

This is an attention-seeking device and the child may be reacting to emotional stress— for instance, he may be jealous of a new baby. Those affected are usually intelligent children with low frustration levels who easily become angry. It is a form of tantrum.

Treatment: Do not give in to the child. Slapping and other punishments don't work. Try to relieve frustrations: for instance, he may need help coping with jealousy of new baby. Divert his attention when an attack seems imminent. If it persists, see your doctor.

HEAD-BANGING, ROCKING
Some babies start these habits at about the age of nine months. They bang their heads against something hard, such as a cot or a chair, or roll their heads from side to side. They may do it for a sense of security or comfort.

Treatment: Give baby more cuddling and attention. Make sure he can't hurt himself. Pad the cot. If the problem persists, see your doctor.

TEMPER TANTRUMS

The strong-willed two-year-old often clashes with his parents—a reaction to too much or too little discipline.

Treatment: Keep calm; don't shout. Do not slap or punish him. Try leaving him on his own but do not go far away. Be prepared to give him a cuddle when he is over it. Learn to recognise signs of an impending attack and try to divert his attention at that stage. As with breath-holding, it may be a sign of family tension.

THUMB SUCKING

Thumb sucking is normal behaviour; almost all babies suck fingers or thumbs at some time. Some children keep up the habit for years. Babies suck their thumbs because it gives a sense of security. They stop eventually.

Treatment: Don't scold, forcefully remove thumb from mouth or use splints or mittens to restrain baby. If you are worried, try giving him a dummy. Thumb sucking and dummies have little—if any—effect on the child's first teeth.

If baby uses a dummy, clean it thoroughly in hot, soapy water after use; sterilise by boiling or in cold sterilising agent; check that the dummy has not deteriorated. Replace it as needed. As a precaution against accidents, never attach it to the baby's clothes by a ribbon or cord or tie it around the neck.

TICS

Repetitive, irritating nervous twitches, jerky movements of muscles or habits such as rubbing nose or tossing hair back continually. The child may twitch his mouth, wrinkle his forehead, blink, jerk his head or shoulders. Frequency is from several times a minute to a few times a day.

Treatment: Children do not do it on purpose, so scolding, punishment or demanding that the child stop is pointless. The tic usually disappears in time. Those which persist could be signs of emotional tension—in which case it is wise to seek medical advice.

HYPERACTIVITY

A condition in which children are unable to be quiet and sit still for more than a few moments at a time. Controversy surrounds what hyperactivity is and what causes it. Some children are merely more active than others. In extreme cases, the child is constantly in physical motion, annoying and often destructive.

Some evidence suggests that behavioural problems may be related to food fads—say, eating excessive amounts of one particular food. Hyperactivity has been linked with use of artificial additives, artificial colourings and preservatives in food, drinks and drugs. Usually treated with the Feingold Diet which cuts out these and certain other foods.

Treatment: See your doctor who will arrange a complete physical and neurological examination, including vision and hearing tests. Counselling may be recommended for emotional problems thought to be a factor.

SPEECH PROBLEMS, STUTTERING

Children learn to speak at different rates—depending on intelligence, hearing and control of muscles involved in speaking. Most children start saying a few single words at about one year of age and by two have some simple sentences. If, by the age of four, the child is difficult to understand or not using sentences, you should seek medical advice about the situation.

Stuttering is quite common between two and three years, and is not unusual in children aged up to five years.

Treatment: Speak and listen to your baby often. Correct improper speech. See your doctor if stuttering is severe, constant and prolonged. Do not call attention to the stutter. Read, sing and speak to your child as often as possible. Don't force a child to speak more clearly. Have any suspected hearing defect checked at an early stage. Speech therapy may be needed if the child continues to have problems after starting school.

20
EMERGENCIES

QUICK THINKING is the order of the day in an emergency. This section deals with natural disasters, unexpected emergencies such as being caught in an electrical storm or witnessing a car accident, and home hazards. On the basis that prevention is always better than cure, precautions have been included where relevant.

For FIRST AID TREATMENTS see pp. 273–282.

NATURAL DISASTERS

Natural disasters are often referred to as 'Acts of God', although it is hard to think of them as such when they take a heavy toll. You usually get some kind of warning, however brief, before bushfires, cyclones and floods. Taking the correct precautions, being prepared and knowing the right and wrong ways to act in the face of such disasters will maximise your chances of survival.

BUSHFIRES

In many parts of Australia, the summer bushfire threat is part of everyday life. When the weather is hot and dry, the winds strong, and undergrowth tinder-dry, a whole State can come under a fire ban.

The first precaution, even if you live in a built-up area, is to take note of and obey fire bans.

It is not true that houses spontaneously 'explode' during an intense bushfire. Rather, houses ignite at a number of points and may burn to destruction in 15 minutes. Radiation from bushfires can ignite furnishings of houses through openings or even through closed windows. But more often flying brands or sparks enter openings in the roof or walls or under-floor area and ignite the buildings, preheated by radiation and hot winds.

Older weatherboard houses can be ignited by flying embers which lodge in warped, cracked and unpainted cladding or window frames. Apart from that, in very severe bushfires there is little difference in risk to brick, asbestos-cement or timber houses.

The main danger spots are the outskirts of large towns and cities where homes adjoin bushland; homes on the fringes of many country towns; isolated bushland homes and settlements; and farms with crops or vegetation too close to the homestead.

The most dangerous places to live are those surrounded by dense bush, or on a ridgetop above a steep, wooded slope, because fire travels faster uphill.

The following are guidelines to help protect yourself and your property in a bushfire.

GENERAL PRECAUTIONS

• Rake a fire break. Reduce thick scrub growth within a radius of 30 metres from the house.

• Remove garden rubbish.

• Store fuel away from the house.

• Cut back branches which overhang the house.

• Remove shrubs growing too close to the house.

• Clear the guttering of leaves.

• Enclose the eaves.

• Fit wire screens to doors, windows and vents.

• Enclose the area under the house.

• Install and maintain the garden taps and long hoses.

FIRE APPROACHING

• Fill buckets, baths and basins with water. Connect a hose to an interior tap. Take the garden hose inside with you.

• Close all windows and doors, wind up car windows and move cars away from the house to open ground.

• Stuff downpipes with rags and fill roof gutters with water. (Don't forget you will want to remove them when the danger has passed.)

• Put a ladder up to the manhole in the ceiling and a bucket of water near the manhole, and put another ladder up to the roof outside the house.

• Dress in woollen clothes and heavy boots if possible and cover your head. Do not wear synthetics.

• Douse nearby shrubs and grass with water and turn on the roof sprinkler if one is fitted.

• Immediately extinguish burning leaves or bits of bark that blow towards the house.

• Watch the roof, gutters and ceiling space for outbreaks of fire.

• Stay inside the house for the few minutes it takes for the flame front to pass, then recheck the roof, ceiling space, exposed timbers, garage and cars.

IN YOUR CAR

If you are your car and are overtaken by a

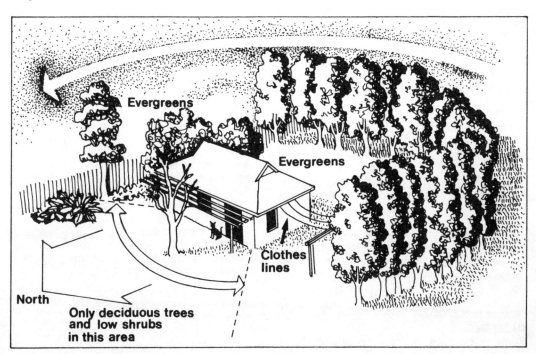

bushfire realise that the car's bodywork provides your best chance of survival. Do not panic and flee from your refuge. Radiant heat does not penetrate solid substances and is easily reflected.

Do not drive a car blindly through thick smoke. Turn on the headlights and park opposite bare sections of ground beside the road as far as possible from the advancing fire.

Remain calm and have confidence that even in the worst situations it will be some minutes before the vehicle actually catches fire. If someone can survive the flaming period of a forest fire (rarely more than three to four minutes at one spot) or a grass fire (around 30 seconds) there is little danger of succumbing later.

Wind up the windows and shelter from radiation beneath the dashboard, covering your body with a blanket or the floormat. If the car catches fire leave it but keep your skin covered as much as possible.

IN THE OPEN

• Don't panic. Panic will stress your body and make you more susceptible to radiant heat. It can also cause you to act irrationally.

• Try to move to cleared or already burnt ground.

• Do not run uphill or away from the fire unless you know a nearby refuge.

• Move across the slope out of the path of the fire front and work your way down the slope towards the back of the fire.

• Don't attempt to run through flames unless you can see clearly behind them. Lulls in the fire often result in the flames being low enough to step over or run through to burnt ground behind.

• Use every possible means to protect yourself from radiation. On bare areas cover yourself with sand or dirt if possible or lie in wheel ruts, depressions, or behind large rocks or logs.

• Pools, streams or dams can give protection, but do not use water tanks that are on supports in the air because they heat up quickly.

• Breathe close to the ground—the air is purer.

• Don't move immediately after the fire has passed because the ground will still be very hot.

CAMPING

Summer holidays for many people mean a camping trip in the bush. It pays to be aware of the dangers of bushfires. This is a survival plan for campers and bushwalkers.

• Avoid lighting fires—take cold meals and be careful if you are a smoker.

• Stay away from fire danger areas—avoid camping or walking where the bush is dry.

• Think about safe places and escape routes—notice water or areas without combustible material where you could take refuge.

• Carry protective clothing capable of covering as much of your body as possible to guard against the heat of fire.

• Know first aid for burns.

• Co-operate with authorities, obeying their safety instructions.

• Before heading off, check details on fire restrictions by ringing a national park or State recreation area office.

LOW-RISK GARDENS

Living in a bushfire-risk area does not mean you cannot have a garden. Many trees and shrubs are fire-resistant and can be used to catch flying sparks so they do not carry on to a building.

The things to look for when seeking fire-resistant plants are a high leaf moisture content, low resin or oil content and minimal dead matter.

The first line of defence in a garden should be a perennial plant called *Galenia pubescens* which is drought and salt tolerant and burns with great reluctance.

The 'old man' saltbush should come next, followed by 'boobyalla', *Myoporum insulare*, in well-watered areas, or 'boomeralla', *Myoporum montanum*, in drier areas.

Next in line is the Norfolk Island hibiscus, *Lagunaria patersonii*, alternated with the New Zealand mirror plant, *Coprosma repens*.

Finally, a line of fire-resistant eucalypts should be planted which will catch the sparks before they reach the house. The blue box, bloodwood, and *Eucalyptus maculata* are all fire-resistant varieties. *Syncarpia laurifolia* can be added to these.

A low-risk garden must have an abundance of deciduous or non-flammable evergreen trees and receive regular watering to maintain the high water content in the leaves.

CYCLONES

The main target of cyclones in Australia is the northern half of the coastline between November and April. But this is no iron-clad rule. Even in the more southern States cyclones can strike at other times as well.

Causes A critical combination of weather factors can turn an ordinary tropical depression or 'low' into a cyclone.

Summer sun beating on the warm ocean evaporates water, creating a deep layer of moist air. The uplift of this moist air in the centre of a low cools it, causing the intense rain characteristic of tropical cyclones.

High in the atmosphere, the rising air spirals outwards, removing air faster than it flows inwards at low levels.

The result is a falling barometric pressure. The latent heat released by the rain maintains the energy of the storm.

GENERAL PRECAUTIONS
• Ensure there is a transistor radio in the house and that there are fresh spare batteries.
• Make sure the house is sound, particularly the roof.
• Clear property of loose sheet iron, loosely anchored rain water tanks and other potential missiles.
• In case of a storm surge warning, know the nearest safe high areas.
• Collect tinned food, water containers, emergency lighting, candles, essential clothing, first aid kit, medicines.

WHEN THE CYCLONE COMES
• Keep calm, stay inside.
• Shelter in the strongest part of the house (probably the bathroom, internal toilet or central hallway).
• If the house starts to break up, protect yourself with mattress and blankets.
• Anchor yourself to a strong fixture such as water pipes, or get under a strong table or bed.

The 'eye' of the cyclone The winds in a cyclone whirl clockwise around a 'calm' eye. This eye is usually less than 10km in diameter (though it may exceed 30km across). When the wind drops, there is no rain and often very little cloud. You must be aware of this temporary lull, for when it has passed, the wind will return with battering force, probably from another direction. Do not go outdoors

AFTER THE CYCLONE HAS ABATED
- Keep listening to the radio.
- Don't go outside until advised officially or you are positive the cyclone has passed.
- Don't panic.
- Don't stay in the open.
- Don't go sightseeing.
- Do not ignore warnings.

WARNING MESSAGES
Tropical cyclone warning centres at Brisbane, Darwin and Perth keep a round-the-clock watch during cyclone season.

If a tropical cyclone seems likely or a cyclone is detected, the Bureau issues either a cyclone watch, a cyclone warning, or a flash cyclone warning.

Cyclone watch This means a cyclone is approaching but is not expected in your locality for the next 24 hours.

Cyclone warning This means a cyclone is expected to threaten your community within 24 hours.

Flash cyclone warning This is the first warning issued for an area. It is also issued when major changes to previous warnings are necessary.

Wind and tide warnings The warning message will indicate the expected maximum wind gusts near the centre of the cyclone and also the strength of the maximum gusts expected over particular areas in any of the following terms:
- Gales with gusts above 95km/hr.
- Destructive winds with gusts above 130km/hr.
- Very destructive winds with gusts above 180km/hr.

The warning may mention above normal tides. The effect in terms of the risk of flooding at the coast will be described as follows:
- Abnormally high tides could cause minor flooding.
- Abnormally high tides could cause serious flooding.
- Dangerously high tides could cause extensive flooding.

EMERGENCY AND EVACUATION
Emergency kit (to be kept in house)
- Battery-operated transistor radio and torch with fresh batteries. Tinned food. Water in containers. Candles. Matches. Essential clothing.
- Emergency self-contained cooking gear.
- First aid kit. Essential medicines.

Evacuation outfit
- Warm utility clothing.
- Strong footwear (not thongs) to protect against cuts from debris.

FLOODS

Certain areas of Australia are more prone to flooding than others, but floods can occur in many apparently unlikely places. In the 125 years since records have been kept there have been scores of devastating floods throughout the country.

Know the flood history of your area. Check with your local government and find out what official river height means your house will be flooded and where the catchment area is in which rainfall will cause floods near your home. Also ask if there is a local flood evacuation plan.

GENERAL PRECAUTIONS
- Know the whereabouts of the closest high ground and your shortest route to it.
- Keep tuned to the radio when flooding is a possibility.
- Don't listen to rumours—take all instructions from local counter-disaster authorities.

FLOOD APPROACHING
- If time permits, move essential items and furniture to the highest area of your house.
- Disconnect any stationary electrical appliances—but don't touch them if you are wet or standing in water.
- Anchor anything that may float away.
- Don't attempt to protect below-ground or basement areas by stacking sandbags around the outside walls of your house. (This often has a reverse effect.)

EVACUATION
- Follow instructions and advice of authorities. If they tell you to evacuate, do so promptly. Follow all instructions regarding the best routes to use, and the destination. Listen to the radio for information on the locale of emergency housing and food centres.
- Secure your home before leaving. If you have time, bring outside possessions inside the house, or tie them down securely.
- Lock house doors and windows. Park your

car in the garage or driveway, ready for emergency evacuation if need be.

CLEANING UP
Remember that flood waters may be extremely polluted. Follow these rules carefully to minimise risk of infection and sickness.
- Do not use food or drink which has been in contact with flood water.
- Boil all water until supplies have been declared safe.
- Do not handle wet electrical equipment.
- Beware of contracting infectious diseases from paddling in stagnant and/or contaminated water.
- Wear strong shoes when wading in flood water in case you step on sharp sticks, broken glass etc.
- Beware of snakes and spiders which may seek dry conditions in your house.

WALKING AND MOTORING
- Make sure the route you propose to take is open and safe for use.
- Make sure you have enough petrol in your car.
- Follow recommended routes.
- As you travel, keep listening to the radio for additional information and instructions from authorities.
- Be on guard against washed or undermined roadways, land slides, broken sewer or water mains, loose or downed electrical wires, and falling or fallen objects.
- Watch out for areas where waterways may flood suddenly.
- Do not try to cross a waterway unless you are certain that it will not be over your knees, or above the middle of your car's wheels all the way across.

RURAL AREAS
Flooding brings different problems for country and city people. In the country, isolation can add to the hazards of flood, and special rules need to be followed.
- Paint the name of your property on your roof.
- If you have a radio transmitter, paint the call sign and frequencies on the roof.
- Clear a non-flooding area as near as possible to your house for a helicopter landing pad or a site for dropping supplies.
- Maintain levee banks and flood drains.

THE UNEXPECTED

There are some emergencies which defy classification. When you are confronted with one it is the unexpectedness of it all which may make it hard for you to think quickly.

ELECTRICAL STORM

The best place to be in an electrical storm is indoors. If you are in your car during a storm, stay inside and drive to shelter.

If you are caught outside, try to keep as low as possible as lightning will earth itself on the highest available point.

Do not shelter under a tree. If you are in a heavily wooded area, stand near a tree with lots of foliage in preference to one without. Look for a rock or hollow to shelter near and try to keep yourself dry.

CHILDBIRTH

If a pregnant woman begins labour, medical advisers recommend you allow the birth to proceed naturally. If possible, you should obtain medical help quickly. Untrained interference is potentially dangerous.

DEATH AT HOME

If a relative or any other person dies in your house, the first step is to get a death certificate.

If a doctor has treated the deceased within the previous three months he can issue a death certificate. If the death occurs after hours or on a weekend, a night-service doctor may be called in. If a doctor has been treating the patient, the night-service doctor can issue an interim death certificate until the deceased's own doctor issues one. If the deceased hasn't seen a doctor within the previous three months, the police must be called. They must also be called if the death is of a violent or unnatural nature.

The police must file a report for the coroner, then the government contractors take the body to the nearest hospital where a medical practitioner pronounces 'life extinct'. The body is then taken to a morgue.

The coroner decides whether or not to hold an inquest. Once a death certificate is issued you contact a funeral director who will arrange for the body to be taken to the funeral parlour.

The funeral director usually arranges for the death to be registered. However, this is the responsibility of the person in whose house the death occurred and must be done within 28 days. If the person left a will, the solicitor must be contacted and the will read.

MOTOR ACCIDENT

If you witness an accident, do not panic but see what assistance you can offer.

Check the condition of the people involved to see if an ambulance is necessary. If so, get someone to call one. If you are alone, flag down a passing car and ask them to make the call.

If the accident occurs near a bend of the road or in some other areas of reduced visibility, have someone guide oncoming traffic around the scene of the accident.

Check any injured persons. Help anyone who is able to walk from the crash but don't drag unconscious victims from the car unless there is danger of fire. Instead, keep them warm and comfortable. Cover them with a rug or coat, and loosen any tight clothing, particularly around the neck.

If a victim has stopped breathing, apply mouth-to-mouth resuscitation (see p. 281.) If there is considerable bleeding around the mouth, or if the jaw has been damaged, use mouth-to-nose resuscitation. Breath into the nostrils of the victim rather than the mouth.

Check for bleeding. Press a piece of material on the site of the wound to stem the flow of blood. There may be internal bleeding — often signified by a rapid, weak pulse. Patients in this condition must not be moved.

Do not give injured persons anything to eat or drink, not even a cup of tea or aspirin.

Unless you are experienced in first aid, the most sensible action you can take is to keep victims calm and warm until the ambulance arrives.

MISSING PERSON

If someone fails to turn up at your home or at a meeting place, go over the path he or she would be expected to take. If there is no sign, contact the police and report the person missing. A person must be missing for 24 hours before the police will take action. It is always advisable to carry some form of identification so that if you are involved in an accident relatives can be contacted.

BURST MAINS

If a gas main bursts call the relevant authority or the fire brigade who will do so for you. Do not smoke in the area. If a main bursts in your house, don't turn any lights off or on. Leave everything electrical as it is, as an electrical arc may cause gas to ignite.

If a water main explodes, contact the relevant authority, which should provide a 24-hour service. Your state emergency service or equivalent may help if water threatens to flood your house.

TRAPPED IN A LIFT

Lifts in Australia are required to have an emergency bell or telephone. Most modern lifts have a telephone connected to the switchboard in the building. If you are trapped use the emergency phone or button. People trapped in a lift are given priority by lift-maintenance companies. Do not try tampering with the lift equipment or trapdoor on the roof. While waiting for help you may be uncomfortable but you are not in danger. If you start trying to escape you may put yourself in danger.

HOME HAZARDS

It is generally accepted that home is where most accidents happen. There are many reasons for this. It is a place where people may not exercise the care they might when at work under supervision. Also, many parents find it hard to provide the minute-by-minute supervision of children which is possible at school.

FIRE

A fire may occur in any part of a house through a wide variety of causes. All members of the family should know how to get out as quickly as possible if fire breaks out. Where infants and small children are involved, parents and older children should understand how to reach the little ones if normal access through a doorway is impossible.

PRECAUTIONS

Make sure every member of the family knows how to call the fire brigade in an emergency.

Make sure there is a torch in good order at hand in case lights fail.

Make sure that there are clear exits from the house, and windows and fly-screens can be operated freely if needed as emergency exits.

Do not allow anyone in the family to smoke in bed.

Keep lighters and matches out of reach of children.

Check at bedtime for smouldering cigarette butts, particularly after a party in your home.

In the kitchen Do not dry teatowels over the stove.

Do not allow saucepan handles to face outward into the room or over a lighted burner.

If a saucepan catches alight, switch off the heat and smother the saucepan with a lid, damp cloth or correct extinguisher. Never try to put out a fat fire with water.

Outside the home Remove long grass and dry leaves from the area surrounding your home.

Keep gutters and downpipes clean.

Clear fire breaks if necessary.

Never light a fire in windy weather.

Listen to weather forecasts and be guided by them.

Install a suitable fire extinguisher in garage or workshop.

Electricity Do not run extension cords under rugs or over hooked nails.

Do not overload circuits.

Have appliances checked regularly.

Use only the correct size fuse in each socket.

Replace frayed and damaged flexes and cords at once.

Never leave electrical appliances such as heaters, hair driers or shavers near sink, shower or bath.

Electric blankets Electric blankets are not for babies or toddlers. Temperatures only slightly above normal body heat cause them to perspire. They cannot easily replace lost body fluid, and dehydration, a dangerous condition, can quickly occur.

Electric blankets, like all electrical appliances, need care and maintenance to ensure that they continue to function safely for many years. Check the leads for fraying or exposed wires, especially where they enter plugs or terminal blocks. Do not use if there is any sign of wear. Contact the manufacturer for repairs or inspection of blankets.

Blankets must be firmly fastened by the tapes provided and tied correctly. The blanket must be flat and on top of the mattress.

Do not switch on an electric blanket if the blanket is damp.

Do not fold an electric blanket to suit a smaller bed—this is dangerous.

On children's beds check that the electric blanket is flat on the bed and not in a heap at the foot. Children are often restless sleepers.

For storage, leave on the bed or roll.

Do not pile too many covers, pillows or clothes on top of the bed and then leave the blanket on.

Do not leave on during the day or when there is no one at home.

Where an electric blanket is marked as not suitable for laundering, it should not be laundered under any circumstances.

Fires and heaters Make sure fires are well guarded.

Place portable heaters where they cannot be knocked over.

Never carry heaters which are alight.

Keep heaters turned away from curtains and furniture.

Refill heaters out of doors and use only reco-mmended fuel.

Flammable liquids Do not use petrol or kero-sene or any flammable liquid to revive a fire.

Do not use flammable cleaning fluids.

Keep flammable liquids properly labelled and in sealed containers, preferably in a garage or shed. Do not store in plastic containers unless they are designed for this.

Keep flammable liquids out of reach of chil-dren.

Never store flammable liquids in the same room as a water heater.

Never refuel a running motor.

Do not clean engines with petrol or highly flammable material.

Beware of petrol vapour, particularly in boats. Smell is the best method of detection. If odour is present, do not start the motor.

If flammable liquids do catch fire, do not use water to put out the flame. Keep an all-purpose fire extinguisher.

PROCEDURES

Saucepan on fire Most fires in the kitchen start on the stove or in the oven. If fat or oil catches fire, turn off the source of heat, pick up the saucepan lid, and, keeping it between you and the flames, put it on the pan.

Do not throw water on the fire.

Do not pick up the pan to take it outside. The draught created by the movement will cause the flames to fan back and you risk being burnt, setting your clothes alight or dropping the pan and spreading the fire.

Do not lift the lid until it feels cool when you touch it with the back of your fingers.

If a fire starts in the oven turn off the heat. Do not open the oven door. If you open the oven door during cooking and there is an electrical flash, close it immediately. Turn the oven off and allow it to cool. If you have any doubts at all about a fire, contact your local fire station.

If a fire breaks out in your home Get all the family together and out of the house at once, closing as many doors and windows as you can as you leave.

If you discover a fire or smell smoke, tele-phone the fire brigade at once. Never take it for granted someone else will phone.

Realise that even a small fire can get out of control in five minutes.

Close all doors and windows to try to isolate fire, heat and smoke.

Do not attempt to fight the fire unless this can be done without risk.

Where there is heavy smoke, everyone should keep low, as smoke is less dense near the floor and the temperature is lower. Every member of the household should know this.

If there is an invalid in the house, remember that it is possible to move even a heavy person by dragging him along the floor on a blanket.

Remember that if heat can be felt through a closed door, it is too dangerous to open it. Exit must be made through another door or window. If heat and smoke are coming through an open door or window, close it.

CHILD SAFETY

Always keep your child under constant super-vision, especially in the vulnerable years between one and four. Toddlers are notori-ously curious. If you have to leave the room, even for a second, place the child in a playpen.

• All upper windows should be child-proofed with gratings or secure screens.

• Install adhesive rubber mats on the bottom of the bathtub.

• Put a lock on the medicine cabinet.

• Check that the slats on the cot or playpen are no more than 6cm apart.

• In the bathroom and kitchen keep all sub-stances out of the child's reach or preferably in a child-proof cupboard or drawer. This includes any cleaning agents and also

shampoos, make-up, perfume, deodorants etc.
• Never leave small objects lying around. Nuts are a particular hazard.
• Beware of dangling electrical cords. Unplug small appliances when not in use. Caps are available at hardware stores to protect unused electrical outlets.
• The water temperature in the home should be lowered to between 50° and 60° to prevent scalding.
• Use table mats, not tablecloths that children can tug at.
• Turn saucepan handles towards the rear of the stove when cooking. Try to use hot-plates or burners at the rear.
• If you have firearms, always keep them locked up and store unloaded.
• Have sturdy fire-screens around all fire-places in the house.
• In the garden, store tools so they cannot fall down on a child. Insecticides and other products should be kept out of the reach of children.
• Make sure your swimming pool is fenced and has a child-proof gate.

IN THE GARDEN

The most frequent garden accidents are falls from ladders and trees, on broken paths or over garden tools or hoses left lying about.

Thousands more injuries are caused by using tools improperly.

Keep shears, secateurs and knives closed when not in use.

Do not leave hoes and rakes lying on the ground. Stand them upright and upside-down.

Do not cut or prune when you cannot see what you are cutting.

Read instructions before using new electrical gadgets and make sure outside plugs are correctly installed and earthed.

Lock chemicals out of reach of children and animals and label chemicals decanted into other bottles or jars. Always read the maker's label thoroughly.

Familiarise yourself with how your lawn-mower works. Know how to stop it in an emergency. Check the condition of the blade-holder and blades before starting.

Wear protective clothing such as gloves and sensible footwear. Foot injuries are common when using mowers, spades or forks.

Always wear a hat on hot, sunny days.

Keep your back straight and do not bend more than necessary. When lifting, bend the knees and not the back. Use long-handled rakes and hoes and set the lawnmower handle to allow the user to walk upright.

For POOL SAFETY TIPS see p. 206.

SUN

Care should always be taken to avoid sunburn. It is extremely painful and can be just as serious as any other burn. Fair-skinned people and very young children are particularly at risk. If you must get a tan, do it gradually. Start with 10–15 minutes a day.

Avoid sun-bathing between 11am and 3pm, when the sun's rays are most harmful.

Wear a wide-brimmed hat when out in the sun.

Ask your school to encourage the children to wear hats during recess in the summer months.

If you are planning a picnic or a day at the beach, make sure there is adequate shade for you and your family, e.g. a beach umbrella or awning. Tree shade is inadequate for a baby in a bassinet.

Remember that the shade moves during the day and you will need to move with it.

At the beginning of the season your child should be protected with a T-shirt after short exposure to the sun. For fair-skinned children, this practice may need to be continued throughout the summer months.

If you are near a reflecting surface such as sand, water or snow, you will burn more quickly.

A block-out cream should be liberally applied before going out into the sun and re-applied after swimming.

Give children frequent cool drinks. Remember babies cannot tell you when they are thirsty.

Avoid strenuous outdoor activities in the middle of the day. They are best done in the early morning or the cool of the evening.

To protect your eyes, always avoid looking directly at the sun.

Sunburn Over-exposure to the sun can cause sunburn or, more seriously, skin cancer.

For sunburn, apply cool moist compresses to the affected areas. The person should rest in a cool place. Give plenty of fluids to drink. In cases of severe sunburn, seek medical attention.

Skin cancer Everyone should be on the lookout for any of skin cancer's warning signs. See your doctor if you notice any of the following:

• A lump, sore, ulcer or scaly patch on the skin or white patches on the lips or in the mouth, that have been there for more than four weeks.

• Any change in a wart, mole or birthmark, for example itching, a change of shape or colour, or bleeding.

GLASS

Teach children to play ball games well away from windows and doors with glass panels.

Laminated or toughened glass is much safer for doors, large windows and shower screens. Laminated glass cracks but does not break leaving jagged edges. Toughened glass shatters into very small pieces which will not cut deeply.

If you have large areas of glass in your house make sure they are clearly marked with an adhesive strip at eye level—yours and your child's.

Glass tables if not made of laminated or toughened safety glass need protection from direct contact with hot liquid and sharp knocks.

Provide a carrier for milk bottles.

Make sure you bring your empty bottles home from a picnic unless a rubbish bin is provided.

Do not allow young children to carry glass bottles.

Treat aerated cordial bottles with caution. They can explode if shaken too vigorously.

Always sweep up broken glass immediately, and wrap well before putting in the rubbish bin.

It is better to wear shoes in unfamiliar places. Broken glass is not always easily seen.

BURGLARY

Many Australians of the older generation wistfully recall when keys and locks were virtually unknown. Those days, unfortunately, have gone. The rate of home burglaries increases all the time. With thought and some financial outlay you can reduce your chances of being robbed.

Unlocked doors and windows account for nearly 40 per cent of house robberies. Whenever you are leaving your house unoccupied:

Lock all doors and windows.

Take your key with you or leave it with a friend. Do not hide it.

Leave a light burning if you will be returning home after dark. The light should be visible from the street and should suggest someone is home.

Never leave notes. Thieves can read.

Keep blinds and curtains partly open so the house looks occupied.

Consider trimming shrubs growing near the house. They are best kept at window level. If they are overgrown they could be a burglar's hiding place.

Be careful of telling shops or tradesmen that nobody will be home.

Make a list of all valuables in the home, describing them by make, model and serial number. This will make it easier to recover them if they are stolen.

Attach to your insurance policy photographs of valuable items insured. This will help with identification and recovery.

If you think a burglary may have been committed while you have been away from the house, don't investigate. Use a neighbour's phone and call the police. Act quickly. The burglar may still be in the house.

Signs of crime A strange car roaming your district for a suspiciously long time; a stranger entering a neighbour's house; teenagers who don't live in the neighbourhood going into yards; loitering, fighting; a scream; the sound of a window breaking or a broken window; offers of goods at unusually low prices; someone taking a short cut through your yard—he may have just broken into a neighbour's house; uninvited guests at a young people's party—lots of stereo equipment is stolen a week or so afterward, taken by people who have quickly and expertly worked out how the job can be done.

Be suspicious of young people who ring the front door bell then vaguely ask for 'Sharon' or 'Craig' or someone, but cannot readily answer if you question them about surnames and exact addresses. They may be only checking to see if someone is at home before trying a bit of amateur pilfering.

Rented accommodation Under the terms of your lease, a landlord must take reasonable steps to ensure the premises are secure, but

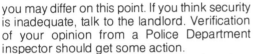

you may differ on this point. If you think security is inadequate, talk to the landlord. Verification of your opinion from a Police Department inspector should get some action.

Advice Your local police station or the crime prevention division of your state Police Department can advise you on the best security measures. Some state departments will send out officers to examine your home and make recommendations free of charge.

SECURITY DEVICES

Numerous devices are supposed to make your home 'burglar proof'. While nothing can guarantee absolute protection, it is worth examining what is available. If you are serious about this, do not skimp in the belief that you have nothing worth stealing. It is unlikely you will feel that way when your possessions have been stolen.

Doors Deadlocks are recommended, preferably those which can be opened from both sides only with a key. The thief, if inside, will then have to get out the same way he got in. Few will risk injury or discovery by attempting to move goods through broken windows.

Door chains are an extra hindrance to burglars and also let you check callers before admitting them.

Sliding doors and windows can be effectively secured by placing a dowel rod in the running rail on the frame.

Windows Key-operated window locks are best, placed as far as possible from the reach of any intruding hand.

Windows can be treated with a special reinforcing film which makes them very difficult to break.

Alarms An alarm acts as an effective back-up system. A thief is unlikely to stay around once an alarm sounds. Some alarms detect movement or sound in an area by emitting radio waves and monitoring reflected signals; others pick up body heat through infra-red beams. Pressure-sensitive mats are also available.

21
FIRST AID

FIRST AID and home treatment are valuable for minor accidents but if pain persists and you are unsure of the cause, or if the condition is manifestly grave, get medical help. In many emergencies the best thing, if possible, is to get the patient to the casualty department of a large hospital. There they have all the equipment and people to cope. If the patient cannot easily be moved by car, call an ambulance. If you call a doctor and wait for his arrival you may only be losing valuable time.

Keep a first aid kit in the house. Keep it in good order and up to date. It is useful to keep a smaller one in the car.

Keep an up-to-date list of emergency numbers near the telephone.

A medical reference book written in lay language detailing simple treatments for common problems is invaluable in every home

FIRST AID KIT

Here is a selection of items that you should have on hand at all times:

Bandages Include three 2.5cm cotton bandages and three 5cm ones. Also, have one or two 7.5cm wide crepe bandages.

Cotton bandages are handy for cuts, abrasions and gashes. They can be cut up into dressings and applied before bandaging; this saves the added cost of buying gauze dressings. After a wound has been cleaned, use a cotton bandage to wrap the injured part.

Crepe bandages are excellent for keeping dressings in place and for bandaging injured limbs, bruised parts or sprained joints, such as ankles and wrists. If there has been bleeding, the pressure they exert often will check this as well as holding the injured parts together while they heal.

Cotton wool Settle for a 50g or 100g roll which will have myriad uses such as for cleansing wounds with dirt in them and as padding under bandages. Don't place cotton wool directly on wounds or burns because it will stick, making removal difficult. Use a dry dressing first, then pad with teased-out cotton wool before bandaging the wound.

Adhesive plaster A 1cm wide roll of adhesive plaster is a good idea to help hold everything in place. As a temporary measure, gaping wounds often can be taped together pending further medical assistance.

Safety pins Have various sizes on hand to hold your bandages together, even though some bandages come with metal fasteners.

Dressing strips Good for minor injuries. Buy a packet of 50 in a variety of sizes and shapes.

Pain-killers Keep a packet of 25 to 50 standard pain-killers handy. Paracetamol tablets (500mg strength) or aspirin (300mg) are suitable. Dosage is written on the label but as a general rule adults should take two tablets after food (either drug), while children 6 to 12 years should have half this dose. Children under five are best given paracetamol elixir.

Antiseptics   A 50mL to 100mL bottle of antiseptic concentrate is a good idea. A small amount added to water will kill off germs in dirty wounds. Directions for use usually are written on the label. Otherwise ask your doctor for advice.

An antiseptic tincture also is handy for small wounds and injuries. Being in a spirit base, it often stings; 25mL is adequate.

Miscellaneous   A pair of good quality scissors, with one blunt and one sharp point. Use the blunt end when cutting off bandages to reduce the risk of cutting the skin.

A pair of sharp-ended splinter forceps. These also can be used to remove bits of debris, gravel and dirt from wounds.

An eye-bath and eye-wash solution.

Calamine lotion.

Syrup of Ipecac to induce vomiting.

TREATMENTS

ABDOMINAL PAIN

Pain in the abdomen, like pain anywhere in the body, is a warning signal that someting is wrong, and should not be ignored. By questioning a child you may soon establish that the 'stomach ache' is due to eating green fuit or too many potato chips. Unless the cause is minor, in adult or child, the matter should be dealt with seriously if pain persists.

Pain could indicate acute appendicitis or it could stem from other vital organs within the abdomen—even from other parts of the body. A heart attack, for example, may cause abdominal pain, so may pneumonia. Abdominal pain may mean a real emergency.

Get medical help. Do not give food until the doctor advises, nor a laxative, and never use a hot-water bottle in the treatment of undiagnosed abdominal pain. This could cause an infected appendix to rupture and spread infection through the abdomen.

BITES AND STINGS

Treat all bites and stings as serious, particularly with children, until you are sure they are not.

Check for allergic reactions, such as itching, flushes, dizziness, nausea or difficulty in breathing.

Check air passages, breathing and circulation of the patient.

If you have doubts about the nature of the bite, or there is a sudden deterioration in the patient, get medical treatment at once.

Arterial tourniquets are no longer recommended as treatment for any type of bite or sting.

Even if a bitten or stung person is already ill when first seen, the application of the pressure/immobilisation method (see snake bites) will prevent further movement of venom from the affected limb.

Animals   Any wound which punctures the skin, whether a cut, graze or animal bite, can become infected. Stop bleeding by pressing wound with a clean cloth as for cuts and scrapes. Seek medical advice on whether an anti-tetanus injection should be given.

Bees and wasps   Never pull or squeeze stinger out of the skin as more venom will be injected. Apply an ice compress or cold cloth to affected area to limit swelling. Using a sterilised needle or knife point, carefully remove stinger by brushing or scraping with a gentle sideways motion. If nothing else is available, use a fingernail. Do not squeeze stinger between finger and thumb as you would do with a thorn.

• If the sting is around the mouth or neck, apply ice packs and seek medical advice, as swelling can cause air passage obstruction.

• If the patient is allergic to such stings, treat as for snake bite.

Bluebottles   Wash the areas where tentacles have touched the patient with vinegar to ease pain. Do not rub sand into affected areas as this aggravates the skin.

Blue-ringed octopus   If touched or provoked, this octopus may bite. The victim does not feel pain at first, but soon experiences difficulty breathing. Urgent medical attention is essential, but until then wash the wound thoroughly and commence resuscitation promptly. Continue resuscitation until medical help is obtained.

Box jelly fish and sea wasp   Pour vinegar (never methylated spirits or alcohol) over the adhering tentacles to inactivate them as soon as possible. Artificial respiration and cardiac massage may be required. The pressure/immobilisation method is NOT recommended. An antivenom is available.

Mosquitoes and flies   Discourage scratching, which could cause infection. Apply cool-water compresses or calamine lotion for temporary relief.

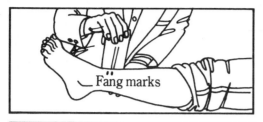

Fang marks

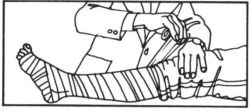

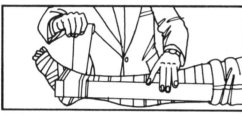

Pressure/immobilisation method

Snakes Immediately apply a broad firm bandage to cover bitten area. If it is a limb, bind as much of it as possible. The bandage should be as tight as for a sprained ankle.

Immobilise limb or area, if possible, with some form of splint. Leave bandage and splint on until you reach medical care. Do not let patient move more than is necessary. This is the pressure/immobilisation method which is now recommended for snake bite.

Do not wash the bitten area. The snake involved may be identified by the detection of venom on the skin. If the snake has been or

can be killed, bring it with the patient.
- Do not apply an arterial tourniquet.
- Do not cut or excise the bitten area.
- Do not try to suck out the venom.

Spiders To treat a Sydney funnel-web spider bite, begin the pressure/immobilisation method outlined in snake bite treatment as soon as possible. Leave the bandage and splint in position until the patient reaches hospital. Recent evidence suggests that funnel-web venom may lose its activity if kept in the bitten limb. Antivenom is now available.

In treating a red-back spider bite, no first aid is recommended as the venom works very slowly and, if its movement is restricted, local pain may become severe.

Other spider bites should be treated with a cold compress. Don't put ice directly on the skin. Seek medical advice.

Stonefish and other stinging fish Do not try to restrict the movement of the injected toxin. Most stings respond to bathing in warm water. Pain relief from severe stings may require local or even general anaesthesia, especially for stonefish stings. Antivenom is available for stonefish stings.

Ticks Do not attempt to squeeze or pull tick out with tweezers or other sharp objects. A common remedy is to pour turpentine or kerosene over the tick and leave for half an hour. If the tick has not come free by then, seek medical attention. If the tick is disengaged, make sure you get it all out. Wash and apply antiseptic to the bitten area.

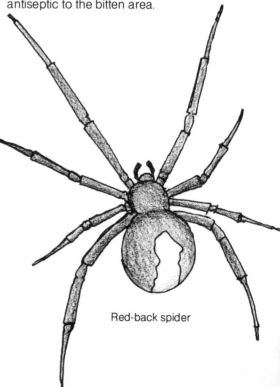

Red-back spider

Name	Description	First aid	Where found in Australia
Tiger snakes	Pale brown or black with yellow stripes; about one metre long	Pressure/immobilisation technique	South-east coast (N.S.W. & Victoria) Tasmania South-west of W.A.
Brown snakes	Light brown, orange or black; slender, streamlined body; up to 2.4 metres long	Pressure/immobilisation technique	All of the mainland
Red-bellied black snakes	Shiny black with red sides and belly; up to 2.5 metres long	Pressure/immobilisation technique	All east-coast All of Victoria and south-east corner of S.A.
Death Adder	Short, thick body with little spiky tail; light brown, reddish-brown or black; up to 2.5 metres long	Pressure/immobilisation technique	All of the mainland except Victoria and south-east corner of S.A.
Taipan	Light brown with creamy yellow belly; up to 3.3 metres long snake	Pressure/immobilisation technique	East coast of N.S.W. North coast of N.T. North-east corner of W.A.
Mulga snake ('King Brown')	Uniform light brown; sometimes olive brown; up to 3 metres long	Pressure/immobilisation technique	All of mainland except south-west corner of W.A., N.S.W. coast and all of Victoria
Small-scaled snake	Deep brown with cream belly; up to 1.93 metres long	Pressure/immobilisation technique	Area centred around common borders of Qld, N.S.W., N.T. & S.A.
Sea snakes	Paddle-shaped tail; 26 types in Australian waters; average length one metre	Pressure/immobilisation technique	Coastal waters from mid-W.A. north around to mid-N.S.W.
Red-back spider	Black with orange-red slash across back	Seek medical care; do not panic as venom acts slowly	All of Australia
Funnel-web spider	All black; slightly hairy legs; one of Australia's largest spiders	Pressure/immobilisation technique	Area covering 160km from centre of Sydney
Australian paralysis tick	Small as a pin's head; when feeding grows to size of a child's finger nail; has the appearance of a blood blister	Soak affected area with turpentine or kerosene; make sure all parts of tick are removed	East coast from northern Qld to N.S.W.–Victorian border
Blue-ringed octopus	Yellow-brown bands with blue circles on arms and body; circles turn bright peacock blue when disturbed	Pressure/immobilisation technique; resuscitation may be needed	All waters of Australia

Name	Description	First aid	Where found in Australia
Box jelly fish	Transparent body with ribbons of tentacles; size of a bucket	Pour vinegar (never methylated spirits) over tentacles on victim's body; resuscitation may be needed	Coastal waters from northern W.A. north to southern Qld
Stonefish	Warty and slimy skin; often found partially buried in sand	Bathe injured area in warm water; seek medical care as anti-venom may be needed	Coastal waters from mid-W.A. north to southern Qld
Cone shells	Conical or cylindrical in shape; light brown with cream contrast; contains fish with poison dart	Pressure/immobilisation technique; resuscitation may be needed	Coastal waters from mid-W.A. north ro mid-N.S.W.
Toad and puffer fish	No scales; grey or whitish in colour; puffs up like a ball out of water	Force vomiting; seek medical care; resuscitation may be needed	All waters of Australia

BLEEDING
(including nosebleeds)
Superficial bleeding will stop spontaneously. Cleanse the wound with water and cover with a dry dressing. Heavy bleeding may kill within three to five minutes if not controlled. To apply pressure is imperative. Place a clean cloth directly over the wound and press firmly with one or both hands, or bandage firmly. Send for urgent medical help.

Heavy bleeding Hold the pressure pad firmly with any strip of material, belt, necktie, but do not tie it so tightly that the pulse throbs near the wound. Raise the bleeding part higher than the rest of the body unless there are broken bones. Keep victim lying down and warm. Use a constrictive bandage only if limb has been crushed or mangled.

To apply a constrictive bandage to stem the bleeding wrap a piece of cloth around the limb above the wound. Protect the skin underneath it with padding. Tie the bandage just tightly enough to stop the bleeding, wait 15 minutes, then loosen the bandage cautiously to see if bleeding has stopped; if not, replace the bandage for a further 15 minutes, then check again. Tell those who take over the patient that a constrictive bandage has been applied.

Nosebleed Sit the patient upright with head forward, keeping still. He must breathe through the mouth. A cork placed between upper and lower back teeth is a help. Firmly press the soft

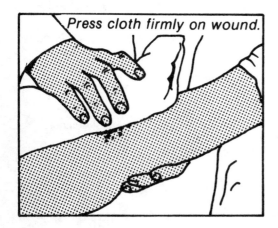

Press cloth firmly on wound.

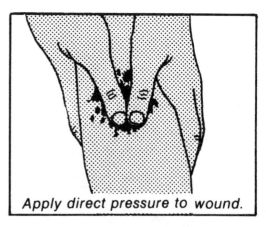

Apply direct pressure to wound.

part of the nose together between finger and thumb for 10 minutes to allow a clot to form. A cloth wrung out in cold water applied to the forehead or back of the neck may help. If bleeding persists for more than 20 minutes, contact the doctor.

Bleeding after tooth extraction Instruct the patient to keep the tongue clear of the socket. Do not attempt to remove the clot in the socket by rinsing, but place a firm pad of gauze over the socket and ask the patient to bite on it firmly.

Bleeding from the ear The patient may be suffering from a fracture of the base of the skull.

Do not plug the ear canal. Let it drain freely. Place the patient in the coma position (see Unconsiousness) with affected ear downward. Seek urgent medical aid.

BROKEN BONES

The following symptoms could indicate a cracked or broken bone (fracture):
- Pain at, or near, the injury.
- Swelling and bruising.
- Inability to use the limb.
- Possible protruding bones or change in shape of the limb (compare with the uninjured limb).
- Often a certain degree of shock.

Sometimes it is difficult to tell whether a bone is broken or not. If there is any doubt, treat the injury as a fracture.

For all fractures Don't try to clean any wounds, but quickly cover with a sterile dressing or clean cloth.

Support the injured area with padding and bandages if possible. Use other parts of the body for support. For example, secure the arm across the chest to support broken ribs.

If the bone is broken, immobilise the joints above and below the injury. Additional bandages may be placed above and below but never over the fracture. Make sure circulation is not restricted.

Obtain medical aid as quickly as possible — the fracture could require special treatment.

Never force a broken limb into a difficult position and never try to set a broken bone yourself.

Wrist or arm breaks Support the arm in the most comfortable position using padding and a sling. A splint can be made of cardboard, rolled or folded newspaper, an umbrella or anything long and firm enough. Cover splint with padding such as a towel, sheet or blanket.

Tie arm to the splint in several places using wide strips of cloth. Make a sling from a large scarf or piece of sheet folded into a triangle.

Leg or ankle breaks Keep the person flat. If necessary to move, improvise a stretcher with a door, ironing board, or anything firm and flat. Use same treatment as for broken arm, using a board, brookstick or something similar for a splint.

Alternatively, bandage the injured leg to the uninjured leg to provide support. Pad generously between legs and apply bandages around the ankles and knees. If available, place additional bandages above and below the injury. Knot all bandages on the uninjured side.

Jaw break Keep air passages clear. To avoid airway obstruction, a conscious patient should either sit or lie flat with the jaw supported. An unconscious person should be turned on to the side.

Finger break Proceed as for a broken arm or leg, using a pencil, ice cream stick or something small and firm for a splint.

Collarbone break Put arm in sling until medical help is obtained.

BURNS AND SCALDS

- If clothes catch alight, smother or extinguish the flame; roll victim on the ground in a rug or blanket.
- Immerse or flood the burnt area in cold water.
- If cold water is not available, remove hot charred remnants of clothing from the area.
- Cover the burn or scald with clean cloth.
- Do not put anything on the burn (butter, oil, ointment or ice).
- Once cool do not attempt to remove clothing or adherent melted material (such as nylon, plastic, glue).
- Seek medical advice immediately.

Chemical burns Such burns are usually caused by a strong acid or by an alkali such as caustic soda.
- Wash the burn under running water. If a large area is affected, use the hose or shower.
- Remove any contaminated clothing.
- Neutralise the chemical if possible. Check the instructions on the container or ring the Poisons Information Centre.
- Cover with a clean dressing.
- If an eye is affected, wash immediately. Pull the lid back to make sure the eye is open under the water. Continue for 15 minutes.
- Seek medical help.

CHOKING

Attempt to remove the object with the finger, but be careful not to push the obstruction down further.

A sharp blow between the shoulder blades with the patient facing down should release the object. Small children may be held upside-down by the feet.

CONVULSIONS

Convulsions must be allowed to run their course. The best thing to do is to try to prevent the person from being hurt. Move any furniture that is in the way, for example.

Check after the convulsion if the patient is breathing. If not, apply mouth-to-mouth resuscitation.

CUTS AND SCRAPES

Stop bleeding by pressing the skin edges of the wound together and applying pressure for ten minutes or so with a clean cloth or sterile dressing. If bleeding continues through dressing, do not remove it but add extra dressings and more pressure for another ten minutes.

Minor cuts and grazes may be cleaned with soap and water or an antiseptic solution before applying a dressing. Large cuts should be cleaned and dressed with gauze pads or bandages.

Use clean hands and sterile dressings whenever possible.

After bleeding has stopped, keep the injured part raised for a while if possible.

Seek medical assistance if: the wound grows more painful, is swollen or discharges pus; a red line extends from the wound; the edges of the cut are separated, or you cannot wash all the dirt out of the wound.

DIABETIC ATTACKS

Diabetic attacks can lead to coma and can be frightening, both for the sufferer and for anybody with them who knows very little about diabetics. Diabetes is a disease caused by a malfunctioning pancreas resulting in a too-high level of sugar in the blood. Occasionally — because they've skipped a meal, perhaps — an attack occurs.

Symptoms: sweating, dizziness, trembling. The cause is too much insulin and low blood sugar (because of that skipped meal) and you must NOT try to give them their usual medication.

Give them sugar — a sweet or a sweet drink (a glucose drink is best). The attack may be over quickly but even so, the diabetic should have a check-up.

DROWNING

• Look around quickly for any object that may assist in rescuing the victim from the water — a rope or a tyre can provide a means of help without introducing risk to the rescuer.

• Only enter the water yourself as a last resort, especially if alone. If others are there, send someone for help.

• If the victim is unconscious when brought ashore, clear the air passage and check for breathing.

• If there are no signs of breathing, immediately turn victim on back and begin mouth-to-mouth resuscitation. (See Resuscitation.)

ELECTRIC SHOCK

Every second counts when a person is in contact with a source of electricity as the longer the contact the less the chance of survival. Never try to pull a victim away from the contact with your bare hands. If you do you'll become the second victim. The human body is an excellent conductor of electricity.

If you are indoors, disconnect the plug or pull the main switch at the fuse box.

If you are outdoors, use a dry pole, branch or thick roll of newspaper that will not conduct electricity. Be sure you are standing on a dry surface. Carefully push or pull the wire off the victim or the victim off the wire.

It is likely the victim will not be breathing when freed; if so, begin mouth-to-mouth resuscitation immediately (see Resuscitation.) and send someone for medical aid.

EPILEPSY

Epilepsy, like diabetes, can be controlled today by medication, but from time to time an epileptic may have an attack. First, move furniture out of the way. Lie the victim on his side to maintain the airways. Wait quietly by the patient until the fit subsides and call an ambulance.

Forget the old wives' tales about putting a wooden spoon in the mouth. This does nothing except, most likely, break the teeth.

FAINTING

You can usually tell when someone is about to faint because the colour drains out of the face and the person looks sick just before blacking out. Most people recover quickly.

• First check the breathing and heart beat. Perform emergency resuscitation if necessary. (See Resuscitation.)

• If resuscitation is not necessary, put patient's feet up and ensure maximum comfort.

FISH HOOKS

Do not attempt to pull the hook out, because it may make the barb more firmly embedded. Instead, push the shank through until barbed hook appears. Cut off the barb with pliers, pull out the shank. Wash the wound with soap and water and treat as for cuts and scrapes.

If hook is embedded in the face, do not attempt to remove it yourself. Get medical help.

FOOD POISONING

Food poisoning may be due to eating food infected with bacteria or a virus or to poisonous substances in the food. Symptoms will be nausea, vomiting, diarrhoea, dehydration, high temperature and rapid, weak pulse. Give nothing by mouth. Get medical help.

FROSTBITE

Frostbite is caused by exposure to extreme cold or bitter winds. The blood vessels closest to the surface of the skin constrict and affected spots become pale, even greyish. Fingers, toes, ears and the nose are particularly vulnerable.

• Cover the frostbitten part and try to get patient indoors.

• Give warm fluids and wrap patient in warm, dry clothes.

• Remove rings or anything constrictive as frostbitten extremities tend to swell when they thaw.

• Try to restore circulation in frostbitten areas by immersing them in warm water. Pat areas dry but never rub them.

• If blisters appear, do not open them. Protect them with a loosely wrapped dressing.

HEART ATTACK

Given proper treatment quickly enough, most heart attack victims recover. But each year many thousands of lives are lost through failure to recognise the onset of a heart attack or to take proper action. The first few hours are vital.

Heart attack symptoms can vary widely and it is difficult to try to simplify them. But the most common are:

• An oppressive pain or unusual discomfort in the centre of the chest, behind the breastbone, lasting for more than 10 minutes.

• The pain may radiate to the shoulder, arm, neck, or jaw.

• Often the pain or discomfort is accompanied by sweating.

• Nausea, vomiting, and shortness of breath may occur.

• Sometimes the symptoms subside and then return.

• Sudden collapse may also indicate heart attack.

The all-important thing to remember is that a chest pain which does not go away after 10 minutes of rest should not be ignored.

Get to the nearest hospital, by ambulance if immediately available, by car if not. The decision to act should not be left to the patient. It is the responsibility of those nearby—wife, husband, relative, bystander or friend. Treat it as a heart attack—there's no harm done if you are wrong.

HEAT EXHAUSTION AND STROKE

These result from overactivity in hot, humid weather. Heat stroke usually occurs when heat exhaustion is not treated promptly. It is a more serious condition, requiring medical aid.

Heat exhaustion Symptoms include patient feeling hot, faint and giddy, nauseous, having muscle cramps, excessive sweating and rapid breathing and pulse.

Help patient to rest in a cool, shaded area or an air-conditioned room. Loosen clothing and sponge exposed skin surfaces with cool water. Give frequent cool drinks—one sip every few minutes for an hour. Sweetened iced coffee or tea may be given when patient revives.

Give salt only on medical advice.

Heat stroke Symptoms include those of heat exhaustion. The skin becomes hot and dry as the patient becomes dehydrated. Headaches and mental disturbance are common before collapse. Body temperature is very high, skin flushed and breathing shallow.

It can be fatal. Treat promptly and arrange for medical aid without delay. Place patient at rest in a cool, shaded area. Remove unnecessary clothing and sponge with quick, light strokes. If possible, wrap in a wet, cold sheet and cool patient with a fan.

If conscious, give frequent drinks, as for heat exhaustion. If unconscious, watch body temperature and repeat cool sponge treatment when temperature rises.

HYPOTHERMIA
When exposed to cold for long periods you can get hypothermia, a condition caused by the body losing heat it cannot replace, when the whole body temperature drops. A person suffering from hypothermia will be lethargic, irrational and will stop shivering because of a lack of energy.
• Wrap victim up with as much clothing as possible. Increase the body temperature gradually by warming slowly.
• Never give victim alcohol or put near a fire. Both cause the blood vessels to open up. Blood flowing to the extremities could kill them.

POISONS
Every year many people, especially children, are poisoned. It is vital to recognise the dangers of poisons and drugs.
General precautions
• Keep all medicine and poisons in a cupboard with a child-proof lock.
• Know what is in your medicine cupboard and keep it tidy.
• Know what is in a product. Find out if it is dangerous for yourself, your child or your pet (ask your pharmacist). Find out if a drug is dangerous in particular circumstances—for example, if taken with alcohol or when pregnant.
• Keep the product in its original container with its label intact.
• Insist that your medicines come in child-proof containers.
• Never put poison in a food or drink container.
• Label all poisonous substances.
There are four main groups of household poisons:
Medicines The medicines most dangerous to children are aspirin, paracetamol, iron pills, heart drugs, sleeping pills, tranquillisers, antidepressants and liniments. Medicines are safe only for the patient for whom they have been prescribed. They should be taken only in the recommended dose.
Pest killers Many weed and pest killers are

very poisonous, and must be kept away from children. They must always be used strictly according to label directions. Protective clothing should be worn where indicated, and the proper dilution should be made before spraying.
Kerosene and petrol products Kerosene, petrol, diesel oil, turps, paint thinners, cleaning fluid and lighter fluid are all very dangerous. Even a small amount swallowed can get into the lungs and cause the victim serious illness.
Household chemicals and cleaners Many household cleaners and polishes are poisonous, especially drain and oven cleaners, caustic soda, acids, bleaches and detergents for automatic dishwashing machines.
First aid for poisoning
• Do not wait and see—the first hour or two are critical. Contact the nearest hospital, Poisons Information Centre, a doctor or chemist immediately for advice.
• If poison is swallowed, give water immediately.
• If poison is on the skin, wash the area well with soap and water.
• If in the eyes, hold the lids apart and flush the eye copiously with water, making sure you wash under the eyelids.
• If poison is inhaled, go straight out to the fresh air and breathe deeply. If the patient is overcome and is not breathing, begin mouth-to-mouth resuscitation immediately.
• If petrol, turpentine or methylated spirits have been swallowed, do not induce vomiting.
• If any other poison has been swallowed, give patient a dose of Ipecac syrup to induce vomiting (a glass of fizzy drink or water will help with this). Vomiting may take up to 20 minutes to occur. Repeat the Ipecac syrup only once after 20 minutes if vomiting has not occurred. If no Ipecac syrup is available, tickle the patient's throat with your finger.
• Take the patient and the container of poison to the hospital or doctor immediately.
Poisons Information Centres
Sydney—(02) 51 0466
Melbourne—(03) 347 5522
Adelaide—(08) 267 4999
Brisbane—(07) 253 8233
Hobart—(02) 38 8485
Perth—(09) 382 8222
Canberra—(062) 43 2154
Darwin—(089) 20 7211

Potentially dangerous substances
The following are potentially dangerous substances found in the home.
Kitchen: drain and oven cleaners, insect repellents, fly sprays, detergents, dishwashing

machine products, disinfectants, room deodo-risers.

Laundry: bleaches, cleansers, pre-wash sprays, soap powders.

Bathroom: lavatory cleansers and deodoriser blocks, medicines, hair products, antiseptics, suntan preparations.

Bedroom: cosmetics, medicines, sleeping pills.

Garden shed: fungicides, herbicides, pesti-cides, snail killer pellets, plant foods.

Garage: petrol, oil, kerosene, brake and battery fluids.

Workshop: paints, strippers, solvents, adhe-sives, soldering flux.

Garden: castor oil plants, oleander, angels trumpets, mushrooms and toadstools.

RESUSCITATION

• Tilt the patient's head backwards and support the jaw. Pinch the nostrils closed or seal with your cheek.

• Take a breath and seal your mouth over the patient's slightly open mouth. For infants, cover both their nose and mouth with yours.

• Breathe into patient's mouth until chest rises.

• Remove your mouth and turn your head to watch, listen and feel for the escape of air from the patient's mouth. Take a breath your-self and continue with regular breaths at a rate of one every four or five seconds until help arrives.

• For infants, gentle puffs must be used, one every three seconds. Puff only enough air for the infant's chest to rise and fall gently.

• If the patient's chest does not rise with each breath, check that the head is fully back and nose completely closed.

• When breathing is occurring unaided, turn the patient onto the side at once, with head, back and jaw supported. An unconscious patient will often vomit during recovery and could choke to death if left lying on the back. Keep the patient under observation until medical help arrives.

Cardiac compression If pulse is still absent after mouth-to-mouth resuscitation, perform cardiac compression with expired air breath-ing. Kneel at the patient's side, placing one hand on the chest and crossing the other over it. Keep the arms straight and lean on chest of patient and compress to squeeze blood out of the heart. Compress 60 to 80 times a minute.

SHOCK

Shock can accompany any accident or sudden illness. It is caused by a reduced flow of blood. With serious bleeding, death can result if untreated.

Symptoms may include feeling faint; having pale, clammy skin, irregular breathing and rapid, faint pulse; nausea, vomiting may occur; thirst (mainly in burns or bleeding); uncon-sciousness; facial sweat.

• Lie patient down, legs raised. Loosen tight clothing. Keep the surroundings quiet and allow plenty of fresh air. Cover patient lightly to maintain normal body temperature.

• Protect the underside of the body from heat or cold. Food and drink should not be given as they could cause vomiting. Calm and reassure patient while checking that all injuries have been found and treated.

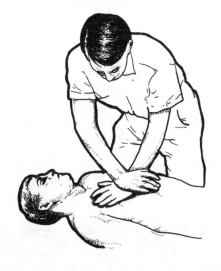

SPORTS INJURIES

Although physical fitness lowers the chances of sports injuries, problems may still arise. It is important to recognise what the injury is to allow for the correct treatment.

A number of sport-related problems are covered elsewhere in this chapter. They include broken bones, cuts and scrapes, heat exhaustion and stroke and frostbite.

Bruises A bruise is caused by a blow and is an extremely common minor injury for athletes.

• Rest, stop exercising.

• Apply ice wrapped in a cloth or towel to the affected area for at least 48 hours, at two-hourly intervals.

• Apply a compression bandage to the area.

- Elevate the area above heart level.
- Never use heat to treat a bruise.

Heat cramps These can occur after strenuous exercise if there is a low concentration of salt in the body or if too much fluid has been lost. Symptoms include muscle spasms, twitches, fatigue, reduced alertness, heavy sweating and cold, clammy skin.

- Rest in a shaded area.
- Drink plenty of cold water.
- Apply pressure to cramped area while muscle is being slowly stretched.

Hernia This is an outward protrusion of normal tissue from its natural position. Some local discomfort and swelling is possible. It can be caused by strain, uncontrolled twisting or weakness in the tissue that covers a muscle. A hernia requires treatment from a doctor.

Ligament injuries Ligaments attach bone to bone. Sprains occur when the joint is forced beyond its normal range of motion. There are three degrees of severity.

First-degree sprain: Sudden pain in the joint then mild disability with some amount of weakness, point tenderness and possible swelling.

Second-degree sprain: Sudden and prolonged pain in the joint with point tenderness, swelling, weakness and some bleeding within the joint which shows up in discolouration.

Third-degree sprain: Sudden pain, loss of motion, tenderness, swelling and haemorrage.

Rest, ice, compression and elevation treatment (as described in bruises) is most effective immediately. For second and third-degree sprains, medical treatment may be required.

Muscle cramps Symptoms are severe and painful uncontrollable contractions of any muscle. The most common causes are salt deficiency from excessive perspiration, overfatigue, sudden changes in temperature, sudden blow to the muscle, impairment of circulation or overstretching of the muscle.

- Loosen any restrictive clothing in the area.
- Administer fluids.
- Massage to restore circulation.
- Do not massage if the cramp is caused by a direct blow or overstretching.

Muscle strains These are caused by an unexpected movement, such as slipping, or an abnormal muscle contraction.

First-degree strain: Localised weakness and tenderness as well as spasm.

Second-degree strain: Symptoms are more severe, with loss of motion, swelling and possible discolouration.

Third-degree strain: Severe spasm, loss of motion, tenderness, swelling and discolouration.

Rest, ice, compression and elevation treatment (see bruises) should be given. For second and third-degree strains, medical treatment may be required.

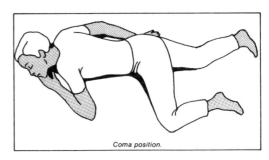

Coma position.

UNCONSCIOUSNESS

Lie the patient on side, tilt head backwards and support jaw at the point of the chin between the thumb and first finger. Quickly clear mouth using fingers.

- Look, listen and feel for signs of breathing, such as escape of air from the patient's mouth and movement of the lower chest and abdomen.
- If the patient is breathing, leave lying on the side.
- If not breathing, turn on to the back and commence resuscitation. (See Resuscitation.)

WOUNDS

Stab and puncture wounds can cause serious, deep injury and may plant infection inside the body. On the surface the injury may seem minor, but these injuries should always be regarded as serious. Do not attempt home treatment. Be on the safe side and get medical help.

INDEX

ACKNOWLEDGEMENTS

The *Australian Women's Weekly* and the Publishers wish to express their gratitude to the following organisations for their invaluable assistance:

AMP Society; Australian Gaslight Company; Australian Institute of Dry Cleaning; Australian Wool Corporation.

Berger Paints (Australia Pty Ltd; Board of Fire Commissioners of New South Wales; Bread Research Institute of Australia; Breville; Building Information Centre, Sydney.

Caroma Doulton Plastics; Coats Patons (Australia) Ltd; Comalco Ltd; Commonwealth Department of Housing and Construction; Commonwealth Institute of Health; Commonwealth Serum Laboratories.

Dairy Promotion Council.

Egg Marketing Board; Email Ltd.

Fibremakers; Finnish Sauna Company of Australia.

Grace Brothers, Sydney; Grafton Galleries.

Health Commission of New South Wales; Rosemary Hemphill.

Kelvinator Australia Ltd.

Law Foundation of New South Wales; Lever and Kitchen Pty Ltd.

Metric Conversion Board; Miele Australia Pty Ltd.

National Health and Medical Research Council; National Roads and Motor Association; National Safety Council of Australia; National Trust of Australia (Tasmania); New South Wales Chamber of Manufacturers; New South Wales Department of Agriculture; New South Wales Department of Consumer Affairs; New South Wales Energy Authority; New South Wales Police Department; New South Wales Home Purchase Advisory Service; Nover and Co. Pty Ltd.

Office of the Commonwealth Ombudsman.

Pet Traders and Fish Importers Association; Phillips Industries; Poisons Information Centre, Sydney; Pork Promotion Centre.

Reckitt and Colman; Roden Products; Royal Alexandra Hospital for Children, Sydney; Royal Automobile Club of Western Australia.

St John Ambulance Association; Selleys Chemical Company; Sharp Corporation; Simpsons Ltd; Socomin International; Standards Association of Australia; Stevenson and Company, Sydney; Surf Life Saving Association of Australia; Swimming Pool and Spa Association (NSW) Ltd; Swimming Pools Association (Victoria) Ltd; Sydney County Council.

Taubmans Pty Ltd; Samuel Taylor.

Victa Ltd.